*Holt Social Studies Curriculum*

GENERAL EDITOR    EDWIN FENTON

# The Humanities in Three Cities

## An Inquiry Approach

**EDWIN FENTON**

Professor of History and
Director, Social Studies Curriculum Center
Carnegie-Mellon University

**JOHN M. GOOD**

Formerly Co-Director,
Social Studies Curriculum Center
Carnegie-Mellon University

**Holt, Rinehart and Winston, Inc.**

New York    Toronto    London    Sydney

For Charlie and Mac

Maps by Viewpoint

# CONTENTS

## UNIT I   *The Humanities in Athens*

# UNIT II The Humanities in Florence

# UNIT III *The Humanities in New York*

## Index     384

## Maps

# To the Student

This is a new kind of textbook. Most social studies texts you have read in the past probably contained information about a particular subject, like civics or geography. The texts were written by one or two authors who organized their material into chapters, each with an important theme. There were numerous illustrations in the form of pictures, graphs, tables, and charts. You read or examined this material to learn the facts and generalizations it presented.

Instead of twenty or thirty chapters written by one or two authors, this text has sixty-two readings. After an introductory chapter entitled "The Humanities: An Introduction," there are three units. Each unit is made up of three chapters, each of which is composed of a number of readings. Each reading contains at least one article or piece of source material, taken from a diary, piece of fiction, historical account, or other publication. An introduction linking one reading with another, and study questions, alerting you to important points and issues, open each reading. Additional questions, designed to alert you to problems raised by specific points in the readings, appear as marginal notes opposite the passages they refer to.

Although maps accompany each unit, you will find few illustrations in the text. However, filmstrips, recordings, and dittoed class handouts have been provided for use with various readings.

Most students are able to study one reading in this text for each night's homework assignment. Because most classes meet about ninety times a semester and there are only sixty-two readings, there will be days when your teacher will not assign readings from this book. On these days, he may give tests, assign supplementary readings, study current events, or hold additional class discussions or individual conferences with students. He may also suggest that many students should spend two days on a particular reading.

Both the text and the audio-visual materials have been designed so that instead of merely memorizing facts and generalizations, you will identify problems, develop hypotheses (or tentative answers to questions), and draw your own conclusions from the evidence. This course in the humanities emphasizes basic questions about the nature of the good man, the good life, and the good society. This course does not aim for consensus about issues such as these. Instead, it has been designed so that each individual can develop his own philosophy.

Modern education helps people to prepare for a career. It should also help them to develop a consistent and satisfying philosophy of life. Everyone working at a job, studying in school or college, or rearing a family ought to know clearly what he believes and why he believes it. Humanistic study provides opportunities to investigate questions about the nature of the good man, the good life, and the good society.

Most of the great humanistic thinkers have lived in cities. At one time or another, a number of cities have made outstanding contributions to philosophy, music, art, literature, or history. We have selected for study three cities at three widely scattered periods of time—ancient Athens, Renaissance Florence, and modern New York City—partly because each one made great contributions to thought about the human condition and partly because the range of this thought was so wide. The variety of ideas you will encounter as you read works written in and about these cities should help you to clarify your own beliefs about yourself and your world. We welcome you to the beginning of a quest which should last a lifetime—the search for personal answers to the great philosophic questions which give meaning to life.

Edwin Fenton
General Editor
Holt Social Studies Curriculum

# How To Use This Book

The text of *The Humanities in Three Cities* consists of sixty-two readings which have been edited from published works or written especially for this course. Each day's assignment follows a common pattern:

1. *An introduction* giving background information and relating the reading to other readings in the same chapter.
2. *Study questions* stressing key points which you should think about to prepare for class discussion.
3. *An article written especially for this course, or a piece of source material* such as a newspaper article, a speech, or an excerpt from a book.

Before coming to class, read the lesson and take notes. Since your teacher will distribute dittoed material from time to time, you should have a three-ring looseleaf notebook which can hold both the material which will be distributed and your homework and classroom notes. Note-taking helps you to remember what the lesson is about, and thus prepares you for class discussion. There are many methods of note-taking. But unless you find from experience that a different method works better, use the following one:

1. *Write the reading number and the title of the reading at the top of a piece of notebook paper.*
2. *Skim the entire reading.* Read the topic sentences of the introduction. Next, read the study questions and fix them in your mind. Then read the topic sentences of the article itself. When you have finished, state in your own words what the reading is about. All this should take no more than two or three minutes.
3. *Read the introduction and take notes as you read.* Pick out the major ideas and necessary information to support those ideas. It will save time if you develop your own method of shorthand, instead of using complete sentences. But remember that you may wish to study from the notes several months later, so take down enough information to make the notes meaningful.

4. *Read the article or source material carefully and take notes as you read.* Put any conclusions you draw in parentheses as a reminder that they are your ideas. Do not underline or mark the text.
5. *Go over your notes, underlining key words or ideas.* This will help you to learn the information in the reading, and prepare for class discussion.
6. *Try to answer the study questions for yourself.* Do not write your answers out. Simply think about them and be prepared to present and defend your answers in class.
7. *Keep a vocabulary list of new words and their definitions.*

It will also help to keep your class notes and your reading notes together in your notebook, so that you can review without flipping through a mass of paper to find material which goes together. If you have trouble with this note-taking method, or if it takes too long, ask your teacher for help.

# Supplementary Readings

At the end of each unit, you will find a list of books, most of them paperbacks, suggested for supplementary reading. In some cases teachers may add titles to the lists of Suggested Readings in order to guide you toward books in your school library on topics that may be of special interest to you. Your teacher may have placed these books in the library or in your classroom. He may require you to read some of them or assign some for extra credit.

Following the author and title of each book, you will find a brief description of the volume. The descriptions will help you decide which volumes you want to read. You may also want to leaf through a number of the books first to get a better idea of what they are like. Some of the volumes are easier to read than others. Many contain numerous illustrations. You should choose something appropriate to your own interests and reading skill.

Your teacher may wish to make special rules and regulations about the Suggested Readings. Some teachers may choose not to use them at all. Others may ask you to submit book reviews based on the volumes you select. Instructions for writing book reviews have been included as a handout in the audio-visual kit.

# PART I: SYNOPSIS AND SCENES FROM *WEST SIDE STORY*

*The Humanities: An Introduction*

This introduction to the humanities will begin with excerpts from a modern musical play, *West Side Story*. Set on the West Side of Manhattan in New York City, the play pits two teenage gangs against each other. It also tells the story of two star-crossed lovers, each of whom belongs to one of the rival gangs, much as Shakespeare's Romeo and Juliet belonged to rival families.

*West Side Story* opened on Broadway in September, 1957. It was a smash hit. Later the play was made into a spectacular motion picture that won ten Academy Awards. *West Side Story's* dramatic excitement, its beautiful music, and its brilliant choreography won widespread popularity and critical acclaim in both its stage and screen versions.

But *West Side Story* is more than outstanding entertainment. It provokes deeper feeling and greater reflection than plays of lower caliber. *West Side Story* compels its audiences to come to grips with basic questions which trouble all men, questions which provide the focus of this course: What is the good man? What is the good life? What is the good society? Part I of this introduction asks you to reflect upon the first and the third of these questions as you read the synopsis of *West Side Story* which follows. Think about the following questions as you read:

1. Do you think the young people in *West Side Story* are good men and women? Why or why not?
2. What social problems contribute to the characters' problems in *West Side Story?* How might they be remedied?
3. What criteria would you use to determine who is a good man and who is a good woman in *West Side Story?* What criteria would you use to determine whether the social setting is a good one? Does *West Side Story* add to the criteria you would use to judge men and societies?

xiii

# West Side Story

Two rival teenage gangs, the Sharks, who are Puerto Rican, and the Jets, composed of a jumble of Caucasian groups, live on the West Side of Manhattan. Their feuding is approaching a blow-up when the play opens. That evening a dance is to be held at the neighborhood gym—considered neutral territory. Riff, the leader of the Jets, now plans to challenge Bernardo, leader of the Sharks, at the dance. With trouble threatening, the Jets naturally look for guidance to one of their founders, Tony, who has recently drifted away from the gang. Riff, the leader of the Jets, declares that Tony's "always come through for us and he will now."

Tony, who has been holding down a job at a neighborhood drugstore, accepts Riff's invitation to join the Jets at the dance with the greatest reluctance. When Tony arrives, the Jets and Sharks are dancing wildly and tensely. In the midst of the excitement, Tony spots a beautiful girl; instantly they are drawn to each other. The girl is Maria, younger sister of Bernardo, who is leader of the Sharks. Bernardo, appalled at his sister and furious at Tony, sends Maria home and then accepts Riff's challenge to meet for a formal declaration of war between the Sharks and the Jets. Tony, dazzled by his new-found love, heads straight to Maria's tenement building and climbs the fire-escape to her family's apartment. On the fire-escape, Tony and Maria sing "Tonight":

MARIA [sings:]

Only you, you're the only thing I'll see forever.
In my eyes, in my words and in everything I do,
Nothing else but you
Ever!

TONY:

And there's nothing for me but Maria,
Every sight that I see is Maria.

MARIA:

Tony, Tony . . .

TONY:

Always you, every thought I'll ever know,
Everywhere I go, you'll be.

MARIA:

All the world is only you and me!

> [And now the buildings, the world fade away, leaving them suspended in space.]

The passages from the play are taken from Arthur Laurents and Stephen Sondheim, **West Side Story**, bound together with William Shakespeare, **Romeo and Juliet** (New York: Dell Publishing Co., 1965), pp. 161–164, 212–214. Lyrics to **West Side Story** are copyright © 1957 by Leonard Bernstein and Stephen Sondheim. Copyright © 1956, 1958 by Arthur Laurents, Leonard Bernstein, Stephen Sondheim and Jerome Robbins. Reprinted by permission of Random House, Inc. and the Leonard Bernstein Foundation (c/o Abraham Friedman, Esq., 17 East 45th St., New York, N.Y.).

Tonight, tonight,
It all began tonight,
I saw you and the world went away.
Tonight, tonight,
There's only you tonight,
What you are, what you do, what you say.

TONY:

Today, all day I had the feeling
A miracle would happen—
I know now I was right.
For here you are
And what was just a world is a star
Tonight!

BOTH:

Tonight, tonight
The world is full of light,
With suns and moons all over the place.
Tonight, tonight,
The world is wild and bright,
Going mad, shooting sparks into space.
Today the world was just an address,
A place for me to live in,
No better than all right,
But here you are
And what was just a world is a star
Tonight!

MAN'S VOICE [*offstage:*]

Maruca!

MARIA:

Wait for me!

[*She goes inside as the buildings begin to come back into place.*]

TONY [*sings:*]

Tonight, tonight,
It all began tonight,
I saw you and the world went away.

MARIA [*returning:*]

I cannot stay. Go quickly!

TONY:

I'm not afraid.

MARIA:

They are strict with me. Please.

TONY [*kissing her:*]

Good night.

MARIA:

*Buenas noches.*

TONY:

I love you.

MARIA:

Yes, yes. Hurry. [*He climbs down.*] Wait! When will I see you?
[*He starts back up.*] No!

TONY:

Tomorrow.

MARIA:

I work at the bridal shop. Come there.

TONY:

At sundown.

MARIA:

Yes. Good night.

TONY:

Good night.

[*He starts off.*]

MARIA:

Tony!

TONY:

Ssh!

MARIA:

Come to the back door.

TONY:

*Sí.*

[*Again he starts out.*]

MARIA:

Tony! [*He stops. A pause.*] What does Tony stand for?

**TONY:**

Anton.

**MARIA:**

*Te adoro,* Anton.

**TONY:**

*Te adoro,* Maria.

[*Both sing as music starts again:*]
Good night, good night,
Sleep well and when you dream,
Dream of me
Tonight.

*Meanwhile, the Jets and the Sharks gather at Doc's drugstore where they insult each other as thoroughly as they know how. Then the two gangs agree to meet the next night for an all-out rumble. At this point Tony steps in and persuades the gangs to let their differences be settled by a simple fist-fight between one man from each gang, Bernardo for the Sharks and Riff for the Jets. The next day Tony meets Maria at the bridal shop where she works. They dream of marriage, and Maria, opposed to any fighting between her brother and the man she loves, pleads with Tony to try to stop even the fistfight.*

*Tony's attempt to stop the fight ends in disaster. The two champions of the rival gangs produce switchblades and Bernardo stabs Riff, who had hesitated in response to Tony's plea. Enraged, Tony takes Riff's knife and rams it into Bernardo. By the time the police arrive and the gangs have fled, Riff and Bernardo are lying dead. Soon after Maria learns of the fight, Tony appears. At first she is hysterical and angry, but then she falls into Tony's arms as he tells her what happened.*

*Later that evening Tony and Maria make plans to run away together. Tony then leaves Maria's apartment and Anita, who was Bernardo's girl, enters. They quarrel as they sing "A Boy Like That" and "I Have a Love."*

**ANITA** [*savagely:*]

And you still don't know: *Tony is one of them!*

[*She sings bitterly:*]
A boy like that who'd kill your brother,
Forget that boy and find another!
One of your own kind—
Stick to your own kind!

A boy like that will give you sorrow—
You'll meet another boy tomorrow!
One of your own kind,
Stick to your own kind!

A boy who kills cannot love,
A boy who kills has no heart.
And he's the boy who gets your love
And gets your heart—
Very smart, Maria, very smart!

A boy like that wants one thing only,
And when he's done he'll leave you lonely.
He'll murder your love; he murdered mine.
Just wait and see—
Just wait, Maria,
Just wait and see!

MARIA [*sings:*]

Oh no, Anita, no—
Anita, no!
It isn't true, not for me,
It's true for you, not for me,
I hear your words—
And in my head
I know they're smart,
But my heart, Anita,
But my heart
Knows they're wrong.

[*Anita reprises the chorus she has just
sung, as Maria continues her song.*]

And my heart
Is too strong,
For I belong
To him alone, to him alone,
One thing I know:
I am his,
I don't care what he is.
I don't know why it's so,
I don't want to know.
Oh no, Anita, no—you should know better!
You were in love—or so you said.
You should know better . . .

I have a love, and it's all that I have.
Right or wrong, what else can I do?

I love him; I'm his,
And everything he is
I am, too.
I have a love and it's all that I need,
Right or wrong, and he needs me too,
I love him, we're one;
There's nothing to be done,
Not a thing I can do
But hold him, hold him forever,
Be with him now, tomorrow
And all of my life!

BOTH:

When love comes so strong,
There is no right or wrong,
Your love is your life!

*Chino, a Shark who has courted Maria, has been hunting for Tony with a gun since Bernardo's slaying. Since leaving Maria's, Tony has been hiding in the drugstore cellar. In the store itself, the Jets have gathered. Anita, carrying a message from Maria for Tony, enters. The Jets taunt her so ruthlessly, however, that she becomes infuriated and tells the Jets that Chino shot Maria. When Tony is told the false message, he stumbles out into the street yelling, "Chino? . . . COME ON: GET ME, TOO!" Then, in the shadows, Tony sees Maria. In joy he rushes toward her, but at that moment Chino appears and fires a single shot. Mortally wounded, Tony falls into Maria's arms. As Tony dies, Maria brushes his lips with her fingers. Then she shouts in anguish, "WE ALL KILLED HIM; and my brother and Riff." Finally she leans over Tony, whispers "Te adoro, Anton," and kisses her dead lover.*

# PART II: SONGS OF THE GOOD LIFE

The songs of *West Side Story* as well as Jerome Robbins's choreography contribute substantially to the development of the plot and atmosphere. Through songs and dances, the authors make their characters more vividly express their feelings about one another and about life in general. Stephen Sondheim's poetic words set to Leonard Bernstein's music express a number of ideas about some of life's most perplexing questions.

The three songs included in Part II of this introduction focus on the second of the three core questions of this course in the humanities: What is the good life? In each of these three songs, the Jets or the Sharks reveal their attitudes toward some aspect of their life on the West Side of Manhattan. Not only do they express their feelings and judgments about life as it is; they also reveal their aspirations for a better life.

As you read and react to these songs from *West Side Story*, reflect upon your own ideas about the nature of the good life. Let these questions guide your thoughts as you read:

1. What words in the "Jet Song" symbolize the nature of the good life for the Jets? What words in "America" symbolize the good life for the Puerto Rican girls? What words in "Somewhere" symbolize the good life for all of the young people in the story?
2. Which of the ideas presented in each song conflict with the ideas presented in the other two? Are there any ideas about the nature of the good life that are expressed in all of the songs?
3. What words would *you* use to describe the nature of the good life? Are these the same words used by the characters in *West Side Story?*

## The Gang and the Good Life

*At the opening of the play, the Jets, one of the rival gangs in* West Side Story, *sing about the virtues of belonging to a gang. Their song reveals their ideas about the good life.*

The passages from the play are from Arthur Laurents and Stephen Sondheim, **West Side Story,** bound together with William Shakespeare, **Romeo and Juliet,** pp. 143–145, 167–169, 200–202.

RIFF [*He sings:*]
    When you're a Jet,
    You're a Jet all the way
    From your first cigarette
    To your last dyin' day.

When you're a Jet,
If the spit hits the fan,
You got brothers around,
You're a family man!
You're never alone,
You're never disconnected!
You're home with your own—
When company's expected,
You're well protected!
Then you are set
With a capital J,
Which you'll never forget
Till they cart you away.
When you're a Jet,
You stay
A Jet!

[*He speaks:*]

I know Tony like I know me. I guarantee you can count him in.

ACTION:

In, out, let's get crackin'.

A-RAB:

Where you gonna find Bernardo?

RIFF:

At the dance tonight at the gym.

BIG DEAL:

But the gym's neutral territory.

RIFF [*sweet innocence:*]

I'm gonna make nice there! I'm only gonna challenge him.

A-RAB:

Great, Daddy-O!

RIFF:

So everybody dress up sweet and sharp. Meet Tony and me at ten.
And walk tall!

[*He runs off:*]

A-RAB:

We always walk tall!

BABY JOHN:

We're Jets!

ACTION:
  The greatest!

[*He sings with Baby John:*]

  When you're a Jet,
  You're the top cat in town,
  You're the gold-medal kid
  With the heavyweight crown!

[*A-rab, Action, Big Deal sing:*]

  When you're a Jet,
  You're the swingin'est thing.
  Little boy, you're a man;
  Little man, you're a king!

[*All:*]

  The Jets are in gear,
  Our cylinders are clickin'!
  The Sharks'll steer clear
  'Cause every Puerto Rican
  'S a lousy chicken!
  Here come the Jets
  Like a bat out of hell—
  Someone gets in our way,
  Someone don't feel so well!
  Here come the Jets:
  Little world, step aside!
  Better go underground,
  Better run, better hide!
  We're drawin' the line,
  So keep your noses hidden!
  We're hangin' a sign
  Says "Visitors forbidden"—
  And we ain't kiddin'!
  Here come the Jets,
  Yeah! And we're gonna beat
  Every last buggin' gang
  On the whole buggin' street!

[*Diesel and Action:*]

  On the whole!

[*All:*]

  Ever—!
  Mother—!
  Lovin'—!
  Street!

  *The Lights Black Out*

# "America": Goods and the Good Life

*The Sharks, a gang of Puerto Rican youths, is the other gang in* West Side Story. *In the following song, Rosalia and Anita, two of the Sharks' girls, debate the advantages of living in Puerto Rico and New York City.*

ROSALIA [*She sings nostalgically:*]

Puerto Rico . . .
You lovely island . . .
Island of tropical breezes.
   Always the pineapples growing,
   Always the coffee blossoms blowing . . .

ANITA [*sings sarcastically:*]

Puerto Rico . . .
You ugly island . . .
Island of tropic diseases.
   Always the hurricanes blowing,
   Always the population growing . . .
   And the money owing,
   And the babies crying,
   And the bullets flying.
I like the island Manhattan—
Smoke on your pipe and put that in!

                         [*All, except Rosalia:*]

I like to be in America!
OK by me in America!
Everything free in America
For a small fee in America!

ROSALIA:

I like the city of San Juan—

ANITA:

I know a boat you can get on.

ROSALIA:

Hundreds of flowers in full bloom—

ANITA:

Hundreds of people in each room!

                         [*All, except Rosalia:*]

Automobile in America,
Chromium steel in America,

Wire-spoke wheel in America—
Very big deal in America!

ROSALIA:

I'll drive a Buick through San Juan—

ANITA:

If there's a road you can drive on.

ROSALIA:

I'll give my cousins a free ride—

ANITA:

How you get all of them inside?

[*All, except Rosalia:*]

Immigrant goes to America,
Many hellos in America;
Nobody knows in America
Puerto Rico's in America.

[*The girls whistle and dance.*]

ROSALIA:

When will I go back to San Juan—

ANITA:

When you will shut up and get gone!

ROSALIA:

I'll give them new washing machine—

ANITA:

What have they got there to keep clean?

[*All, except Rosalia:*]

I like the shores of America!
Comfort is yours in America!
Knobs on the doors in America,
Wall-to-wall floors in America!

[*They whistle and dance.*]

ROSALIA:

I'll bring a TV to San Juan—

ANITA:

If there's a current to turn on.

ROSALIA:

Everyone there will give big cheer!

ANITA:

Everyone there will have moved here!

[*The song ends in a joyous dance*]
*The Lights Black Out*

# The Good Life Is "Somewhere"

*In a dream sequence after the leaders of the two gangs have been killed, the Jets and the Sharks sing of aspirations they share for a better life—"somewhere."*

TONY [*He sings:*]

I'll take you away, take you far far away out of here,
Far far away till the walls and the streets disappear,
Somewhere there must be a place we can feel we're free,
Somewhere there's got to be some place for you and for me.

[*As he sings, the walls of the apartment begin to move off, and the city walls surrounding them begin to close in on them. Then the apartment itself goes, and the two lovers begin to run, battering against the walls of the city, beginning to break through as chaotic figures of the gangs, of violence, flail around them. But they do break through, and suddenly—they are in a world of space and air and sun. They stop, looking at it, pleased, startled, as boys and girls from both sides come on. And they, too, stop and stare, happy, pleased. Their clothes are soft pastel versions of what they have worn before. They begin to dance, to play: no sides, no hostility now; just joy and pleasure and warmth. More and more join, making a world that Tony and Maria want to be in, belong to, share their love with. As they go into the steps of a gentle love dance, a voice is heard singing.*]

OFFSTAGE VOICE [*sings:*]

There's a place for us,
Somewhere a place for us.
Peace and quiet and room and air
Wait for us
Somewhere

There's a time for us,
Someday a time for us,
Time together with time to spare,

Time to learn, time to care
Someday!

Somewhere
We'll find a new way of living,
We'll find a way of forgiving
Somewhere,
Somewhere . . .

There's a place for us,

A time and place for us.
Hold my hand and we're halfway there.
Hold my hand and I'll take you there
Someday,
Somehow,
Somewhere!

> [*The lovers hold out their hands to each other; the others follow suit: Jets to Sharks; Sharks to Jets. And they form what is almost a procession winding its triumphant way through this would-be world, as they sing the words of the song with wonderment. Then, suddenly, there is a dead stop. The harsh shadows, the fire escapes of the real, tenement world cloud the sky, and the figures of Riff and Bernardo slowly walk on. The dream becomes a nightmare: as the city returns, there are brief re-enactments of the knife fight, of the deaths. Maria and Tony are once again separted from each other by the violent warring of the two sides. Maria tries to reach Bernardo, Tony tries to stop Riff; the lovers try to reach each other, but they cannot. Chaotic confusion and blackness, after which they find themselves back in the bedroom, clinging to each other desperately. With a blind refusal to face what they know must be, they reassure each other desperately as they sing.*]

TONY AND MARIA:

Hold my hand and we're halfway there.
Hold my hand and I'll take you there
Someday,
Somehow,
Somewhere!

# Unit I:

# The Humanities in Athens

Artist unknown, *Head of the bronze statue of a youth* (fourth century B.C.)
National Museum, Athens
Photo from Hirmer Fotoarchiv

# Athens and Its Citizens

## STATING THE ISSUE

Men constantly search for symbols to give meaning to their lives. They turn to religious scriptures to find symbols that express morals and values, and ideas about the origin and destiny of man. They look to secular political documents for ideas about the good society. The works of painters, sculptors, dramatists, and poets often symbolize ideas about the good man and the good life. Sometimes men seek symbols for what is good in the lives of heroes and leaders.

Sometimes a "golden age" illuminates the essence of men's values. Since the end of the Middle Ages, western men have regarded the fifth century B.C. as the golden age of Athens. In little more than one hundred years, Athens produced some of the most elegant architecture, most beautiful sculpture, most compelling drama, and most profound philosophy the world has ever known. The ancient Greeks were not content merely to survive; they sought to survive in style. In doing so, they considered directly the nature of the good man, the good life, and the good society.

What sort of men were those ancient Athenians who produced a golden age? What values inspired them? What qualities did they admire? What were their lives like? The answers to these questions begin to reveal symbols that can give any man's life greater purpose. These questions provide the focus of this chapter.

CHAPTER

1

3

# 1 A TOUR OF ATHENS

High on a craggy rock overlooking the modern city of Athens stand the ruins of ancient temples. As the twentieth-century visitor walks among them, their graceful lines and magnificent proportions gratify his senses. The entire Acropolis, and particularly the Parthenon, the temple built to honor the patron goddess of Athens, leads the visitor to wonder what manner of men would expend so much energy and lavish such care on the creation of beauty. For beauty crowned the city.

In ancient Athens, the hill called the Acropolis was the city's religious center. ("Acro" means topmost, and "polis" can mean city.)

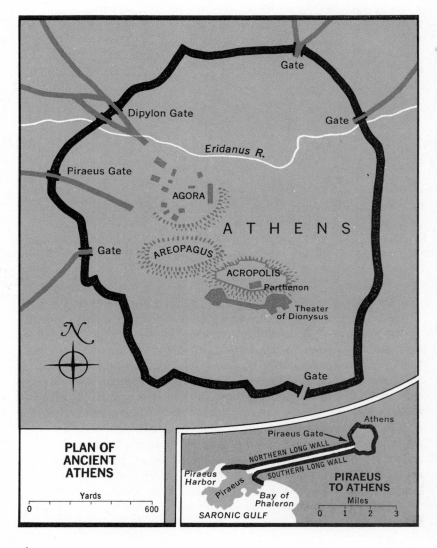

Gate

Dipylon Gate

Gate

Gate

*Eridanus R.*

Piraeus Gate

AGORA

A T H E N S

AREOPAGUS

ACROPOLIS

Parthenon

Gate

Theater of Dionysus

Gate

**PLAN OF ANCIENT ATHENS**

Yards

0          600

Athens

Piraeus Gate

NORTHERN LONG WALL

SOUTHERN LONG WALL

*Piraeus Harbor*

*Piraeus*

*Bay of Phaleron*

**PIRAEUS TO ATHENS**

Miles

0   1   2   3

SARONIC GULF

The ancient Athenians were city dwellers. To them, life outside the polis, or city-state, seemed hardly worth living—a dreary and solitary existence cut off from all that mattered. But in a city, men could congregate to share ideas. A city could marshal its resources to build a magnificent temple, stage an exciting new play in a public theater, or commission great sculpture. And a city could set up a government in which each citizen shared in determining his own destiny. Only cities, thought the Athenians, enabled man to cultivate the human spirit rather than struggle endlessly merely to survive.

If a modern visitor could somehow be transported to the days when temples stood whole upon the hill, he would be caught up in a life of extraordinary vitality. As he toured the city and met its people, he would begin to understand the values that inspired Athenians. Reading 1 attempts to convey the sights, sounds, and smells that the visitor would have encountered as he toured Athens more than two thousand years ago. As you take this tour, keep the following questions in mind:

1. What sorts of activities took place in Athens? In what ways were these activities similar to or different from those of a modern city?
2. What were the settings for various activities in the city? To what extent do you think certain types of buildings and other settings in the city affected the activities that took place there?
3. What kinds of people met on the city streets? What seem to have been their major interests?
4. Do you think that you would have liked living in a city like the one described in this reading? Explain your answer.

The Athenian polis comprised the city of Athens and the surrounding countryside. Some wealthy Athenians owned country estates as well as houses in the city.

# A Visit to the Ancient City

It is very early in the morning. . . . Long since, little market boats have rowed across the narrow strait from Salamis, bringing the island-farmers' produce, and other farmers from the plain and the mountain slopes have started for market. In the ruddy light the marble temples on the lofty Acropolis rising ahead of these hurrying rustics are standing out clearly; the spear and helmet of the great brazen statue of . . . Athena . . . are flashing from the noble citadel, as a kind of day beacon, beckoning onward toward the city. From the Peiraeus, the harbor town, a confused hum of mariners lading and unlading the vessels is even now rising. . . . Our route is to follow the farmers bound for market.

The most direct road from the Peiraeus to Athens . . . leads between the towering ramparts of the "Long Walls," two mighty

William Stearns Davis, **A Day in Old Athens** (Boston: Allyn & Bacon, Inc., 1914), pp. 9–19, 22–23. Reprinted by permission.

Athena was the patron goddess of Athens.

5

barriers which run parallel almost four miles from the inland city to the harbor, giving a guarded passage in wartime and making Athens safe against starvation from any land blockade; but there is an outside road leading also to Athens from the western farmsteads, and this we can conveniently follow. Upon this route the crowd which one meets is certainly not aristocratic, but it is none the less Athenian. Here goes a drover, clad in skins, his legs wound with woolen bands in lieu of stockings; before him and his wolf-like dog shambles a flock of black sheep or less manageable goats, bleating and baaing as they are propelled toward market. After him there may come an unkempt, long-bearded farmer flogging on a pack ass or a mule attached to a clumsy cart with solid wheels, and laden with all kinds of market produce. . . . There are still other companies bound toward the city: countrymen bearing cages of poultry; others . . . driving pigs; swarthy Oriental sailors, with rings in their ears, bearing bales of Phoenician goods from the Peiraeus; respectable country gentlemen, walking gravely in their best white mantles and striving to avoid the mud and contamination; and perhaps also a small company of soldiers, just back from foreign service, . . . clattering shields and spear staves.

The crowds grow denser as everybody approaches the frequented "Peiraeus Gate," for nearly all of Attica which lies within easy reach of Athens has business in the Market Place every morning. . . . There are few late risers at Athens. . . . The plays in the theater, which, however, are given only on certain festivals, begin . . . at sunrise. The philosophers say that "the man who would accomplish great things must be up while yet it is dark." . . .

The Market Place attracts the great masses, but by no means all; . . . sturdy slave girls, carrying graceful pitchers on their heads, are hurrying towards the fountains which gush cool water at most of the street corners. Theirs is a highly necessary task, for few or no houses have their own water supply. . . . Many in the street crowds are rosy-cheeked schoolboys. . . . Close behind, carrying their writing tablets, follow the faithful "pedagogues," the body-servants appointed to conduct them to school, give them informal instruction, and, if need be, correct their faults in no painless manner. . . .

Progress is slower near the Market Place because of the extreme narrowness of the streets. They are only fifteen feet wide or even less, . . . and dirty to boot. Sometimes they are muddy, more often extremely dusty. Worse still, they are contaminated by great accumulations of filth; for the city is without an efficient sewer system or regular scavengers. Even as the crowd elbows along, a house door will frequently open, an ill-favored slave boy show his

Attica comprised the city of Athens and the surrounding countryside. The word referred to the geographic area (not the political unit) of the Athenian polis.

Vases and pitchers for the Greeks were both practical equipment and art objects. They were used for carrying water and storing olive oil. Many were also beautifully painted.

Pedagogue comes from the Greek words "paido" for boy, and "agogos" for leader. Thus a pedagogue was a leader of boys, or a teacher.

6

head, and with the yell, "Out of the way!" slap a bucket of dirty water into the street. . . . It is fortunate indeed that the Athenians are otherwise a healthy folk, or they would seem liable to perpetual pestilence; even so, great plagues have . . . harried the city.

The first entrance to Athens will thus bring to a stranger, full of the city's fame and expectant of meeting objects of beauty at every turn, almost instant disappointment. . . . One can readily be lost in a labyrinth of filthy little lanes the moment one quits the few main thoroughfares. High over head, to be sure, the red crags of the Acropolis may be towering, crowned with the red, gold, and white tinted marble of the temples, but all around seems only monotonous squalor. The houses seem one continuous series of blank walls; mostly of one, occasionally of two stories, and with flat roofs. These walls are usually spread over with some dirty gray or perhaps yellow stucco. For most houses, the only break in the street walls are the simple doors, all jealously barred and admitting no glance within. There are usually no street windows, if the house is only one story high. . . .

It is clear we are entering a city where nine tenths of what the twentieth century will consider the "essential conveniences" of life are entirely lacking. . . . When we investigate, we will find conditions like these—houses absolutely without plumbing, beds without sheets, rooms as hot or as cold as the outer air, only far more drafty. . . . We must fasten on our clothes (or rather our "two pieces of cloth") with two pins instead of with a row of buttons; we must wear sandals without stockings (or go barefoot); must warm ourselves over a pot of ashes; judge plays or lawsuits on a cold winter morning sitting in the open air; we must study poetry with very little aid from books, geography without real maps, and politics without newspapers; and lastly, [as a modern scholar has put it] "we must learn how to be civilized without being comfortable!"

. . . The contrast between the dingy, dirty streets and [the] magnificent public plaza [of the Agora] is startling. The Athenians manifestly care little for merely private display, rather they frown upon it; their wealth, patriotism, and best artistic energy seem all lavished upon their civic establishments and buildings.

The Agora is a square of spacious dimensions, planted here and there with graceful bay trees. . . . Ignoring for the time the teeming noisy swarms of humanity, let our eyes be directed merely upon the encircling buildings. The place is almost completely inclosed by them, although not all are of equal elegance or pretension. Some are temples. . . . Others are governmental buildings. . . . The majority of these buildings upon the Agora, however, are covered promenades, porticoes, or stoae.

▶ How much do you think civilization depends on material comfort?

7

The **stoae** (plural of **stoa**) were open galleries, walled at the back and with columns in front.

The stoae are combinations of rain shelters, shops, picture galleries, and public offices. Turn under the pillars of the "Royal Stoa" upon the west, and you are among a whispering, nudging, intent crowd of listeners, pushing against the barriers of a low court. . . .

In the open spaces of the plaza itself are various altars . . . to the . . . Gods, . . . and innumerable statues of local worthies. . . .

. . . The whole square is abounding with noisy activity. If an Athenian has no actual business to transact, he will at least go to the Agora to get the morning news— . . . the last rumor as to the foreign policy of Thebes; whether it is true that old King Agesilaus had died at Sparta; whether corn is likely to be high, owing to a failure of crops in the Euxine (Black Sea) region; whether the "Great King" of Persia is prospering in his campaign against Egypt. The crowd is mostly clad in white, though often the cloaks of the humbler visitors are very dirty, but there is a sprinkling of gay colors,—blue, orange, and pink. Everybody is talking at once. . . . The southern part of the square is covered with little booths of boards and wicker work, very frail and able to be folded up, probably every night. There are little lanes winding amid these booths; and each manner of huckster has its own especial "circle" or section of the market. . . . Trade is mostly on a small scale,—the stock of each vender is distinctly limited in its range. . . . Behind each low counter, laden with its wares, stands the proprietor, who keeps up a din from leathern lungs: "Buy my oil!" "Buy charcoal!" "Buy sausage!" etc., until he is temporarily silenced while dealing with a customer. . . .

Evidently Athens, more than many later-day cities, draws clear lines between the workers and the "gentlemen of leisure." There is no distinction of dress between the numerous slaves and the humbler free workers and traders; but there is obvious distinction between the artisan of bent shoulders . . . with his scant garments girded around him, and the graceful gentleman of easy gestures and flowing drapery. . . . There is a great *political* democracy in Athens, but not so much *social* democracy. "Leisure," *i.e.* exemption from every kind of sordid, money-getting, hard work, is counted the true essential for a respectable existence, and to live on the efforts of others and to devote oneself to public service or to letters and philosophy is the open satisfaction or the private longing of every Athenian.

▶ Do you think that a man can justify slavery by arguing that enslaving others permits him to devote his life to public service?

A great proportion of these, therefore, who frequent the Agora are not here on practical business, unless they have official duties at the government offices. But in no city of any age has the gracious art of doing nothing been brought to such perfection. The Athenians are an intensely gregarious people. Everybody knows everybody else. Says an orator, "It is impossible for a man to be either a rascal or an honest man in this city without your all knowing it." Few men walk long alone. . . . The morning visit to the Agora "to tell or to hear some new thing" will be followed by equally delightful idling and conversation later in the day at the Gymnasia, and later still, probably, at the dinner-party.

The Gymnasia functioned like an athletic club. Men gathered there to exercise and to talk. Toward the end of the fourth century B.C., the Gymnasia became more an educational center for Athenian youths.

# 2 THE LIFE OF AN ATHENIAN LEADER: PERICLES

In a democracy, leaders often symbolize the values of the people who follow them. Americans remember George Washington, Thomas Jefferson, and Abraham Lincoln as more than great Presidents. These three leaders symbolize qualities that Americans admire—Washington's integrity and courage, Jefferson's idealism and intelligence, Lincoln's humility and compassion. At our best moments, we choose great men to lead us.

Pericles, the most prominent Athenian political leader during the fifth century B.C., perhaps best symbolizes the values of Athens's golden age. The following account of Pericles's life was written by Plutarch, a Greek turned Roman citizen. Although Plutarch lived nearly four hundred years after Pericles, scholars agree that Plutarch's view of the "Olympian," as Pericles was known to his followers, conforms generally to what is now known of Athenian values during the fifth century B.C. As you read this biography of Pericles, consider the following questions:

1. What adjectives would you use to describe Pericles? To what extent do they represent your ideals of the good man?
2. How would you describe the kind of life that Pericles lived? Does his way of life appeal to you? Why or why not?
3. To what extent do you think that a man could be like Pericles today? What social conditions are necessary to produce a man like Pericles?
4. How did Pericles resemble American political leaders? How did he differ?

## Plutarch's Life of Pericles

As a young man of Athens, Pericles was wary of the people. Because of his wealth, his distinguished family and influential friends, and his striking resemblance to a tyrant of the past,

John W. McFarland, Pleasant F. Graves, Jr., and Audrey Graves, **Lives from Plutarch** (New York: Random House, Inc., 1966), pp. 49–51, 53–54, 56–58, 60, 68–69. Copyright © 1966 by John W. McFarland, Pleasant F. Graves, Jr., and Audrey Graves. Reprinted by permission of Random House, Inc.

9

By vote of six thousand citizens, a man could be forced to leave Athens for ten years. This procedure, called **ostracism**, was meant to curb leaders who were considered politically dangerous or personally obnoxious. Aristides, Themistocles, and Cimon were leading Athenian politicians.

The sophists were professional teachers, some quite learned, others much less so. Because they were available for hire, and because their teachings often conflicted with traditional values, the sophists were highly controversial.

The assembly was the main legislative body of Athens. All citizens could take part in its discussions.

he feared he might be considered a dangerous person and subsequently ostracized. But when Aristides was dead, Themistocles driven out, and Cimon usually abroad on expeditions, Pericles became the spokesman for the common people rather than for the aristocrats. By nature he was far from democratic; actually he chose the party of the people to protect himself from any suspicion that he wanted arbitrary power. Also, the people's party seemed the most likely source of support in his political contest with Cimon, who had great power with the aristocracy. . . .

Under the pretense of teaching him only music, the sophist Damon . . . trained Pericles to be a young athlete of politics. Zeno, . . . who taught natural philosophy with a tongue like a double-edged weapon, instructed Pericles in the art of silencing opponents in argument, no matter which side he might take. But it was Anaxagoras . . . who inspired him to nobility of purpose and character. Anaxagoras was the first philosopher to teach that the order of the world was the work of a conscious intelligence rather than the result of chance. Pericles held Anaxagoras in high esteem; he filled himself with his tutor's lofty thought. He developed, under the influence of Anaxagoras, a sustained, even tone of voice which was extremely effective. More importantly, Anaxagoras inspired in the young Pericles a composure, serenity, and majestic dignity which nothing could disturb.

. . . Pericles carefully reserved the effectiveness of his own appearances for great occasions. . . . He did not speak on every occasion, nor did he attend the assembly at each meeting. Matters of lesser importance were taken care of by friends or other speakers. He was never seen walking in public except when he went to the marketplace or the council hall. He declined all invitations to supper, all friendly visits and indeed any intimate association which might weaken the public impression of his superiority and gravity. He knew well that dignity is not easy to preserve in the familiarity of comradeship or drinking.

Pericles was very careful of what and how he would speak—so much so that before he addressed the people he prayed to the gods that no word might slip unawares from his lips which might be unsuitable to the occasion. When he did appear to harangue them, they spoke of his "thunder and lightning" and the "dreadful thunderbolt in his tongue." . . . But it was his study of philosophy which gave his eloquence what Plato calls "that all-commanding power." With this quality he surpassed all other orators of his time, and earned his nickname, "The Olympian." The poet Ion criticized Pericles for being haughty and arrogant; but Zeno urged those who sneered at his gravity to affect the same sort of pride themselves, saying that by imitating it they might in time come to possess it naturally.

. . . Pericles made it his policy to gratify the desires of the people. He arranged to always have some great public show, banquet, or procession in town to please them—coaxing and managing his countrymen like children with such delights. Many have said that Pericles encouraged and led the people to bad habits; that by his public indulgences he changed the Athenians from a sober, thrifty people, who were self-sufficient, into lovers of expense, intemperance and license. On the other hand, Thucydides described

▶ Can a political leader justify the use of tax revenues for public shows or buildings to win political support?

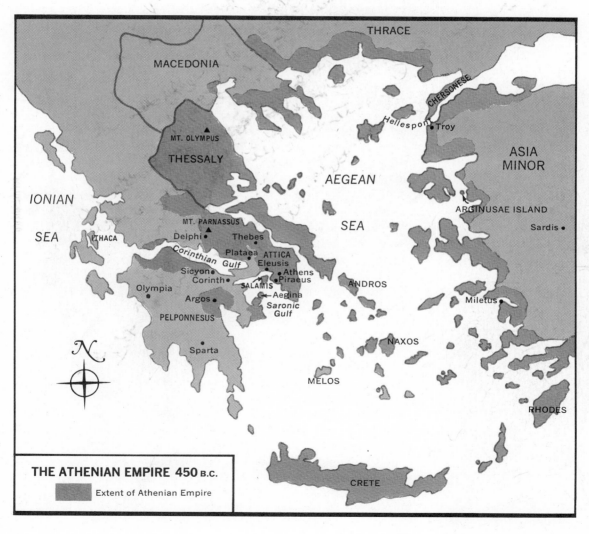

THRACE

MACEDONIA

CHERSONESE

Hellespont • Troy

ASIA MINOR

▲ MT. OLYMPUS

THESSALY

AEGEAN

IONIAN

SEA

SEA

• ARGINUSAE ISLAND

Sardis •

▲ MT. PARNASSUS

ITHACA    Delphi •    • Thebes

Corinthian Gulf   Plataea   ATTICA
                            Eleusis
      Sicyon •              • Athens
      Corinth •            • Piraeus
                   SALAMIS
Olympia •          ← Aegina         ANDROS
        Argos •    Saronic
                   Gulf            Miletus •
PELPONNESUS

NAXOS

Sparta •

MELOS

RHODES

**THE ATHENIAN EMPIRE 450 B.C.**

Extent of Athenian Empire

CRETE

11

the rule of Pericles as an aristocratical government which, though it was called a democracy, was in fact the supremacy of a single great man. Every year Pericles sent out sixty galleys, each carrying many citizens who were paid for eight months while they learned the art of seamanship. To further ease the city of an idle, restless crowd, he sent a thousand citizens into the Chersonese as planters, . . . five hundred more to the isle of Naxos, a thousand into Thrace, and others to Andros and Italy. In this way he both met the needs of poor Athenians and intimidated their allies by, in effect, posting garrisons in the midst of them.

But it was the construction of public and sacred buildings which Pericles ordered that gave the most pleasure to the Athenians and astonished all strangers. . . . Yet this was the policy for which Pericles was most criticized. His enemies denounced him: "Our Greek allies cannot but resent it as an insufferable affront, if not open tyranny, when they see the treasure they contributed for the Persian war wantonly lavished by us upon our own city. We use their money to gild Athens and adorn her like some vain woman bedecked with precious stones, to sculpt figures and temples which cost a thousand talents!"

But Pericles informed the men of Athens that so long as they maintained the defense of their Greek allies and kept the Persians from attacking, Athens was in no way obliged to make any accounting. "Those we defend do not supply so much as one horse or man or ship, but only money. If we uphold our side of the agreements," he said, "that money is not theirs who give it, but ours who receive it." Pericles wanted not only eternal glory for Athens, but also work and immediate prosperity for the undisciplined multitude of workers who stayed at home while those who were eligible earned public pay in military service. With the variety of workmanship needed to erect these great works of Athens, almost everyone in the city, either directly or indirectly, was on the public payroll. . . .

When [his enemies] denounced Pericles for squandering the public money, Pericles rose in open assembly and put the question to the people whether they thought he had spent too much. They answered, "Too much, a great deal!" "Then," he said, "since it is so, let the cost be charged not to your account, but to mine; and let the inscriptions upon the buildings carry my name." When they heard this, whether from surprise at his generosity or from a determination to share in the glory, they cried aloud, urging him to spend what he thought fit from the public purse, and to spare no cost till all work was finished.

. . . With the people no longer divided, he got all of Athens and all affairs that pertained to the Athenians into his own hands. He controlled their tributes, their armies, their galleys, the islands, the sea, and the far-flung power and leadership they exercised over other Greeks as well as barbarians.

After Pericles had consolidated all political power, he was no longer the same man he had been before—he was not so tame, gentle and familiar with the people, nor so ready to comply with their wild and capricious desires. He turned from indulgence in courting their support to the austerity of aristocratic and regal rule. By being honorable, firm, and consistent in the city's best interest, he was able to lead the people along and show them what should be done. Sometimes, though, he had to urge them forward and force them against their will to do what was for their best advantage. . . .

Actually, Pericles' influence was due not only to his eloquence but also . . . to the whole fabric and reputation of his life, the confidence felt in his character, his manifest freedom from every kind of corruption, and his superiority to all considerations of money. . . . Nor did greatness come to Pericles as the lucky windfall of some happy chance of fate, nor as the brief bloom of a policy that flourished for a season only. For forty years he was first among statesmen, and after the banishment of Thucydides, for fifteen more years he held continuous command [as] general. During this entire period he preserved his integrity unspotted.

Yet Pericles was not indifferent to earning money. Indeed, he was neither idle nor careless in looking after the property he inherited from his father, but managed his business so it would not absorb his time and attention, yet not suffer from neglect. Each year's produce he sold in a single sale. From the proceeds, he supplied everything needed for his family until the next year's sale. Every expenditure was ordered and set down from day to day with great exactness; no money was spent except from profits already in hand. His sons and their wives objected to scanty allowances and minute calculation of daily expenditures; and claimed they should be able to enjoy some of the luxury customary to so great a family with such a large estate.

This tight, parsimonious personal economy of Pericles was very unlike the conduct of his philosopher-tutor Anaxagoras, who, in contempt of wealth, left his house and his fields untended, insisting that one employed in purely intellectual contemplation should be independent of external and material things. Pericles, however, dedicating himself to the service of society and the business of life, found use for material wealth in helping the poor. To him, therefore, wealth was not only useful but also honorable and good. It is said that in the involvement of public business Pericles forgot Anaxagoras, who finding himself neglected and deserted in his old age,

The tributes were annual assessments Athens made on the member states of its imperial alliance. Tribute money was supposed to pay for Athens's defense of the alliance against other states.

▶ Should the government provide pensions for old people when they retire?

wrapped himself up, intending to starve. Pericles, hearing this, ran immediately to him and earnestly entreated him to give up his purpose, if not for his own sake, then so that Pericles and Athens would not be deprived of such a faithful and able counselor. Unfolding his robes, Anaxagoras replied, "Ah, Pericles! Those who have need of a lamp take care to supply it with oil!"

As a military leader, Pericles gained a great reputation for prudence. He would not willingly engage in any fight which he believed was unduly risky. He did not envy the glory of generals whose rash adventures were by chance crowned with success. . . .

▶ Should mature people divorce and remarry when their children are grown and they are no longer happy together?

When Pericles and his first wife no longer agreed nor liked to live together, they parted by mutual consent, and she married another man. She had borne Pericles two sons, Xanthippus and Paralus. Pericles then took himself Aspasia, a woman who captivated the greatest statesmen and provoked much comment from the philosophers. Some say Pericles visited Aspasia on account of her knowledge and skill in politics. She had the reputation for being interested in only the most powerful men, and having taught public speaking to many famous Athenians; even Socrates sometimes went to visit her. . . . She was not an Athenian, but a Milesian by birth, who became famous throughout the Mediterranean world. Pericles loved her very much, and every day as he left and returned from the marketplace he greeted and kissed her. She bore him a son, who lacked full Athenian citizenship because of his mother's foreign birth. . . .

Pericles was a man to be admired for his kind, just, dispassionate nature and the patience with which he accepted the conflicting humors of the Athenians, while persevering in working for Athens. Though his power was nearly absolute, he never used it to gratify himself nor did he ever treat an enemy as if he were irreconcilable. His unblemished integrity and irreproachable conduct during his whole administration made that otherwise absurd and arrogant title "Olympian" fitting and becoming. . . .

According to Greek mythology, the gods dwelled on Mount Olympus in eastern Greece. The title "Olympian" implied that Pericles was fit to be a god.

The events that followed his death made the Athenians sharply aware of the loss of Pericles. Those who, while he lived, resented his great authority because it overshadowed their own, were soon disillusioned with other orators and statesmen. They soon began to acknowledge that for all his majestic power, no man had ever been more moderate, and that none had ever given to moderation such impressive authority. Corruption and vice, which Pericles had kept under control, grew, through licentious impunity, to become a flood of wrongdoing. Only then was the wisdom and restraint with which Pericles had exercised his great power recognized as having been the chief bulwark of Athenian democracy.

# 3 ATHENIAN EDUCATION

Education gives children the knowledge, attitudes, and skills that society believes they will need in order to assume adult responsibilities. American students, for example, learn reading, writing, and arithmetic because these skills are necessary to hold a job, be a good citizen, and manage one's personal affairs. Not every society has placed a high priority on these skills. For example, a primitive agricultural society which obtains its food from small family plots would depend upon fathers to teach their sons the techniques of farming rather than have them learn reading, writing, and arithmetic in a school.

Education plays a vital role in a society's efforts to develop good men, to help them lead the good life, and to have them support the ideals of the good society. American schools try to teach moral principles partly by punishing students when they break rules of good conduct. At least part of an American boy's education stresses vocational skills so that he can get a job which will let him support a family and contribute to the economy. American educational institutions teach students about American government so that they can participate intelligently in the democratic process.

Reading 3 describes the way in which Athenian citizens were educated during the fifth century B.C. Using this information, you should be able to determine how Athens tried to develop individuals who were imbued with its ideals. Not every child in Athens received the kind of education described in the selection which follows, however. Only those who would eventually become citizens ever received this kind of schooling. Consequently girls, the children of slaves, and resident foreigners were excluded from Athenian schools. Moreover, only wealthy citizens could afford to send their children through the educational system, since the state did not provide free public education. Keep these exceptions in mind as you read the selection which follows, and use the questions below to guide you.

1. What subjects were taught to Athenian boys in school? Which of these subjects are still taught in American schools?
2. How were children taught? What effect would these teaching techniques have on Athenian boys?
3. What do you think was the purpose of schooling in Athens?
4. Would Athenian education contribute to developing the good man? Would it produce individuals who could lead the good life and work for the good society?

# Schools for Citizens

By John M. Good.

In Athens, as everywhere, boys grew to become men. But in the ancient city, the process of growth involved much more than physical maturation. The adult male was a citizen, and Athenian citizens had many more responsibilities than their wives, servants, or slaves. The ideal citizen had to learn, as he grew, to weigh the arguments of a debate and reach a decision. He had to learn to express his own views eloquently and persuasively. He was expected to become an able judge of sculpture, architecture, and drama, for he might be asked to judge artistic works in some of the many competitions which Athens sponsored. He also had to acquire the physical strength and skills to defend his city as a soldier. And most important, he had to learn the values by which Athenians guided their lives.

The education of the citizen began in the home. As in all societies, child-rearing in Athens set many of the patterns for adult life. The child in his earliest years learned respect for his elders, the basic principles of proper behavior, and his duties to other members of his family. From infancy, the child learned that his father was absolute master of the household. But there is evidence that Athenian parents were somewhat more lenient than their counterparts in other societies. Themistocles, for example, joked that his son was the real ruler of Athens, for Themistocles, the most powerful man in the city was ruled by his wife, and his wife was ruled by their child. Even the toys and games of the young influenced what kind of adults they would become. Boys learned early to be competitive; even before they reached school age they played games in which the object was to triumph over a rival. The boy's toy box nearly always contained a set of clay soldiers which he manipulated in great mock-battles. Boys began to learn military tactics at an early age.

▶ Should women receive the same formal education as men?

Girls never went to school. They received all their education in the home, learning the necessary skills of womanhood—embroidery, spinning, weaving, and other "domestic sciences." Wives of citizens often taught their daughters to read and write, and many girls learned to dance, sing, and play a musical instrument. Some men argued that women should receive more formal education. "Is there anyone with whom you hold fewer discussions than with your wife?" they asked. Perhaps home life would not be so intellectually boring, they contended, if girls learned some of the things that boys began to learn at the age of six—the age that Athenians believed marks the beginning of rationality. The boys did not go to free, public schools, for Athens had none. They were educated at their fathers' expense. Yet Athens valued education highly, and fathers were expected to see that their sons received formal education. In fact, Athenian law stipulated that a son need not care for his aged father if his father had not provided for his education.

The schools were run by professional schoolmasters, stern men who did not spare the rod if a boy misbehaved, or even if he merely stumbled over a recitation of his A, B, C's. Elementary-school teaching was not a respected vocation in Athens. An Athenian proverb defines a man who has fallen on ill fortune as one who is "either dead or teaching A, B, C's."

Once he acquired a certain amount of literacy, the boy began to read the poets, particularly Homer. He was made to memorize long passages from both the *Iliad* and the *Odyssey* and a few of the brightest boys even memorized all of the two works. Not only did the boy have to memorize the passages; he was also expected to recite them with intelligence and expression. Athenians believed that this type of instruction would not only cultivate oratorical skills in the young, but also imbue boys with the ideals symbolized by the heroes of Homer's great epics.

Schoolboys also learned arithmetic in their first years at school. Mathematics was not only useful for keeping accounts; it also was the basis of many aspects of Greek culture. The Athenians knew that much about the world could be understood best by the application of mathematical logic—proportion in architecture, musical harmonies, symmetry and unity in design. Hence, Athenian schoolboys learned arithmetic to become capable of making aesthetic and logical judgments. They did not learn to figure, as later generations would, mainly in order to conduct business affairs or to inquire in the empirical sciences.

About the time that a boy reached the age of thirteen his musical education began. He was taught to sing and to play a musical instrument, generally the lyre, a small harp. Music occupied an important part in the curriculum because Athenians believed that it cultivated the feelings. The Greeks believed that music produced specific emotional reactions, and that these reactions were governed by mathematical structures which defined harmony, phrasing, and tonal scales. Music properly cultivated feelings because it released emotions only within a rational structure. It provided that proper balance and relationship between passion and reason which was the Greek ideal.

Physical training also played an important part in the boys' education. Most of the training was devoted to running, leaping, wrestling, hunting, driving chariots, and hurling javelins—skills which contributed to the boys' ability to defend the city. Physical

▶ Can a society expect excellent people to teach school if it refuses to give teachers the status and respect given to members of other professions?

The Athenians had very few books. In societies where the written word is rare, long epic poems have been memorized and transmitted orally through many generations.

Though only a few fragments of Greek music survive, many theoretical writings on music are available. The Greeks approached music with mathematical logic and powerful emotions. In this respect, Greek music resembled classical Indian music.

▶ What should be the function of physical education in a high school?

training also involved learning to use the weapons of the day, the bow and the sling. The development of skill, strength, and a competitive spirit took place in the gymnasia, and the boys would continue to go there for exercise and conversation even after they became grown men. A large proportion of Athenian boys were too poor to continue formal education after the age of sixteen. These sons of less wealthy parents went to work, while the more fortunate paid handsomely for advanced education with the great "professors" of the day. Many studied rhetoric, for the ability to express oneself well increased his status, prestige, and power. These young men also studied philosophy, aesthetics, and mathematics. Physical training also continued, as the boys went to professional coaches of wrestling, boxing, spear-throwing, and riding to increase their skills.

At the age of eighteen all young men began their formal military training. In impressive ceremonies, perhaps a thousand or more eighteen-year-olds marched to a temple and recited the Ephibic Oath:

> I will not disgrace the sacred arms, nor will I abandon the man next to me, whoever he may be. I will bring aid to the ritual of the state, and to the holy duties, both alone and in company with many. I will transmit my native commonwealth not lessened, but larger and better than I have received it. I will obey those who from time to time are judges; I will obey the established statutes, and whatever other regulations the people shall enact. If anyone shall attempt to destroy the statutes I will not permit it, but will repel him both alone and with all. I will honor the ancestral faith.

The inductees then marched off to the Piraeus, for garrison duty and military training for several months. They ate at a common mess with the other members of their tribe, hopefully developing the *esprit de corps* and loyalty to their fellows which Athenians believed so essential to the life of the city. For men might legitimately disagree with each other on what should be done, but they were expected to be of one heart in their affection, pride, and devotion to their polis. Upon conclusion of their garrison duty and training young men marched back to Athens. Before an assembly held in the great theater each man was presented with a spear and a shield. Together they marched off again, this time to patrol the frontiers of the polis. While on duty they received instruction in marching, digging trenches, building fortifications, and using siege weapons.

Their tour of duty over at about the age of twenty, the young men returned again to the city, this time to take their places as citizens. Having completed their formal education, they returned as highly capable and interesting young men.

Rhetoric is the art of speaking or writing effectively.

Trans. in G. W. Botsford and E. G. Sihler, **Hellenic Civilization** (New York: Columbia University Press, 1915), p. 478. **Ephibi** came to mean those young men who were completing their education to become citizens.

# 4 THE PLACE OF WOMEN

Most people in the ancient world toiled endlessly for little reward. A large proportion of Athenian citizens, however, enjoyed the leisure to participate in the city's rich cultural life. But not all Athenians were citizens. In Pericles's day, only about 50,000 male offspring of two native-born parents enjoyed the privileges of citizenship and therefore full participation in Athenian life. Approximately 20,000 resident foreigners, 125,000 slaves, and the wives and children of citizens were denied these privileges.

Athens did not take a thorough census, so these population figures are educated guesses.

The slaves, working long hours in the fields, silver mines, shops, and households of citizens, led the hardest lives of all Athenians. Resident foreigners, most of whom engaged in business, enjoyed more material comfort than slaves. They were heavily taxed, however, and could not participate fully in political, economic, and cultural affairs. Although scholars agree that women were excluded from full participation in Athenian life, they disagree about the exact status women achieved in the Athenian social structure. Some students of Greek history believe that women were little more than prisoners in the households of their husbands. Others contend that women had an honored place in society.

This dispute among modern scholars about the place of women in Athenian society may reflect disagreement among Athenian men. The selection that follows presents only one Athenian thinker's view of the role and status of women. You will examine other attitudes in class.

Xenophon, author of the following selection, was a historian, an essayist, and a soldier. His *Oeconomicus* was a treatise on estate management. Along with other matters, he naturally discussed the role of the lady of the manor. The essay is written in the form of a dialogue between Socrates and Ischomachus, who owned a country estate. As you read, try to answer the following questions:

1. What does Ischomachus consider to be the special abilities and dispositions of women? What role does he think these abilities and dispositions fit them for?
2. What status did Ischomachus give his wife? What privileges did she have? what duties?
3. How would you describe the relationship between Ischomachus and his wife?
4. If all Athenian men had treated their wives as Ischomachus treated his, what kind of life would the wives have led? Do you think it would have been a good life? Why or why not?

19

# Lessons for a Young Wife

Xenophon, **Oeconomicus,** trans. by H. G. Dakyns. From **Readings in the History of the Ancient World,** ed. by William C. McDermott and Wallace E. Caldwell (New York: Holt, Rinehart and Winston, Inc., 1951), pp. 205–208. Reprinted by permission.

▶ Should parents play a major role in choosing their children's mates?

. . . But to answer your question, Socrates (he proceeded), I certainly do not spend my days indoors, if for no other reason, because my wife is quite capable of managing our domestic affairs without my aid.

Ah! (said I), Ischomachus, that is just what I should like particularly to learn from you. Did you yourself educate your wife to be all that a wife should be, or when you received her from her father and mother was she already a proficient well skilled to discharge the duties appropriate to a wife?

Well skilled! (he replied). What proficiency was she likely to bring with her, when she was not quite fifteen at the time she wedded me, and during the whole prior period of her life had been most carefully brought up to see and hear as little as possible, and to ask the fewest questions? or do you not think one should be satisfied, if at marriage her whole experience consisted in knowing how to take the wool and make a dress, and seeing how her mother's handmaidens had their daily spinning-tasks assigned them? For (he added), as regards control of appetite and self-indulgence, she had received the soundest education, and that I take to be the most important matter in the bringing-up of man or woman. . . .

*Socrates:* Pray, narrate to me, Ischomachus, I beg of you, what you first [taught] her. . . .

Why, Socrates (he answered), when after a time she had become accustomed to my hand, that is, was tamed sufficiently to play her part in a discussion, I put to her this question: "Did it ever strike you to consider, dear wife, what led me to choose you as my wife among all women, and your parents to entrust you to me of all men? It was certainly not from any difficulty that might beset either of us to find another bedfellow. That I am sure is evident to you. No! it was with deliberate intent to discover, I for myself and your parents in behalf of you, the best partner of house and children we could find, that I sought you out, and your parents, acting to the best of their ability, made choice of me. If at some future time God grant us to have children born to us, we will take counsel together how best to bring them up, for that too will be a common interest, and a common blessing if haply they shall live to fight our battles and we find in them hereafter support and succour when ourselves are old. But at present there is our house here, which belongs alike to both. It is common property, for all that I possess goes by my will into the common fund, and in the same way all that you deposited was placed by you to the common fund. We need not stop to calculate in figures which of us contributed most, but rather let us lay to heart this fact that whichever of us proves the better partner, he or she at once contributes what is most worth having. . . .

"God made provision from the first shaping, as it seems to me, the woman's nature for indoor and man's for outdoor occupations. Man's body and soul He furnished with a greater capacity for enduring heat and cold, wayfaring and military marches; or, to repeat, He laid upon his shoulders the outdoor works.

"While in creating the body of woman with less capacity for these things," I continued, "God would seem to have imposed on her the indoor works; and knowing that He had implanted in the woman and imposed upon her the nurture of new-born babes, He endowed her with a larger share of affection for the new-born child than He bestowed upon man. And since He had imposed on woman the guardianship of the things imported without, God, in His wisdom, perceiving that a fearful spirit was no detriment to guardianship, endowed the woman with a larger measure of timidity than He bestowed on man. Knowing further that he to whom the outdoor works belonged would need to defend them against malign attack, He endowed the man in turn with a larger share of courage.

"And seeing that both alike feel the need of giving and receiving, He set down memory and carefulness between them for their common use, so that you would find it hard to determine whether of the two, the male or the female, has the larger share of these. So, too, God set down between them for their common use the gift of self-control, where needed. . . . And for the very reason that their natures are not alike adapted to like ends, they stand in greater need of one another; and the married couple is made more useful to itself, the one fulfilling what the other lacks.

"Now, being well aware of this, my wife," I added, "and knowing well what things are laid upon us . . . by God Himself, must we not strive to perform, each in the best way possible, our respective duties? Law, too, gives her consent—law and the usage of mankind, by sanctioning the wedlock of man and wife; and just as God ordained them to be partners in their children, so the law establishes their common ownership of house and estate. Custom, moreover, proclaims as beautiful those excellences of man and woman with which God gifted them at birth. Thus for a woman to bide tranquilly at home rather than roam abroad is no dishonour; but for a man to remain indoors, instead of devoting himself to outdoor pursuits, is a thing discreditable. But if a man does things contrary to the nature given him by God, the chances are, such insubordination escapes not the eye of Heaven; he pays the penalty, whether of neglecting his own works, or of performing those appropriate to woman. . . .

21

Xenophon was describing a country estate that was, for the most part, economically self-sufficient. Compare it to an eighteenth-century plantation in Virginia.

▶ Should a woman be able to find fulfillment only through her family and her household duties?

"You will need in the same way to stay indoors, despatching to their toils without those of your domestics whose work lies there. Over those whose appointed tasks are wrought indoors, it will be your duty to preside; yours to receive the stuffs brought in; yours to apportion part for daily use, and yours to make provision for the rest, to guard and garner it so that the outgoings destined for a year may not be expended in a month. It will be your duty, when the wools are introduced, to see that clothing is made for those who need; your duty also to see that the dried corn is rendered fit and serviceable for food.

"There is just one of all these occupations which devolve upon you," I added, "you may not find so altogether pleasing. Should any of our household fall sick, it will be your care to see and tend them to the recovery of their health."

"Nay," she answered, "that will be my pleasantest of tasks, if careful nursing may touch the springs of gratitude and leave them friendlier than heretofore." . . .

"But there are other cares, you know, and occupations," I answered, "which are yours by right, and these you will find agreeable. This, for instance: to take some maiden who knows naught of carding wool and to make her a proficient in the art, doubling her usefulness; or to receive another quite ignorant of housekeeping or of service, and to render her skilful, loyal, serviceable, till she is worth her weight in gold; or again, when occasion serves, you have it in your power to requite by kindness the well-behaved whose presence is a blessing to your house; or maybe to chasten the bad character, should such a one appear. But the greatest joy of all will be to prove yourself my better; to make me your faithful follower; knowing no dread lest as the years advance you should decline in honour in your household, but rather trusting that, though your hair turn gray, yet, in proportion as you come to be a better helpmate to myself and to the children, a better guardian of our home, so will your honour increase throughout the household as mistress, wife, and mother, daily more dearly prized. Since," I added, "it is not through excellence of outward form, but by reason of the lustre of virtues shed forth upon the life of man, that increase is given to things beautiful and good."

That, Socrates, or something like that, as far as I may trust my memory, records the earliest conversation which I held with her.

# Athens: The Ideals

## STATING THE ISSUE

By any standard, the Athenians left a rich heritage to modern man. Their philosophy, embodied in the works of Plato, Aristotle, and many others, still helps to shape western thought. Their temples, though few in number and small in size, stand as enduring monuments of excellence. Modern theatrical companies still perform their plays, which continue to offer penetrating insights into basic human dilemmas. Their democratic political system, which offered all citizens a voice in shaping the community, remains a standard by which modern men judge their own governments.

Perhaps the Greek heritage endured because ancient Athenians faced squarely the most significant questions that confront men in all ages. Athenians boldly asked themselves what is good. They examined critically their assumptions about truth, beauty, and justice. Because they confronted these issues honestly and intelligently, they left the modern world a treasure of philosophy, art, and literature concerned with man's most important problems.

The eagerness of Athenians to probe the meaning of life grew in part from their great confidence in man. They believed that man, through the use of his reason and the liberation of his spirit, could find answers to history's most profound questions. Consequently, they were far more willing than most other peoples, before or since, to speculate about the meaning of existence. Can man lead a good life on earth? What does a good man owe to his family, to his companions, and to strangers? What do a society's ideals reveal about its conceptions of what is good? Should a man obey society's laws if he thinks that they are basically wrong? These are the major issues of Chapter 2.

CHAPTER

2

# 5 GREEK CONCEPTS
# OF THE AFTERLIFE

Men have always sought immortality. Unwilling to accept the idea that a man's existence ends with his final heartbeat, they have clung tenaciously to belief in an afterlife. Some men, such as Christians, think that life in an eternal paradise lies beyond the grave. Others, such as Hindus, contend that men's souls leave them at death to enter the bodies of other earthly creatures. Still others believe that man achieves immortality only through the memories of men who live after him. All these beliefs influence the ways in which men spend their earthly existence. Indeed, preparation for death shapes much of what men do in this world.

The Greeks sought immortality as much as men of any age. Consequently, they asked themselves questions about the afterlife and about the relationship between the afterlife and life on this earth. On these questions, as on so many fundamental issues, no single Greek view prevailed. Adept and passionate thinkers, the Greeks often pursued different lines of thought to different conclusions. Reading 5 presents the afterlife as seen by three Greeks—a ninth-century-B.C. poet and two fourth-century-B.C. philosophers. As you read, keep the following questions in mind:

1. How is the afterlife defined in Homer's story of Odysseus in Hades? How do Epicurus and Socrates define it?
2. According to Homer, is the afterlife something to be desired? Does Socrates believe the afterlife is something to strive for? How about Epicurus?
3. Does each believe that the afterlife is a reward for having lived a good life on earth?
4. What does each of these three views of the afterlife imply about how a man should live on earth? What does each imply about the central purpose of this life?

## The Afterlife According to Homer

*For Athenians the epic poetry of Homer was a prime source of history, national spirit, religion, and entertainment. Homer's two great works, the* Iliad *and the* Odyssey, *tell the heroic story of the Trojan War, fought between the Greeks and the Trojans, a people who dominated western Asia Minor. Homer composed his poems around 800 B.C., nearly four centuries after the Trojan*

*War. The* Iliad *and the* Odyssey *became fountainheads of Greek culture. In the fifth century nearly all Athenians knew Homer's stories; Athenian schoolchildren studied Homer and memorized long passages from his works.*

*In the following selection from the* Odyssey, *Homer describes a visit by Odysseus, a Greek war-hero, to Hades, the place where the Greeks believed all souls went after death. Odysseus, however, is not yet dead; he goes to Hades to get directions for a safe passage home from the war to his family in Greece. Once in Hades, Odysseus meets the soul of his mother, whom he has not seen since leaving for the war, and then the soul of Achilles, another Greek hero of the Trojan War. As Odysseus relates the story, he first questions his mother.*

" 'But do tell me, really and truly, what was the cause of your death? how did you die? Was it a long disease? or did Artemis Archeress [goddess of the hunt] kill you with her gentle shafts? And tell me about my father.' . . .

. . . " '[Y]our father stays there in the country and never comes to town. His bedding is not glossy rugs and blankets on a bedstead, but in winter he sleeps among the hinds in the house, in the dust beside the fire, and wears poor clothes: when summer comes and blooming autumn, he lies on the ground anywhere about the slope of his vineyard, on a heap of fallen leaves. There he lies sorrowing and will not be comforted, longing for your return; old age weighs heavy upon him.

" 'And this is how I sickened and died. The Archeress did not shoot me in my own house with those gentle shafts that never miss; it was no disease that made me pine away: but I missed you so much, and your clever wit and your gay merry ways, and life was sweet no longer, so I died.'

"When I heard this, I longed to throw my arms round her neck. Three times I tried to embrace the ghost, three times it slipt through my hands like a shadow or a dream. A sharp pang pierced my heart, and I cried out straight from my heart to hers:

" 'Mother dear! Why don't you stay with me when I long to embrace you? Let us relieve our hearts, and have a good cry in each other's arms. Are you only a phantom which awful Persephoneia [goddess of the underworld] has sent to make me more unhappy than ever?'

"My dear mother answered:

" 'Alas, alas, my child, most luckless creature on the face of the earth! Persephoneia is not deceiving you, she is the daughter of Zeus; but this is only what happens to mortals when one of us dies.

Homer, **The Odyssey,** trans. by W. H. D. Rouse (New York: The New American Library, Inc., 1937), pp. 119-120, 124-125. Reprinted by permission. English rights controlled by Thomas Nelson & Sons, Ltd. This translator decided that the poetry of Homer could most effectively be rendered in English through prose.

▶ How often should children visit aged parents?

As soon as the spirit leaves the white bones, the sinews no longer hold flesh and bones together—the blazing fire consumes them all; but the soul flits away fluttering like a dream. Make haste to the light; but do not forget all this, tell it to your wife by and by.' . . .

"As we two stood talking together of our sorrows in this mournful way, other ghosts came up: Achilles and Patroclos, and Antilochos, the man without stain and without reproach, and Aias, who was most handsome and noble of all next to the admirable Achilles. [These four men were Greek warriors.] The ghost of Achilles knew me, and said in plain words:

"'Here is Prince Odysseus who never fails! O you foolhardy man! Your ingenious brain will never do better than this. How did you dare to come down to Hades, where dwell the dead without sense or feeling, phantoms of mortals whose weary days are done?'

"I answered him, 'My lord Achilles . . . , our chief and our champion before Troy! I came to ask Teiresias if he had any advice or help for me on my way to my rugged island home. For I have not yet set foot in my own country, since trouble has ever been my lot. But you, Achilles, are most blessed of all men like the gods; and now you are a potentate in this world of the dead. Then do not deplore your death, Achilles.'

"He answered at once, 'Don't bepraise death to me, Odysseus. I would rather be a plowman to a yeoman farmer on a small holding than lord paramount in the kingdom of the dead.'"

Teiresias was a blind prophet. You will meet him again when you read **Antigone.**

# Epicurus on Life and Death

*The following selection comes from the* Golden Maxims *of Epicurus, a philosopher of the fourth century* B.C. *Unlike most Greek thinkers, Epicurus had little use for the gods; his name, in fact, became the Hebrew word for "atheist."*

Epicurus, **Golden Maxims,** in Walter R. Agard, **The Greek Mind** (Princeton: D. Van Nostrand Company, Inc., 1957), p. 162. Reprinted by permission.

Accustom yourself to think that death means nothing to us. For what is good and bad is a matter of sensation, and death is an end of sensation. Grasping this principle makes human life pleasant, not by giving us any promise of immortality, but by freeing us from any desire for immortality. For there is nothing in life to be afraid of for a man who understands that he need not be afraid of its extinction. So death, usually regarded as the greatest of calamities, is actually nothing to us; for while we are, death is not, and when death is here, we are not. So death means nothing to either the living or the dead, for it has nothing to do with the living and the dead do not exist.

# Socrates Contemplates His Death

*In the year 399 B.C., Socrates, the great Athenian philosopher, was tried and condemned to death on the charge of corrupting the minds of the youth of Athens. In this selection, written by his student, Plato, we find Socrates reflecting upon death and the afterlife as he awaits his execution in his cell.*

. . . [T]hose of us who think that death is an evil must needs be mistaken. I have a clear proof that that is so. . . .

. . . [W]e may well hope that death is a good. For the state of death is one of two things: either the dead man wholly ceases to be and loses all consciousness or, as we are told, it is a change and a migration of the soul to another place. And if death is the absence of all consciousness, and like the sleep of one whose slumbers are unbroken by any dreams, it will be a wonderful gain. For if a man had to select that night in which he slept so soundly that he did not even dream, and had to compare with it all the other nights and days of his life, and then had to say how many days and nights in his life he had spent better and more pleasantly than this night, I think that a private person, nay, even the Great King of Persia himself, would find them easy to count, compared with the others. If that is the nature of death, I for one count it a gain. For then it appears that all time is nothing more than a single night. But if death is a journey to another place, and what we are told is true—that all who have died are there—what good could be greater than this? . . . [W]hat would you not give to converse with Orpheus and Musaeus and Hesiod and Homer? . . . I am willing to die many times if this be true. . . . I could spend my time in examining those who are there, as I examine men here, and in finding out which of them is wise, and which of them thinks himself wise when he is not wise. . . .

And you too . . . must face death hopefully, and believe this one truth, that no evil can happen to a good man, either in life or after death. His affairs are not neglected by the gods; and what has happened to me today has not happened by chance. I am persuaded that it was better for me to die now, and to be released from trouble; and that was the reason why the guide never turned me back. And so I am not at all angry with my accusers or with those who have condemned me to die. Yet it was not with this in mind that they accused me and condemned me, but meaning to do me an injury. So far I may blame them.

Yet I have one request to make of them. When my sons grow up, punish them, my friends, and harass them in the same way that I

Plato, **Euthyphro, Apology, Crito,** trans. by F. J. Church and R. D. Cummings (New York: Liberal Arts Press, Inc., 1956), pp. 47–49.

These four men were famous Greek singers and poets of the past.

27

▶ Do you believe that excellence should be pursued at the expense of material comfort? Or should one strive for some of each?

have harassed you, if they seem to you to care for riches or for any other thing more than excellence; and if they think that they are something when they are really nothing, reproach them, as I have reproached you, for not caring for what they should, and for thinking that they are something when really they are nothing. And if you will do this, I myself and my sons will have received justice from you.

# 6 THE HERO AND THE GOOD LIFE

Heroes shape our conceptions of the good man and the good life. Nathan Hale, Martin Luther King, Babe Ruth, and John Glenn symbolize qualities of the good man to many Americans. In similar fashion, the lives of people as diverse as the Beatles and the Kennedys influence our thoughts about the nature of the good life. So long as man can learn and has memory, past and present heroes will subtly mold his world.

The selections in Reading 6 present four models that influenced ancient Athenians. The first, Odysseus, was the hero of Homer's *Odyssey,* an epic tale that describes the adventures of Odysseus on his return to Greece after the Trojan War. Odysseus was one of the most important legendary heroes in the Greek tradition. The three that follow, Tellus, Cleobis, and Biton, were more simple folk. They figured in a conversation about the nature of happiness between Solon, the Athenian wise man and reformer, and Croesus, a fabulously wealthy king in Asia Minor. As you read these two selections, let the following questions guide your thinking:

1. What are the characteristics of the good man according to Homer's story of Odysseus and the Cyclops?
2. Do you think the standards of the good man suggested by the example of Odysseus provide a satisfactory guide to human behavior?
3. What qualities did Croesus and Solon believe make men happy? What qualities did they believe a good man should demonstrate?
4. Which provides a better model for a good man and a good life, someone who is famous or a humble man with more modest attainments?

# Odysseus and the Cyclops

*In the following selection Odysseus tells of his encounter with the Cyclops, the giant, one-eyed monster. After having been blown off course, Odysseus and his men landed on the island inhabited by the Cyclops and were captured. Odysseus tells how he plotted to free his men.*

" 'Who are you?' [the Cyclops] called out. 'Where do you come from over the watery ways? Are you traders, or a lot of pirates ready to kill and be killed, bringing trouble to foreigners?'

"While he spoke, our hearts were wholly broken within us to see the horrible monster, and to hear that beastly voice. But I managed to answer him:

" 'We are Achaians [Greeks] from Troy, driven out of our course over the broad sea by all the winds of heaven. We meant to sail straight home, but we have lost our way altogether: such was the will of Zeus, I suppose. We have the honour to be the people of King Agamemnon [of the Achaians]. . . , whose fame is greatest of all men under the sky, for the strong city he sacked and the many nations he conquered. But we have found you, and come to your knees, to pray if you will give us the stranger's due or anything you may think proper to give to a stranger. Respect the gods, most noble sir; see, we are your suppliants! Strangers and suppliants have their guardian strong, God walks with them to see they get no wrong.'

"He answered me with cruel words: 'You are a fool, stranger, or you come from a long way off, if you expect me to fear gods. Zeus Almighty be damned and his blessed gods with him. We Cyclopians care nothing for them, we are stronger than they are. I should not worry about Zeus if I wanted to lay hands on you or your companions. But tell me, where did you moor your ship—far off or close by? I should be glad to know that.'

"He was just trying it on, but I knew something of the world and saw through it; so I answered back, 'My ship was wrecked by Poseidon Earthshaker, who cast us on the rocks near the boundary of your country; the wind drove us on a lee shore. But I was saved with these others.'

"The cruel monster made no answer, but just jumped up and reached out towards my men, grabbed two like a pair of puppies and dashed them on the ground: their brains ran out and soaked into the earth. Then he cut them up limb by limb, and made them ready for supper. He devoured them like a mountain lion, bowels and flesh and marrow-bones, and left nothing. We groaned aloud,

Homer, **The Odyssey,** trans. by W. H. D. Rouse (New York: The New American Library, Inc., 1937), pp. 98-101. Reprinted by permission. English rights controlled by Thomas Nelson & Sons, Ltd.

In a world undotted with motels and other public accommodations, one was expected to greet a stranger with hospitality.

Poseidon was the god of the sea.

Note this vivid, if gory, example of Homer's imagery. Homer often described the unfamiliar by a precise comparison to something that was more easily imaginable. Here he implies that the Cyclops is as powerful compared to man as man is to a puppy.

29

lifting our hands to Zeus, when we saw this brutal business; but there was nothing to be done.

"When Goggle-eye had filled his great belly with his meal of human flesh, washed down with a draught of milk neat, he lay and stretched himself among the sheep. But I did not lose heart. I considered whether to go near and draw my sharp sword and drive it into his breast; I could feel about till I found the place where the midriff encloses the liver. But second thoughts kept me back. We should have perished ourselves in that place, dead and done for; we could never have moved the great stone which he had planted in the doorway. So we lay groaning and awaited the dawn.

"Dawn came. He lit the fire, milked his flocks, all in order, put the young under each, then he grabbed two more men and prepared his breakfast. That done, he drove out the fat flocks, moving away the great stone with ease; but he put it back again, just as you fit cover to quiver. With many a whistle Goggle-eye turned his fat flocks to the hills; but I was left brooding and full of dark plans, longing to have my revenge if Athena would grant my prayer.

"Among all my schemes and machinations, the best plan I could think of was this. A long spar was lying beside the pen, a sapling of green olive-wood; Goggle-eye had cut it down to dry it and use as a staff. It looked to us about as large as the mast of a twenty-oar ship . . . ; it was about that length and thickness. I cut off a fathom of this, and handed it over to my men to dress down. They made it smooth, then I sharpened the end and charred it in the hot fire, and hid it carefully under the dung which lay in a great mass all over the floor. Then I told the others to cast lots who should help me with the pole and rub it into his eye while he was sound asleep. The lot fell on those four whom I would have chosen myself, which made five counting me.

"In the evening, back he came with his flocks. This time he drove them all into the cave, and left none outside in the yard; whether he suspected something, or God made him do it, I do not know. Then he lifted the great stone and set it in place, sat down and milked his ewes and nannies bleating loudly, all in order, put her young under each, and when all this was done, grabbed two more men and made his meal.

"At this moment I came near to Goggle-eye, holding in my hand an ivy-wood cup full of the red wine, and I said:

"'Cyclops, here, have a drink after that jolly meal of mans-mutton! I should like to show you what drink we had on board our ship. I brought it as a drink-offering for you, in the hope that you might have pity and help me on my way home. But you are mad beyond all bearing! Hard heart, how can you expect any other men to pay you a visit? For you have done what is not right.'

"He took it and swallowed it down. The good stuff delighted him terribly, and he asked for another drink:

"'Oh, please give me more, and tell me your name this very minute! I will give you a stranger's gift which will make you happy! Mother earth does give us wine in huge bunches, even in this part of the world, and the rain from heaven makes them grow; but this is a rivulet of nectar and ambrosia!'

"Then I gave him a second draught. Three drinks I gave him; three times the fool drank. At last, when the wine had got into his head, I said to him in the gentlest of tones:

"'Cyclops, do you ask me my name? Well, I will tell you, and you shall give me the stranger's due, as you promised. Noman is my name; Noman is what mother and father call me and all my friends.'

"Then the cruel monster said, 'Noman shall be last eaten of his company, and all the others shall be eaten before him! that shall be your stranger's gift.'

"As he said this, down he slipt and rolled on his back. His thick neck drooped sideways, and all-conquering sleep laid hold on him; wine dribbled out of his gullet with lumps of human flesh, as he belched in his drunken slumbers. Then I drove the pole deep under the ashes to grow hot, and spoke to hearten my men that no one might fail me through fear.

"As soon as the wood was on the point of catching fire, and glowed white-hot, green as it was, I drew it quickly out of the fire while my men stood round me: God breathed courage into us then. The men took hold of the stake, and thrust the sharp point into his eye; and I leaned hard on it from above and turned it round and round. As a man bores a ship's timber with an auger, while others at the lower part keep turning it with a strap which they hold at each end, and round and round it runs: so we held the fire-sharpened pole and turned it, and the blood bubbled about its hot point. The fumes singed eyelids and eyelashes all about as the eyeball burnt and the roots crackled in the fire. As a smith plunges an axe or an adze in cold water, for that makes the strength of steel, and it hisses loud when he tempers it, so his eye sizzled about the pole of olive-wood.

"He gave a horrible bellow till the rocks rang again, and we shrank away in fear. Then he dragged out the post from his eye dabbled and dripping with blood, and threw it from him, wringing his hands in wild agony, and roared aloud to the Cyclopians who lived in caves round about among the windy hills. They heard his

▶ How should we treat strangers who have had an accident or need help?

31

cries, and came thronging from all directions, and stood about the cave, asking what his trouble was:

"'What on earth is the matter with you, Polyphemos?' they called out. 'Why do you shout like this through the night and wake us all up? Is any man driving away your flocks against your will? Is any one trying to kill you by craft or main force?'

"Out of the cave came the voice of mighty Polyphemos: 'O my friends, Noman is killing me by craft and not by main force!'

"They answered him in plain words:

"'Well, if no man is using force, and you are alone, there's no help for a bit of sickness when heaven sends it; so you had better say your prayers to Lord Poseidon your father!'

"With these words away they went, and my heart laughed within me to think how a mere nobody had taken them all in with my machinomanations!"

# The Good Life: A View of Happiness

*The following selection is taken from Herodotus's Histories, which tell of the fifth-century-B.C. wars between the Persians, who ruled most of Asia Minor, and the Greeks. Herodotus did not record the following conversation firsthand; in fact, he may well have made it up. In any case, Herodotus used the story of Croesus and Solon as an opportunity to present an Athenian view of the good man and the good life.*

Herodotus, **The Histories**, trans. by Aubrey de Selincourt (London: Penguin Books, Ltd., 1954), pp. 23–26. Reprinted by permission.

Croesus entertained [Solon] hospitably in the palace, and three or four days after his arrival instructed some servants to take him on a tour of the royal treasuries and point out the richness and magnificence of everything. When Solon had made as thorough an inspection as opportunity allowed, Croesus said: "Well, my Athenian friend, I have heard a great deal about your wisdom, and how widely you have travelled in the pursuit of knowledge. I cannot resist my desire to ask you a question: who is the happiest man you have ever seen?"

The point of the question was that Croesus supposed himself to be the happiest of men. Solon, however, refused to flatter, and answered in strict accordance with his view of the truth. "An Athenian," he said, "called Tellus."

Croesus was taken aback. "And what," he asked sharply, "is your reason for this choice?"

"There are two good reasons," said Solon, "first, his city was prosperous, and he had fine sons, and lived to see children born to each

▶ Could you be happy if your parents were ashamed of you?

32

of them, and all these children surviving; and, secondly, after a life which by our standards was a good one, he had a glorious death. In a battle with the neighbouring town of Eleusis, he fought for his countrymen, routed the enemy, and died like a soldier; and the Athenians paid him the high honour of a public funeral on the spot where he fell."

All these details about the happiness of Tellus, Solon doubtless intended as a moral lesson for the king; Croesus, however, thinking he would at least be awarded second prize, asked who was the next happiest person whom Solon had seen.

"Two young men of Argos," was the reply; "Cleobis and Biton. They had enough to live on comfortably; and their physical strength is proved not merely by their success in athletics, but much more by the following incident. The Argives were celebrating the festival of Hera, and it was most important that the mother of the two young men should drive to the temple in her ox-cart; but it so happened that the oxen were late in coming back from the fields. Her two sons therefore, as there was no time to lose, harnessed themselves to the cart and dragged it along, with their mother inside, for a distance of nearly six miles, until they reached the temple. After this exploit, which was witnessed by the assembled crowd, they had a most enviable death—a heaven-sent proof of how much better it is to be dead than alive. Men kept crowding around them and congratulating them on their strength, and women kept telling the mother how lucky she was to have such sons, when, in sheer pleasure at this public recognition of her sons' act, she prayed the goddess Hera, before whose shrine she stood, to grant Cleobis and Biton, who had brought her such honour, the greatest blessing that can fall to mortal man.

"After her prayer came the ceremonies of sacrifice and feasting; and the two lads, when all was over, fell asleep in the temple— and that was the end of them, for they never woke again.

"The Argives had statues made of them, which they sent to Delphi, as a mark of their particular respect."

Croesus was vexed with Solon for giving the second prize for happiness to the two young Argives, and snapped out: "That's all very well, my Athenian friend; but what of my own happiness? Is it so utterly contemptible that you won't even compare me with mere common folk like those you have mentioned?"

"My Lord," replied Solon, "I know God is envious of human prosperity and likes to trouble us; and you question me about the lot of man. Listen then: as the years lengthen out, there is much both to see and to suffer which one would wish otherwise. . . . [T]he total of days for your seventy years is 26,250, and not a single one

Argos was a Greek city. By choosing Greeks for both of his examples, Solon may have been rubbing it in, as Croesus was not Greek.

Delphi, located at the foot of Mount Parnassus, was the home of the chief shrine to the god Apollo.

33

of them is like the next in what it brings. You can see from that, Croesus, what a chancy thing life is. You are rich, and you rule a numerous people; but the question you asked me I will not answer, until I know that you have died happily. Great wealth can make a man no happier than moderate means unless he has the luck to continue in prosperity to the end. . . . [T]hough the rich have the means to satisfy their appetites and to bear calamities, and the poor have not, the poor, if they are lucky, are more likely to keep clear of trouble, and will have besides the blessings of a sound body, health, freedom from trouble, fine children, and good looks.

▶ Forced to a choice, would you rather be rich or healthy?

"Now if a man thus favoured dies as he has lived, he will be just the one you are looking for: the only sort of person who deserves to be called happy. But mark this: until he is dead, keep the word 'happy' in reserve. Till then, he is not happy, but only lucky.

"Nobody of course can have all these advantages, any more than a country can produce everything it needs: whatever it has, it is bound to lack something. The best country is the one which has most. It is the same with people: no man is ever self-sufficient—there is sure to be something missing. But whoever has the greatest number of the good things I have mentioned, and keeps them to the end, and dies a peaceful death, that man, my lord Croesus, deserves in my opinion to be called happy.

"Look to the end, no matter what it is you are considering. Often enough God gives a man a glimpse of happiness, and then utterly ruins him."

These sentiments were not of the sort to give Croesus any pleasure; he let Solon go with cold indifference, firmly convinced that he was a fool. For what could be more stupid than to keep telling him to look at the "end" of everything, without any regard to present prosperity?

# 7 THE ROGUE

Good men, both the famous and the humble, mirror a society's ideals. Their lives serve as models for others. Parents and teachers parade their achievements for the young to emulate. Legends, folk songs, and biographies record their good deeds. They are everywhere honored in the land.

Villains and rogues can play a similar role; but instead of models to emulate, they become examples of all that is bad and to be avoided at all costs. The bad can reveal the good, however. A list

34

of the characteristics of villains and rogues can be transformed by antonyms into a character sketch of the good man.

A fourth-century-B.C. writer named Theophrastus sketched some of Athens's most unpleasant character types. For all of their achievements, the Athenians, as Theophrastus delighted in showing, were not invariably heroic and charming. In portraying the darker side of Athenian character, Theophrastus was part of a great comic tradition that leaned heavily on wit, satire, and bawdiness. As you read excerpts from his character sketches, keep the following questions in mind:

1. What qualities did Theophrastus attack in these character sketches?
2. What qualities do the sketches imply that a good man should have? (You may wish to find an antonym for each of the characteristics you identify.)
3. Which of Theophrastus's characters have you met in modern dress in your own city or town? How "modern" does Theophrastus seem?
4. How should a good person deal with the sorts of people Theophrastus described?

# A Gallery of Rogues

### THE TOADY, OR FLATTERER

Flattery may be thought of as an attitude or relationship which is degrading in itself, but profitable to the one who flatters.

The toady is the sort of person who will say to the man he is walking with, "Do you notice how people look at you? You're the only man in Athens they study in that way." Or perhaps, "You were being complimented yesterday in the Arcade. There was a group of thirty or more sitting talking; and the question cropped up, Who was our best citizen? Starting from that, we all came back finally to your name." While he is going on like this, he picks a stray thread off the other's cloak; or if a bit of chaff has blown into his hair, he takes it out, and says with a laugh, "Look at that! Because I haven't seen you for two days, you've got a beard full of grey hairs; though if anyone's hair keeps its colour in spite of years, yours does." Then he will tell the company to keep silent while the great man is speaking; he will praise him when he is listening; and when he pauses in his talk he will back him up with "Hear, hear!" When his patron makes a feeble joke he laughs, stuffing his

Theophrastus, **The Characters**, bound together with Menander, **Plays and Fragments**, both trans. by Philip Vellacott (London: Penguin Books, Ltd., 1967), pp. 27–29, 37–38, 41–42, 48–50. Reprinted by permission.

cloak into his mouth as if he couldn't contain his merriment. He asks people they meet in the street to wait until "He" has passed. He buys apples and pears, brings them in and gives them to the children when their father is watching, kisses them and says, "Well, youngsters, you've got a splendid father." If he goes with his patron to help him buy some shoes, he remarks that the foot is more shapely than the shoe. If the other is on his way to visit some friend, the toady will run ahead and tell the friend, "He's coming to see you," and then turn back and say, "I have announced you." He is even capable of running errands, at a moment's notice, to the women's market. . . . Then in the theatre, he will take the cushions from the slave, and himself arrange them on his patron's seat. His patron's house, he will say, is beautifully built; his land has been nicely planted; and his portrait is an excellent likeness.

### THE CHATTERER

Chatter is the churning-out of long-winded, unconsidered talk.

The chatterer is the sort of man who sits down beside someone he doesn't know and begins by delivering a panegyric on his own wife; continues with an account of his dream of the night before; then describes in detail what he had for supper. Next, getting into his stride, he remarks how far inferior men of the present day are to the ancients; how reasonable wheat is now in the shops; how full of foreigners Athens is getting. He observes that since the Dionysia it has been good sailing weather; and that if only Zeus would send more rain it would be better for the farmers. Then he tells you what part of his land he will put down to crops next year; and how difficult it is to live; and that Damippus has set up an enormous torch at the Mysteries; and "How many columns has the Odeion?" and "I was violently sick yesterday"; and "What day of the month is it today?" Then he tells you that the Mysteries are in September, the Apaturia in October, and the Rural Dionysia in December. In fact, if you put up with him, he will never stop.

### THE UNSEASONABLE MAN

Unseasonableness is an annoying faculty for choosing the wrong moment.

The unseasonable man is the kind who comes up to you when you have no time to spare and asks your advice. He sings a serenade to his sweetheart when she has influenza. . . . If he is going to give evidence he turns up when judgement has just been pronounced. When he is a guest at a wedding he makes derogatory remarks

A panegyric is a formal oration of praise.

The Dionysia, the Mysteries, the Apaturia, and the Rural Dionysia were all annual religious and civic festivals. The Odeion, or Odeon, which has given its name to countless modern theaters, was a public building devoted to poetical and musical contests. It was built by Pericles.

about the female sex. When you have just reached home after a long journey he invites you to come for a stroll. He is certain to bring along a buyer who offers more, when you have just sold your house. When people have heard a matter and know it by heart, he stands up and explains the whole thing from the beginning. He eagerly undertakes a service for you which you don't want performed but which you have not the face to decline. . . . When a friend's slave is being beaten he will stand there and tell how he once had a slave who hanged himself after a similar beating. If he takes part in an arbitration, he will set everyone at blows again just when both sides are ready to cry quits. And after dancing once, will seize as partner another man who is not yet drunk.

## A CHIP ON THE SHOULDER, OR THE MAN WITH A GRIEVANCE

To have a "chip on the shoulder" means to complain unduly about the lot which life has assigned to one.

The man with a grievance is the kind of man who, when . . . his sweetheart is caressing and kissing him he says to her, "I wonder if you genuinely love me as much as you seem to." He is resentful against Zeus, not for sending rain, but for sending it too late. If he finds a purse in the road, he says, "But a fortune—no! I've never found *that*." When he has bought a slave cheap after much haggling, "I wonder, now," says he, "whether for that money I can have bought anything worth having." When someone comes to him with the good news, "You've got a son," he replies, "If you add to that, 'And away goes half my property,' you'll be telling the truth." . . . When his friends have contributed to provide him with a loan, and one of them says, "Now you can feel cheerful," "Can I indeed," he answers, "when I've got to give every one of you his money back, and on top of that show gratitude, as if I'd been done a favour!"

## COWARDICE

Cowardice, let us say, is a sort of shrinking of the soul due to fear.

The coward is the sort of man who, when at sea, is sure that the cliffs just sighted are pirate vessels; . . . or looks up at the steersman to ask if he is on mid-course, or what he thinks of the weather; and explains to the man next to him that his fear is due to a dream he had. . . . On military service, . . . when he hears shouting and sees men falling, he tells those standing next to him that in his hurry he forgot his sword; and he runs back to the tent, and sends his slave out, telling him to look and see where the enemy are; and meanwhile he hides his sword under his pillow, and then spends a long time looking for it; and while he's in the tent he sees a wounded man being brought in—one of his friends; so he runs to him, tells him to cheer up, and lends a hand to carry him. Then he looks after him, washes him, sits down beside him, and flicks the flies off his wound—in fact, anything rather than fight the enemy. When the trumpet sounds the advance, he remains sitting in the tent, and says, "To hell with you! Can't you let the man get a bit of sleep—always blaring away!" Then, covered with blood from the other man's wound, he meets the men as they come back from the battle, and recounts how—at some risk to himself—he has "saved one of our comrades"; and he brings the men of his tribe in to see the patient, and describes to each of them how with his own hands he brought the man back to the tent.

## THE AUTHORITARIAN

Authoritarianism, or the oligarchic temperament, may be described as an arrogant relish for power and profit.

The authoritarian is the sort of person who, when the Assembly is discussing what men to appoint as assistants to the Archon in organizing the procession at the Great Dionysia, will come forward and state his opinion that those appointed should be given unconditional powers; and if someone else proposes ten assistants, he will answer, "One is enough, but he must be a *man*." Of the poems of Homer there is one single line he has made his own: "From many rulers no good comes; let one man rule." Of all the rest of Homer he knows nothing. Typical of him are utterances like this: "We must get together by ourselves and discuss these matters, out of the reach of the rabble and the street-corner. It's time we stopped kowtowing to every jack-in-office, and ourselves accepting the kicks or compliments from them. Either they or we must run this city." He will go out about midday, with his cloak thrown well back, his hair tastefully trimmed, his nails precisely pared, and strut about declaiming statements like this: "These blackmailers make Athens impossible to live in"; or "In the law-courts we are simply slapped down by corrupt juries"; or "People who meddle in politics—I can't imagine what they want"; or "The working class—they're always the same: ungrateful, and ready to obey anyone who offers a bribe or a bonus." Or he will tell you how ashamed he feels in the Assembly, when some mean-looking, scruffy citizen sits down next to him. "The rich are being bled to death," he says, "with subsidizing the navy, the theatre, the festivals, and everything else. When is it going to end? Democratic agitators—how I detest them!"

The Great Dionysia was the annual dramatic festival of Athens. **Archons** were high office-holders. This sketch suggests that all Athenian people did not share a high opinion of democracy.

# 8 GREEK ART AND IDEAS

Perhaps no other people in history devoted so much attention to their artistic environment as the Athenians. Modern man often judges his architecture in terms of how functional it is; the ancient Greeks judged a building in terms of its beauty. Today, most paintings and sculpture are inside private homes or museums, where only those willing to make an extra effort can see them; the Athenians displayed works of art in public places where people gathered to conduct their business, participate in religious festivals, or discuss public issues. Modern Americans must pay to see a Broadway play; Greek tragedies and comedies were free to all.

Athenian citizens diligently cultivated a sense of beauty. Athens expected every citizen to contribute to the arts by creating an artistic work or by giving money to support an artist, build a temple, or finance a play. The nature of beauty was the subject of serious inquiry. Philosophers such as Plato and Aristotle, and mathematicians such as Pythagoras and Euclid, devoted much of their attention to defining the beautiful.

In the following essay William Fleming, professor of art at Syracuse University, discusses three ideas that he believes are expressed in all Greek art. As you read, think about the following questions:

1.  How does the author define the concepts of humanism, idealism, and rationalism?
2.  How were humanism, idealism, and rationalism expressed in Greek art?
3.  What do the ideas of humanism, idealism, and rationalism reveal about the Greek conception of the good man, the good life, and the good society?
4.  To what extent do the concepts of humanism, idealism, and rationalism symbolize your own values?

## Humanism, Idealism, and Rationalism in Greek Art

Certain recurring themes appear in each of the arts of the Hellenic [Greek] period as artists sought to bring their ideals to expression. Out of these themes emerges a trio of ideas—humanism, idealism, and rationalism—that recur continually in Athenian thought and action. These three ideas, then, provide the framework

William Fleming, **Arts and Ideas,** 3rd ed. (New York: Holt, Rinehart and Winston, Inc., 1968), pp. 33–34, 36–39. Reprinted by permission.

39

that surrounds the arts and encloses them in such a way that they come together into a significant unity.

## HUMANISM

▶ What does the expression "man is the measure of all things" imply about the goals of a society?

"Man," said Protagoras, "is the measure of all things." And, as Sophocles observed, "Many are the wonders of the world, and none so wonderful as man." This, in essence, is humanism. With himself as yardstick, Hellenic man conceived his gods as perfect beings, immortal and free from physical infirmities but, like himself, subject to very human passions and ambitions. The gods likewise were personifications of human ideals: Zeus stood for masculine creative power, Hera for maternal womanliness, Athena for wisdom, Apollo for youthful brilliance, Aphrodite for feminine desirability, and so on down the list. And because of his resemblance to the gods, Hellenic man gained greatly in self-esteem. When gods were more human, as the saying goes, men were more divine.

The principal concern of the Greeks was with human beings—their social relationships, their place in the natural environment, and their stake in the universal scheme of things. In such a small city-state as Athens, civic duties devolved on each individual. Every responsible person had to concern himself with politics, which Aristotle considered to be the highest social ethics. Participation in public affairs was based on the need to subordinate personal aspirations to the good of the whole state. A man endowed with great qualities of mind and body was honor-bound to exercise his gifts in the service of his fellow men. Aeschylus, Socrates, and Sophocles were men of action who served Athens on the battlefield as well as in public forums and theaters. One responsibility of a citizen was to foster the arts, and under Athenian democracy the state itself, meaning the people as a whole, became the principal patron of the arts. . . .

Particularly congenial to this humanistic mode of thought was the art of sculpture. With the human body as the point of departure, such divinities as Athena and Apollo appeared as idealized images of perfect feminine and masculine beauty. Equally imaginative were such deviations from the human norm as the goat-footed Pan, the half-human half-horse centaurs, and the myriads of fanciful creatures and monsters that symbolized the forces of nature. The Greeks were more thoroughly at home in the physical world than the later Christian peoples who believed in a separation of flesh and spirit. The Greeks greatly admired the beauty and agility of the human body at the peak of its development. In addition to studies in literature and music, Greek youth was trained from childhood for

40

competition in the Athenian and Olympic games. Since it was through the perfection of their bodies that men most resembled the gods, the culture of the body was a spiritual as well as a physical activity. The nude body in action at gymnasiums was a fact of daily experience, and sculptors had ample opportunity to observe its proportions and musculature. . . .

## IDEALISM

When an artist faces the practical problems of representation, he has two main courses open to him: he can choose to represent objects either as they appear to the physical eye or as they appear to the mind's eye. In one case, he emphasizes nature, in the other, imagination; the world of appearances as opposed to the world of essences; reality as contrasted with ideality. The avowed realist is more concerned with *concretion*—that is, with rendering the actual, tangible object that he sees with all its particular and peculiar characteristics. The idealist, on the other hand, accents *abstraction*, which is to say he eliminates all extraneous accessories and concentrates on the inner core, the essential qualities of things. A realist, in other words, tends to represent things as they are; an idealist, as they might or should be. . . .

The case for idealism is argued in Plato's dialogues. He assumes a world of eternal verities . . . but recognizes that perfect truth, beauty, and goodness can exist only in the mental world of forms and ideas. Phenomena observed in the visible world are but reflections of these invisible forms. By way of illustration, parallelism is a concept, and two exactly parallel lines will, in theory, never meet. It is impossible, however, to find anything approaching true parallelism in nature, and, no matter how carefully a draftsman draws them, two lines will always be unparallel to a slight degree and, hence, will meet somewhere this side of infinity. But this does not destroy the concept of parallelism, which still exists in the mental image or idea of it. Plato's *Republic*, to cite another example, is an intellectual exercise in projecting an ideal state. No one knew better than the author that such a society did not exist in fact and probably never would. But this does not lessen the value of the activity, and the important thing was to set up goals that would approach his utopian ideal more closely than did any existing situation. . . .

Aristotle, for his part, distinguished between various approaches in art. In his *Poetics*, he observes that "it follows that we must represent men either as better than real life, or as worse, or as they are. It is the same in painting. . . ." Aristotle also applied the same standard to drama, pointing out that "Comedy aims at repre-

During the Greek Olympics, held once every four years, there was a truce between Greek states so that athletes could come to Olympia. Victors in the games won only a branch of wild olive, but they were also celebrated as heroes in songs and poems.

41

senting men as worse, Tragedy as better than in actual life." In the visual arts, the distinction, then, is between making an idealized image, a realistic image, or a caricature. And it is clearly implied that the true artist should be concerned only with the ideal.

At its high point in the latter half of the fifth century B.C., the Hellenic style was dominated by the idealistic theory. The Greek temple was designed as an idealized dwelling place for a perfect being, and by its logical interrelationship of lines, planes, and masses, it achieves something of permanence and stability in the face of the ephemeral and haphazard state of nature. In portraying an athlete, a statesman, or a god, the Hellenic sculptor concentrated on typical or general qualities rather than on the unique or particular. This was in line with the Greek idea of personality, which it was felt was better expressed in the dominating traits and characteristics than in individual oddities or peculiarities. In sculpture, as well as in all the other arts, the object was to rise above transitory sensations to capture the permanent, the essential, the complete. Thus the sculptor avoided representing the human being in infancy or old age, since these extremes of immaturity and postmaturity implied incompleteness or imperfection and hence were incompatible with the projection of ideal types. The range of representations extends from athletes in their late teens through images of Hermes, Apollo, and Athena, who are conceived in their early maturity, to Zeus, father of the gods, who appears as the fully developed patriarch in all the power of mature manhood. It must also be remembered that few of the Hellenic sculptor's subjects were intended to represent human beings as such. The majority were fashioned to represent gods, who, if they were to be cast in human form, must have bodies of transcendent beauty. . . .

## RATIONALISM

Pythagoras was a Greek philosopher, mathematician, and astronomer who founded a religious and moral brotherhood that became a political force in a Greek colony in southern Italy. Among Pythagoras's ideas were that all matter corresponds to numbers, and that numbers have quasi-mystical properties.

Anaxagoras was the Greek philosopher who taught Pericles. See Reading 2.

Rational and irrational forces exist within every society as well as every person. The question remains whether the state or individual tries to solve problems by reason or emotion. "Things are numbers," Pythagoras is supposed to have said, and by this statement to have affirmed that something solid and permanent underlies the shifting appearances of things. A few generations later, Anaxagoras went a step farther by stating that "mind has power over all things that have life." His disciple Socrates continued the argument and kindled in his followers a burning love of truth, not because truth was useful for worldly success but because it is an ideal to be pursued for its own sake. . . .

. . . [T]he Hellenic artists were no less concerned than Plato with the pursuit of an ideal order, which they felt could be grasped by the mind through the medium of the senses. Greek architecture, in retrospect, turns out to be a high point in the rational solution to building problems. The post-and-lintel system of construction, as far as it goes, is eminently reasonable and completely comprehensible. All structural members fulfill their logical purpose, and nothing is hidden or mysterious. The orderly principle of repetition on which Greek temple designs are based is as logical in its way as one of Euclid's geometry propositions or Plato's dialogues. It accomplishes for the eye what Plato was trying to achieve for the mind. The tight unity of the Greek temple met the Greek requirement that a work of art be complete in itself. Its carefully controlled but flexible relationships of verticals and horizontals, solids and voids, structural principles and decorative embellishments give it an inexorable internal consistency. And the harmonic proportions of the Parthenon reflect the Greek image of a harmoniously proportioned universe quite as much as a logical system.

Sculpture likewise avoided the pitfalls of rigid mathematics and succeeded in working out principles adapted to its specific needs. When Polyclitus [a sculptor] said, "the beautiful comes about, little by little, through many numbers," he was aiming at a rational theory of art in which the parts and whole of a work could be expressed in mathematical proportions. But he also allowed for flexible application of the rule, depending on the pose or line of vision. By such a reconciliation of the opposites of order and freedom, he reveals the sculptor's kinship with his philosophical and political colleagues who were trying to do the same for other aspects of Athenian life.

Post-and-lintel construction is placing stones horizontally on top of supporting columns.

# 9 GREEK POETRY

Poetry often expresses strong or delicate feelings and intense perceptions better than other forms of literature. By using powerful images and compact, rhythmic language, a poet can say in a few words what a novelist would need a volume to explain. Greek poets used verse to express a wide range of thoughts and feelings. Many of their poems deal with values and touch upon the concepts of humanism, idealism, and rationalism that were discussed in Reading 8.

The works that follow are examples of Greek lyric poetry. "Lyric" comes from "lyre," the stringed musical instrument to whose music lyric poems were originally sung. These poems are usually short, and focus on a single theme, in contrast to the far-ranging narrative of epics such as the *Iliad* and the *Odyssey*.

Most of the authors of the following poems spent at least part of their lives in Athens. Athenians heard and memorized nearly all of the poems that follow. As you read them, think about the following questions:

1. What is each poem's theme? What is each poet trying to say? How is he trying to say it?
2. How do the ideals and feelings expressed in each poem compare with the ideals and feelings expressed in Readings 5–8?
3. Which of the poems best express your own ideals? Which do not? Why?

The poems by Hybrias, Simonides, Pindar, and Praxilla are from **Greek Lyrics,** trans. by Richmond Lattimore (Chicago: University of Chicago Press, rev. ed., 1960), pp. 49, 55–56, 61, 49, respectively. Reprinted by permission. The poems by Theognis, Eupolis, Phrynichus, and Menander are from T. F. Higham and C. M. Bowra, eds., **The Oxford Book of Greek Verse in Translation** (Oxford: Clarendon Press, Inc., 1938), pp. 227, 515, 515, 526 respectively. Reprinted by permission. The poem by Sappho is from Sappho, **Poems and Fragments,** trans. by Guy Davenport (Ann Arbor: Copyright © by The University of Michigan, 1965). Reprinted by permission.

Pittakos was a Greek statesman, general, and sage.

▶ What role does luck play in determining a person's chances to lead a good life?

# Nine Lyric Poems

### A boastful drinking song, by HYBRIAS

My wealth is great; it is a spear and a sword,
and the grand hairy shield to guard my body.
With these I plow, with these I harvest,
with these I tread the sweet wine from the grapevine,
with these I am called master of the rabble.

And they who dare not carry the spear and the sword
and the grand hairy shield to guard their bodies,
all these fall down before me, kiss my knee, hail me
their high king and master.

### On trying to live the good life, by SIMONIDES

*To be a good man, without blame and without question,*
*foursquare founded hand and foot, mind also*
*faultless fashioned, is difficult.*

Thus the word of Pittakos, but it does not
run right, though it was a wise man who said it:
that it is difficult to be excellent. Not difficult;
only a god could have this privilege; it is not *possible*
for a man not to go bad
when he has more bad luck than he can handle.
Any man is good while his luck is good,
bad when bad, and for the most part they are best
whom the gods love.

44

Therefore, I will not throw away my time and life
into unprofitable hope and emptiness, the search
for that object which cannot possibly be,
the Utterly Blameless Man among all of us who enjoy
man's food on the wide earth.
But if I find one, I will let you know.
No, I admire all, am a friend of any
who of his own will does nothing shameful. Against
necessity not even the gods can fight.

I do not like to find fault.
Enough for me if one is not
bad, not too unsteady, knows
what is right and good for his city,
a sound man. I will not
look out his faults. For the generation
of fools is endless. Take anything as good
which is not soiled with shame.

## A different view from a poet short on funds, by THEOGNIS

Poverty, Kyrnos, breaks a gallant man
More than white hairs or shivering fevers can.
To flee it, Kyrnos, in the deep sea drown,
Or from a towering precipice leap down;
Broken by poverty, a man's denied
All power of speech and act: his tongue is tied.

This is one of a series
of poems in which Theognis
offers advice to his young
friend Kyrnos.

## An un-Homeric view of war, by PINDAR

War is sweet to those who have not tried it. The experienced
man is frightened at the heart to see it advancing.

## A eulogy to a statesman, by EUPOLIS

In eloquence no man could equal him—
When Pericles arose and took the floor,
By ten good feet our common orators
As by an expert runner were outstript.
Not only voluble, but with persuasion
Sitting upon his lips. He bound a spell,
And had this power, alone of orators,—
To prick men's hearts and leave behind the sting.

You will find an example
of Pericles's eloquence
in Reading 13.

### A eulogy to a poet, by PHRYNICHUS

Readings 10–11 consist
of one of Sophocles's
greatest tragedies.

How blessed Sophocles, who, dying old,
Was old in happiness and skill of hand.
Beautiful were his Tragedies, and many;
And beautiful his end, who lived untroubled.

### On life and death, by MENANDER

This translation of
Menander's poem is by
Lord Byron.

Whom the gods love die young.

### A lady poet's song to Aphrodite, by SAPPHO

Aphrodite, whom the
Romans called Venus, was
the goddess of love. The
apple was one of her
symbols.

Come out of Crete
And find me here,
Come to your grove,
Mellow apple trees
And holy altar
Where the sweet smoke
Of libanum is in
Your praise,

**Libanum** means incense.

Where leaf melody
In the apples
Is a crystal crash,
And the water is cold.
All roses and shadow,
This place, and sleep
Like dusk sifts down
From trembling leaves.
Here horses stand
In flowers and graze.
The wind is glad
And sweet in its moving.
Here, Kypris

Aphrodite was also known
as Kypris.

Pour nectar in the golden cups
And mix it deftly with
Our dancing and mortal wine.

### On beauty found in simple things, by PRAXILLA

Loveliest of what I leave behind is the sunlight,
and loveliest after that the shining stars, and the moon's face,
but also cucumbers that are ripe, and pears, and apples.

# 10–11 GREEK DRAMA

Ancient Athenians enjoyed the theater as modern Americans enjoy television and movies. Men and women, citizens and slaves, flocked to the great open-air theater on the slope of the Acropolis. Public funds and private contributions supported the theater and the plays that were performed there.

Athenian drama brought together nearly every strain of Greek culture. The plays themselves were written mostly in poetic form. Dramatists took themes from the Homeric legends and, occasionally, from historical events and mythology; their characters included the gods themselves. Actors needed such admired skills as public speaking, singing, and dancing. Leading artists made statues and painted scenery for the performances.

The Athenians found the theater peculiarly suited to their own concerns. In their comedies, Athenian playwrights poked fun at the gods, more serious playwrights, philosophers, and politicians. In their tragedies, they posed seemingly irreconcilable conflicts, showing what happens when men dare to act like the gods, and dealing with such matters as free will and death. Of the hundreds of plays written for the spring religious festivals in Athens, only the comedies of Aristophanes and the tragedies of Aeschylus, Sophocles, and Euripides remain. Even many of the plays by those four authors are lost.

Readings 10–11 consist of the complete text of a modern translation of one of the greatest Greek tragedies, Sophocles's *Antigone*. More perfectly than any other Greek playwright, Sophocles fused two Greek views of how to live the good life. His characters look to the gods and to religious laws for guidance, but they are always individual human beings with full responsibility for working out their own destinies.

Sophocles's *Antigone* is the last in a series of three plays chronicling the downfall of the ruling family of the Greek city of Thebes. Sophocles based the plays on legends familiar to every Athenian. The first two plays, *Oedipus Rex* and *Oedipus at Colonus*, tell the story of Antigone's father, King Oedipus of Thebes. Wishing to end a plague that has struck his city, Oedipus consults the Delphic oracle, a prophetic power that gives information through a priestess at a temple in Delphi. The oracle, traditionally long on wisdom and short on practical suggestions, tells Oedipus to find the murderer of his predecessor, King Laios. As he investigates the murder, Oedipus gradually learns that he himself, unknowingly, killed King Laios, who was his father, and married Queen Iocaste, who was his mother. Upon his revelation, Iocaste kills herself, and in anguish

Sigmund Freud invented the term "Oedipus complex" to describe the intense jealousy four- and five-year-old boys often feel toward their fathers, and the intense love they feel for their mothers. Most people outgrow this stage in childhood; a few do not. King Oedipus, according to Sophocles, did not even know who his father and mother were; thus it could be said that he did not suffer from the complex named after him— at least not consciously.

47

Oedipus tears out his own eyes. After the downfall of Oedipus, his sons vie for the throne and in the ensuing war kill each other. Antigone and her sister, Ismene, are the only surviving members of the family; their maternal uncle, Creon, becomes king.

When Antigone protests Creon's decree that one brother was a traitor who must be left lying on the plain unburied, the conflict of *Antigone* begins. Burial rites were of vast religious importance to nearly every Greek, and to be denied them was a punishment of overwhelming terror. An unburied body was an offense to the gods, and the tormented souls of the unburied were believed to haunt and plague their survivors instead of going to their proper resting place in Hades.

Both Antigone and Creon are unswerving in their devotion to what they believe is the correct view of the good man, the good life, and the good society. Sophocles took no sides. His greatness was his power to make both Antigone and Creon complex and sympathetic individuals.

Aristotle spelled out the psychological functions of tragedy in his **Poetics.**

By involving the spectator in a compelling story, Sophocles hoped to provoke him to deep thought and emotion. As you read, keep the following questions in mind:

1. On what values does Antigone base her defiance of Creon? On what values does Creon base his position?
2. Is either Antigone or Creon clearly in the wrong? Do you agree with one more than with the other? Why?
3. Do you think Antigone and Creon are stubborn and prideful? Or are they noble in refusing to change their ideals? Why?
4. Can a good society tolerate citizens who defy its laws? Why? Can a good man obey what he believes is an unjust law? Why?

# Sophocles's *Antigone*

CHARACTERS:

| | | |
|---|---|---|
| ANTIGONE | CREON | A SENTRY |
| ISMENE | HAIMON | A MESSENGER |
| EURYDICE | TEIRESIAS | CHORUS |

SCENE:

*Before the palace of Creon, King of Thebes. A central double door, and two lateral doors. A platform extends the length of the façade, and from this platform three steps lead down into the "orchestra," or chorus-ground.* TIME: *dawn of the day after the repulse of the Argive army from the assault on Thebes.*

48

# PROLOGUE

*[ANTIGONE and ISMENE enter from the*
*central door of the Palace.]*

ANTIGONE:

Ismene, dear sister,
You would think that we had already suffered enough
For the curse on Oedipus:
I cannot imagine any grief
That you and I have not gone through. And now—
Have they told you of the new decree of our King Creon?

ISMENE:

I have heard nothing: I know
That two sisters lost two brothers, a double death
In a single hour; and I know that the Argive army
Fled in the night; but beyond this, nothing.

The Argive army was one
of the armies allied with
Polyneices, brother of
Antigone and Ismene.

ANTIGONE:

I thought so. And that is why I wanted you
To come out here with me. There is something we must do.

ISMENE:

Why do you speak so strangely?

ANTIGONE:

Listen, Ismene:
Creon buried our brother Eteocles
With military honors, gave him a soldier's funeral,
And it was right that he should; but Polyneices,
Who fought as bravely and died as miserably,—
They say that Creon has sworn
No one shall bury him, no one mourn for him,
But his body must lie in the fields, a sweet treasure
For carrion birds to find as they search for food.
That is what they say, and our good Creon is coming here
To announce it publicly; and the penalty—
Stoning to death in the public square! There it is,
And now you can prove what you are:
A true sister, or a traitor to your family.

ISMENE:

Antigone, you are mad! What could I possibly do?

ANTIGONE:

You must decide whether you will help me or not.

ISMENE:

I do not understand you. Help you in what?

ANTIGONE:

Ismene, I am going to bury him. Will you come?

ISMENE:

Bury him! You have just said the new law forbids it.

ANTIGONE:

He is my brother. And he is your brother, too.

ISMENE:

But think of the danger! Think what Creon will do!

ANTIGONE:

Creon is not strong enough to stand in my way.

ISMENE:

Ah sister!
Oedipus died, everyone hating him
For what his own search brought to light, his eyes
Ripped out by his own hand; and Iocaste died,
His mother and wife at once: she twisted the cords
That strangled her life; and our two brothers died,
Each killed by the other's sword. And we are left:
But oh, Antigone,
Think how much more terrible than these
Our own death would be if we should go against Creon
And do what he has forbidden! We are only women,
We cannot fight with men, Antigone!
The law is strong, we must give in to the law
In this thing, and in worse. I beg the Dead
To forgive me, but I am helpless: I must yield
To those in authority. And I think it is dangerous business
To be always meddling.

ANTIGONE:

If that is what you think,
I should not want you, even if you asked to come.
You have made your choice, you can be what you want to be.
But I will bury him; and if I must die,
I say that this crime is holy: I shall lie down
With him in death, and I shall be as dear
To him as he to me. It is the dead,
Not the living, who make the longest demands:

▶ Are there circumstances under which the individual should not yield to those in authority? If so, what are they?

We die forever. . . You may do as you like,
Since apparently the laws of the gods mean nothing to you.

ISMENE:

They mean a great deal to me; but I have no strength
To break laws that were made for the public good.

ANTIGONE:

That must be your excuse, I suppose. But as for me,
I will bury the brother I love.

ISMENE:

Antigone,
You have yourself to consider, after all.
I am so afraid for you!

ANTIGONE:

You need not be:
You have yourself to consider, after all.

ISMENE:

But no one must hear of this, you must tell no one!
I will keep it a secret, I promise!

ANTIGONE:

Oh tell it! Tell everyone!
Think how they'll hate you when it all comes out
If they learn that you knew about it all the time!

ISMENE:

So fiery! You should be cold with fear.

ANTIGONE:

Perhaps. But I am doing only what I must.

ISMENE:

But can you do it? I say that you cannot.

ANTIGONE:

Very well: when my strength gives out, I shall do no more.

ISMENE:

Impossible things should not be tried at all.

ANTIGONE:

Go away, Ismene:
I shall be hating you soon, and the dead will too,

For your words are hateful. Leave me my foolish plan:
I am not afraid of the danger; if it means death,
It will not be the worst of deaths—death without honor.

ISMENE:

Go then, if you feel that you must.
You are unwise,
But a loyal friend indeed to those who love you.

[*Exit into the Palace.* ANTIGONE *goes off,
L. Enter the* CHORUS.]

In most Greek tragedies
the chorus, itself de-
tached from the central
action of the play, com-
ments on the characters
and events, interpreting
them to the audience.
Sometimes, as here, the
chorus fills in plot
information. The chorus-
leader was called the
**choragos**. In effect, the
function of the Greek
chorus was the same as
that of the chorus in a
modern musical comedy.
That fact is not surprising,
for the Greeks invented
not only the chorus, but
the very idea of theater.

CHORUS:

Now the long blade of the sun, lying
Level east to west, touches with glory
Thebes of the Seven Gates. Open, unlidded
Eye of golden day! O marching light
Across the eddy and rush of Dirce's stream,
Striking the white shields of the enemy
Thrown headlong backward from the blaze of morning!

CHORAGOS:

Polyneices their commander
Roused them with windy phrases,
He the wild eagle screaming
Insults above our land,
His wings their shields of snow,
His crest their marshalled helms.

CHORUS:

Against our seven gates in a yawning ring
The famished spears came onward in the night;
But before his jaws were sated with our blood,
Or pinefire took the garland of our towers,
He was thrown back; and as he turned, great Thebes—
No tender victim for his noisy power—
Rose like a dragon behind him, shouting war.

CHORAGOS:

For God hates utterly
The bray of bragging tongues;
And when he beheld their smiling,
Their swagger of golden helms,
The frown of his thunder blasted
Their first man from our walls.

52

CHORUS:

We heard his shout of triumph high in the air
Turn to a scream; far out in a flaming arc
He fell with his windy torch, and the earth struck him.
And others storming in fury no less than his
Found shock of death in the dusty joy of battle.

CHORAGOS:

Seven captains at seven gates
Yielded their clanging arms to the god
That bends the battle-line and breaks it.
These two only, brothers in blood,
Face to face in matchless rage,
Mirroring each the other's death,
Clashed in long combat.

CHORUS:

But now in the beautiful morning of victory
Let Thebes of the many chariots sing for joy!
With hearts for dancing we'll take leave of war:
Our temples shall be sweet with hymns of praise,
And the long night shall echo with our chorus.


## SCENE I

CHORAGOS:

But now at last our new King is coming:
Creon of Thebes, Menoikeus' son.
In this auspicious dawn of his reign
What are the new complexities
That shifting Fate has woven for him?
What is his counsel? Why has he summoned
The old men to hear him?

> [*Enter* CREON *from the Palace, C. He ad-
> dresses the* CHORUS *from the top step.*]

CREON:

Gentlemen: I have the honor to inform you that our Ship of State, which recent storms have threatened to destroy, has come safely to harbor at last, guided by the merciful wisdom of Heaven. I have summoned you here this morning because I know that I can depend upon you: your devotion to King Laios was absolute; you never hesitated in your duty to our late ruler Oedipus; and when Oedipus died, your loyalty was transferred to his children. Unfortunately, as you know, his two sons, the princes Eteocles and Poly-neices, have killed each other in battle; and I, as the next in blood, have succeeded to the full power of the throne.

I am aware, of course, that no Ruler can expect complete loyalty from his subjects until he has been tested in office. Nevertheless, I say to you at the very outset that I have nothing but contempt for the kind of Governor who is afraid, for whatever reason, to follow the course that he knows is best for the State; and as for the man who sets private friendship above the public welfare,—I have no use for him, either. I call God to witness that if I saw my country headed for ruin, I should not be afraid to speak out plainly; and I need hardly remind you that I would never have any dealings with an enemy of the people. No one values friendship more highly than I; but we must remember that friends made at the risk of wrecking our Ship are not real friends at all.

These are my principles, at any rate, and that is why I have made the following decision concerning the sons of Oedipus: Eteocles, who died as a man should die, fighting for his country, is to be buried with full military honors, with all the ceremony that is usual when the greatest heroes die; but his brother Poly-neices, who broke his exile to come back with fire and sword against his native city and the shrines of his fathers' gods, whose one idea was to spill the blood of his blood and sell his own people into slavery—Polyneices, I say, is to have no burial: no man is to touch him or say the least prayer for him; he shall lie on the plain, un-buried; and the birds and the scavenging dogs can do with him whatever they like.

This is my command, and you can see the wisdom behind it. As long as I am King, no traitor is going to be honored with the loyal man. But whoever shows by word and deed that he is on the side of the State,—he shall have my respect while he is living, and my reverence when he is dead.

CHORAGOS:

If that is your will, Creon son of Menoikeus,
You have the right to enforce it: we are yours.

CREON:

That is my will. Take care that you do your part.

CHORAGOS:

We are old men: let the younger ones carry it out.

CREON:

I do not mean that: the sentries have been appointed.

54

CHORAGOS:

Then what is it that you would have us do?

CREON:

You will give no support to whoever breaks this law.

CHORAGOS:

Only a crazy man is in love with death!

CREON:

. And death it is; yet money talks, and the wisest
Have sometimes been known to count a few coins too many.

[*Enter* SENTRY *from L.*]

SENTRY:

I'll not say that I'm out of breath from running, King, because
every time I stopped to think about what I have to tell you, I felt
like going back. And all the time a voice kept saying, "You fool,
don't you know you're walking straight into trouble?"; and then
another voice: "Yes, but if you let somebody else get the news to
Creon first, it will be even worse than that for you!" But good sense
won out, at least I hope it was good sense, and here I am with a
story that makes no sense at all; but I'll tell it anyhow, because,
as they say, what's going to happen's going to happen, and—

CREON:

Come to the point. What have you to say?

SENTRY:

I did not do it. I did not see who did it. You must not punish
me for what someone else has done.

CREON:

A comprehensive defense! More effective, perhaps,
If I knew its purpose. Come: what is it?

SENTRY:

A dreadful thing . . . I don't know how to put it—

CREON:

Out with it!

SENTRY:

      Well then;
The dead man—Polyneices—

        [*Pause. The* SENTRY *is overcome, fumbles
        for words.* CREON *waits impassively.*]
        out there—someone—

New dust on the slimy flesh!

> [*Pause. No sign from* CREON.]

Someone has given it burial that way, and
Gone. . .

> [*Long pause.* CREON *finally speaks with
> deadly control.*]

CREON:

And the man who dared do this?

SENTRY:

> I swear I

Do not know! You must believe me! Listen:
The ground was dry, not a sign of digging, no,
Not a wheeltrack in the dust, no trace of anyone.
It was when they relieved us this morning: and one of them,
The corporal, pointed to it. There it was,
The strangest—Look:
The body, just mounded over with light dust: you see?
Not buried really, but as if they'd covered it
Just enough for the ghost's peace. And no sign
Of dogs or any wild animal that had been there.
And then what a scene there was! Every man of us
Accusing the other: we all proved the other man did it,
We all had proof that we could not have done it.
We were ready to take hot iron in our hands,
Walk through fire, swear by all the gods,
*It was not I!*
*I do not know who it was, but it was not I!*

> [CREON'S *rage has been mounting stead-
> ily, but the* SENTRY *is too intent upon his
> story to notice it.*]

And then, when this came to nothing, someone said
A thing that silenced us and made us stare
Down at the ground: you had to be told the news,
And one of us had to do it! We threw the dice,
And the bad luck fell to me. So here I am,
No happier to be here than you are to have me:
Nobody likes the man who brings bad news.

CHORAGOS:

I have been wondering, King: can it be that the gods have done
this?

This passage refers to
an ordeal by torture to
demonstrate honesty. It
was not used in the fifth
century B.C. in Greece.

CREON:                                                [*Furiously*]

Stop!
Must you doddering wrecks
Go out of your heads entirely? "The gods!"
Intolerable!
The gods favor this corpse? Why? How had he served them?
Tried to loot their temples, burn their images,
Yes, and the whole State, and its laws with it!
Is it your senile opinion that the gods love to honor bad men?
A pious thought!—No, from the very beginning
There have been those who have whispered together,
Stiff-necked anarchists, putting their heads together,
Scheming against me in alleys. These are the men,
And they have bribed my own guard to do this thing.
Money!                                              [*Sententiously*]
There's nothing in the world so demoralizing as money.
Down go your cities,
Homes gone, men gone, honest hearts corrupted,
Crookedness of all kinds, and all for money!

                                                [*To* SENTRY:]
                        But you—!
I swear by God and by the throne of God,
The man who has done this thing shall pay for it!
Find that man, bring him here to me, or your death
Will be the least of your problems: I'll string you up
Alive, and there will be certain ways to make you
Discover your employer before you die;
And the process may teach you a lesson you seem to have missed;
The dearest profit is sometimes all too dear:
That depends on the source. Do you understand me?
A fortune won is often misfortune.

SENTRY:

King, may I speak?

CREON:

                    Your very voice distresses me.

SENTRY:

Are you sure that it is my voice, and not your conscience?

CREON:

By God, he wants to analyze me now!

SENTRY:

It is not what I say, but what has been done, that hurts you.

57

CREON:

You talk too much.

SENTRY:

Maybe; but I've done nothing.

CREON:

Sold your soul for some silver: that's all you've done.

SENTRY:

How dreadful it is when the right judge judges wrong!

CREON:

Your figures of speech
May entertain you now; but unless you bring me the man,
You will get little profit from them in the end.

[*Exit* CREON *into the Palace.*]

SENTRY:

"Bring me the man"—!
I'd like nothing better than bringing him the man!
But bring him or not, you have seen the last of me here.
At any rate, I am safe!

[*Exit* SENTRY.]

CHORUS:

In this celebrated ode ·
to man, note Sophocles's
use of concrete and
precise images.

Numberless are the world's wonders, but none
More wonderful than man; the stormgray sea
Yields to his prows, the huge crests bear him high;
Earth, holy and inexhaustible, is graven
With shining furrows where his plows have gone
Year after year, the timeless labor of stallions.

The lightboned birds and beasts that cling to cover,
The lithe fish lighting their reaches of dim water,
All are taken, tamed in the net of his mind;
The lion on the hill, the wild horse windy-maned,
Resign to him; and his blunt yoke has broken
The sultry shoulders of the mountain bull.

Words also, and thought as rapid as air,
He fashions to his good use; statecraft is his,
And his the skill that deflects the arrows of snow,
The spears of winter rain: from every wind
He has made himself secure—from all but one:
In the late wind of death he cannot stand.

58

O clear intelligence, force beyond all measure!
O fate of man, working both good and evil!
When the laws are kept, how proudly his city stands!
When the laws are broken, what of his city then?
Never may the anarchic man find rest at my hearth,
Never be it said that my thoughts are his thoughts.


## SCENE II

[*Re-enter* SENTRY *leading* ANTIGONE.]

CHORAGOS:

What does this mean? Surely this captive woman
Is the Princess, Antigone. Why should she be taken?

SENTRY:

Here is the one who did it! We caught her
In the very act of burying him.—Where is Creon?

CHORAGOS:

Just coming from the house.

[*Enter* CREON, *C.*]

CREON:

What has happened?
Why have you come back so soon?

[*Expansively*]
O King,
A man should never be too sure of anything:
I would have sworn
That you'd not see me here again: your anger
Frightened me so, and the things you threatened me with;
But how could I tell then
That I'd be able to solve the case so soon?
No dice-throwing this time: I was only too glad to come!
Here is this woman. She is the guilty one:
We found her trying to bury him.
Take her, then; question her; judge her as you will.
I am through with the whole thing now, and glad of it.

CREON:

But this is Antigone! Why have you brought her here?

SENTRY:

She was burying him, I tell you!

CREON:                                                         [*Severely*]

                    Is this the truth?

SENTRY:

   I saw her with my own eyes. Can I say more?

CREON:

   The details: come, tell me quickly!

SENTRY:

                              It was like this:
   After those terrible threats of yours, King,
   We went back and brushed the dust away from the body.
   The flesh was soft by now, and stinking.
   So we sat on a hill to windward and kept guard.
   No napping this time! We kept each other awake.
   But nothing happened until the white round sun
   Whirled in the center of the round sky over us:
   Then, suddenly,
   A storm of dust roared up from the earth, and the sky
   Went out, the plain vanished with all its trees
   In the stinging dark. We closed our eyes and endured it.
   The whirlwind lasted a long time, but it passed;
   And then we looked, and there was Antigone!
   I have seen
   A mother bird come back to a stripped nest, heard
   Her crying bitterly a broken note or two
   For the young ones stolen. Just so, when this girl
   Found the bare corpse, and all her love's work wasted,
   She wept, and cried on heaven to damn the hands
   That had done this thing. And then she brought more dust
   And sprinkled wine three times for her brother's ghost.
   We ran and took her at once. She was not afraid.
   Not even when we charged her with what she had done.
   She denied nothing. And this was a comfort to me,
   And some uneasiness: for it is a good thing
   To escape from death, but it is no great pleasure
   To bring death to a friend. Yet I always say
   There is nothing so comfortable as your own safe skin!

CREON:                                              [*Slowly, dangerously*]

   And you, Antigone,
   You with your head hanging,—do you confess this thing?

ANTIGONE:

   I do. I deny nothing.

60

CREON:                                              [*To* SENTRY:]

                    You may go.

                                                   [*Exit* SENTRY.]
                                                   [*To* ANTIGONE:]

Tell me, tell me briefly:
Had you heard my proclamation touching this matter?

ANTIGONE:

It was public. Could I help hearing it?

CREON:

And yet you dared defy the law.

ANTIGONE:

                        I dared.
It was not God's proclamation. That final Justice
That rules the world below makes no such laws.
Your edict, King, was strong,
But all your strength is weakness itself against
The immortal unrecorded laws of God.
They are not merely now: they were, and shall be,
Operative for ever, beyond man utterly.
I knew I must die, even without your decree:
I am only mortal. And if I must die
Now, before it is my time to die,
Surely this is no hardship: can anyone
Living, as I live, with evil all about me,
Think Death less than a friend? This death of mine
Is of no importance; but if I had left my brother
Lying in death unburied, I should have suffered.
Now I do not. You smile at me. Ah Creon,
Think me a fool, if you like; but it may well be
That a fool convicts me of folly.

CHORAGOS:

Like father, like daughter: both headstrong, deaf to reason!
She has never learned to yield.

CREON:

                        She has much to learn.
The inflexible heart breaks first, the toughest iron
Cracks first, and the wildest horses bend their necks
At the pull of the smallest curb. Pride? In a slave?
This girl is guilty of a double insolence,
Breaking the given laws and boasting of it.
Who is the man here,
She or I, if this crime goes unpunished?

▶ Should a person sometimes obey a "higher law" in defiance of his government?

61

Sister's child, or more than sister's child,
Or closer yet in blood—she and her sister
Win bitter death for this!

[*To servants:*]

Go, some of you,
Arrest Ismene. I accuse her equally.
Bring her: you will find her sniffling in the house there.
Her mind's a traitor: crimes kept in the dark
Cry for light, and the guardian brain shudders;
But how much worse than this
Is brazen boasting of barefaced anarchy!

ANTIGONE:

Creon, what more do you want than my death?

CREON:

Nothing.

That gives me everything.

ANTIGONE:

Then I beg you: kill me.
This talking is a great weariness: your words
Are distasteful to me, and I am sure that mine
Seem so to you. And yet they should not seem so:
I should have praise and honor for what I have done.
All these men here would praise me
Were their lips not frozen shut with fear of you.

[*Bitterly*]

Ah the good fortune of kings,
Licensed to say and do whatever they please!

CREON:

You are alone here in that opinion.

ANTIGONE:

No, they are with me. But they keep their tongues in leash.

CREON:

Maybe. But you are guilty, and they are not.

ANTIGONE:

There is no guilt in reverence for the dead.

CREON:

But Eteocles—was he not your brother too?

ANTIGONE:

My brother too.

CREON:

And you insult his memory?

ANTIGONE: [*Softly*]

The dead man would not say that I insult it.

CREON:

He would: for you honor a traitor as much as him.

ANTIGONE:

His own brother, traitor or not, and equal in blood.

CREON:

He made war on his country. Eteocles defended it.

ANTIGONE:

Nevertheless, there are honors due all the dead.

CREON:

But not the same for the wicked as for the just.

ANTIGONE:

Ah Creon, Creon,
Which of us can say what the gods hold wicked?

CREON:

An enemy is an enemy, even dead.

ANTIGONE:

It is my nature to join in love, not hate.

CREON: [*Finally losing patience*]

Go join them, then; if you must have your love,
Find it in hell!

CHORAGOS:

But see, Ismene comes:

[*Enter* ISMENE, *guarded.*]

Those tears are sisterly, the cloud
That shadows her eyes rains down gentle sorrow.

CREON:

You too, Ismene,
Snake in my ordered house, sucking my blood
Stealthily—and all the time I never knew
That these two sisters were aiming at my throne! Ismene,
Do you confess your share in this crime, or deny it?
Answer me.

ISMENE:

Yes, if she will let me say so. I am guilty.

ANTIGONE: [*Coldly*]

No, Ismene. You have no right to say so.
You would not help me, and I will not have you help me.

ISMENE:

But now I know what you meant; and I am here
To join you, to take my share of punishment.

ANTIGONE:

The dead man and the gods who rule the dead
Know whose act this was. Words are not friends.

ISMENE:

Do you refuse me, Antigone? I want to die with you:
I too have a duty that I must discharge to the dead.

ANTIGONE:

You shall not lessen my death by sharing it.

ISMENE:

What do I care for life when you are dead?

ANTIGONE:

Ask Creon. You're always hanging on his opinions.

ISMENE:

You are laughing at me. Why, Antigone?

ANTIGONE:

It's a joyless laughter, Ismene.

ISMENE:

But can I do nothing?

ANTIGONE:

Yes, save yourself. I shall not envy you.
There are those who will praise you; I shall have honor, too.

ISMENE:

But we are equally guilty!

ANTIGONE:

No more, Ismene.
You are alive, but I belong to Death.

CREON:                                    [*To the* CHORUS:]

Gentlemen, I beg you to observe these girls:
One has just now lost her mind; the other,
It seems, has never had a mind at all.

ISMENE:

Grief teaches the steadiest minds to waver, King.

CREON:

Yours certainly did, when you assumed guilt with the guilty!

ISMENE:

But how could I go on living without her?

CREON:
                                                 You are.
She is already dead.

ISMENE:

                            But your own son's bride!

CREON:

There are places enough for him to push his plow.
I want no wicked women for my sons!

ISMENE:

O dearest Haimon, how your father wrongs you!

CREON:

I've had enough of your childish talk of marriage!

CHORAGOS:

Do you really intend to steal this girl from your son?

CREON:

No; Death will do that for me.

CHORAGOS:

                            Then she must die?

CREON:                                            [*Ironically*]

You dazzle me.—But enough of this talk!

                                                 [*To* GUARDS:]

You, there, take them away and guard them well:
For they are but women, and even brave men run
When they see Death coming.

                    [*Exeunt* ISMENE, ANTIGONE, *and* GUARDS.]

Just as Creon has accused
his nieces of promoting
anarchy in the state, so
here he accuses them of
suffering anarchy in
their minds. In both
cases, Creon's concern
is with order and reason.

65

**CHORUS:**

Fortunate is the man who has never tasted God's vengeance!
Where once the anger of heaven has struck, that house is shaken
For ever: damnation rises behind each child
Like a wave cresting out of the black northeast,
When the long darkness under sea roars up
And bursts drumming death upon the windwhipped sand.

I have seen this gathering sorrow from time long past
Loom upon Oedipus' children: generation from generation
Takes the compulsive rage of the enemy god.
So lately this last flower of Oedipus' line
Drank the sunlight! But now a passionate word
And a handful of dust have closed up all its beauty.

What mortal arrogance
Transcends the wrath of Zeus?
Sleep cannot lull him, nor the effortless long months
Of the timeless gods: but he is young for ever,
And his house is the shining day of high Olympos.
All that is and shall be,
And all the past, is his.
No pride on earth is free of the curse of heaven.

The straying dreams of men
May bring them ghosts of joy:
But as they drowse, the waking embers burn them;
Or they walk with fixed eyes, as blind men walk.
But the ancient wisdom speaks for our own time:
*Fate works most for woe*
*With Folly's fairest show.*
Man's little pleasure is the spring of sorrow.

## SCENE III

**CHORAGOS:**

But here is Haimon, King, the last of all your sons.
Is it grief for Antigone that brings him here,
And bitterness at being robbed of his bride?

[*Enter* HAIMON.]

**CREON:**

We shall soon see, and no need of diviners.—Son,
You have heard my final judgment on that girl:

Many of the Greek legends that are the basis of tragedies deal with the terrible fates of several generations of a family.

Mount Olympos, or Olympus, in eastern Greece, was believed to be the home of the gods.

66

Have you come here hating me, or have you come
With deference and with love, whatever I do?

HAIMON:

I am your son, father. You are my guide.
You make things clear for me, and I obey you.
No marriage means more to me than your continuing wisdom.

CREON:

Good. That is the way to behave: subordinate
Everything else, my son, to your father's will.
This is what a man prays for, that he may get
Sons attentive and dutiful in his house,
Each one hating his father's enemies,
Honoring his father's friends. But if his sons
Fail him, if they turn out unprofitably,
What has he fathered but trouble for himself
And amusement for the malicious? So you are right
Not to lose your head over this woman.
Your pleasure with her would soon grow cold, Haimon,
And then you'd have a hellcat in bed and elsewhere.
Let her find her husband in Hell!
Of all the people in this city, only she
Has had contempt for my law and broken it.
Do you want me to show myself weak before the people?
Or to break my sworn word? No, and I will not.
The woman dies.
I suppose she'll plead "family ties." Well, let her.
If I permit my own family to rebel,
How shall I earn the world's obedience?
Show me the man who keeps his house in hand,
He's fit for public authority. I'll have no dealings
With law-breakers, critics of the government:
Whoever is chosen to govern should be obeyed—
Must be obeyed, in all things, great and small,
Just and unjust! O Haimon,
The man who knows how to obey, and that man only,
Knows how to give commands when the time comes.
You can depend on him, no matter how fast
The spears come: he's a good soldier, he'll stick it out.
Anarchy, anarchy! Show me a greater evil!
This is why cities tumble and the great houses rain down,
This is what scatters armies!
No, no: good lives are made so by discipline.
We keep the laws then, and the lawmakers,

▶ Does a man owe his first
allegiance to his father
or to his wife?

And no woman shall seduce us. If we must lose,
Let's lose to a man, at least! Is a woman stronger than we?

CHORAGOS:

Unless time has rusted my wits,
What you say, King, is said with point and dignity.

HAIMON:                                                 [*Boyishly earnest*]

Father:
Reason is God's crowning gift to man, and you are right
To warn me against losing mine. I cannot say—
I hope that I shall never want to say—that you
Have reasoned badly. Yet there are other men
Who can reason, too; and their opinions might be helpful.
You are not in a position to know everything
That people say or do, or what they feel:
Your temper terrifies them—everyone
Will tell you only what you like to hear.
But I, at any rate, can listen; and I have heard them
Muttering and whispering in the dark about this girl.
They say no woman has ever, so unreasonably,
Died so shameful a death for a generous act:
"She covered her brother's body. Is this indecent?
She kept him from dogs and vultures. Is this a crime?
Death?—She should have all the honor that we can give her!"
This is the way they talk out there in the city.
You must believe me:
Nothing is closer to me than your happiness.
What could be closer? Must not any son
Value his father's fortune as his father does his?
I beg you, do not be unchangeable:
Do not believe that you alone can be right.
The man who thinks that,
The man who maintains that only he has the power
To reason correctly, the gift to speak, the soul—
A man like that, when you know him, turns out empty.
It is not reason never to yield to reason!
In flood time you can see how some trees bend,
And because they bend, even their twigs are safe,
While stubborn trees are torn up, roots and all.
And the same thing happens in sailing:
Make your sheet fast, never slacken,—and over you go,
Head over heels and under: and there's your voyage.
Forget you are angry! Let yourself be moved!

▶ Is a person who has knowledge that a crime is to be committed and does nothing to prevent it as guilty as the criminal himself?

68

I know I am young; but please let me say this:
The ideal condition
Would be, I admit, that men should be right by instinct;
But since we are all too likely to go astray,
The reasonable thing is to learn from those who can teach.

CHORAGOS:

You will do well to listen to him, King,
If what he says is sensible. And you, Haimon,
Must listen to your father.—Both speak well.

CREON:

You consider it right for a man of my years and experience
To go to school to a boy?

HAIMON:

It is not right
If I am wrong. But if I am young, and right,
What does my age matter?

CREON:

You think it right to stand up for an anarchist?

HAIMON:

Not at all. I pay no respect to criminals.

CREON:

Then she is not a criminal?

HAIMON:

The City would deny it, to a man.

CREON:

And the City proposes to teach me how to rule?

HAIMON:

Ah. Who is it that's talking like a boy now?

CREON:

My voice is the one voice giving orders in this City!

HAIMON:

It is no City if it takes orders from one voice.

CREON:

The State is the King!

▶ Why is it sometimes so difficult for parents to discuss vital issues reasonably and on a basis of equality with their children?

Note the weight given here to public opinion, even though the play is set in a monarchy.

HAIMON:

Yes, if the State is a desert.

[*Pause*]

CREON:

This boy, it seems, has sold out to a woman.

HAIMON:

If you are a woman: my concern is only for you.

CREON:

So? Your "concern"! In a public brawl with your father!

HAIMON:

How about you, in a public brawl with justice?

CREON:

With justice, when all that I do is within my rights?

HAIMON:

You have no right to trample on God's right.

CREON: [*Completely out of control*]

Fool, adolescent fool! Taken in by a woman!

HAIMON:

You'll never see me taken in by anything vile.

CREON:

Every word you say is for her!

HAIMON: [*Quietly, darkly*]

And for you.
And for me. And for the gods under the earth.

CREON:

You'll never marry her while she lives.

HAIMON:

Then she must die.—But her death will cause another.

CREON:

Another?
Have you lost your senses? Is this an open threat?

HAIMON:

There is no threat in speaking to emptiness.

70

CREON:

I swear you'll regret this superior tone of yours!
You are the empty one!

HAIMON:                              If you were not my father,
I'd say you were perverse.

CREON:

You girlstruck fool, don't play at words with me!

HAIMON:

I am sorry. You prefer silence.

CREON:

                              Now, by God—!
I swear, by all the gods in heaven above us,
You'll watch it, I swear you shall!

                              [*To the* SERVANTS:]
                    Bring her out!
Bring the woman out! Let her die before his eyes!
Here, this instant, with her bridegroom beside her!

HAIMON:

Not here, no; she will not die here, King.
And you will never see my face again.
Go on raving as long as you've a friend to endure you.
                              [*Exit* HAIMON.]

CHORAGOS:

Gone, gone.
Creon, a young man in a rage is dangerous!

CREON:

Let him do, or dream to do, more than a man can.
He shall not save these girls from death.

CHORAGOS:

                              These girls?
You have sentenced them both?

CREON:

                              No, you are right.
I will not kill the one whose hands are clean.

CHORAGOS:

But Antigone?

CREON: [*Somberly*]

       I will carry her far away
Out there in the wilderness, and lock her
Living in a vault of stone. She shall have food,
As the custom is, to absolve the State of her death.
And there let her pray to the gods of hell:
They are her only gods:
Perhaps they will show her an escape from death,
Or she may learn, though late,
That piety shown the dead is pity in vain.

[*Exit* CREON.]

CHORUS:

This choral ode is a hymn to
Aphrodite, goddess of love.

Love, unconquerable
Waster of rich men, keeper
Of warm lights and all-night vigil
In the soft face of a girl:
Sea-wanderer, forest-visitor!
Even the pure Immortals cannot escape you,
And mortal man, in his one day's dusk,
Trembles before your glory.

Surely you swerve upon ruin
The just man's consenting heart,
As here you have made bright anger
Strike between father and son—
And none has conquered but Love!
A girl's glance working the will of heaven:
Pleasure to her alone who mocks us,
Merciless Aphrodite.

## SCENE IV

CHORAGOS: [*As* ANTIGONE *enters guarded:*]

But I can no longer stand in awe of this,
Nor, seeing what I see, keep back my tears.
Here is Antigone, passing to that chamber
Where all find sleep at last.

ANTIGONE:

Look upon me, friends, and pity me
Turning back at the night's edge to say
Good-by to the sun that shines for me no longer;

Now sleepy Death
Summons me down to Acheron, that cold shore:
There is no bridesong there, nor any music.

CHORUS:

Yet not unpraised, not without a kind of honor,
You walk at last into the underworld;
Untouched by sickness, broken by no sword.
What woman has ever found your way to death?

ANTIGONE:

How often I have heard the story of Niobe,
Tantalos' wretched daughter, how the stone
Clung fast about her, ivy-close: and they say
The rain falls endlessly
And sifting soft snow; her tears are never done.
I feel the loneliness of her death in mine.

CHORUS:

But she was born of heaven, and you
Are woman, woman-born. If her death is yours,
A mortal woman's, is this not for you
Glory in our world and in the world beyond?

ANTIGONE:

You laugh at me. Ah, friends, friends,
Can you not wait until I am dead? O Thebes,
O men many-charioted, in love with Fortune,
Dear springs of Dirce, sacred Theban grove,
Be witnesses for me, denied all pity,
Unjustly judged! and think a word of love
For her whose path turns
Under dark earth, where there are no more tears.

CHORUS:

You have passed beyond human daring and come at last
Into a place of stone where Justice sits.
I cannot tell
What shape of your father's guilt appears in this.

ANTIGONE:

You have touched it at last: that bridal bed
Unspeakable, horror of son and mother mingling:
Their crime, infection of all our family!
O Oedipus, father and brother!

Acheron, in Greek mythology, was a river that led to Hades.

Niobe, a lesser goddess who mothered six children, boasted that she was the equal of a more powerful goddess who had but two children. In revenge, other gods destroyed Niobe's children and turned her into a stone.

In Greek mythology, Dirce was a queen who was killed by being tied to the horns of a bull. Then, near Thebes, she was turned into a spring that bore her name.

Your marriage strikes from the grave to murder mine.
I have been a stranger here in my own land:
All my life
The blasphemy of my birth has followed me.

CHORUS:

Reverence is a virtue, but strength
Lives in established law: that must prevail.
You have made your choice,
Your death is the doing of your conscious hand.

ANTIGONE:

Then let me go, since all your words are bitter,
And the very light of the sun is cold to me.
Lead me to my vigil, where I must have
Neither love nor lamentation; no song, but silence.

[CREON *interrupts impatiently:*]

CREON:

If dirges and planned lamentations could put off death,
Men would be singing for ever.

[*To the* SERVANTS:]

Take her, go!
You know your orders: take her to the vault
And leave her alone there. And if she lives or dies,
That's her affair, not ours: our hands are clean.

ANTIGONE:

O tomb, vaulted bride-bed in eternal rock,
Soon I shall be with my own again
Where Persephone welcomes the thin ghosts underground:
And I shall see my father again, and you, mother,
And dearest Polyneices—dearest indeed
To me, since it was my hand
That washed him clean and poured the ritual wine:
And my reward is death before my time!
And yet, as men's hearts know, I have done no wrong,
I have not sinned before God. Or if I have,
I shall know the truth in death. But if the guilt
Lies upon Creon who judged me, then, I pray,
May his punishment equal my own.

CHORAGOS:

O passionate heart,
Unyielding, tormented still by the same winds!

Persephone, also spelled
Persephoneia, was goddess
of the underworld.

74

CREON:

Her guards shall have good cause to regret their delaying.

ANTIGONE:

Ah! That voice is like the voice of death!

CREON:

I can give you no reason to think you are mistaken.

ANTIGONE:

Thebes, and you my fathers' gods,
And rulers of Thebes, you see me now, the last
Unhappy daughter of a line of kings,
Your kings, led away to death. You will remember
What things I suffer, and at what men's hands
Because I would not transgress the laws of heaven.

[*To the* GUARDS, *simply:*]

Come: let us wait no longer.

[*Exit* ANTIGONE, *L., guarded.*]

CHORUS:

All Danae's beauty was locked away
In a brazen cell where the sunlight could not come:
A small room, still as any grave, enclosed her.
Yet she was a princess too,
And Zeus in a rain of gold poured love upon her.
O child, child,
No power in wealth or war
Or tough sea-blackened ships
Can prevail against untiring Destiny!

And Dryas' son also, that furious king,
Bore the god's prisoning anger for his pride:
Sealed up by Dionysus in deaf stone,
His madness died among echoes.
So at the last he learned what dreadful power
His tongue had mocked:
For he had profaned the revels,
And fired the wrath of the nine
Implacable Sisters that love the sound of the flute.

And old men tell a half-remembered tale
Of horror done where a dark ledge splits the sea
And a double surf beats on the gray shores:
How a king's new woman, sick
With hatred for the queen he had imprisoned,

In the following verses
the chorus illustrates
the futility of opposing
the will of the gods.
Danae's uncle, warned by
an oracle that his niece's
son would grow up to kill
him, sealed Danae in a
bronze chamber. Angered,
Zeus impregnated Danae
"in a rain of gold."
Danae's son fulfilled
the prophecy by killing
his mother's uncle.

Lycurgus, son of Dryas,
attacked Dionysus, son
of Zeus and founder of
an ecstatic cult that
appealed to women (the
nine Implacable Sisters).
Dionysus was quick to take
revenge on Lycurgus.

Ripped out his two sons' eyes with her bloody hands
While grinning Ares watched the shuttle plunge
Four times: four blind wounds crying for revenge,

Crying, tears and blood mingled.—Piteously born,
Those sons whose mother was of heavenly birth!
Her father was the god of the North Wind
And she was cradled by gales,
She raced with young colts on the glittering hills
And walked untrammeled in the open light:
But in her marriage deathless Fate found means
To build a tomb like yours for all her joy.

## SCENE V

[*Enter blind* TEIRESIAS, *led by a boy. The opening speeches of* TEIRESIAS *should be in singsong contrast to the realistic lines of* CREON.]

TEIRESIAS:

This is the way the blind man comes, Princes, Princes,
Lock-step, two heads lit by the eyes of one.

CREON:

What new thing have you to tell us, old Teiresias?

TEIRESIAS:

I have much to tell you: listen to the prophet, Creon.

CREON:

I am not aware that I have ever failed to listen.

TEIRESIAS:

Then you have done wisely, King, and ruled well.

CREON:

I admit my debt to you. But what have you to say?

TEIRESIAS:

This, Creon: you stand once more on the edge of fate.

CREON:

What do you mean? Your words are a kind of dread.

TEIRESIAS:

Listen, Creon:
I was sitting in my chair of augury, at the place
Where the birds gather about me. They were all a-chatter,

76

As is their habit, when suddenly I heard
A strange note in their jangling, a scream, a
Whirring fury; I knew that they were fighting,
Tearing each other, dying
In a whirlwind of wings clashing. And I was afraid.
I began the rites of burnt-offering at the altar,
But Hephaistos failed me: instead of bright flame,
There was only the sputtering slime of the fat thigh-flesh
Melting: the entrails dissolved in gray smoke,
The bare bone burst from the welter. And no blaze!
This was a sign from heaven. My boy described it,
Seeing for me as I see for others.
I tell you, Creon, you yourself have brought
This new calamity upon us. Our hearths and altars
Are stained with the corruption of dogs and carrion birds
That glut themselves on the corpse of Oedipus' son.
The gods are deaf when we pray to them, their fire
Recoils from our offering, their birds of omen
Have no cry of comfort, for they are gorged
With the thick blood of the dead. O my son,
These are no trifles! Think: all men make mistakes,
But a good man yields when he knows his course is wrong,
And repairs the evil. The only crime is pride.
Give in to the dead man, then: do not fight with a corpse—
What glory is it to kill a man who is dead?
Think, I beg you:
It is for your own good that I speak as I do.
You should be able to yield for your own good.

*Hephaistos was the god of fire.*

CREON:

It seems that prophets have made me their especial province.
All my life long
I have been a kind of butt for the dull arrows
Of doddering fortune-tellers! No, Teiresias:
If your birds—if the great eagles of God himself
Should carry him stinking bit by bit to heaven,
I would not yield. I am not afraid of pollution:
No man can defile the gods. Do what you will,
Go into business, make money, speculate
In India gold or that synthetic gold from Sardis,
Get rich otherwise than by my consent to bury him.
Teiresias, it is a sorry thing when a wise man
Sells his wisdom, lets out his words for hire!

TEIRESIAS:

Ah Creon! Is there no man left in the world—

CREON:

To do what?—Come, let's have the aphorism!

TEIRESIAS:

No man who knows that wisdom outweighs any wealth?

CREON:

As surely as bribes are baser than any baseness.

TEIRESIAS:

You are sick, Creon! You are deathly sick!

CREON:

As you say: it is not my place to challenge a prophet.

TEIRESIAS:

Yet you have said my prophecy is for sale.

CREON:

The generation of prophets has always loved gold.

TEIRESIAS:

The generation of kings has always loved brass.

CREON:

You forget yourself! You are speaking to your King.

TEIRESIAS:

I know it. You are a king because of me.

CREON:

You have a certain skill; but you have sold out.

TEIRESIAS:

King, you will drive me to words that—

CREON:

                              Say them, say them!
Only remember: I will not pay you for them.

TEIRESIAS:

No, you will find them too costly.

CREON:

                         No doubt. Speak:
Whatever you say, you will not change my will.

TEIRESIAS:

Then take this, and take it to heart!

The time is not far off when you shall pay back
Corpse for corpse, flesh of your own flesh.
You have thrust the child of this world into living night,
You have kept from the gods below the child that is theirs:
The one in a grave before her death, the other,
Dead, denied the grave. This is your crime:
And the Furies and the dark gods of Hell
Are swift with terrible punishment for you.
Do you want to buy me now, Creon? Not many days,
And your house will be full of men and women weeping,
And curses will be hurled at you from far
Cities grieving for sons unburied, left to rot
Before the walls of Thebes.
These are my arrows, Creon: they are all for you.

The Furies were hellish
spirits of the vengeance
of the gods.

                                        [*To* BOY:]

But come, child: lead me home.
Let him waste his fine anger upon younger men.
Maybe he will learn at last
To control a wiser tongue in a better head.

                                        [*Exit* TEIRESIAS.]

CHORAGOS:

The old man has gone, King, but his words
Remain to plague us. I am old, too,
But I cannot remember that he was ever false.

CREON:

That is true. . . . It troubles me.
Oh it is hard to give in! But it is worse
To risk everything for stubborn pride.

CHORAGOS:

Creon: take my advice.

CREON:

                        What shall I do?

CHORAGOS:

Go quickly: free Antigone from her vault
And build a tomb for the body of Polyneices.

CREON:

You would have me do this?

CHORAGOS:

                        Creon, yes!
And it must be done at once: God moves
Swiftly to cancel the folly of stubborn men.

79

CREON:

It is hard to deny the heart! But I
Will do it: I will not fight with destiny.

CHORAGOS:

You must go yourself, you cannot leave it to others.

CREON:

I will go.—Bring axes, servants:
Come with me to the tomb. I buried her, I
Will set her free. Oh quickly!
My mind misgives—
The laws of the gods are mighty, and a man must serve them
To the last day of his life!

[*Exit* CREON.]

CHORAGOS:

God of many names

CHORUS:

O Iacchos
son
of Kadmeian Semele
O born of the Thunder!
Guardian of the West
Regent
of Eleusis' plain
O Prince of maenad Thebes
and the Dragon Field by rippling Ismenos:

CHORAGOS:

God of many names

CHORUS:

the flame of torches
flares on our hills
the nymphs of Iacchos
dance at the spring of Castalia:
from the vine-close mountain
come ah come in ivy:
*Evohe evohe!* sings through the streets of Thebes

CHORAGOS:

God of many names

The chorus, fearing the worst for its city, is here invoking the god Dionysus by his many names. Dionysus, god of wine and the focus of an ecstatic religious cult, was a patron god of Thebes.

CHORUS:

                    Iacchos of Thebes
heavenly Child
              of Semele bride of the Thunderer!
The shadow of plague is upon us:
                          come
with clement feet
              oh come from Parnasos
down the long slopes
                across the lamenting water

At the foot of Mount Parnasos, or Parnassus, lay the shrine of Delphi, home of the Delphic oracle.

CHORAGOS:

Io Fire! Chorister of the throbbing stars!
O purest among the voices of the night!
Thou son of God, blaze for us!

CHORUS:

Come with choric rapture of circling Maenads
Who cry *Io Iacche!*
        *God of many names!*
            [*Enter* MESSENGER, *L.*]

MESSENGER:

Men of the line of Kadmos, you who live
Near Amphion's citadel: I cannot say
Of any condition of human life "This is fixed,
This is clearly good, or bad." Fate raises up,
And Fate casts down the happy and unhappy alike:
No man can foretell his Fate. Take the case of Creon:
Creon was happy once, as I count happiness:
Victorious in battle, sole governor of the land,
Fortunate father of children nobly born.
And now it has all gone from him! Who can say
That a man is still alive when his life's joy fails?
He is a walking dead man. Grant him rich,
Let him live like a king in his great house:
If his pleasure is gone, I would not give
So much as the shadow of smoke for all he owns.

Kadmos was the legendary founder of the city of Thebes. Amphion, according to legend, built the first wall surrounding Thebes.

CHORAGOS:

Your words hint at sorrow: what is your news for us?

MESSENGER:

They are dead. The living are guilty of their death.

CHORAGOS:

Who is guilty? Who is dead? Speak!

MESSENGER:

Haimon.
Haimon is dead; and the hand that killed him
Is his own hand.

CHORAGOS:

His father's? or his own?

MESSENGER:

His own, driven mad by the murder his father had done.

CHORAGOS:

Teiresias, Teiresias, how clearly you saw it all!

MESSENGER:

This is my news: you must draw what conclusions you can
from it.

CHORAGOS:

But look: Eurydice, our Queen:
Has she overheard us?

[*Enter* EURYDICE *from the Palace, C.*]

EURYDICE:

I have heard something, friends:
As I was unlocking the gate of Pallas' shrine,
For I needed her help today, I heard a voice
Telling of some new sorrow. And I fainted
There at the temple with all my maidens about me.
But speak again: whatever it is, I can bear it:
Grief and I are no strangers.

MESSENGER:

Dearest Lady,
I will tell you plainly all that I have seen.
I shall not try to comfort you: what is the use,
Since comfort could lie only in what is not true?
The truth is always best. I went with Creon
To the outer plain where Polyneices was lying,
No friend to pity him, his body shredded by dogs.
We made our prayers in that place to Hecate
And Pluto, that they would be merciful. And we bathed
The corpse with holy water, and we brought
Fresh-broken branches to burn what was left of it,
And upon the urn we heaped up a towering barrow

Hecate was a goddess of
sorcery and witchcraft;
Pluto was king of Hades.

Of the earth of his own land. When we were done, we ran
To the vault where Antigone lay on her couch of stone.
One of the servants had gone ahead,
And while he was yet far off he heard a voice
Grieving within the chamber, and he came back
And told Creon. And as the King went closer,
The air was full of wailing, the words lost,
And he begged us to make all haste. "Am I a prophet?"
He said, weeping, "And must I walk this road,
The saddest of all that I have gone before?
My son's voice calls me on. Oh quickly, quickly!
Look through the crevice there, and tell me
If it is Haimon, or some deception of the gods!"
We obeyed; and in the cavern's farthest corner
We saw her lying:
She had made a noose of her fine linen veil
And hanged herself. Haimon lay beside her,
His arms about her waist, lamenting her,
His love lost under ground, crying out
That his father had stolen her away from him.
When Creon saw him the tears rushed to his eyes
And he called to him: "What have you done, child? Speak to me.
What are you thinking that makes your eyes so strange?
O my son, my son, I come to you on my knees!"
But Haimon spat in his face. He said not a word,
Staring—And suddenly drew his sword
And lunged. Creon shrank back, the blade missed; and the boy,
Desperate against himself, drove it half its length
Into his own side, and fell. And as he died,
He gathered Antigone close in his arms again,
Choking, his blood bright red on her white cheek.
And now he lies dead with the dead, and she is his
At last, his bride in the houses of the dead.

[*Exit* EURYDICE *into the Palace.*]

CHORAGOS:

She has left us without a word. What can this mean?

MESSENGER:

It troubles me, too; yet she knows what is best,
Her grief is too great for public lamentation,
And doubtless she has gone to her chamber to weep
For her dead son, leading her maidens in his dirge.

CHORAGOS:

It may be so: but I fear this deep silence.          [*Pause*]

MESSENGER:

I will see what she is doing. I will go in.

[*Exit* MESSENGER *into the Palace.*]
[*Enter* CREON *with attendants, bearing*
HAIMON's *body.*]

CHORAGOS:

But here is the King himself: oh look at him,
Bearing his own damnation in his arms.

CREON:

Nothing you say can touch me any more.
My own blind heart has brought me
From darkness to final darkness. Here you see
The father murdering, the murdered son—
And all my civic wisdom!
Haimon my son, so young, so young to die,
I was the fool, not you; and you died for me.

CHORAGOS:

That is the truth; but you were late in learning it.

CREON:

This truth is hard to bear. Surely a god
Has crushed me beneath the hugest weight of heaven,
And driven me headlong a barbaric way
To trample out the thing I held most dear.
The pains that men will take to come to pain!

[*Enter* MESSENGER *from the Palace.*]

MESSENGER:

The burden you carry in your hands is heavy,
But it is not all: you will find more in your house.

CREON:

What burden worse than this shall I find there?

MESSENGER:

The Queen is dead.

CREON:

O port of death, deaf world,
Is there no pity for me? And you, Angel of evil,
I was dead, and your words are death again.
Is it true, boy? Can it be true?
Is my wife dead? Has death bred death?

84

MESSENGER:

You can see for yourself.

[*The doors are opened, and the body of*
EURYDICE *is disclosed within.*]

CREON:

Oh pity!
All true, all true, and more than I can bear!
O my wife, my son!

MESSENGER:

She stood before the altar, and her heart
Welcomed the knife her own hand guided,
And a great cry burst from her lips for Megareus dead,
And for Haimon dead, her sons; and her last breath
Was a curse for their father, the murderer of her sons.
And she fell, and the dark flowed in through her closing eyes.

CREON:

O God, I am sick with fear.
Are there no swords here? Has no one a blow for me?

MESSENGER:

Her curse is upon you for the deaths of both.

CREON:

It is right that it should be. I alone am guilty.
I know it, and I say it. Lead me in,
Quickly, friends.
I have neither life nor substance. Lead me in.

CHORAGOS:

You are right, if there can be right in so much wrong.
The briefest way is best in a world of sorrow.

CREON:

Let it come,
Let death come quickly, and be kind to me.
I would not ever see the sun again.

CHORAGOS:

All that will come when it will; but we, meanwhile,
Have much to do. Leave the future to itself.

CREON:

All my heart was in that prayer!

Megareus, a son of Creon, died in the war between the brothers of Antigone. Megareus fought on the side of Eteocles, who defended Thebes against the assault of Polyneices.

▶ Can suicide be justified by great personal loss?

CHORAGOS:

Then do not pray any more: the sky is deaf.

CREON:

Lead me away. I have been rash and foolish.
I have killed my son and my wife.
I look for comfort; my comfort lies here dead.
Whatever my hands have touched has come to nothing.
Fate has brought all my pride to a thought of dust.

> [As CREON *is being led into the house,
> the* CHORAGOS *advances and speaks di-
> rectly to the audience:*]

CHORAGOS:

There is no happiness where there is no wisdom;
No wisdom but in submission to the gods.
Big words are always punished,
And proud men in old age learn to be wise.

# 12 THE GOOD CITY:

# PLATO'S *REPUBLIC*

Plato and Aristotle have had the most profound influence of all the Greek philosophers on western thought. They spent their lives wrestling with basic questions: What is good? What is real? What is beauty? They sought answers to these questions through the use of inquiry and logic. Their writings have stimulated western man throughout the centuries primarily because they identified clearly so many basic humanistic issues. If the Greeks did not find all the answers, they at least posed many of the questions.

Plato believed that if man could know the truth, he would know what is good. To him, knowing the truth meant to know the universal and absolute forms upon which all earthly objects, moral standards, and institutions could be based. For example, although man cannot create a perfect circle, he can imagine a perfect circle upon which to base a drawing. Similarly, man cannot create a perfect society, but he can use his reason to conceive of an ideal society upon which to model his own institutions.

To Plato the search for the ideal form of the state meant a search for the ideal of justice. But justice involved far more than the fair settlement of disputes in a court of law. Plato believed that justice would be achieved when the people in a society adhered to three basic virtues—wisdom, courage, and self-control. He believed that a society governed by these three virtues would make it possible for men to live the good life. Moreover, such a society would create good men by encouraging them to observe basic moral standards.

To Plato it was self-evident that the ideal state should be ruled by the best men. The best men, for Plato, were the most virtuous. These best men were not necessarily born to the best parents. Plato believed in an aristocracy of talent, not an aristocracy of birth. On the crucial question of how the best men were to be identified, Plato was vague. Some scholars believe that Plato wanted all people to have the same education, so that those who proved themselves through education could be made rulers. Others point out that in one of the following excerpts Plato suggests that the rulers should be able to identify infants as members of the future ruling class. The evidence, at any rate, is not conclusive. We can, however, be sure that Plato believed rulers should prove themselves to be virtuous.

Plato's *Republic*, from which Reading 12 is taken, discusses nearly every aspect of the ideal state—from child-rearing to political decision-making. Like all of Plato's philosophical works, *The Republic* was written in the form of a dialogue between Plato's own spokesman, Socrates, and the spokesmen for other views. As you read, keep the following questions in mind:

1. In Plato's *Republic*, who makes political decisions? Why are these particular men chosen to make the decisions?
2. What criteria would Plato use to determine whether or not a decision was good?
3. On what basis does Plato's *Republic* determine the role an individual citizen will play in society? What does the answer to this question imply about the obligations of citizens to the society? What does it imply about the nature of the good man and the good life?
4. What do you think Plato would think of democracy? Would he think it is capable of achieving the basic purposes of the state? Why or why not?

## The Republic

A city is formed because men are not self-sufficient but have many wants. So each looks to others for help in supplying his various wants, and many associates and helpers come together in one place and call it a city. Everyone who gives or takes in exchange does so in the belief that he is thus serving his own best

Plato, **The Republic**, in Walter R. Agard, **The Greek Mind** (Princeton: D. Van Nostrand Company, Inc., 1957), pp. 127–130. Reprinted by permission.

interests. It follows that more and better of everything will be produced, and more easily, when each person works at his own specialty according to his own peculiar talent, and at the proper time, without interfering with other tasks. . . .

We shall tell our people the following myth. "All of you are brothers, but when you were created God mixed gold in the composition of those of you who are qualified to govern; in those fitted to be guardians he mixed silver; and in the farmers and artisans he mixed baser metals. It is therefore the first duty of our rulers to see which of these metals enters into the composition of each child that is born; and if a child of baser metal is born in the golden class they are to have no pity on it, but shall put it into the class of farmers and artisans; if, on the other hand, among that class a child of gold or silver is born, they are to raise it to its proper status. For an oracle has declared that when a city is ruled by men of baser metal it shall perish." . . .

When anyone who is by nature an artisan or other kind of producer is inflated by the wealth he has acquired or other material advantage so as to try to join the soldier-guardian class; or when a soldier tries to join the class of philosopher-rulers; or when one person attempts to be all three at one time, you will agree with me, will you not, that such changes in status and such interference will ruin the state?

I most certainly do agree, said [Glaucon].

This, then [continued Socrates], is injustice. But when each of these groups—workers, soldier-guardians, and philosopher-rulers, keeps in its place and performs its own function, then justice will prevail. . . .

Our object in constructing our state is not to make any one class pre-eminently happy, but to guarantee the welfare of the whole community as far as possible. . . .

Unless either philosophers become rulers, or those who rule become lovers of wisdom, and so political power and philosophy are united, there can be no respite from calamity for states or for mankind. . . .

Shall we not require for our rulers men who are by nature of good memory, speedy in learning, high-minded, gracious in manner, friends and brothers of truth, justice, courage, and self-control? . . .

Twenty-year-old youths of exceptional ability must receive special educational opportunities; the separate branches of knowledge must be developed so as to show their interrelationship and the nature of reality. At the age of thirty this group must be tested in terms of ability at dialectic, in order to discover who can advance further toward a true understanding of reality. . . .

Plato is here explaining how the people living in the ideal city should be educated. Plato used myths in a manner similar to the way Jesus used parables.

▶ Do you think that public officials should have the power to determine what social class people should belong to?

By philosophers, here, Plato meant the most virtuous and intelligent men.

Dialectic here refers to the type of logically proceeding dialogue of which Plato was particularly fond. Through deductive reasoning, Plato believed, the truth could be discovered.

Democracy arises when the poor come to power, killing and exiling some of the opposing party, but admitting the rest to equal participation in government. Usually the officials are determined by lot. In such a city are not men free, and does not liberty of speech and action flourish, and is not every man allowed to do what he wishes? This might seem to be the most beautiful constitution of all, decorated, so to speak, with every variety of character as a dress is embroidered with every kind of flower. . . .

But may we not say that democracy, like oligarchy, is destroyed by its unrestrained craving for what it considers the supreme good? In the case of oligarchy, it is wealth; in a democracy it is freedom. For excessive freedom leads to anarchy, which in turn results in despotism, the most burdensome and most brutal slavery. . . .

A man who has joined the select company of philosophers and has come to realize how delightful and blessed is their lot, and has seen how mad the multitude is, how corrupt their politics, and how impossible for a just man to save them from folly, or his own life should he try to do so, this man will refrain from political activity and tend to his own affairs, like a traveler who finds shelter under a wall during a whirlwind. How much better it would be, however, if the philosopher had been fortunate enough to belong to a society which appreciated him; for then he would be able to save the community as well as himself.

**Oligarchy** meant irresponsible government by the few. For Plato it was the corruption of aristocracy, just as anarchy was the corruption of democracy.

▶ Can too much freedom destroy a democracy?

▶ Will philosophers necessarily be the best politicians?

# 13 THE GOOD CITY:
# PERICLES'S DEMOCRACY

Plato lived in Athens, a city noted for its democratic institutions. Yet he questioned some of the fundamental assumptions upon which Athenian democracy was based. Consequently, he envisioned an ideal state in which an elite would make major decisions about public policy. Moreover, he drastically restricted the freedom of individuals in his ideal state.

Athenian democracy, however, had its champions as well as its philosophical critics. Perhaps the most articulate defender of the Athenian way of life was Pericles. At a time when the very life of Athens was threatened by Sparta, a city governed by autocratic institutions, he spoke in praise of his native city and its political organization. Like Lincoln at Gettysburg, Pericles chose to defend democracy in an oration honoring those who had fallen in battle.

**Sparta,** a city-state on the Peloponnesian peninsula south of Athens, did almost everything differently from Athens. Spartan citizens, ethnically different from their slaves and servants, were separated from their families from age seven to thirty and educated to be soldiers. Sparta was little interested in trade or culture, a fact which has not endeared it to later historians. Its forte was order and discipline.

His defense was not so much a description of the Athenian government as an explanation of its ideals. Just as Plato's *Republic* attempted to base an ideal state on assumptions about the nature of truth and the nature of man, Pericles's justification of democracy rested on certain broad principles. Plato and Pericles argued that the purpose of the good society was to create the good life and encourage moral conduct in men. But they disagreed about the nature of the good life, the characteristics of the good man, and the way in which society would provide for these.

The following reading presents Pericles's version of these ideals as they were recorded (and perhaps heavily edited) by Thucydides, the Greek historian. As you read the speech, keep the following questions in mind:

1. Who made political decisions in Athens? How were leaders chosen? What assumption underlay this method of recruiting leaders? Would Plato have agreed with this assumption?
2. What criteria did Athenians use to determine whether or not a decision was good? Would Plato have agreed with these criteria?
3. Who determined the role a person would play in Athenian society? On what basis were these roles determined? Were there any limits on a citizen's freedom to determine his role? What do the answers to these questions imply about Athenian assumptions regarding the good life and the good man?
4. What would Pericles have thought of Plato's *Republic*? On what basic assumptions did Pericles and Plato disagree?

## In Praise of Athens

Thucydides, The **Peloponnesian War,** trans. by Benjamin Jowett (New York: Bantam Books, Inc., 1963), pp. 116–119. Reprinted by permission.

▶ Should citizens of a democracy always obey elected officials?

"Our form of government does not enter into rivalry with the institutions of others. We do not copy our neighbors, but are an example to them. It is true that we are called a democracy, for the administration is in the hands of the many and not the few. But while the law secures equal justice to all alike in their private disputes, the claim of excellence is also recognized; and when a citizen is in any way distinguished, he is preferred [for] the public service, not as a matter of privilege, but as the reward of merit. Neither is poverty a bar, but a man may benefit his country whatever . . . his condition. There is not exclusiveness in our public life, and in our private intercourse, a spirit of reverence pervades our public acts; we are prevented from doing wrong by respect for the authorities and for the laws, having an especial regard to those which are ordained for the protection of the injured as well as to those unwritten laws which bring upon the transgressor of them the reprobation of the general sentiment.

"And we have not forgotten to provide for our weary spirits many relaxations from toil; we have regular games and sacrifices throughout the year; our homes are beautiful and elegant; and the delight which we daily feel in all these things helps to banish melancholy. Because of the greatness of our city the fruits of the whole earth flow in upon us; so that we enjoy the goods of other countries as freely as of our own.

"Then, again, our military training is in many respects superior to that of our adversaries. Our city is thrown open to the world, and we never expel a foreigner or prevent him from seeing or learning anything of which the secret if revealed to an enemy might profit him. We rely not upon management or trickery, but upon our own hearts and hands. And in the matter of education, whereas they from early youth are always undergoing laborious exercises which are to make them brave, we live at ease, and yet are equally ready to face the perils which they face. And here is the proof: The [Spartans] come into Attica not by themselves, but with their [allies] following; we go alone into a neighbor's country; and although our opponents are fighting for their homes and we on a foreign soil, we have seldom any difficulty in overcoming them. Our enemies have never yet felt our united strength; the care of a navy divides our attention, and on land we are obliged to send our own citizens everywhere. But they, if they meet and defeat a part of our army, are as proud as if they had routed us all, and when defeated they pretend to have been vanquished by us all.

"If then we prefer to meet danger with a light heart but without laborious training, and with a courage which is gained by habit and not enforced by law, are we not greatly the gainers?—since we do not anticipate the pain, although, when the hour comes, we can be as brave as those who never allow themselves to rest; and thus too our city is equally admirable in peace and in war. For we are lovers of the beautiful, yet simple in our tastes, and we cultivate the mind without loss of manliness. Wealth we employ, not for talk and ostentation, but when there is a real use for it. To avow poverty with us is no disgrace; the true disgrace is in doing nothing to avoid it.

"An Athenian citizen does not neglect the state because he takes care of his own household; and even those of us who are engaged in business have a very fair idea of politics. We alone regard a man who takes no interest in public affairs, not as a harmless, but as a useless character; and if few of us are originators, we are all sound judges of a policy. The great impediment to action is, in

▶ How much leisure should a citizen of a democracy be willing to give up in order to spend part of his time in politics?

our opinion, not discussion, but the want of that knowledge which is gained by discussion preparatory to action. For we have a peculiar power of thinking before we act and of acting too, whereas other men are courageous from ignorance but hesitate upon reflection. And they are surely to be esteemed the bravest spirits who, having the clearest sense of both the pains and pleasures of life, do not on that account shrink from danger. In doing good, again, we are unlike others; we make our friends by conferring, not by receiving favors. Now he who confers a favor is the firmer friend, because he would . . . by kindness keep alive the memory of an obligation; but the recipient is colder in his feelings, because he knows that in [repaying] another's generosity he will not be winning gratitude but only paying a debt. We alone do good to our neighbors not upon a calculation of interest, but in the confidence of freedom and in a frank and fearless spirit.

**Hellas** is the Greek word for Greece.

"To sum up: I say that Athens is the school of Hellas, and that the individual Athenian in his own person seems to have the power of adapting himself to the most varied forms of action with the utmost versatility and grace. This is not a passing and idle word, but truth and fact; and the assertion is verified by the position to which these qualities have raised the state. For in the hour of trial Athens alone among her contemporaries is superior to the report of her. No enemy who comes against her is indignant at the reverses which he sustains at the hands of such a city; no subject complains that his masters are unworthy of him. And we shall assuredly not be without witnesses; there are mighty monuments of our power which will make us the wonder of this and of succeeding ages; we shall not need the praises of Homer or of any other panegyrist whose poetry may please for the moment, although his representation of the facts will not bear the light of day. For we have compelled every land and every sea to open a path for our valor, and have everywhere planted eternal memorials of our friendship and of our enmity. Such is the city for whose sake these men nobly fought and died; they could not bear the thought that she might be taken from them; and every one of us who survive should gladly toil on her behalf.

"I have dwelt upon the greatness of Athens because I want to show you that we are contending for a higher prize than those who enjoy none of these privileges, and to establish . . . the merit of these men whom I am now commemorating. Their loftiest praise has been already spoken. For in magnifying the city I have magnified them, and men like them whose virtues made her glorious. . . .

"Such was the end of these men; they were worthy of Athens, and the living need not desire to have a more heroic spirit, although

they may pray for a less fatal issue. The value of such a spirit is
not to be expressed in words. Any one can discourse to you forever
about the advantages of a brave defense, which you know already.
But instead of listening to him I would have you day by day fix
your eyes upon the greatness of Athens, until you become filled
with the love of her; and when you are impressed by the spectacle
of her glory, reflect that this empire has been acquired by men
who knew their duty and had the courage to do it, who in the hour
of conflict had the fear of dishonor always present to them, and
who, if ever they failed in an enterprise, would not allow their
virtues to be lost to their country, but freely gave their lives to her
as the fairest offering which they could present at her feast. The
sacrifice which they collectively made was individually repaid to
them; for they received again each one for himself a praise which
grows not old, and the noblest of all sepulchers—I speak not of
that in which their remains are laid, but of that in which their
glory survives, and is proclaimed always and on every fitting occasion in both word and deed. For the whole earth is the sepulcher
of famous men. . . ."

# 14 CITY AND EMPIRE:
# A VALUE DILEMMA

Athens's war with Sparta was part of the Athenian struggle to preserve an empire centering on the Aegean Sea. Led by
Pericles, Athens had subjugated much of the Greek world and
forced the conquered states to pay tribute. To protect themselves,
many of the Greek states that remained free had formed an alliance with Sparta against Athens.

Melos, an island-state in the Aegean Sea, had been settled by
Spartans hundreds of years before. Like other Greek colonies,
Melos was an independent state, though many Melians felt a senti-
mental attachment to their mother country of Sparta. In the war
between Athens and Sparta, Melos at first tried to remain neutral.
But later, after Athenian forces raided Melian territory, Melos became an open enemy of Athens.

Soon Athens sent a large army to Melos. Before attacking, however, the Athenians sent representatives to try to negotiate a Melian
surrender. Instead of inviting these representatives to speak before
their entire citizenry, the Melian leaders brought them before their

governing body. Thucydides recorded the dialogue that took place. As usual, Thucydides's version of the dialogue is not word for word. It is, however, eloquent, and captures the sense of the conflict as at least one intelligent Athenian understood it. As you read, think about the following questions:

1.  What are the basic arguments offered by the Athenians and the Melians?
2.  How do the Athenian arguments square with the Athenian ideals expressed by Pericles?
3.  Would you like to live in a city that behaved as Athens did toward a weaker power? Can an imperial city be a good city? Give reasons for your answers.
4.  Were the Melians foolish in their decision? Had they any real choice? Why or why not?

# The Melian Dialogue

Thucydides, **History of the Peloponnesian War,** trans. by Rex Warner (Baltimore: Penguin Books, Inc., 1955), pp. 359–366. Reprinted by permission.

*Athenians:* So we are not to speak before the people, no doubt in case the mass of the people should hear once and for all and without interruption an argument from us which is both persuasive and incontrovertible, and should so be led astray. This, we realize, is your motive in bringing us here to speak before the few. . . .

The Council of the Melians replied as follows:

*Melians:* No one can object to each of us putting forward our own views in a calm atmosphere. That is perfectly reasonable. What is scarcely consistent with such a proposal is the present threat, indeed the certainty, of your making war on us. We see that you have come prepared to judge the argument yourselves, and that the likely end of it all will be either war, if we prove that we are in the right, and so refuse to surrender, or else slavery. . . .

*Athenians:* Then we on our side will use no fine phrases saying, for example, that we have a right to our empire because we defeated the Persians, or that we have come against you now because of the injuries you have done us—a great mass of words that nobody would believe. . . . Instead we recommend that you should try to get what it is possible for you to get, taking into consideration what we both really do think; since you know as well as we do that, when these matters are discussed by practical people, the standard of justice depends on the equality of power to compel and that in fact the strong do what they have the power to do and the weak accept what they have to accept.

▶ Does might make right, as this passage implies?

*Melians:* Then in our view (since you force us to leave justice out of account and to confine ourselves to self-interest)—in our view it is at any rate useful that you should not destroy a principle that is to the general good of all men—namely, that in the case of all who fall into danger there should be such a thing as fair play and just dealing, and that such people should be allowed to use and to profit by arguments that fall short of a mathematical accuracy. And this is a principle which affects you as much as anybody, since your own fall would be visited by the most terrible vengeance. . . .

*Athenians:* As for us, even assuming that our empire does come to an end, we are not despondent about what would happen next. One is not so much frightened of being conquered by a power which rules over others, as Sparta does . . . as of what would happen if a ruling power is attacked and defeated by its own subjects. So far as this point is concerned, you can leave it to us to face the risks involved. What we shall do now is to show you that it is for the good of our own empire that we are here and that it is for the preservation of your city that we shall say what we are going to say. We do not want any trouble in bringing you into our empire, and we want you to be spared for the good both of yourselves and of ourselves.

*Melians:* And how could it be just as good for us to be the slaves as for you to be the masters?

*Athenians:* You, by giving in, would save yourselves from disaster; we, by not destroying you, would be able to profit from you.

*Melians:* So you would not agree to our being neutral, friends instead of enemies, but allies of neither side?

*Athenians:* No, because it is not so much your hostility that injures us; it is rather the case that, if we were on friendly terms with you, our subjects would regard that as a sign of weakness in us. . . .

*Melians:* Is that your subjects' idea of fair play—that no distinction should be made between people who are quite unconnected with you and . . . rebels whom you have conquered?

*Athenians:* So far as right and wrong are concerned they think there is no difference between the two, that those who still preserve their independence do so because they are strong, and that if we fail to attack them it is because we are afraid. So that by conquering you we shall increase not only the size but the security of our empire. We rule the sea and you are islanders, and weaker islanders too than the others; it is therefore particularly important that you should not escape. . . . This is no fair fight, with honour on one side and shame on the other. It is rather a question of saving your lives and not resisting those who are far too strong for you.

95

*Melians:* Yet we know that in war fortune sometimes makes the odds more level than could be expected from the difference in numbers of the two sides. And if we surrender, then all our hope is lost at once, whereas, so long as we remain in action, there is still a hope that we may yet stand upright.

*Athenians:* Hope, that comforter in danger! If one already has solid advantages to fall back upon, one can indulge in hope. It may do harm, but will not destroy one. But hope is by nature an expensive commodity, and those who are risking their all on one cast find out what it means only when they are already ruined; it never fails them . . . when such a knowledge would enable them to take precautions. Do not let this happen to you, you who are weak and whose fate depends on a single movement of the scale. And do not be like those people who, as so commonly happens, miss the chance of saving themselves in a human and practical way, and, when every clear and distinct hope has left them in their adversity, turn to what is blind and vague, to prophecies and oracles and such things which by encouraging hope lead men to ruin.

*Melians:* It is difficult, and you may be sure that we know it, for us to oppose your power and fortune, unless the terms be equal. Nevertheless we trust that the gods will give us fortune as good as yours, because we are standing for what is right against what is wrong. . . .

*Athenians:* So far as the favour of the gods is concerned, we think we have as much right to that as you have. Our aims and our actions are perfectly consistent with the beliefs men hold about the gods and with the principles which govern their own conduct. Our opinion of the gods and our knowledge of men lead us to conclude that it is a general and necessary law of nature to rule wherever one can. . . . You will see that there is nothing disgraceful in giving way to the greatest city in Hellas when she is offering you such reasonable terms—alliance on a tribute-paying basis and liberty to enjoy your own property. And, when you are allowed to choose between war and safety, you will not be so insensitively arrogant as to make the wrong choice. This is the safe rule—to stand up to one's equals, to behave with deference towards one's superiors, and to treat one's inferiors with moderation. . . .

The Athenians then withdrew from the discussion. The Melians, left to themselves, reached a conclusion which was much the same as they had indicated in their previous replies. Their answer was as follows:

*Melians:* Our decision, Athenians, is just the same as it was at first. We are not prepared to give up in a short moment the liberty

► Is it more "natural" to rule people than to permit free people to govern themselves?

96

which our city has enjoyed from its foundation for 700 years. We put our trust in the fortune that the gods will send and which has saved us up to now, and in the help of men—that is, of the Spartans; and so we shall try to save ourselves. But we invite you to allow us to be friends of yours and enemies to neither side, to make a treaty which shall be agreeable to both you and us, and so to leave our country.

The Melians made this reply, and the Athenians, just as they were breaking off the discussion, said:

*Athenians:* Well, at any rate, judging from this decision of yours, you seem to us quite unique in your ability to consider the future as something more certain than what is before your eyes, and to see uncertainties as realities, simply because you would like them to be so. As you have staked most on and trusted most in Spartans, luck, and hopes, so in all these you will find yourselves most completely deluded.

The Athenian representatives went back to the army, and the Athenian generals, finding that the Melians would not submit, immediately commenced hostilities and built a wall completely round the city of Melos, dividing the work out among the various states. . . . Siege operations were carried on vigorously and, as there was also some treachery from inside, the Melians surrendered unconditionally to the Athenians, who put to death all the men of military age whom they took, and sold the women and children as slaves. Melos itself they took over for themselves, sending out later a colony of 500 men.

# Athens: Ideal and Reality

CHAPTER
3

The ideal Athenian combined a remarkable number of excellent qualities. He could debate profound philosophical issues, following the twists and turns of a subtle Socratic dialogue. He could face an enemy, sword in hand, in defense of his city. He volunteered his private fortune to build a theater or train men for the navy. He gave his time to make the laws and see that they were carried out. He spent his leisure enjoying music, athletics, and drama, and passed many an evening with friends surrounded by good food, fine wines, and dancing girls. He helped to educate his sons and to choose suitable mates for his daughters. What city would not be proud to boast of men with qualities like these?

These qualities imply criteria for a good life, and for a good society in which to lead it. For a good life, a man needed a healthy body, an income large enough to give him leisure, a family, and a host of good friends. His society had to supply an economic organization that could feed, clothe, and shelter him and his family and provide additional goods and services for civic projects. He also needed a government receptive to the demands of citizens and organized to translate desires into legislation. And he needed a social structure in which men with courage, temperance, justice, and wisdom could rise to positions of honor in the city.

The Greeks were well aware of the problems and the potential of the city. They strove to make the city promote their ideals. To what extent did they succeed? Did the city provide opportunities for every man to develop all of his potential? To what extent did Athens fail to promote that ideal? These are the central questions to be considered in Chapter 3, which examines the social setting of Athenian culture.

# 15 THE GEOGRAPHIC SETTING

To what degree have ice and cold shaped the culture of Eskimos? How much impact has hot, steamy weather had on the civilization of people in the Congo? We can ask similar questions about ancient Athens. Perhaps there is some relationship between land form and climate on the one hand, and the texture of Greek civilization on the other.

Some geographers argue that nature decisively shapes man's culture. Small states rather than large nations emerge where mountains cut up the terrain, they say. Toiling on stony mountainsides and fighting fierce storms in small boats breeds strong bodies and courageous spirits. But other geographers challenge these views. If geography determines culture, why did the dozens of American Indian tribes on the flat expanse of the Great Plains fail to unite? And how could Great Britain, with such limited natural resources, take the lead in industrialization?

Reading 15 raises many of the issues involved in this controversy about geography and culture. Its author, C. M. Bowra of Oxford University, suggests ways in which geography may have shaped Greek culture and character. As you read, keep the following questions in mind:

1. For what sorts of activities were the Greek land and climate suited? How could some of the disadvantages stemming from poor soil be overcome?
2. How does Bowra think geographic factors influenced Greek politics, economics, philosophy, and art? Does the evidence he gives convince you that he is right? Are his assertions provable or disprovable? Give reasons for your answers.
3. What Athenian values, if any, do you think may have been shaped by geographic factors? In what way, if any, has American geography helped to shape the national character?

## Landscape and Culture

. . . In Greece the configuration and the character of the landscape have been a primary influence in shaping the destiny of its people ever since the first Greek tribes moved down from the north into the lands which still belong to their descendants. . . . [O]n the whole Greece is physically much the same today as it was four thousand years ago: a land of mountains, which are not huddled together in ungainly lumps but flaunt their peaks in proud

C. M. Bowra, **The Greek Experience** (Cleveland: The World Publishing Company, 1957), pp. 4–5, 9–13. Reprinted by permission of The World Publishing Company and George Weidenfeld & Nicolson Ltd.

independence, and of islands, which are themselves mountains, with roots engulfed in the sea. It presents dramatic contrasts between barren marble or limestone masses and watered valleys, between rain and snow in winter and unbroken sunshine in summer, between an unequalled magnificence of wild flowers and blossoming trees in March and April and parched, crumbling earth from June to October. . . .

Greece is a land of contrasts, but not of extremes. Even in winter there is abundant sunshine; the heat is intense in summer, but lacks the humidity which saps energy and effort; districts, near enough to each other as the crow flies, may be separated by almost impassable mountains, but often have easy communications by sea; though most Greek rivers become barren, stony gullies in summer, in winter they are hurtling torrents, whose water is stored in pools and wells; even the rudest shores may have safe harbours or sandy reaches on which boats can be moored. Greece is indeed a hard land, capable of maintaining only a small population, but if this population faces its tasks with decision, it will reap its rewards. The country is still incapable of feeding flocks or herds on any large scale. Olive-oil takes the place of butter, preservatives, and cooking fats. Fruit and vegetables can be grown only in a few fertile plains or in terraces and holes carved in hill-sides and held by stone embankments; fish is not nearly so common or so various as in northern seas; meat is rare and more likely to be kid than beef or mutton. Yet the Greek larder has its compensations. Wine is abundant; in a land of many flowers honey yields an ample supply of sugar; the goat gives milk and cheese; the mountains have their hares and wild birds, the sea its mullets, lobsters, and squids. Scarcity of food has never prevented the Greeks from being healthy and vigorous; and the very difficulties which attend its supply have stimulated their efforts and their ingenuity.

Such a land demands that its inhabitants should be tough, active, enterprising, and intelligent. When the Greeks exposed unwanted children at birth, they showed how seriously they interpreted the exacting conditions of their existence, and followed the example of nature, which exerts its own selection and control by allowing only the strongest to survive. The physical capacity of the Greeks is clear enough from their many male statues, whose sturdy, muscular frames and limbs are combined with slim waists and competent hands. Men living in such circumstances needed more than the usual qualities of workers in fields, since much of their labour lay on mountain-slopes and in rocky hollows. They must be able to climb easily, to carry heavy loads up and down hill, to be handy with the shifting and shaping of stones, to travel long distances on

The custom of leaving unwanted children outside to die was not practiced in fifth-century Athens. It originated in an earlier and harsher age, when an extra mouth to feed could mean the starvation of a family.

100

foot, to drive ploughs through obstinate, stony soil, to tame horses and mules, to repel the onslaughts of wild animals, and to endure alike sun and storm. This physical equipment must be supplemented by unflagging industry, careful foresight, skill in essential handicrafts, and all the age-old virtues of the farmer who works on difficult land. As labour in the fields promotes endurance and strength of body, so the handling of ships demands quickness of eye and hand, agility and lightness of movement, unresting vigilance, and rapidity of decision. Geographical circumstances formed the Greek character by forcing it to make the most of its natural aptitudes in a hard struggle with the earth and the elements. . . .

In Greece . . . geography shaped the pattern of political life. . . . The most marked feature of Greek politics is the division of the country into a number of small states, each with its own independent government and its own local character. This was imposed by a landscape in which men lived in valleys divided from one another by mountains, or on uplands which presented few entrances to the outer world, or on islands which were largely self-sufficient and self-contained. Each district developed its own life and customs and local pride, because it was separate, complete, and difficult to control from without. Mountainous barriers were not enough to prevent invasion, but they were enough to prevent one state from being merged into another. From time to time states might fall under the dominion of aggressive and powerful neighbours or be forced into union with one another, but they still maintained something of their political independence and many of their own institutions.

It is customary to speak of the units of Greek polity as city-states, and the phrase is apt enough if we recognize that such a state consisted of a good deal more than a city. If the city, usually walled, was the centre of government and justice and of the many handicrafts and trades, other activities went on outside. If there were fertile plains, people would live in villages near their work. Beyond the plains was rising land, usually covered by scrub, hard to cultivate except in patches and pockets, and useful chiefly for pasturing goats. Beyond this, and still higher up, were the rough slopes of the mountains, perhaps here and there enclosing some isolated hamlet, but for the most part desolate, the haunt of hunters in summer and snow-covered winter. Since many Greek cities lay close to the sea, there would be ports where ships could be built and harboured and a maritime population could have its home. In general, the inhabitants of a city-state would be formed of farmers, craftsmen, and sailors, and many would combine two or even three of the roles. Because all members of a city-state lived in close

▶ Does overcoming hardships necessarily strengthen character?

101

proximity within a more or less enclosed space, they had a strong sense of unity and kinship. This did not save them from internecine [within the group] struggles or from class-war, but it meant that respect for local tradition made them look on the men of other cities as somehow different from themselves. . . .

No less powerful was the influence which the Greek scene had on the Greek eye and the Greek mind. The traveller who comes from the west or the north to Greece for the first time may feel a slight twinge of disappointment at the nakedness of its outline and its lack of exuberant colour, but he will soon see that he is faced by a commanding beauty which makes no ready concessions to his appreciation but forces itself slowly and unforgettably on him. What matters above all is the quality of the light. Not only in the cloudless days of summer but even in winter the light is unlike that of any other European country, brighter, cleaner, and stronger. It sharpens the edges of the mountains against the sky, as they rise from valleys or sea; it gives an ever-changing design to the folds and hollows as the shadows shift on or off them; it turns the sea to opal at dawn, to sapphire at midday, and in succession to gold, silver, and lead before nightfall; it outlines the dark green of the olive-trees in contrast to the rusty or ochre soil; it starts innumerable variations of colour and shape in unhewn rock and hewn stone-work. The beauty of the Greek landscape depends primarily on the light, and this had a powerful influence on the Greek vision of the world. Just because by its very strength and sharpness the light forbids the shifting, melting, diaphanous [filmy] effects which give so delicate a charm to the French or the Italian scene, it stimulates a vision which belongs to the sculptor more than to the painter, which depends not so much on an intricate combination or contrast of colours passing into each other as on a clearness of outline and a sense of mass, of bodies emphatically placed in space, of strength and solidity behind natural curves and protuberances. Such a landscape and such a light impose their secret discipline on the eye, and make it see things in contour and relief rather than in mysterious perspective or in flat spatial relations. They explain why the Greeks produced great sculptors and architects, and why even in their painting the foundation of any design is the exact and confident line.

Nor is it perhaps fanciful to think that the Greek light played a part in the formation of Greek thought. Just as the cloudy skies of northern Europe have nursed the huge, amorphous progeny [offspring] of Norse mythology or German metaphysics, so the Greek light surely influenced the clear-cut conceptions of Greek philosophy. If the Greeks were the world's first true philosophers

▶ How important a role does the beauty of nature play in living a good life?

102

in that they formed a consistent and straightforward vocabulary for abstract ideas, it was largely because their minds, like their eyes, sought naturally what is lucid and well defined. Their senses were kept lively by the force of the light, and when the senses are keenly at work, the mind follows no less keenly and seeks to put in order what they give it. . . .

If the light is the first element in the Greek scene, the second is the sea. Its "watery ways," as Homer calls them, bind most districts in Greece, whether mainland or islands, to one another. It plays a larger part there than in any other European country because for most places it is the best, and for many the only, means of communication. There are few districts from which it is not somewhere visible. Often in isolated solitudes among the mountains a man will feel that he has lost sight of it, only to see it again round the next corner. Mastery of it was indispensable to survival, and once mastery was gained, new vistas inspired to adventure. The Greeks were sailors from the dawn of their history, and, because they were bred to ships, they were saved from sinking into the narrow, parochial round which would otherwise have been the lot of dwellers in small city-states. The sea drew alike those who wanted profit and those who wanted excitement, and was the chief means by which the Greeks expanded their knowledge of men and manners. But it was more than this. Its special enchantment, "the multitudinous laughter of the sea-waves," of which Aeschylus speaks, took hold of the Greek consciousness and helped to shape some of its most characteristic convictions. At times no sea can be more alluring than the Aegean with its rippling waves or its halcyon calm, and then indeed it presents an image of that celestial radiance which the Greeks regarded as the most desirable state of man. But even when it seems to be most welcoming, it suddenly changes its temper and menaces with ruin on hidden reefs from merciless winds and mounting waves. By its unpredictable moods and its violent vagaries it provides a lesson on the precarious state of human life, which in the very moment when all seems to be lapped in golden calm is overwhelmed in unforeseen disaster. It is not surprising that when Sophocles sang of the unique achievements of man, he put seafaring first in his list:

> He makes the winter wind carry him
> Across the grey sea
> Through the trough of towering waves.

This quotation, translated differently from the version in Readings 10–11, is from the choral ode at the end of Scene I of **Antigone**.

Command of the sea was indeed something of which to be proud, and it left an indelible mark on the Greek character.

103

# 16 THE ATHENIAN ECONOMY

Man's wants are infinite; his resources are limited: hence he must make choices. The citizens of an ancient city, given a limited quantity of marble, had to decide whether to use it to construct a palace for a king or to build a public theater for everyone. Available manpower could be used to build a temple or increase the supply of wheat in the granary. Potters might use their tools to turn out artistically decorated vases or simple, functional urns; the artistic pieces took longer to make.

Like all ancient cities, Athens depended upon the surrounding countryside to produce agricultural products. Instead of being grown chiefly for home consumption, the main products, olives and grapes, were mostly exported in the form of olive oil and wine and exchanged for wheat from the Black Sea, metals from Italy and North Africa, and other products from the Mediterranean area. One other natural resource played an important role in the prosperity of Athens—silver. Silver from the mines near the city was converted into Athens's most important capital resource—the ships, or triremes, as they were called, which carried the goods of Athenian commerce. As for human resources, Athenian citizens owned their own labor, plus that of approximately 125,000 slaves. More than half of these slaves worked as domestic servants in the homes of wealthy Athenians. The remainder labored in workshops, along with poor Athenian citizens, and in the silver mines.

How a society uses its natural, human, and capital resources depends largely upon its values. The ancient Egyptians employed a huge proportion of their resources to build tombs for the pharoahs because they valued the afterlife more than life on earth. The Greeks, on the other hand, valued this life, and most of their resources went to making it more worth living. How Athenians allocated their resources is the subject of Reading 16, written by another Oxford professor, Alfred E. Zimmern. Let the following questions guide your study:

1. What were the Athenian ideas of private and public property? From what early social organization did these ideas evolve?
2. What did Athenians consider when deciding what goods and services to produce? How did they distribute goods and services? How did they use them?
3. How did Athenian economic decisions about what to produce reflect the values of the society?
4. Do you think the Athenian economy promoted the good life and the good society according to Athenian standards? according to your standards?

# The Greek Commonwealth

The Greeks set out from a different starting point [from us]. In their early world of tribes and brotherhoods and families no one thought of his own "rights" or questioned the claims of society. Practically everything that he had belonged to his kin. He would not claim his own life for himself, if they asked it of him in time of need. Why should he dream of claiming his house or his field or his cattle? They were indeed his own, for he needed them daily and could not live without them. He had made them his own by making use of them, and his chief claim upon them was that no one else could use them . . . so well as he, the father of the family or head of the clan. . . . He held his wealth in trust for the little society round him: and if it belonged to him, as head of the family, rather than to them, this was simply because, in the slow evolution of generations, it had been discovered that private ownership, in this limited and primitive form, was better for the community as a whole. Property held in this way did not involve rights; it simply bestowed duties. . . .

. . . [T]he Greek property-owner grew in zeal and enterprise as he became increasingly conscious of the larger society in which he was working, and of the purposes for which the city required his wealth. . . . The duties that used to be paid to the family or the clan were now paid to the city, which united all these lesser loyalties: and if he was now free to give away his riches as he liked, and even, within limits, to bequeath them, he was willing, nay, eager, that the city should ever be the first to profit by his generosity. She had a claim upon his wealth, as she had upon his time. We have seen that he gave her far more than a tithe of his working hours. His wealth was as freely and as generously lavished. . . .

So it is not difficult to see why the Greek democracies always shrunk, unless they were driven to it by necessity, from direct taxation. It was regarded as derogatory to the dignity of a free citizen. Resident aliens and freedmen might pay a poll-tax and be thankful for the privilege; but the citizen must be left free to help the city in his own way. Every kind of indirect tax he was indeed willing to pay, taxes in time as well as in money; but the only direct contribution he made as a citizen to the State's resources was by preference a free gift, or what was called at Athens and elsewhere a "liturgy" or "public work." A large part of the public expenses of the Athenian State, the mounting of its plays, the equipment of its ships, the arrangements for its games and festivals, its chariot and horse and torch races, its musical contests and regattas both in city and township, were defrayed by private citizens, who came forward voluntarily, and took pride in vying with

Alfred E. Zimmern, **The Greek Commonwealth: Politics and Economics in Fifth-Century Athens,** 5th edition (Oxford: Clarendon Press, 1931), pp. 285–290, 292–295. Reprinted by permission.

▶ Is it fair to run a government by depending on gifts, if some people who could afford to contribute do not choose to do so?

105

their predecessors or with a crowd of rivals in their performance of the task. . . . To talk of taxes in such an atmosphere is a blunder as well as a sacrilege, for a tax is a payment which leaves a man poorer: a "liturgy" leaves him richer. He still possesses what he has given, and yet has added to the common store. For, to quote Pericles . . . , "national greatness is more for the advantage of private citizens than any individual well-being coupled with public need." . . .

But here we are concerned not so much with the feeling that prompted this constant stream of generosity as with its effect upon the economy of the city which it enriched. It produced what is to us an entirely unfamiliar relation between public and private riches, between the resources of the city and the private resources of the citizens. In a community so poor as an ordinary Greek State the city not only tends to possess far larger permanent resources (quite apart from her annual revenue from gifts and taxes) than any individual citizen, but may easily, with all her public lands and temple-treasures, be wealthier than her individual citizens put together. . . .

Demosthenes was a famous orator and politician.

. . . Fifth-century Athens presented a . . . striking contrast. You would gaze with admiration, says Demosthenes, on her temples and colonnades, her armouries and her dockyards, and on those immortal buildings upon her Acropolis which, as you passed to and fro in the city, flashed over the edge of the rock on every side; but when you asked for the house of Themistocles or Cimon or Aristeides or any other of the great ones whose names were on all men's lips, you would find that men hardly knew it, and, when you reached it at last, that it was just like their next door neighbour's—a plain villa of sunbaked brick. Their real wealth, in fact, was not laid up in their own houses, where moth and rust do corrupt and thieves break through the flimsy party wall and steal, but was shared with their fellow-citizens and embodied for all to enjoy in the works of their artists. For such a society, however poor, will know how to use the talents of its architects and sculptors and painters. It may be without wealthy patrons; but its public will have the zeal and its artists the inspiration. . . .

▶ Do you think that a father should reduce his family's standard of living in order to give money to the symphony or to charity?

. . . [T]heir material equipment was sadly defective, and called for the best of spirits to put up with it. Strange indeed is the contrast between the city as mistress of men's lives and as manager of their affairs, between Athens as the source of energy and dispenser of wisdom and Athens as a mere municipality. . . .

The Great Plague struck Athens during the Peleponnesian War. Thucydides described the epidemic brilliantly.

. . . Water indeed she had, thanks to the tyrants: although even that almost indispensable condition of Greek city life was not extended to the Piraeus, which up to the time of the Great Plague relied wholly upon cisterns. Her streets narrow and crooked, dirty, unlighted, and ill-paved. She had no sewers, or even cesspools, and over the whole department of sanitation it is best to draw a veil. Most of the police were amateurs, and the rest Scythian barbarians, the laughing-stock of freeborn citizens. State-paid detectives she had never heard of, and their place is taken by private spies or "sycophants" who, in a society full of tittle-tattle, create more mischief than they discover. Postmen we do not expect, though the Persians, and later the Ptolemies, had a national post. But it is a surprise, especially if we come fresh from the national systems of education in Plato and Aristotle, to find that the Athens of Pericles paid no attention whatever to her children (who did not indeed become hers till they reached their eighteenth year), and provided no national schoolmasters except the citizens who drilled the recruits. . . . Another surprise is to find that the city was too lazy to collect her own money. The imperial treasury, where her ideals were vitally concerned, was carefully looked after in every particular, and if the contributions were late there were officials to hasten them in. But all the mere municipal moneys, the foreigners' poll-tax, the customs, the market dues, and all the various licences, were simply farmed out to "publicans," who made a profit on their contract. . . .

No doubt all these [defects], Pericles would tell us, are non-essentials on which we ought not to dwell. We should accept . . . the magnificence and let the squalor rest in peace; go straight for the big things, as he did, and ignore the rest. What matters is the finished work of Athenian civilization, not the infinite petty obstacles with which it was daily contending.

The Scythians lived on the northern shore of the Black Sea. The Greeks considered all non-Greeks barbarians. However, the Greeks did not consider "barbarian" a term of contempt; they simply meant by it anyone who made noises like "bar bar" rather than speaking the intelligible language of Greek.

▶ How can each individual develop to the limit of his abilities if there is no public school system and all parents cannot afford tutors?

Tax collection was done by private enterprise instead of by a treasury or a department of internal revenue. This system of tax-farming has been rejected by most modern states.

# 17 THE ATHENIAN POLITICAL SYSTEM

The Athenians assumed that men could govern themselves. Most ancient peoples rejected this assumption. Because they thought man was little more than an animal, they believed that he needed an absolute ruler to keep him in control. The Athenians, however, placed man closer to the gods than to brutes. Hence, they believed that men were able to control their own destinies.

Athens ruled itself by a direct democracy. All citizens participated in making political decisions as members of the Assembly, the major governmental institution in Athens. But only adult males born of native Athenian parents were citizens; slaves, women, and children, as well as foreigners who had taken up residence in the city, had no vote. Despite these restrictions, however, Athenians still put greater trust than any other ancient people in man's ability to run his own affairs.

The Athenians set high standards for their government. Not only was it charged with keeping peace and order, but it was responsible for creating a good society as well. For Athenians, a government was worthless unless it created an environment in which a man could develop his full potential.

To what extent did the Athenians live up to these standards? Did Athenian democracy create the good society? Reading 17, written by H. D. F. Kitto, a leading English classicist, explores these questions. As you read, keep the following questions in mind:

1. How did the Athenians choose their leaders? How did they make political decisions? What were the institutions by which they governed themselves? What was the role of the individual citizen? What part did ideology play in the political system?
2. To what extent do you think the Athenian political system helped create the good society? In what ways did the government promote the ideals of the Greeks? In what ways did it fall short of the Athenian ideals?
3. To what extent did the Athenian political system live up to the ideal depicted by Pericles in the Funeral Oration?

# Athenian Democracy

H. D. F. Kitto, **The Greeks** (London: Penguin Books, Ltd., 1957), pp. 126–131. Reprinted by permission.

The Areopagus was an aristocratic advisory council. The archons were high officeholders.

[The] Assembly, a mass-meeting of all the native male residents of Attica, was the sole legislative body, and had, in various ways, complete control of the administration and judicature. First, the administration. The old Areopagus, composed of ex-archons, did nothing [in the fifth century B.C.] except deal with cases of homicide. The archons, once so powerful, were now chosen by annual ballot from the Assembly. Any citizen, any year, might find himself one of the nine archons: this meant, naturally, that the archonship, although it had administrative responsibility, had no real power. Power remained with the Assembly. The Assembly met once a month, unless specially convened to settle something of importance. Any citizen could speak—if he could get the Assembly to listen; anybody could propose anything, within certain strict constitutional safeguards. But so large a body needed a committee to prepare its business and to deal with matters of urgency. This committee was the Council ("boule") of five hundred, not elected, but chosen by ballot, fifty from each tribe. Since this Council was chosen haphazard, and was composed of entirely different people each year, it could develop no corporate feeling. That was the whole idea: nothing must overshadow the Assembly. Most of the administrative boards ("Government departments") were manned by members of the Boule. But since five hundred men could not be in constant session, and were too many to make an efficient executive committee, there was an inner council, the "prytany," composed, in turn, of the fifty men drawn from each of the ten tribes, which remained in session one-tenth of the year. Of these, one was chosen by ballot to be chairman each day. If there was a meeting of the Assembly, he presided: for twenty-four hours he was titular Head of the State. (It happened, Greece being an essentially dramatic country, that Socrates held this position one day towards the end of the war when the Assembly ran amok—as sometimes happened, but not often—and quite illegally demanded to impeach the whole of the Board of Generals for failing to rescue survivors of the successful naval battle of Arginusae. Socrates defied the mob, and refused to put the irregular proposal to the vote.) As a further check on the Administration, all outgoing magistrates had to submit to the Assembly an account of their official acts, and their responsibility did not end until they had passed this "audit." Until they had done this they might neither leave Athens nor sell property.

One important office could not be left to the hazard of the ballot —the command of the forces, on land or afloat. The ten Strategoi ("generals" or "admirals" indifferently) were elected—but annually, though re-election was permissible and indeed normal: but it was no unusual thing for an Athenian to be a general in one campaign and a private soldier in the next. This was an extreme case of the basic conception of democracy, "to rule and to be ruled in turn." It was as if the trade-union official of one year automatically returned to his bench the next. Being the only officials expressly elected on the grounds of special competence, and holding offices of such importance, the strategoi naturally wielded great influence in the city's affairs. It was through this office, and through his personal ascendency in the Assembly, that Pericles led the Athenians for so long.

The Assembly controlled not only legislation and administration, but justice as well; as there were no professional administrators, so there were no professional judges or pleaders. The principle was preserved that the aggrieved man appealed directly to his fellow-citizens for justice—in the local courts for trivial matters, in Athenian courts for important matters, criminal or civil. The jury was virtually a section of the Assembly, varying in size from 101 to 1,001, according to the importance of the case. There was no judge, only

▶ Could a large modern democracy permit every citizen to participate directly in devising legislation? Would the costs of such an arrangement be compensated for by the chance each citizen would have to develop his full potential as a legislator?

109

a purely formal chairman, like our "foreman." There were no pleaders: the parties conducted their own case, though in fact, a plaintiff or defendant might get a professional "speech-writer" to make up his speech; but then he learnt it and gave it himself. This popular jury was judge both of law and of fact, and there was no appeal. If the offence was one for which the law laid down no precise penalty, then—since a large jury could not conveniently fix the sentence—the prosecutor, if he won his case, proposed one penalty, the accused proposed an alternative, and the jury had to choose one of the two. . . .

This survey, brief though it is, will bring out one essential point, that public affairs in Athens were run, so far as possible, by amateurs. The professional was given as little scope as possible; indeed, the expert was usually a public slave. Every citizen was, in turn, a soldier (or sailor), a legislator, a judge, an administrator—if not as archon, then certainly as member of the Boule. The extraordinary use made of amateurs may strike the reader as ludicrous: it was indeed severely criticized by Socrates and Plato, though not so much because it was inefficient as because it entrusted to men entirely ignorant of it the major function of "the political art," namely, to make men better. But this is by the way.

Beneath this general aversion to the professional there was a more or less conscious theory of the polis: namely that the duty of taking part, at the appropriate season of life, in all the affairs of the polis was one that the individual owed both to the polis and to himself. It was part of that full life which only the polis could provide: the savage, living for himself alone, could not have it, nor the civilized "barbarian" living in a vast empire ruled by a King and his personal servants. To the Athenian at least, self-rule by discussion, self-discipline, personal responsibility, direct participation in the life of the polis at all points—these things were the breath of life.

And they were incompatible with a representative government administering a large area. This is the reason why Athens could not grow as Rome did, by incorporating other poleis. To the Athenian, the responsibility of taking his own decisions, carrying them out, and accepting the consequences, was a necessary part of the life of a free man. This is one reason why the popular art of Athens was the tragedy of Aeschylus and Sophocles and the comedy of Aristophanes, while ours is the cinema. The Athenian was accustomed to deal with things of importance: an art therefore which did not handle themes of importance would have seemed to him to be childish.

. . . It was government by amateurs in the strict sense of this word: that is to say, by people who liked government and ad-

"Poleis" is the plural of "polis."

110

ministration. To put it in this way is perhaps misleading, because the words "government" and "administration" have, among us, acquired capital letters: they are things in themselves, pursuits to which some misguided persons devote their lives. To the Greeks, they were merely two sides of that many-sided thing, the life of the polis. To attend to the business of the polis was not only a duty which a man owed to the polis: it was also a duty which a man owed to himself—and it was an absorbing interest too. It was part of the complete life. This is the reason why the Athenian never employed the professional administrator or judge if he could possibly help it. The polis was a kind of super-family, and family life means taking a direct part in family affairs and family counsels. This attitude to the polis explains, too, why the Greek never, as we say, "invented" representative government. Why should he "invent" something which most Greeks struggled to abolish, namely being governed by someone else?

But was it amateurish in the other sense? Was it inefficient, or inconsequent? To this question, I think, we can say no, if our standard is not perfection, but government as it is normally found among men. The regime was stable, recovering quite easily from two oligarchic revolutions made possible by the stress of unsuccessful war. It won and managed an empire: it collected its taxes; it managed its economy, its finances and its currency with notable firmness: it seems to have maintained a standard of public justice which certain governments of our time have not reached. It lost a critical war, not from lack of nerve or spirit, but from serious errors in judgment, and to these any form of government is liable. Judged by all these, the ordinary standards of efficiency, this experiment in logical democracy must be pronounced not unsuccessful.

The Athenian would have accepted all these tests of efficiency as legitimate, but would have added another: did it secure for the ordinary citizen a reasonably good life? That is to say, besides doing what we today expect from our government, did it stimulate his intellect and satisfy his spirit? In answering this question there can be no hesitation whatsoever. A much more searching test was applied by philosophers like Socrates and Plato: did this form of government train men in virtue? Plato says, in the *Gorgias,* that Themistocles, Cimon, and Pericles "filled the city with fortifications and rubbish of that sort," but failed miserably in the stateman's first duty, of making the citizens more virtuous. But efficiency of this kind is what very few governments have aimed at.

In considering efficiency of the grosser sort, two points must be borne in mind. One is the small scale of the state. This Athenian district-meeting, the Assembly, like a vigorous local council today, was for the most part dealing with problems of which many of its

▶ Should a government take responsibility for stimulating the intellects and satisfying the spirits of its citizens?

members at least had direct personal knowledge. Further, the complexity of things was much less than it is today—not indeed the intellectual or moral complexity of things, which is always the same, but the complexity of organization. If war was declared, it was not a matter of "mobilizing the entire resources of the nation," with endless committees and an enormous consumption of paper: it was a matter simply of every man going home for his shield, his spear and his rations, and reporting for orders. The Assembly made its worst mistakes in making decisions on matters outside its personal knowledge. Thus, in the middle of the war it made the disastrous resolution to invade Sicily, though (as Thucydides remarks) very few knew where Sicily was, nor how big it was.

Then one must remember that all the members of this Assembly, other than the youngest, had first-hand experience of administration in the various local and tribal offices and in law-courts, and that five hundred new men every year served in the Boule, drafting laws for submission to the Assembly, receiving foreign embassies, dealing with finance, and all the rest of it. If we take 30,000 as a reasonable estimate of the normal number of citizens, it will be seen that any one citizen was more likely than not to serve his year on the Boule. The Assembly, in fact, was for the most part composed of men who knew what they were talking about, from personal experience.

# 18 THE ATHENIAN SOCIAL SYSTEM

A society's values interact in complicated ways with its social structure. Values help to determine the status of individual members of a society and to shape the interaction between them. At the same time, the ways in which men group themselves and interact with each other help to mold values. To understand the values of a society one must analyze the degree to which its social structure conforms to ideas of the good man, the good life, and the good society.

Urbanization was one of the most significant social movements to influence the values of the ancient Greeks. Like most ancient peoples, the early Greeks had been organized in tribes; social relationships had been governed largely by kinship ties. As the Greeks began to establish cities, the importance of family connections began to diminish. Out of this changing social pattern evolved the values of the fifth-century Athenians.

Reading 18 examines the social effects of urbanization in ancient Greece. As you read, keep the following questions in mind:

1. What were the most important social changes involved in the transition from a tribal to an urban culture? How did these changes affect the values of the people?
2. How did Greek society control its members' behavior? How did these mechanisms of social control promote or detract from the attainment of Athenian ideals?
3. To what extent do the same forces that shaped the values of the ancient Greeks shape the values of modern urban dwellers? To what extent should these forces influence values?
4. To what degree do you think Athenian social structure reflected the ideals of the culture? To what extent did the social structure make the attainment of Athenian ideals more difficult?

# From Tribe to Polis

Between the ninth and the sixth centuries B.C., the Greeks experienced one of the greatest social revolutions in the history of mankind—the breakdown of tribalism and the development of urban communities. Unlike other peoples of their day, the Greeks in general, and the Athenians in particular, responded to this revolution in ways that encouraged the development of freedom, individualism, and equality. Out of their responses to the breakdown of tribalism grew the unique social arrangements that encouraged the development of Greek values. And as these values became the measuring stick for Greek society, the democratization of political institutions and social arrangements was accelerated.

Prior to the development of cities, kinship ties shaped almost every aspect of a man's life. Kinship defined a man's fundamental loyalties. It determined when and against whom he waged war, where he lived, and what goods and services he produced. Kinship also determined whom he married; from whom he obtained justice; and from whom he learned the work skills, rituals, and traditions of the culture.

Leaving tribalism meant leaving a world in which most decisions were closely regulated by a set of unexamined and unexaminable rules. To leave tribalism meant entering a world of wider choice concerning marriage, trade, personal loyalties, and political alliances. Perhaps most important, men could determine the very rules by which they lived once they broke the tribal bonds. In tribal societies men were only rule-breakers, not rule-makers.

By John M. Good. An adaptation from pp. 78-107 of Enter Plato, by Alvin W. Gouldner, ©1965 by Basic Books, Inc., Publishers, New York. Reprinted by permission also of Routledge & Kegan Paul, Ltd., London.

Many African societies today are going through similar developments.

113

Most ancient cultures did not trust large bodies of men to legislate for themselves, even when urban societies developed. Instead, they gave that power to a tiny elite. More often than not, the rule-makers in ancient societies were those who had the military might to enforce their decisions. Most of those who had such military might owned enough land to be able to purchase soldiers, armor, weapons, and horses. And because they owned the instruments of war, they were able to acquire and protect the land needed to finance their military strength. This vicious circle did not develop in Greece, however, where landholdings were relatively small. As a consequence, the breakdown of tribalism in Greece created a more open and unstructured society than in other parts of the ancient world.

**Mores** are fixed, binding customs.

The Greek kinship system itself helped to prevent men from accumulating large landholdings to finance large armies. The mores of the Greek kinship system required that a father divide his land equally among his sons. As generation after generation passed, and as the population grew, the land became subdivided into smaller and smaller parcels. Moreover, only a small portion of Greece was arable. Consequently, no one man or even one tribe could produce enough surplus food to pay for enough soldiers and weapons to subdue all neighboring tribes. Greece remained a land of many tribes, instead of becoming a unified kingdom.

Nevertheless, the ancient Greeks were a warlike people. Since the agricultural surplus was small, the Greeks were unable to purchase many metal products and other essential goods. Instead, they often acquired these necessities by war and piracy. As a consequence, they placed a high value on such military virtues as courage, strength, skill in using weapons, and loyalty to one's fellow soldiers.

These peculiar economic and military conditions in Greece fostered a social structure more mobile than most in the ancient world. Rather than giving status to those who owned large tracts of land, the Greeks gave status to those who possessed military virtues. Hence, social status could not be passed on from father to son in the form of land. It had to be earned by demonstrating one's courage, strength, skill, and devotion in battle. As centuries passed, excellence in more peaceful pursuits, such as oratory, art, athletics, philosophy, and politics, was also rewarded with high status. So, too, was wealth. Even in fifth-century Athens, however, a man's achievements in warfare contributed heavily to his social status. Such great men as Pericles, Thucydides, and even Socrates demonstrated their prowess on the battlefield.

As the Greeks passed from a tribal to an urban culture, the achievement system gradually replaced kinship as the major social

114

regulator. A man's excellence—measured by his achievements rather than by his position in the family—came mainly to determine his position in society. With the weakening of tribal ties and the growth of an urban economy, the Greeks had to establish new rules for assessing the worth of a man. The establishment of these new criteria led, in turn, to new rules for governing a man's conduct and for determining the direction of his life.

Generally speaking, a man's reputation was the criterion used to judge his worth under the achievement system. A man's family position, while never meaningless, counted for less in the polis than it did in the tribe. Consequently, the Athenian's greatest ambition was for fame—to perform acts that would receive the accolades of his fellow citizens.

▶ Is status worth anything if it is inherited rather than earned?

The quest for fame promoted the development of a "contest system" as a mechanism for determining who would be recognized and who would not. The most famous of these contests, of course, were the Olympic games. Athens and other states also sponsored festivals in which the best dramatists and actors competed. The contest system, however, reached far beyond these formal competitions. Competitiveness became a way of life in Athens. Citizens competed for public office, for the purchase of a valuable item, for victory in debate, for the most perfect demonstration of a philosophical or mathematical theorem, for the most elegant dinner party, or for the privilege of supporting the best play or the largest warship.

While the Greeks used fame as a positive incentive to achieve, they also used shame as a punishment to discourage men from dropping out of the competitive life. As Pericles stated in his Funeral Oration: "To avow poverty with us is no disgrace; the true disgrace is in doing nothing to avoid it." In short, it is shameful not to try to get rich. Shame as much as fame depended upon the opinions of others. To the Greeks shame was not a matter of whether or not your conscience bothered you; it was a matter of whether or not your neighbors thought that you were negligent, unfaithful, lazy, stupid, stingy, or weak. The Athenians even developed a mechanism by which those of relatively low status could make their opinions felt. First, they gave all citizens, however poor in material possessions or reputation, the right to vote upon community policy. Second, the citizenry as a whole could periodically decide whether a particular man should be ostracized, or exiled, from the city's limits. Thus shame as well as fame depended upon the opinions of all the citizens.

These social mechanisms of fame and shame largely replaced the kinship system as a means of ordering society. Although Athenians developed individual talents and interests, they were

▶ Which influences you more effectively, striving for fame or trying to avoid shame?

115

deeply concerned about the opinions of others, for the opinions of others determined an Athenian's social status. The effect of these opinions on status, in turn, influenced the norms of behavior, or the standards of conduct. Public opinion rather than tradition of a ruler defined good and bad behavior and used the mechanisms of fame and shame to give its definitions force. In such a society behavior and status were not governed mainly by the dead hand of tradition or by kinship. Under the achievement system a man's status could change if he earned the accolades or reprimands of his fellow citizens. For the ancient world, Athens was a relatively mobile society. The very rules of conduct in Athenian society were flexible as well. There was no generally accepted "right way." Many of the traditions that remained were sharply challenged. Athenian society was bubbling with new ideas and new norms of behavior. The Athenian citizen of the fifth century B.C. therefore faced a world of greater choices than his ancestors had in their traditional tribal world.

Athens was far from a thorough-going democracy. The citizenry made up an elite. Women, children, slaves, and resident foreigners were less free; their lives were more closely governed by tradition, as well as by the rules agreed upon by citizens. Still, among the citizen-elite, life patterns were shaped by the mobility and freedom characteristic of democratic social systems. And in fifth-century Athens the citizenry comprised a far larger proportion of the population than in any other society of the time.

# 19 THE GOOD MAN AND THE GOOD LIFE: A SUMMARY

Modern Americans often equate the good life with material comfort and define the good man in terms of moral standards derived from religion. The conditions of Athenian life made definitions like these impossible. In the first place, Athenians lacked the scientific and technical knowledge that makes modern material prosperity possible. Secondly, their religion was not centered around moral behavior. Yet, more than any other ancient people, the Greeks struggled to define the good man and the good life.

During the past weeks you have been studying the culture of the ancient Greeks. Many of the readings have been translated from original sources written by the Greeks themselves. You have been asked to develop your own conception of Athenian definitions of the good man, the good life, and the good society. The last two readings in this unit consist of analyses of Greek society written by modern scholars. Each reading will give you an opportunity to test your own conclusions. As you read the following excerpt, think about these questions:

1. What is the Greek definition of the good man, according to Bowra? Is the good man defined chiefly in terms of morality or proficiency?
2. What is the Greek definition of the good life, according to Bowra? To what extent does this definition depend upon material prosperity?
3. What evidence is there for Bowra's assertions? In the earlier readings of this unit, have you encountered evidence that contradicts Bowra's conclusions?
4. To what extent do the Greek definitions of the good man and the good life appeal to you? What relevance do those Greek definitions have to twentieth-century America?

## The Good Man and the Good Life

. . . [For the Greeks there were] four cardinal virtues— courage, temperance, justice, and wisdom. The English words do not quite represent their Greek originals, and we must not read too many associations or subtleties into them. The establishment of this quartet is thought to have been the work of Pythagoras, and even if he inherited it from traditional wisdom, he may have given it a neater form and a wider currency. . . . It embodied what the Greeks admired in theory and sought in practice, and most of them would have thought that, if a man exercises these virtues and applies them to each situation as it arises, he does as much as can be expected of him.

The list . . . has no special authority, but it represents average opinion on character and conduct and is a fair guide to the standards by which the Greeks judged each other and themselves. Originally, perhaps, the list looked at men from four different angles, physical, aesthetic, moral, and intellectual, and reflected the concept of the "four-square" man in all its fullness and balance. Physical courage was highly valued at all times by a people much given to war, and we cannot doubt that the average man would not trouble himself with niceties about its nature, but respond with admiration to its imaginative-appeal. . . . Temperance was largely a matter of style, of doing things without display or vulgarity, of

C. M. Bowra, **The Greek Experience**, pp. 86–87, 89, 91–96, 98. Reprinted by permission.

Recall Simonides's poem in Reading 9.

▶ Should the good man try
always to be balanced
and controlled?

behaving without arrogance. If it was highly regarded in aristocratic circles as an essential element in good manners, it was also
something that Pericles praised in the Athenians: "Our love of what
is beautiful does not lead us to extravagance; our love of the things
of the mind does not make us soft." Justice is essentially of a moral
quality, the natural tendency to obey the rules and laws of a
civilized society and to treat other men to their deserts, and is well
described by Simonides as "rendering to every man his due." It is
primarily social in its application. The word *dike,* which we translate "justice," seems to be derived from the boundaries of a man's
land and conveys metaphorically the notion that he should keep
within his own sphere and respect that of his neighbour. Wisdom
is certainly an intellectual quality. In early days it is applied to
any activity of the mind and denotes skill in the arts, to say nothing
of capacity for philosophy, science, or politics. Obviously it was not
easy to find all four virtues equally prominent in a single man, but
it was not impossible, and a respect for them certainly indicated
a well-balanced view of what a man ought to be. . . .

If the four virtues stood for an ideal of a balanced and controlled
personality, their antithesis lay in those faults which destroy such
a balance and work havoc both in individuals and in societies.
. . . In general it was thought that not only the individual virtues
but their unity and balance were destroyed by *hybris* or arrogance.
It might well reflect an inner lack of courage; it certainly meant a
defiance of self-control and temperance; it led inevitably to injustice in its disregard for the rights of others; it often ended in
folly when its possessor thought that he could by unjust methods
secure the impossible. The Greeks gave this vile eminence to arrogance because, more than anything else, it defied their ideal of a
harmonious and restrained self, and their deep political distrust
of it was equalled by their moral condemnation. They saw that it
grows with feeding and creates other evils as great as itself. . . .

When we turn from the notion of the good man to that of the
good life, it is clear that the word "good" has another sense. We
may take as our text an Attic drinking-song which lays down the
four best goods:

> For a man health is the first and best possession,
> Second best to be born with shapely beauty,
> And the third is wealth honestly won,
> Fourth are the days of youth spent in delight with friends. . . .

The Greeks prayed for health as the first of blessings because
not only did the lack of it ruin happiness as they conceived it, but
they were at the mercy of disease. Medicine had indeed begun to

make an impressive appearance by the end of the sixth century, but though it approached its task in a strictly scientific spirit, it had much to learn and could not cure all evils in a society which had almost no hygiene and fell an easy victim to any new infection. How appalling a disease could be can be seen from Thucydides' account of the plague which attacked Athens in 430 B.C. and has been variously identified with typhus and measles. . . .

The desire for health was inextricably connected with the Greek cult of the body. This was essentially a religious activity. Through their bodies men resembled the gods, and the gods guided and guarded their development. . . . The whole process of birth and growth was directed and watched by gods, and at each stage it was the young body that called for their care, whether it was strengthened at the beginning by being passed over a fire or later by being exercised in games and dances, or tested by initiation ceremonies. If health was the first of good things, it was because the gods gave it and fostered it in those whom they loved.

The belief in health passes imperceptibly into the belief in beauty, which is equally derived from the notion that through it men and women resemble the gods. Indeed, the Greeks could not think any physical form beautiful unless it was healthy. They had no morbid taste for decay, and old age was for them not beautiful but either impressive or pathetic. The beauty which they admired and celebrated with many statues of naked young men and well-clothed maidens was that of the body when it is passing into manhood or womanhood. . . .

The Attic song names wealth as the third good. The Greeks enjoyed the pursuit of money as much as any men, and had an undoubted talent for it, but it was thought mean to treat it as an end in itself, nor were the rich respected just because they were rich. A normal attitude was that a good man needs money to help him to lead the good life, as Cephalus said to Socrates: "If it is true that a good man will not find it easy to endure old age and poverty together, no more will riches ever make a bad man contented and cheerful." It followed that the Greeks saw no virtue in poverty and regarded it as a condition which degrades those whose lot it is. . . .

Recall Theognis's poem in Reading 9.

The fourth good named by the Attic song is to be young among friends, and what this means can be seen from the delight which Greek sculptors and painters take in representing the pastimes and indulgences of young men. They keep their bodies fit by wrestling, playing ball, practising what looks very like hockey, jumping over sticks, and throwing the discus. . . . They exercise horses in a field or listen, in unashamed dandyism, to a lyre-player. They have also their convivial relaxations. A party gathers and

119

soon becomes gay. The young men rush to the mixing-bowl and fill their cups. They play on flutes to each other or to girls, who dance for them. In the end it is too much for them, and they pay for it by vomiting, while fatherly elders or decorous girls look after them. . . . The Greeks did not expect young men always to behave with restraint and were content that at times they should release their ebullience in happy abandonment. This was part of the glory of youth. . . .

# 20 THE GOOD SOCIETY: THE POLIS

The ancient Greeks believed that the world was made up of two kinds of people—themselves and the barbarians. What distinguished Greeks from the barbarians was the polis. "Polis" is most often translated into English as "city-state," but it was far more than a geographical concept. The Greeks thought of the polis as a way of life. It was the particular way the Greeks governed themselves, educated their children, produced their goods and services, and pursued their cultural life. In short, Greeks thought of the polis as the good society.

The selection in this reading comes again from the work of the modern scholar H. D. F. Kitto. Working primarily from the writings of dramatists, philosophers, and historians, he has attempted to summarize the Greek ideals of the polis. Keep the following questions in mind as you read the concluding selection of this unit:

1. According to Kitto what were the characteristics of the polis? Why did the Greeks believe that these characteristics were essential to the good society?
2. To what extent was the polis related to the Greek ideas of the good man and the good life?
3. Are Kitto's assertions about the Greek definition of the good society supported by evidence contained in earlier readings? Does any of the evidence contradict Kitto's conclusions?
4. To what extent is the Greek definition of the good society relevant to modern society? Does the size of modern nations make these ideals impractical, as Kitto suggests? Which of these ideals can be applied as standards for judging modern society?

# The Polis

"Polis" is the Greek word which we translate "city-state." It is a bad translation, because the normal polis was not much like a city, and was very much more than a state. But translation, like politics, is the art of the possible; since we have not got the thing which the Greeks called "the polis," we do not possess an equivalent word. . . .

It is important to realize . . . [the size] . . . [of the polis]. The modern reader picks up a translation of Plato's *Republic* or Aristotle's *Politics;* he finds Plato ordaining that his ideal city shall have 5,000 citizens, and Aristotle that each citizen should be able to know all the others by sight; and he smiles, perhaps, at such philosophic fantasies. But Plato and Aristotle are not fantasts. Plato is imagining a polis on the normal Hellenic scale; indeed he implies that many existing Greek poleis are too small—for many had less than 5,000 citizens. Aristotle says, in his amusing way—Aristotle sometimes sounds very like a don—that a polis of ten citizens would be impossible, because it could not be self-sufficient, and that a polis of a hundred thousand would be absurd, because it could not govern itself properly. . . .

To think on this scale is difficult for us, who regard a state of ten million as small, and are accustomed to states which, like the U.S.A. and the U.S.S.R., are so big that they have to be referred to by their initials; but when the adjustable reader has become accustomed to the scale, he will not commit the vulgar error of confusing size with significance. The modern writer is sometimes heard to speak with splendid scorn of "those petty Greek states, with their interminable quarrels." Quite so; Plataea, Sicyon, Aegina and the rest are petty, compared with modern states. The Earth itself is petty, compared with Jupiter—but then, the atmosphere of Jupiter is mainly ammonia, and that makes a difference. We do not like breathing ammonia—and the Greeks would not much have liked breathing the atmosphere of the vast modern State. They knew of one such, the Persian Empire—and thought it very suitable, for barbarians. Difference of scale, when it is great enough, amounts to difference of kind.

. . . The entire life of the polis, and the relation between its parts, were much easier to grasp, because of the small scale of things. Therefore to say "It is everyone's duty to help the polis" was not to express a fine sentiment but to speak the plainest and most urgent common sense. (It did not, of course, follow that the Greek obeyed common sense any oftener than we do.) Public affairs had an immediacy and a concreteness they cannot possibly have for us.

H. D. F. Kitto, **The Greeks** (London: Penguin Books, Ltd., 1957), pp. 64–67, 73–75, 78–79. Reprinted by permission.

▶ Should a citizen of a large representative democracy take as much personal interest in the society as a member of the polis?

121

One specific example will help. The Athenian democracy taxed the rich with as much disinterested enthusiasm as the British, but this could be done in a much more gracious way, simply because the State was so small and intimate. Among us, the [taxpayer] . . . writes his cheque and thinks, "There! *That's* gone down the drain!" In Athens, the man whose wealth exceeded a certain sum had, in a yearly rota, to perform certain "liturgies"—literally, "folk-works." He had to keep a warship in commission for one year (with the privilege of commanding it, if he chose), or finance the production of plays at the Festival, or equip a religious procession. It was a heavy burden, and no doubt unwelcome, but at least some fun could be got out of it and some pride taken in it. There was satisfaction and honour to be gained from producing a trilogy worthily before one's fellow-citizens. So, in countless other ways, the size of the polis made vivid and immediate, things which to us are only abstractions or wearisome duties. Naturally this cut both ways. For example, an incompetent or unlucky commander was the object not of a diffused and harmless popular indignation, but of direct accusation; he might be tried for his life before an Assembly, many of whose past members he had led to death.

Refer to Pericles's speech in Reading 13.

Pericles's Funeral Speech, recorded or recreated by Thucydides, will illustrate this immediacy, and will also take our conception of the polis a little further. Each year, Thucydides tells us, if citizens had died in war—and they had more often than not—a funeral oration was delivered by "a man chosen by the polis." To-day, that would be someone nominated by the Prime Minister, or the British Academy, or the B.B.C. In Athens it meant that someone was chosen by the Assembly who had often spoken to that Assembly; and on this occasion Pericles spoke from a specially high platform, that his voice might reach as many as possible. Let us consider two phrases that Pericles used in that speech.

He is comparing the Athenian polis with the Spartan, and makes the point that the Spartans admit foreign visitors only grudgingly, and from time to time expel all strangers, "while we make our polis common to all." "Polis" here is not the political unit; there is no question of naturalizing foreigners—which the Greeks did rarely, simply because the polis was so intimate a union. Pericles means here: "We throw open to all our common cultural life," as shown by the words that follow, difficult though they are to translate: "nor do we deny them any instruction or spectacle"—words that are almost meaningless until we realize that the drama, tragic and comic, the performance of choral hymns, public recitals of Homer, games, were all necessary and normal parts of "political" life. This is the sort of thing Pericles has in mind when he speaks of "instruction and spectacle," and of "making the polis open to all."

But we must go further than this. A perusal of the speech will show that in praising the Athenian polis Pericles is praising more than a state, a nation, or a people: he is praising a way of life; he means no less when, a little later, he calls Athens the "school of Hellas."—And what of that? Do not we praise "the English way of life?" The difference is this; we expect our State to be quite indifferent to "the English way of life"—indeed, the idea that the State should actively try to promote it would fill most of us with alarm. The Greeks thought of the polis as an active, formative thing, training the minds and characters of the citizens; we think of it as a piece of machinery for the production of safety and convenience. The training in virtue, which the medieval state left to the Church, and the polis made its own concern, the modern state leaves to God knows what.

▶ Should a government try to shape the lives of its citizens?

"Polis," then, originally "citadel," may mean as much as "the whole communal life of the people, political, cultural, moral"— even "economic," for how else are we to understand another phrase in this same speech, "the produce of the whole world comes to us, because of the magnitude of our polis"? This must mean "our national wealth." . . .

. . . The polis was a living community, based on kinship, real or assumed—a kind of extended family, turning as much as possible of life into family life, and of course having its family quarrels, which were the more bitter because they were family quarrels.

Anthropologists distinguish between the nuclear family, which includes only a father and mother and their children, and an extended family, which can include grandparents, aunts, uncles, cousins, and in-laws as well.

This it is that explains not only the polis but also much of what the Greek made and thought, that he was essentially social. In the winning of his livelihood he was essentially individualist: in the filling of his life he was essentially "communist." Religion, art, games, the discussion of things—all these were needs of life that could be fully satisfied only through the polis—not, as with us, through voluntary, associations of like-minded people, or through *entrepreneurs* appealing to individuals. (This partly explains the difference between Greek drama and the modern cinema.) Moreover, he wanted to play his own part in running the affairs of the community. When we realize how many of the necessary, interesting and exciting activities of life the Greek enjoyed through the polis, all of them in the open air, within sight of the same acropolis, with the same ring of mountains or of sea visibly enclosing the life of every member of the state—then it becomes possible to understand Greek history, to understand that in spite of the promptings of commonsense the Greek could not bring himself to sacrifice the polis, with its vivid and comprehensive life, to a wider but less interesting unity. We may perhaps record an Imaginary Conversation between an Ancient Greek and a member of the Athenaeum. The member regrets the lack of political sense shown by the Greeks.

The Athenaeum is a London gentlemen's club with an exclusive membership and an interest in the arts.

123

# SUGGESTED READINGS

Listings preceded by an asterisk (*) are published in paperback. If the paperback imprint differs from the hardback imprint, the paperback imprint is in parentheses.

## General Histories

* BOWRA, C. M., **The Greek Experience.** New York: World Publishing Co., 1958 (Mentor). A lengthy, affectionate, and often lyrical essay on the nature of Greek civilization.

* BURN, A. R., **The Pelican History of Greece.** Baltimore, Md.: Penguin Books, Inc., 1965 (Pelican). A lively and comprehensive 415-page history of Greece aimed at the general reader.

* BURN, A. R., **Pericles and Athens.** New York: The Macmillan Company, Inc., 1948 (Collier). A readable analysis of a political leader and his relationship to his polis.

* DICKINSON, G. LOWES, **The Greek View of Life.** Ann Arbor, Mich.: University of Michigan Press, 1958 (Collier). Essays on religion, the state, the individual, and art relating these expressions to how Greeks faced day-to-day problems.

* FINLEY, MOSES I., **The Ancient Greeks: An Introduction to their Life and Thought.** New York: The Viking Press, Inc., 1963 (Compass). A brief and handsomely illustrated survey of dominant themes in Greek history and thought.

* HAMILTON, EDITH, **The Greek Way.** New York: W. W. Norton & Company, Inc., 1930. A sensitive, well-written, and wide-ranging essay on Greek culture and its value to twentieth-century man.

* HERODOTUS, **The Histories,** tr. by AUBREY DE SÉLINCOURT. Baltimore, Md.: Penguin Books, Inc., 1954. The first great historian's brilliant and entertaining account of the fifth-century wars between Greece and Persia.

* KITTO, H. D. F., **The Greeks.** Baltimore, Md.: Penguin Books, Inc., 1951 (Pelican). A witty and highly readable study of Greek society and the Greek character.

* LLOYD-JONES, HUGH, ed., **The Greek World.** Baltimore, Md.: Penguin Books, Inc., 1965 (Pelican). A collection of essays by modern scholars on topics from politics to science.

* ROBINSON, CYRIL E., **Hellas: A Short History of Ancient Greece.** Boston: Beacon Press, Inc., 1955. A narrative of the development of Greek civilization which concentrates more on ideas than events.

* THUCYDIDES, **The Peloponnesian War,** tr. by REX WARNER. Baltimore, Md.: Penguin Books, Inc., 1954. The masterful history of the war that was the turning point in Athenian history by a participant and critic. Analytical, highly interpretive, and brilliant.

* TOYNBEE, ARNOLD J., ed., **Greek Civilization and Character.** New York: New American Library, Inc., 1954 (Mentor). A collection of short essays on aspects of Greek life collected by a major twentieth-century historian.

## Picture Histories

BOWRA, C. M., **Classical Greece.** New York: Time, Inc. (Time-Life Books), 1965. A beautifully illustrated and sound examination of Greek culture, with emphasis on the fine arts.

HALE, W. H., **Horizon Book of Ancient Greece.** Garden City, N.Y.: Doubleday & Company, Inc. (American Heritage), 1965. Another sound survey of Greek culture. Profusely and beautifully illustrated.

## Philosophy and Religion

* AGARD, WALTER R., **The Greek Mind.** Princeton, N.J.: D. Van Nostrand Company, Inc., 1957. A brief analysis of the major ideas of the ancient Greeks, followed by excerpts from their writings illustrating these ideas.

* CORNFORD, F. M., **Before and After Socrates.** New York: Cambridge University Press, 1932. A clearly-written introduction to the major ideas of the greatest Greek philosophers.

* KAPLAN, JUSTIN, ed., **The Dialogues of Plato.** New York: Washington Square Press, Inc., 1961. Well-chosen excerpts from Plato's dialogues furnishing a useful introduction to his thought.

* KAPLAN, JUSTIN, ed., **The Pocket Aristotle.** New York: Washington Square Press, Inc., 1962. Excerpts from all of the major works of Plato's greatest student.

* PLATO, **Euthyphro, Apology, Crito,** tr. by F. J. CHURCH and ROBERT D. CUMMINGS. Indianapolis, Ind.: Bobbs-Merrill Company, Inc., 1956 (Liberal Arts). Three dialogues of Plato presenting his version of Socrates's ideas and responses as he faced conviction and execution, accused of being an agitator by the Athenian ruling class.

* ROSE, H. J., **Religion in Greece and Rome.** New York: Harper & Row, Publishers, Inc., 1959 (Torchbook). A brief and authoritative account of the relationship between man and the gods in ancient Greece.

* ROUSE, W. H. D., **Gods, Heroes, and Men of Ancient Greece.** New York: New American Library, Inc., 1957 (Signet). An analysis of the major myths of ancient Greece and their relationship to life and thought.

*Literature*

* ANOUILH, JEAN, **Antigone,** in ANOUILH, **Five Plays,** vol. 1. New York: Hill & Wang, Inc., 1958 (Dramabooks). A modern version of the Greek myth of Antigone, written during World War II by a leading French playwright. Witty, compelling, and a fascinating example of the significance of the Greek view of life to the twentieth century.

* AUDEN, W. H., ed., **The Portable Greek Reader.** New York: The Viking Press, Inc., 1948. A compact and thoughtful selection from Greek literature by a leading twentieth-century poet. Includes a complete dialogue of Plato's and four complete plays, as well as poems and excerpts from philosophical, scientific, dramatic, and historical works.

* **Greek Lyrics,** revised edition, tr. by RICHMOND LATTIMORE. Chicago: University of Chicago Press, 1960 (Phoenix). Readable and graceful modern translations of more than a hundred lyric poems and poetic fragments.

* GRENE, DAVID and RICHMOND LATTIMORE, eds., **The Complete Greek Tragedies.** Chicago: University of Chicago Press, 1953–1956 (Washington Square). One of the best collections of modern translations of the tragedies of Aeschylus, Sophocles, and Euripides. Bound in nine handsome and inexpensive paperbacks.

* HOMER, **The Iliad,** tr. by W. H. D. ROUSE. New York: New American Library, 1954 (Mentor). A swift-moving prose translation of the epic poem describing the heroes, gods, and battles of the Trojan War.

* HOMER, **The Odyssey,** tr. by W. H. D. ROUSE. New York: New American Library, 1937 (Mentor). Warner's prose translation of Homer's second great epic, which tells the story of Odysseus's long, adventurous, and frustrating journey home from the Trojan Wars.

# Unit II:

# The Humanities
# in Florence

Donatello, *The David of the Casa Martelli* (c. 1435)
National Gallery of Art, Widener Collection

# Florence and Its Citizens

## STATING THE ISSUE

Just as Athens symbolizes the pinnacle of ancient Greek civilization, Florence epitomizes the Italian Renaissance. Rome, Venice, Pisa, Milan, and a dozen other cities contributed to the great culture that western man calls the Renaissance. Florence, however, dominated the age. In the process, its citizens left a rich heritage to western humanism.

People in Renaissance Florence saw the world from a number of different vantage points. Their perspective was sometimes an accident of birth. Some were born the heirs of merchant princes who ruled the city; others were the sons of unskilled laborers and had little chance to rise above their father's station. Perspective varied with talent. A poor boy whose brush could make a canvas vibrant with color might be preferred to his neighbor whose clumsy fingers could only grasp a hoe. Perspective also depended upon a person's role in society and the social class to which he belonged. Men and women, rich and poor, artisan and merchant, painter and writer, often defined what was good in different ways. As in all societies, no man's thinking was identical with another's; and Renaissance Florence particularly encouraged the expression of individual temperament. Because Florentine society was so diverse, no one person or group could define the good man, the good life, or the good society to the satisfaction of all.

Chapter 1 examines the lives of various Florentines. The first reading describes the city itself. It is followed by accounts of the lives of a princely young ruler, an artist, women, workers, slaves, and servants. How did each of these persons or groups define the good man, the good life, and the good society? How did perspective on what is good differ with place in the social structure? These are the major issues raised in Chapter 1.

129

# 1 A TOUR OF RENAISSANCE FLORENCE

Cities never died in medieval Italy as they did in most of the rest of medieval Europe. Throughout northern Europe, raids by the Germans and Vikings, the development of a feudal society based on agriculture, and the resulting decline in trade reduced the number and size of cities until most of them disappeared. In Italy, however, none of these forces operated to the same degree. Port cities such as Venice, Genoa, and Pisa traded with the Near East throughout the Middle Ages; inland towns such as Florence and Milan continued to manufacture goods and carry on overland commerce. By the thirteenth century these ancient Italian cities had a commercial life far more vigorous than that of their northern neighbors.

The place in which a man lives often helps to reveal his values. An American home full of fine furniture, books, and paintings implies one conception of the good life. A Japanese home with a few simple furnishings and one art object on display at a time reveals a different conception. In the same way, the physical appearance of a city parades the values of its citizens. Large buildings set aside for public use may dominate the skyline or be lost among festering slums. A city's plan may embrace the countryside or exclude it. Streets may invite a leisurely stroll or stimulate a pell-mell rush to get from one place to another. Plazas may be filled with fountains or with traffic.

Reading 1 describes Florence in the fifteenth century. It was written by a modern French author, who based his descriptions on accounts by fifteenth-century Florentines. As you read, think about the following questions:

1. What kinds of buildings dominated Florence? What does your answer reveal about Florentine conceptions of the good life and the good society?
2. What were the city streets like? What activities happened there that might seem unusual in a modern city? What do you think these activities reveal about the lives of fifteenth-century Florentines?
3. What sorts of people lived in the city? Were there a number of social classes or only one?
4. What might men of different occupations think about the nature of the good life?

# A Tour of Florence

Since the Middle Ages the City of the Flower [Florence] had grown continuously. Its suburbs . . . stretched out beyond the Arno. It had overflowed from the ancient walls, which had been replaced by a second wall at the end of the twelfth century, and by a third, of which remnants still survive, in 1284.

In the fifteenth century the city's appearance was as follows. Some sixty square towers rose from . . . ramparts which were more than two leagues all round. There were as many inside the walls. Seen from a distance, the city was shaped like a spindle, narrow at the ends, very broad in the middle. Along the walls, at intervals of about 327 yards, there was a tower; but . . . from time to time . . . these old towers . . . were broken down and turned into dwelling-houses.

. . . [F]our fine stone bridges spanned the Arno. Starting from the east, there was the Rubaconte bridge, . . . built in 1237. Six massive piles supported houses, shops and a little chapel. . . . The Ponte Vecchio [Old Bridge] had been rebuilt in 1345. It was longer and broader than the others and was covered with shops and houses. The Ponte Santa Trinità [Bridge of the Holy Trinity], dating from 1250, was very handsome. . . . Finally the Ponte alla Carraja, so called from the name of an ancient city gate, had no houses on it. . . .

In the sixteenth century Benedetto Varchi conceived the happy notion of describing the city. The streets, says this famous historian, are "fairly wide," and nearly all paved with flagstones. . . . On each side was a footpath, and a gutter to carry rain-water down to the Arno, so that the streets remained dry and free from the mud and slime which you found elsewhere in winter. In summer, on the other hand, the flagstones radiated the heat, and from noon until evening one could only remain cool in the usually spacious ground-floor rooms of the houses.

Varchi next takes us on a visit to the gates. . . . There were six on . . . [one] side of Florence, and five on the [other]. . . .

Let us now cross the Arno. If you wanted to go to Pisa, over forty miles away, you would leave by the Porta San Friano, where there was a monastery and a suburb, and away beyond, very agreeable villas. . . . If you went out by the Porta San Pietro Gattolini, you saw a great number of villas, palaces, gardens, and fountains, and these commanded a superb view of Florence. . . .

. . . [F]rom the Porta [gate] San Miniato, you could see, silhouetted on the hilltop, the fortress-church raised to the glory of San Minias, one of the few Florentine saints; while the last gate on

J. Lucas-Dubreton, **Daily Life in Florence in the Time of the Medici**, trans. by A. Lytton Sells (New York: The Macmillan Co., 1961), pp. 87–96, 98–100. Reprinted with permission of The Macmillan Company from **Daily Life in Florence in the Time of the Medici** by J. Lucas-Dubreton. Copyright © 1961, Librairie Hatchette. World rights controlled by Librairie Hatchette. British rights controlled by George Allen & Unwin Ltd.

The Romans, who founded Florence in about the first century B.C., called it Florentia, "City of the Flower." In Italian this name became Fiorenza, and then Firenze, the present name.

Benedetto Varchi, a sixteenth-century Italian scholar, wrote a history of Florence commissioned by one of the city's rulers.

The valley formed by the Chianti Mountains is still noted for the dry red wines popular as an accompaniment to Italian food.

The figure 70,000 is almost certainly an underestimate. Most historians put the population of fifteenth-century Florence at 90,000 or 100,000.

Monks belonged to religious orders that, unlike the regular clergy, took vows of poverty and believed that isolation from the world was necessary for spiritual perfection. Orders of friars, such as the Franciscans and Dominicans, arose in the thirteenth century. Friars, too, took vows of poverty, but they believed that active involvement in life was the best way to bring people close to God.

▶ Should a good society provide free medical care? If so, who should pay for it?

The Romans built forums, or public squares, in the towns they founded during the heyday of the empire.

this side, the Porta San Niccolò, was a very busy one, because it led to the valley of Chianti, "famous for the number of exquisite wines that were produced there, and worthy of admiration because it is harsh and rocky."

. . . Varchi tells us that seven or eight children, rather fewer girls than boys, were baptised every day at the Church of San Giovanni, where the civic register had been kept since 1450. Prior to that, people had been simply required to drop a black pea into a box for a boy and a white pea for a girl, to record births. Now counting the number of "hearths," which was 10,000, and excluding the suburbs, the resident population was estimated at 70,000, including the religious—monks and *frati*—who were continually increasing.

In spite of its libertines and free-thinkers, the city contained over a hundred convents, including forty-nine for women. Since the thirteenth century the Dominican and Franciscan orders had imparted a great impetus to monastic life. . . .

Let us now consider the palaces, some of which had retained the aspect of a medieval fortress. . . . [T]he great era of palace-building dates from the fifteenth century. Between 1450 and 1478 thirty new ones were raised, and the movement continued to grow in the years that followed. . . .

One should add that the more distinguished families possessed near their palaces, a *loggia* or *casolaro*, an open-air . . . [enclosure] with an arbour and colonnades. Here citizens would come to converse, or arrange business-deals, or play games. . . .

Florence was particularly proud of its hospitals, where the invalids of both sexes were lodged and treated free of charge. The oldest and wealthiest, thanks to an accumulation of endowments, was the hospital of Santa Maria Nuova, which controlled all the others. These included San Pagolo, near Santa Maria Novella, the hospital of the Incurables in the Via San Gallo, the small receiving-centres for poor folk and travellers, and especially the great hospital of the Innocents, with its gardens, where, "through the hole of a little window," foundlings were taken in. There were over a thousand there, in Varchi's time.

The busiest centre remained where the Roman Forum had once stood. . . . Here you might see the greengrocers with their movable booths, the butchers and their open stalls, the fishmongers and innkeepers. . . . Here and there barbers are shaving people in the open, except on Sundays when they have to remain in their shops. . . . The din is like that of a poultry-yard; people hailing each other or quarrelling, and the barber threatening the apothecary whom he looks on as a competitor.

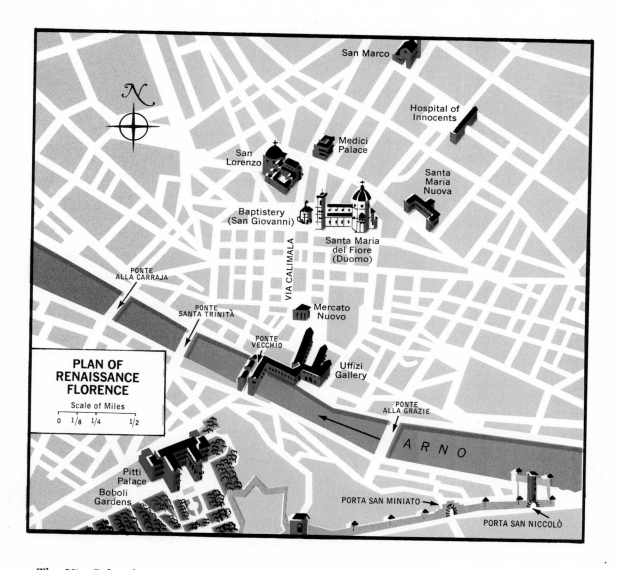

PLAN OF RENAISSANCE FLORENCE

Scale of Miles

0   1/8   1/4   1/2

The Via Calimala is noisy with the shouts of apprentices. Here the first printing-press was founded. This street leads us to the Piazza Or San Michele, to the palace of the wool-merchants and thence by a sloping alley to the Mercato Nuovo. Here the murmur of voices is different. In shops or under awnings, the dealers in silk and other textiles ply their trade, while the money-changers sit gravely at their desks. . . .

In the course of time all these streets became more open and ornate. Buildings were replaced with a constant eye for beauty. . . .

133

[T]he house in Renaissance style . . . replaced the fortress-dwelling; a taste for elegance, luxury and comfort prevailed over notions of war and strife.

Florence already possessed open spaces, some fifty squares, or *piazze,* . . . as well as 138 gardens and vegetable plots. But there were sombre spots like the *Stinche,* the state-prison, "a stinking gaol," according to Machiavelli, "where the walls harbour vermin so huge and swollen that you might compare them to butter-flies." . . .

The Florentine normally lived in the open. In good weather he would sit in the street which served as the outer room of his house, and there he would play at chess or dice. The bystanders commented on every move, but, owing to the restricted space, the least untoward incident might occasion a panic. . . .

The . . . [merchant's] house, as compared with the palace, was still a very splendid residence. The home of a notable in the wool trade, for example, had a vaulted portico, two galleries paved with marble, and three floors. Beside it was the *Loggia* surrounded by colonnades. When the sun was hot, you took refuge on the first floor in a room with glass windows and curtains to hide you from the street. More modest houses also had their comforts—terraces, court-yards, stables, passages, antichambers and at least one well of fresh water. Better still, a fairly well-to-do Florentine owned a *casa,* or dwelling-house, a shop where he worked, and a villa or farm in the country. . . .

Thus the city stretched far beyond its walls. Florence, according to . . . [a Renaissance architect], "is surrounded by innumerable villas where the air is pure as crystal, the landscape most pleasant, the views wonderful. In those parts there are no fogs or harmful winds. Everything is good, the very water is pure and wholesome." Bird-songs and fresh verdure gladden the heart, "the streams go leaping down or hide under tunnels of overhanging herbage" . . . .

This countryside was endowed with every blessing. In his country-farm the merchant cultivated cereals and vegetables; it also provided him with wine, oil, forage and wood. It supplied all his needs and he sold the surplus. . . .

Let us take the case of Agnolo Pandolfini, a cultured merchant whose ancestors had made a fortune in trade at Naples. He owns the fine villa of Signa, where he has everything a gentleman could desire: dogs, falcons and various kinds of nets for small game or fishes. He receives and lodges everyone; he even goes out into the road and invites the wayfarer in, gives him water to wash, seats him at his table, and when he has lunched, thanks him and sends him on his way, as he does not wish to embarrass him. . . .

▶ How important to a good life are sunshine and fresh air?

▶ Should everyone be this generous to strangers? Is such generosity possible today?

134

The peasant, or *contadino,* whom you meet can be recognized by his long grey garment without a cloak and often without trunk-hose, by a broad belt and a cape with flaps hanging down on each side. He is no ordinary peasant, tied to the soil, but ranks as a free man and is more comfortably off than the peasants of other lands.

There was no real barrier in Tuscany between the city and the village. Many small towns were inhabited by peasants who, on returning from the fields, called themselves citizens. A shepherd . . . could leave his flock and join a trade-guild in Florence. There was constant communication between town and country; the contadino benefited from the prosperity of the merchant; and if he were a tenant he could by signing a contract with the proprietor become a free farmer. Peasants' revolts were unknown in Tuscany. . . .

. . . [On the other hand, t]he countryman knew how to defend his rights [against greedy landowners]. . . .

The cultured . . . [merchant] holds the peasant in low esteem or even regards him as a sink of corruption. According to Pandolfini, . . . the peasant gives his whole mind to cheating you. He never makes a mistake to his disadvantage and always tries to get the better in a bargain. Even if he had more money than the owner, he would complain more loudly. When the harvest is good, he keeps two-thirds of the best for himself; when the yield is poor, owing to storms or other mishaps, he always makes you pay for the loss. However, says Pandolfini, it would be a mistake to avoid contact with these cunning rustics who teach one how to contend with scheming townsmen and remain vigilant. They are professors of distrust, and in the end their tricks amuse one.

On the whole, therefore, the Florentine . . . [merchant] did not regard the peasant with . . . scorn. . . . "His shoes are rough, but his brain is subtle." Although violent on occasion he is by nature independent, cheerful and gay. His amusements are simple. At a country fête he brings out a donkey with cymbals tied to its back and a thistle under its tail, so that it is constantly fidgeting and making music for everyone to dance to. . . .

To draw a complete picture of the environs of Florence, we should have to push as far as the subject-cities of Pisa, Volterra, Pistoia, Arezzo and Cortona, the many territories where the gates "were closed at night and opened in the morning." As a mark of submission and by way of tribute, the hundred wealthiest territories were required, on Midsummer Day, to offer . . . a roll of cloth which served as a prize for the races that were run on that festival [day]. The poorer lands, to the number of thirty, gave a candle as symbol.

Tuscany is the region in central Italy of which Florence is the principal city.

# 2  THE MAGNIFICENT:
# LORENZO DE' MEDICI

In 1250 Florence had officially become a free republic, governed by an elected council drawn from three groups: old, aristocratic families, newly rich bankers and merchants, and the guilds. In practice, however, the aristocrats and the new rich held the actual power, often through such ruses as enrolling in the guilds for political convenience.

The old aristocrats feared the growing wealth and power of the merchants and bankers. Feuds broke out between these rival groups; political parties struggled to control the government. Under these unstable conditions, civil tumult often resulted. Workers revolted, and assassinations became commonplace.

Florence could ill afford this insecurity. It had expanded until it ruled most of the surrounding territory. The city needed strong leadership to protect itself and its territories from outside attack, as well as to maintain internal peace.

Finally, Florence found a leader—Cosimo de' Medici, the head of a prominent family grown newly rich in the woolen industry, trade, and banking. He had been exiled from Florence through the efforts of a powerful aristocrat who feared Cosimo's wealth. But the Medici fortune survived, and the pope intervened on Cosimo's behalf. In 1434 the heads of the city council recalled Cosimo to Florence. Although he refused to accept any official titles, his recall was tantamount to putting the government in his hands. A popular ruler, he gained the favor of the common people by supporting many of the small, less powerful guilds, by taxing the rich heavily and the poor not at all, and by patronizing many artists and scholars.

Cosimo's son Piero succeeded him; Piero was followed by his son Lorenzo, called The Magnificent. Hence, the Medici ruled Florence during the greatest century in the city's history. By Lorenzo's time a Medici was the equivalent of a prince.

Lorenzo's education was preparation for this high position, but it was not unlike the education of other elite Florentines. The way Lorenzo's family reared him gives insights into the way they viewed their place in the world. As you read the selections that follow, think about these questions:

1. How was Lorenzo educated? Who was responsible for Lorenzo's education?

The chief threat to Florence was the growing power of neighboring Milan, ruled by a succession of tyrannical dukes from the Visconti family.

Piero ruled from 1464 to 1469; Lorenzo, from 1469 to 1492.

136

2. Do you think his education prepared him adequately to meet his responsibilities? Explain.

3. Did Lorenzo lead a good life as a boy? Did he turn out to be a good man according to the two assessments that conclude this reading? Explain.

4. What does Lorenzo's education imply about the Medici's conception of the good society?

## Lorenzo's Education

*The following account has been taken from a modern biography of Lorenzo.*

It was among a large and united family circle that Lorenzo received his first lesson in the art of living. Piero . . . , Lorenzo's father, . . . found his chief pleasure in classifying and adding to the collection of manuscripts, jewels, cameos, vases and other antiques which became the glory of the Medici Palace. He was an affectionate if somewhat austere father, holding before Lorenzo his own high standard of duty and taking pains to see that his heir was not spoiled. . . .

For the child Lorenzo the most important members of the family were his grandmother and his mother—Contessina dei Bardi and Lucrezia Tornabuoni. Both came from wealthy merchant houses, but otherwise they represented two diverse types of Florentine womanhood. Contessina was the complete housewife; . . . Lucrezia belonged to a new generation, whose interests spread beyond the family. She was the friend and patron of scholars and herself a writer of verse. . . . Her intelligence, her literary tastes and, not least, her deep piety made her a formative influence in her son's life. . . . Lorenzo's only brother, Giuliano, was four years his junior, and he had three sisters. . . .

Lorenzo's education began at the age of five. . . . A letter from Lucrezia to her husband describes her nine-year-old son busily learning the verses set him by his master and teaching them to his little brother. Three years later, when Piero was away from home, . . . [Lorenzo's tutor] reported to him that Lorenzo "is well on with Ovid, and has read four books of Justinus." That the boy was no bookworm is seen from the remark: "Do not ask how he enjoys his studies. In all other matters he is obedient, and now you are away, the fear of transgressing makes him more diligent." The appointment of Argyropulos as Reader of Greek in the University in 1456 gave a new impetus to Hellenic studies; it was said that the

Cecilia M. Ady, **Lorenzo dei Medici and Renaissance Italy** (New York: Collier Books, 1962), pp. 23–29, 32–33. Reprinted with permission of The Macmillan Company from **Lorenzo dei Medici and Renaissance Italy** by Cecilia M. Ady. First Collier edition copyright © 1962. World rights controlled by English Universities Press Ltd.

Ovid (43 B.C.–c. 17 A.D.) was a Roman poet. Justinus, who lived in the third century A.D., wrote a popular summary of history from ancient Greece to the beginnings of Rome.

Johannes Argyropulos, a fifteenth-century Greek, taught in Florence and Rome; he translated some works of Aristotle into Latin. The University of Florence was founded in 1349.

"Vulgar tongue" means the vernacular, here the ordinary Italian as opposed to the Latin generally preferred by medieval scholars for poetry and other formal writing.

young men whom he taught talked Greek so fluently that Florence might have been Athens. Lorenzo as he grew older was among the enthusiastic band of pupils who gathered round him. Two distinguished men had an influential share in Lorenzo's education—Cristoforo Landino, one of the foremost Latin scholars of his day, and Marsilio Ficino, the Platonist. It was fortunate that these masters, each supreme in his own sphere, did not despise the vulgar tongue, but encouraged their pupil in his natural bent for Italian poetry. . . .

Classical studies were treated by humanist educators as the basis of a system which aimed at the development of man's entire personality, body, mind and spirit. Thus Lorenzo's education was not confined to Greek and Latin. His day began by hearing Mass with his tutor, and at his mother's wish he was often taken to meetings of the confraternity of San Paolo, an association formed for common prayer and worship and the furtherance of good works among its members. He was taught to sing to his own accompaniment on the lyre, a form of music which commended itself to the times owing to the opportunities it gave for individual expression. . . . To live in Florence in the middle of the fifteenth century was in itself an artistic education for a clever boy. . . . Nearly all that is best in Florentine art was there for the young Lorenzo to see. At home he could . . . hear the talk of patrons and artists on all that was being done or contemplated in the city. . . .

Within the Medici palace in Florence the standard of living conformed to the simple ways of a citizen family. Magnificence was reserved for the entertainment of guests, and to this the hosts contributed according to their age and capacity. . . . At a banquet given by the Republic to Leonora of Aragon . . . after Lorenzo had succeeded to the first place in the city, he and his brother waited upon the guests. Florentine society knew no rigid class barriers and the younger citizens took their pleasures together. In winter boys and girls snowballed each other in the streets, and the young men played Calcio, the Florentine equivalent of Rugby football. There were many practices before the great match in Carnival time, which attracted crowds of spectators. . . . In summer there were picnic parties in the country, and at all seasons the young people danced and made love. . . .

▶ Why should a member of the elite learn to do manual work?

Lorenzo's training for public life began when he was fifteen, on the death of his grandfather. . . . Piero wrote to tell Lorenzo and Giuliano of Cosimo's last days, saying that the time had now come for them to "take up your share of the burden in good heart as God has ordained, and having been boys make up your minds to be men." During the next two years Lorenzo was sent on three missions. The first was to Pisa to meet Federico, the second son of King Ferrante of Naples. . . . The visit was one of courtesy, and the chief subject of discussion between the two lads appears to have been the respective merits of classical and vernacular poetry. It bore fruit in Lorenzo's first literary effort, a letter on the Tuscan poets which he sent to Federico with a collection of their works. . . . The next mission was to Milan, where Lorenzo was to represent his father at . . . [a] wedding. On his way he visited Bologna, Venice and Ferrara, gaining an insight into Italian social and political life and also into the working of the Medici business. . . .

Piero was satisfied that his son had done well enough on his Milanese mission to be entrusted with more important business, and in 1466 he was sent to Rome to negotiate with Paul II about a contract relating to the recently discovered alum mines at Tolfa. Alum was essential to the Florentine textile industry, as it was used for dyeing wool and silk in the most popular colours. Supplies hitherto had come chiefly from the Levant, and the concession which Lorenzo now obtained for the Medici to work the papal mines proved most profitable to them. . . .

. . . In 1468, the long-drawn-out attempt to overthrow Piero's government was finally defeated.

During the war Lorenzo had remained in Florence, taking no part in the fighting. The Medici were not soldiers but businessmen, and training in the profession of arms had no place in his education. Owing to his failing health, Piero grew increasingly reluctant to let his son out of his sight; without him, he complained, he was a man without hands. Since his grandfather's death Lorenzo had gained valuable experience of the nature of the task which lay before him when he became head of the family. . . . He had already shown that he possessed gifts which rendered him peculiarly fitted for the part he had to play, not least among them being the capacity for making friends in whatever company he found himself.

## An Assessment of Lorenzo

*In the brief passage that follows, Ferdinand Schevill, a modern historian who specialized in the Renaissance, assesses the character and influence of Lorenzo.*

. . . Lorenzo . . . [was] the most notable link in the Medici succession, the finest flowering to which the family attained. . . . [H]e commanded a sum of talents and covered a range of activities that . . . establish his claim to be numbered among the outstanding

The Medici family business was no easy subject to master. It included banking and silk and wool manu-facturing, and had branches in nine cities—one in distant London.

Paul II was pope from 1417 to 1471.

The Levant was the collective name for the countries on the eastern coast of the Mediterranean, from Egypt to Turkey.

Ferdinand Schevill, **The Medici** (New York: Harcourt, Brace & World, Inc., 1949), pp. 165–168.

men of his age. . . . [F]ar from contenting himself with his absorbing political tasks, he was a passionate sportsman, personally looked after his many farm properties, actively cultivated the classical and philosophical movements of his generation, patronized the arts and crafts with a rare discrimination, and, after spurring Italian literature to new efforts, led the way by his own works to a fresh outburst of native poetry. This by the standard of any period constitutes a record that has not often been excelled.

. . . [H]is leading trait . . . [was] an unquenchable zest for life. Instead of his many activities getting into each other's way, each stimulated its neighbor. . . . [H]e had the capacity to give himself easily and without confusion to the many separate interests that made up his average day. It was not at all unusual for him in the course of a single morning to write or dictate a dozen letters, to draw up instructions for an ambassador departing on an important mission, to join a discussion among experts of a moot doctrine of Greek philosophy, to examine a medal or cameo with a view to

▶ Does such variety contribute to a happier life, or does it merely rob a person of time for contemplation?

RENAISSANCE
ITALY
AND THE
MEDITERRANEAN
Scale of Miles
0  25  50  100

140

adding it to his collection, and to make the arrangements for a happy hunting expedition with a group of friends. . . . [H]e was not inhibited by an awkward self-consciousness but was of an open nature, courteous, and accessible to high and low alike. . . .

. . . [H]e interpreted the humanism to which he was devoted not only as a new and stimulating form of intellectuality but also as a nobler social order, under which the surviving remnants of feudal barbarism would be replaced by a code of softer and more urbane relationships. He was therefore, although exercising a form of tyranny, a ruler eminently humane and free from rancor. Among his earliest acts was the recall from exile of the families that had been the victims of the revolution that had put his grandfather, Cosimo, at the head of the government. . . .

The striking mental and moral balance which defines Lorenzo's unique personality enabled him successfully to blend the Catholicism into which he was born with . . . humanism. . . . He never fell into the . . . radical wing of his contemporaries who let themselves be persuaded that to adopt the free outlook of the ancients necessitated the rejection of the Christian faith. . . . His earnest and unfaltering concern was to bring about that fusion of ancient thought and medieval faith which was the best hope of a healthily expanding European culture.

## Another View of Lorenzo

*Here Francesco Guicciardini, a sixteenth-century Florentine historian, political scientist, and practicing politician, evaluates Lorenzo's career somewhat differently.*

Francesco Guicciardini, "A Portrait of Lorenzo de' Medici," trans. by James Bruce Ross, in **The Portable Renaissance Reader,** ed. by James Bruce Ross and Mary Martin McLaughlin (New York: The Viking Press, Inc., 1953), pp. 269–276.

There were in Lorenzo many and most excellent virtues; there were also in him some vices, due partly to nature, partly to necessity. . . .

He had the good judgment of a wise man, but nevertheless not of a quality comparable to his genius; and he was seen to commit various acts of rashness, such as the war with Volterra, which, through his desire to win out over the people of Volterra in regard to the alum mines, forced her to rebel and lit a fire capable of turning all Italy upside down, although in the end it turned out well. Also, after the revolt of 1478, if he had borne himself gently with the pope and king, perhaps they would not have broken out into war against him, but by wishing to act the injured one and not wishing to conceal the injury received, he precipitated a war which caused the greatest damage . . . to himself and to the city. . . .

He desired glory and excellence beyond that of anyone else, and in this he can be criticized for having had too much ambition even

Volterra, a town in Tuscany, rebelled against Florentine rule in 1472. Lorenzo retook the city for its valuable alum mines.

In the revolt of 1478, usually called the Pazzi conspiracy, a Florentine family, the Pazzi, tried to seize power from the Medici. Assassins stabbed Lorenzo and his brother Giuliano during Mass. Lorenzo was wounded, Giuliano killed.

in regard to minor things; he did not wish to be equalled or imitated by any citizen even in verses or games or exercises, turning angrily against any who did so. He was too ambitious even in great affairs, inasmuch as he wished in everything to equal or emulate all the princes of Italy. . . .

. . . [H]e neglected no show of magnificence, even at the greatest expense and loss, by which he might influence great men. And so, through such display and lavishness, his expenditures multiplied in Lyons, Milan, Bruges, and in the various centres of his trade and his company, while his profits diminished from being neglected by incompetent agents. . . . His accounts were not well kept because he did not understand commerce or pay enough attention to it, and as a result his affairs more than once fell into such disorder that he was on the point of bankruptcy, and it was necessary for him to help himself out both with money from his friends and with public funds. . . .

He was considered by some as naturally cruel and vindictive because of the harshness he showed in dealing with the Pazzi conspiracy, imprisoning the innocent young men of the family and not wishing the young girls to be married, after so much slaughter had taken place in those days. This event was so bitter, however, that it was no wonder he was extraordinarily angered by it. . . .

But the trait in him which was more serious and annoying than anything else was suspicion. This came perhaps not so much from his nature as from the knowledge that he had to hold down a free city, and one in which what was done had to be done . . . according to the laws of the city and under the appearance and form of liberty. . . .

. . . Nevertheless, this was not a free city and a private citizen, but a city in servitude and a tyrant. And finally one must conclude that under him the city was not free, but, nevertheless, it would have been impossible for it to have had a better or more pleasing tyrant.

# 3   THE ARTIST AS INDIVIDUAL:
## BENVENUTO CELLINI

Benvenuto Cellini was born in 1500 in Florence, where his family, originally landowners, had been settled for three generations. His father was a musician and a craftsman who made musical instruments. Although Benvenuto's father tried to persuade him to become a musician, the boy developed such a love for design and metalwork that his father apprenticed him to a goldsmith at the age of fifteen. He later studied music and sculpture with several other masters.

Even at an early age Cellini was constantly in trouble. While still in his teens he was banished from Florence for misbehavior, and by his nineteenth birthday he had lived in Siena, Bologna, Pisa, and Rome between trips back to his native city. In each of these cities he practiced his craft and found patrons, among them popes, kings, and members of the Medici family. For them Cellini designed medals and coins, set jewels, created statues, and made all sorts of objects, both decorative and functional. Although much of this work has been lost, a few of the most distinguished pieces remain. After living all over Europe for most of his life, he returned more or less permanently to Florence in 1545, where he supported a widowed sister and her six daughters. He died in 1571, leaving behind at least eight children of his own, only one of whom was legitimate.

"Men like Benvenuto, unique in their profession, stand above the law," Pope Paul III said of Cellini. Cellini thought so, too. His life was full of brawls. He killed a number of men who displeased him, insulted other artists and patrons right and left, flew into violent fits of temper, lied whenever the mood suited him, and made enemies by the score. But at the same time he was a hardworking and talented artist, one of the greatest goldsmiths the world has ever seen.

In 1558 Cellini began his *Autobiography.* Its pages hold insights into Cellini's character, Renaissance society, and the place of the artist in that society. Cellini's egotism was unbounded and unabashed. He believed in his own genius; he delighted in his victories; he vilified his enemies. In an age of outstanding personalities, Cellini's was one of the most noticeable. Needless to say, his character was unique and not typical of Renaissance artists. His exuberant and theatrical *Autobiography,* however, gives a brilliant account of the artist as an individual. As you read the following passages from Cellini's *Autobiography,* consider these questions:

1. How did Cellini define his obligations to himself and to the society of which he was a part? What were his conceptions of the good man, the good life, and the good society?
2. How did Cellini's patrons treat him? What does this treatment reveal about their conceptions of the good man and the good life?
3. How far did Cellini believe an individual should go to develop his talents and express his personality? How far do you think

an individual should go to develop his talents? What should be a person's duties to others—to those who are dear to him, to strangers who cross his path, and to unknown members of his society?

# Cellini's *Autobiography*

*In the opening passages of his* Autobiography, *Cellini told why he was writing it and provided an insight into the nature of individualism in the Renaissance.*

Benvenuto Cellini, **Autobiography,** trans. by George Bull (Baltimore: Penguin Books, Ltd., 1956), pp. 15, 99–100, 106, 120, 292, 312–313, 343–348. Reprinted by permission.

No matter what sort he is, everyone who has to his credit what are or really seem great achievements, if he cares for truth and goodness, ought to write the story of his own life in his own hand; but no one should venture on such a splendid undertaking before he is over forty. Now that I am leaving the age of fifty-eight behind me and find myself in my native place, Florence, my thoughts naturally turn to such a task. Like all other men I have often had to struggle hard with fortune; but now I am less troubled by adversity than at any time before in my life and, in fact, I believe that my mind is more at rest and that I am enjoying better health than ever. I remember some of the delightful and some of the indescribably terrible things that have happened to me, and when I think back to them I am startled to realize that I really am fifty-eight years old and, with God's help, am prosperously growing older. . . .

*Making a living for an artist took ingenuity during the Renaissance, just as it does today. Here is one way Cellini secured a living.*

When I took [a piece I was working on] along to the Pope he could not praise me highly enough.

"If only I were a rich emperor," he said, "I would give my Benvenuto as much land as his eye could reach. But nowadays we princes are poor and bankrupt. All the same I'll at least make sure he has enough bread to satisfy his few wants."

I waited for this torrent to exhaust itself, and then, as one of the posts of mace-bearer was vacant, I asked him if I could have it. He replied by saying that he meant to give me something much more important than that. And then I said that, for the time being, perhaps he would grant me what I had asked as a sort of security.

He burst out laughing and said that he was only too willing to give it to me, but that he did not want me to fill the post in an active capacity, and that I should arrange this with the mace-

Mace-bearer was an honorary court position. The mace, an ornamental spiked staff, was carried before a ruler as a symbol of authority.

144

bearers. . . . It was all arranged. This post I was given brought me in just under two hundred crowns a year. . . .

*Cellini's temper was explosive. In this next passage he describes how he took vengeance upon a soldier who had killed Cellini's brother in a brawl.*

I began to keep a close watch on the arquebusier who had smashed my brother, as if he were a girl I was madly in love with. . . .

I realized that the constant state of passion I was in from seeing him so often was keeping me from my food and sleep, and I was becoming a wreck. So I stopped debating with myself whether what I had in mind was too degrading and dishonourable and one evening I made up my mind to rid myself of my torment.

The fellow had lodgings near to a place called Torre Sanguigna, next door to the house of one of the most popular courtesans in Rome, called Signora Antea. It was nightfall, and the clock had just struck the hour. The arquebusier had finished supper and was standing in his doorway with his sword in his hand. I crept upon him, grasping a Pistoian dagger, and aimed a sudden back-stroke with the idea of cutting his head clean off. But he turned in a flash and the blow landed on the edge of his left shoulder, shattering the bone. He staggered up, was so dazed by the terrible pain that he let go his sword, and then took to flight. I went after him and caught him up in a few steps. Then I raised my dagger above his bent head and drove it exactly between his neckbone and the nape of his neck. The dagger went in so deeply that although I used tremendous force it was impossible to withdraw it, because just then four soldiers, with drawn swords in their hands, burst out from Antea's lodgings, and I was forced to draw my own sword to defend myself. I abandoned the dagger and took to my heels. . . .

*Cellini's love affairs were plentiful and passionate. The following passage indicates some of his attitudes toward women and love.*

At that time, as young men do, I had fallen in love with a very beautiful young Sicilian girl; and she too showed that she felt very affectionately towards me. But her mother discovered this, and began to suspect what was going to happen. To tell the truth I had been planning to elope with the girl to Florence for a year, without telling her mother a word. Well, she discovered the plan and one night she left Rome secretly and went off in the direction of Naples. She gave it out that she was going by Civitavecchia, but she went by Ostia. I followed them to Civitavecchia and made an utter fool of myself trying to find her. It would take too long to tell the whole

An arquebusier was a soldier who used an arquebuse, a light cannon or musket fired from a tripod.

"Courtesan" originally meant the mistress of a courtier. By Cellini's time, the term had become synonymous with "prostitute."

145

In Italian **scorzone** means a rustic or unpolished person.

The **Fontainebleau** (called the **Nymph of Fontainebleau**) and the two **Victories** were bronze figures designed by Cellini to ornament a doorway in the Fontainebleau Palace of the king of France. The **Nymph** is now in the Louvre in Paris.

▶ Is it all right to permit a child to live in a foster home so long as his parents provide money for support?

Cosimo I de' Medici (1519–1574) was the nephew of the Cosimo who was Lorenzo's grandfather. Cosimo I was a cruel ruler, far less popular than his uncle.

Perseus, a mythological Greek hero, cut off the snake-haired head of a monster called Medusa. Cellini's sculpture shows Perseus holding Medusa's head.

story in detail; all I need say is that I was on the verge of either going mad or dying. At the end of two months she wrote and told me that she was in Sicily, and that she was very unhappy. In the meantime I was indulging in every imaginable pleasure and had taken a new love, merely to drown the other. . . .

I found myself a poor young girl, about fifteen years old, [to work as a model]. She was very beautifully formed, and rather swarthy. Since she was inclined to be wild, spoke very little, was swift in her movements, and had brooding eyes, all this led me to give her the name Scorzone; her real name was Gianna. With the help of this delightful girl I finished the Fontainebleau to my satisfaction in bronze, as well as the two Victories for the door.

This young girl was untouched, and a virgin, and I got her pregnant. She bore me a daughter on the seventh of June, at the thirteenth hour of the day, 1544; and that was just the forty-fourth year of my own life. I gave her the name Costanza. . . . This as far as I remember was the first child I ever had. For her endowment I assigned the girl as much money as an aunt of hers—into whose care I gave her—would agree to: and that was the last I had to do with her. . . .

*Throughout his artistic career Cellini worked for patrons. The excerpts below illustrate his relationship with one of his patrons, and the excitement and mastery with which he attacked one of his artistic projects.*

The Duke [Cosimo I de' Medici] greeted me with tremendous affection, and then he and the Duchess asked me about the work I had done. . . . While I was talking . . . the Duke twisted and turned and looked as if he could not wait for me to finish. When I did finish he said: "If you do some work for me, I'll treat you so generously that I imagine you'll be astonished: provided your work pleases me, and of that I have no doubt at all."

Then I . . . in my eagerness . . . said in reply that I would be only too pleased to make him a great statue, either in marble or bronze, for that fine piazza of his. He answered that all he wanted as my first work for him was a Perseus; he had been wanting this for a long time, and he begged me to make him a little [wax] model of it.

I gladly set to work on the model and in a few weeks I had finished it. . . .

I made a start by ordering several loads of . . . pine. . . . While waiting for them to arrive I clothed my [wax] Perseus with the clays I had prepared some months previously in order to ensure that they would be properly seasoned. . . . I built round my

146

Perseus a funnel-shaped furnace. It was built, that is, round the mould itself, and was made of bricks piled one on top of the other, with a great many gaps for the fire to escape more easily. Then I began to lay on wood, in fairly small amounts, keeping the fire going for two days and nights.

When all the wax was gone and the mould well baked, I at once began to dig the pit in which to bury it. . . . That done, I took the mould and carefully raised it up by pulleys and strong ropes. . . . Very, very slowly I lowered it to the bottom of the furnace and set it in exact position with the utmost care: and then, having finished that delicate operation, . . . I turned my attention to the furnace. . . .

The pine logs were heaped on, and what with the greasy resin from the wood and the excellence of my furnace, everything went so merrily that I was soon rushing from one side to another, exerting myself so much that I became worn out. But I forced myself to carry on.

To add to the difficulties, the workshop caught fire and we were terrified that the roof might fall in on us, and at the same time the furnace began to cool off because of the rain and wind that swept in at me from the garden.

I struggled against these infuriating accidents for several hours, but the strain was more than even my strong constitution could bear, and I was suddenly attacked by a bout of fever—the fiercest you can possibly imagine—and was forced to throw myself on to my bed.

Very upset, forcing myself away from the work, I gave instructions to my assistants, of whom there were ten or more. . . .

And then, very miserably, I left them and went to bed. . . .

In the middle of this dreadful suffering I caught sight of someone making his way into my room. His body was all twisted, just like a capital S, and he began to moan in a voice full of gloom, like a priest consoling a prisoner about to be executed.

"Poor Benvenuto! Your work is all ruined—there's no hope left!"

On hearing the wretch talk like that I let out a howl that could have been heard echoing from the farthest planet, sprang out of bed, seized my clothes, and began to dress. My servants, my boy, and everyone else who rushed up to help me found themselves treated to kicks and blows, and I grumbled furiously at them:

"The jealous traitors! This is deliberate treachery—but I swear by God I'll get to the root of it. Before I die I'll leave such an account of myself that the whole world will be dumbfounded!"

As soon as I was dressed, I set out for the workshop in a very nasty frame of mind, and there I found the men I had left in such

To cast a sculpture in bronze, the sculptor first made a wax model. Then he packed clay around the wax and put the whole thing into a furnace. The clay baked into a mold, and the wax melted and ran out through holes. Then through the holes, into the clay mold, he poured liquid bronze, an alloy of about ninety per cent copper and ten per cent tin or zinc. The holes were plugged. When the bronze alloy hardened, the clay exterior was chipped off.

▶ Should a person work hard solely to become famous?

147

high spirits all standing round with an air of astonished dejection.

"Come along now," I said, "listen to me. As you either couldn't or wouldn't follow the instructions I left you, obey me now that I'm here with you to direct my work in person. I don't want any objections—we need work now, not advice." . . .

I went at once to inspect the furnace, and I found that the metal had all curdled, had caked as they say. I ordered two of the hands to go over to Capretta, who kept a butcher's shop, for a load of young oak that had been dried out a year or more before. . . . When they carried in the first armfuls I began to stuff them under the grate. . . . Then, when it was licked by those terrible flames, you should have seen how that curdled metal began to glow and sparkle! . . .

Then I had someone bring me a lump of pewter, weighing about sixty pounds, which I threw inside the furnace on to the caked metal. . . . And when I saw that despite the despair of all my ignorant assistants I had brought a corpse back to life, I was so reinvigorated that I quite forgot the fever that had put the fear of death into me.

At this point there was a sudden explosion and a tremendous flash of fire, as if a thunderbolt had been hurled in our midst. Everyone, not least myself, was struck with unexpected terror. When the glare and noise had died away, we stared at each other, and then realized that the cover of the furnace had cracked open and that the bronze was pouring out. I hastily opened the mouths of the mould and at the same time drove in the two plugs.

Then, seeing that the metal was not running as easily as it should, I realized that the alloy must have been consumed in that terrific heat. So I sent for all my pewter plates, bowls, and salvers [trays], which numbered about two hundred, and put them one by one in front of the channels, throwing some straight into the furnace. When they saw how beautifully the bronze was melting and the mould filling up, everyone grew excited. They all ran up smiling to help me, and fell over themselves to answer my calls, while I —now in one place, now another—issued instructions, gave a hand with the work, and cried out loud: "O God, who by infinite power raised Yourself from the dead and ascended into heaven!" And then in an instant my mould was filled. So I knelt down and thanked God with all my heart.

Then I turned to a plate of salad that was there on some bench or other, and with a good appetite ate and drank with all my band of helpers. Afterwards I went to bed, healthy and happy, since it was two hours off dawn, and so sweetly did I sleep that it was as if I hadn't a thing wrong with me.

Cellini added pewter here because pewter is largely tin. Apparently too much of the tin in his bronze alloy had been consumed.

# 4  WOMEN IN
## RENAISSANCE FLORENCE

Throughout history, men have never granted equality to women. Women were expected to be mothers, housekeepers, and cooks, to work on the farm or tend the loom, and most of all, to wait on their husbands when needed and keep out of the way the rest of the time. This conception of the role of women began to change among the upper classes during the late Middle Ages, but it still remained dominant when the Renaissance began in Italy. Then the movement toward female emancipation picked up pace considerably.

The Renaissance did not emancipate any woman completely. Legal restrictions and powerful customs still held her in dependence. But a few women—the wives and companions of the elite —did make significant gains toward equality during the two centuries of the Florentine Renaissance. The majority of women, however, were little freer at the end of this period than they were at its beginning. Like most of the developments of the Renaissance, female emancipation was for the rich and wellborn, who enjoyed leisure and some education.

Renaissance cities brought women, as well as men, into contact with a world far more varied than life on a feudal manor. Many women adopted the views of their fathers, husbands, or lovers. Many relaxed their obedience to the teachings of the Church, which seemed to many less relevant.

The following reading was written by a modern scholar from fifteenth-century sources. It describes the attitudes and behavior of some Renaissance women. As you read, keep these questions in mind:

1. What were the characteristics of a "good woman" of the upper classes of Florentine society during the fifteenth century? How would these characteristics differ from those of her counterpart in the eleventh century? from those of a woman of the lower classes in the fifteenth century?
2. How did a Florentine woman of the upper classes define the good life? the good society?
3. Why do you think these conceptions of the good woman, the good life, and the good society emerged during the Renaissance? Are they worthy conceptions for the twentieth century? Explain.

# The Life of a Florentine Woman

J. Lucas-Dubreton, **Daily Life in Florence in the Time of the Medici**, pp. 222–233.

"Telling her beads" means saying the rosary. A prayer is said on each rosary bead.

Matteo Bandello (c. 1480–1562), a Dominican friar, wrote many long tales called **novelle.** Shakespeare drew on them for some of his plots, including that of **Romeo and Juliet.**

Petrarch, Ariosto, and Aretino were widely read Italian poets of the Renaissance. Boccaccio was a fourteenth-century Italian scholar who wrote the **Decameron,** a collection of tales from which you will read selections in Chapter 2.

In Italy, as elsewhere in the Middle Ages, . . . [w]hat was required of [a] woman was not to be graceful but to be physically capable of bearing fine children. Her virtue lay in not walking in the streets or going into shops, in not meddling in business, in not gazing out of the window, but in feeding the babies, telling her beads, mending the linen and looking after the keys.

The Renaissance destroyed this narrow outlook, and freed and raised the dignity of woman. She now had warm advocates, and the old-fashioned type of husband was thoroughly well trounced.

"You regard women as slaves and servants rather than companions, which is what justice requires; and this is so . . . contrary to the natural order of things that no other animal than man has the audacity to do it." This opinion . . . was shared by most of the Italian writers of the sixteenth century. "A husband," wrote the novelist Matteo Bandello, "should bear his wife company at all times, dress her according to his means and grant her that decent liberty which befits her rank." . . .

. . . The enlightened Italian of that time was a resolute feminist, and was not even shocked when someone argued that it would not perhaps be a bad thing to let women govern cities, make laws and control armies. Did they not attain excellence in all the arts to which they applied themselves?

Even the less determined feminists admitted that the progress in the education of girls was tending to establish equality among young people, and a grave author quoted *Genesis* and Aristotle to demonstrate that woman possesses the same moral dignity as man.

"It is very cruel of you," wrote Bandello, "to wish to do everything that comes into your head and not recognize that women have the same right. If they venture to do something that displeases us, we very quickly have recourse to rope, dagger or poison." Such barbarism was no longer fitting in a civilized community, where, at least among the well-to-do classes, woman was being emancipated and asserting her personality. The highest praise one could bestow on a woman was to say that she had the mind and soul of a man. Old people were still amazed at the change that had taken place. . . .

It was not merely a question of philosophy and rhetorics. These ladies read Petrarch, Ariosto and . . . Aretino. But beauty was their principal interest, and on this matter they had first-rate advisers in Florence itself. Boccaccio had already given his opinion as to what constitutes feminine beauty. The head should be fairly large, the eyebrows should not form two curves but a single line; a slightly aquiline nose, a broad bosom, a white hand which looks well against a scarlet cloak, a smooth, straight forehead (not bulging, as had once been fashionable), brown, almond-shaped eyes with a gaze that could be serious, or lively, or even roguish, a round neck and small feet—such were the constituents of a beautiful woman. But in the sixteenth century Boccaccio was to be outdone by another Tuscan, who became a sort of professional theorist of beauty . . . , Agnolo Firenzuola. . . .

Firenzuola (1493–c. 1545) was a poet.

Charm, in the eyes of Firenzuola, is a woman's gift for bearing herself, or moving, or acting, harmoniously. Grace is like a hidden light, an indefinable gift conferred by some secret privilege and arising out of a harmony of the whole person. Here are the characteristics of a beautiful countenance: the hair should be fair but golden-tinted and verging on brown. ("Blonde" is the queen of colours and can be obtained by artifice. Venetian women are expert in the matter.) The skin should be bright, not dull; the eyebrows, full in the middle and tapering off towards the nose and the ears; the eyes large, slightly protuberant, the eyelids white and marked with scarcely perceptible red veins. The white of the eye should be slightly bluish, the eyelashes not too long or too thick or too dark. The brow should be white, rather like a mirror but not so shining as to reflect objects. The borders of the eye must be red and shining, like a pomegranate seed. The pink on the cheeks is more marked round the curves. The nose becomes more slender, but by insensible degrees, towards the top. The mouth should be rather small, and should not display more than six teeth when the lips (which should have a dimple and not be too thin) are half open. The gums should remind one of red velvet: they should not be too dark.

As for the body—the neck should be white, round, and too long rather than too short. The leg should be long and slender, and firm at the calf; the foot small but not thin. A white hand large and fairly broad, a pink palm not too deeply marked with lines, shining finger-nails, pink also, and "not extending beyond the fingers by more than the breadth of the back of a knife." The bosom must be ample and shining, and not show any bones. . . .

This and the following quotations on beauty and charm are from Firenzuola and other Renaissance writers on the subject.

As regards manners, a woman should cultivate a reserved and not a provocative attitude; in her movements she should display what is beautiful and conceal what is less so. By wearing gloves, or playing chess or cards, or again at table, she may display her hand, if it is pretty, to advantage. She may give a glimpse of her leg, skilfully and in moderation, when walking, fishing, hunting or leaping some small ditch; and in a salon too she may show "just a little of her leg, especially if she has pretty velvet slippers and very clean stockings." It is all a matter of skill and moderation. One should not wear too many jewels. A necklace of white pearls, a tastefully enamelled collar worth fifteen crowns or so, and a diamond ring on the left-hand finger, will be enough. Scents should not be too strong, nor should they be mixed.

Do not display too keen a taste for balls, fêtes, games and other social functions, which might disquiet your husband, but simply a natural and innocent inclination. When amusing yourself, preserve your usual outer demeanour. Do not talk too much, and think before you speak. "One needs a hundred eyes, a hundred ears, but only one mouth." In this way you will refrain from slanderous gossip and avoid many worries. Do not on the other hand display excessive timidity or prudishness; and do not withdraw if the conversation becomes a little broad. . . . And do not give yourself such airs as to allow people to say: "Do you think that the flies buzzing round are in love with you?" Avoid affectation, be smiling and gracious and, especially, charming. "If Italian ladies do not surpass the French for their figures, charm at least makes them queens of the world."

▶ Is it important for a good woman to strive for beauty and charm?

Beauty, personal merit, balls, games, and society functions are all nothing without love. They are like a "fine house in winter where there is no fire." Renaissance literature is full of hymns to love. "From love spring all good things, all virtues and all pleasant customs." . . .

In former days a notary named Francesco da Barberino had warned young women to distrust the pitfalls of love and had advised them as to how they might preserve their modesty:

Beware of those long-bearded pilgrims who come with their begging bowls and sit beside the women and prophesy things that ensnare young fools. Beware of the physician who pays less heed to the sickness than to the charms of the patient. Be on your guard against the tailor who offers his services free and, while taking your measurements, walks round you and admires you. Do not go to Church or to the baths at night; be prudent. If you want to go to a ball where there will be young men ready to dance, let it be by daylight or at least when the lights are bright enough for you to see those who are tickling the palm of your hand.

To the girl who had been placed when very young in a convent and who was now proud of her emancipation, all this seemed dusty and out-of-date. . . . Let us now hear what advice was given by that experienced matron Raffaella . . . to young Margherita. The latter's husband is "the best fellow in the world" but, being very busy, is often away from home. Margherita, being left a good deal to herself, to her sewing and embroidery, dreams of another kind of life; and Raffaella gives her very different instructions from those of old Barberino:

One must not waste the years of one's youth and, to avoid greater scandal, you should consent to some small backsliding, because, if you do not yield a little to the attraction of pleasure, despair will deliver you bodily to the devil. Honour rests only on public esteem, and that is why a woman should use all her ability to prevent people from talking scandal of her. Honour, in fact, does not consist in what one does or does not do, but in the impression one gives of oneself, advantageous or otherwise. Sin if you can't resist, but maintain your good reputation. . . .

▶ Does honor consist only in not getting caught?

Wives who were imbued with Raffaella's maxims might readily enough look for illicit love, and their infidelities rarely ended in catastrophe. People even came to regard them as legitimate when they were provoked by a husband's faithlessness. It was the law of tit for tat, and when the vengeance was in proportion to the outrage, the public did not hesitate to applaud. . . .

The cultured and emancipated Florentine was not always interested in physical passion. The learned scholars and commentators had told her about the spiritual kind of love associated with Platonism, and this opened new horizons, as we shall see from the example of Costanza Amaretta.

During the Easter festivities of 1523 in Florence, this amiable young lady met a refined and cultured young man named Celso. He was her ideal. They appealed to each other and lived under the same roof in perfect chastity. After Easter they, with two other couples who had formed similar unions, left for Celso's country-house, and here they led the most delightful existence that could be imagined. During meals they chatted or listened to music; then they would walk or ride out to some agreeable spot, where the view was charming, and improvise verses. . . .

One result, in any case, of the decrial of marriage was the success of the courtesans. It had begun in the second half of the fifteenth century and increased at the beginning of the sixteenth. These persons were of course of different types. . . .

. . . The high-class courtesan was a well-bred and cultured woman, sometimes a poetess too and a musician; she was witty, knew how to receive in a courteous manner, and was in short a woman of the world. Florence contained fewer of such women than Rome, Venice and Naples, but the names of some have been recorded.

Nannina Zingera, for example, had a voice so sweet and gentle that it might, people thought, move mountains and calm the wind. Her manners were those of a great lady, and "as shadows vanish before the sun, so everything base and vile flees from her approach." Zafolina was sharp-witted, gay and piquant; "both by nature and experience" she was redolent of the Tuscan land, and appreciated by the nobility. When the honest courtesan paid a visit or went to a fête or to the baths, she was taken for a lady of quality. She had the bearing and reserve of one. She attended Mass and Vespers,

Vespers is an evening prayer service in Christian religions. Lent is a forty-day period of fasting and penitence prior to Easter. Ember Days are certain Wednesdays, Fridays, and Saturdays on which Catholics are expected to fast, although recently the Church has eased the requirements for their observance.

gave her opinion on the preacher's eloquence, observed Lent and the Ember-Days by remaining quiet or at home. She could be invited to dinner without anxiety. She ate and drank slowly, delicately and in moderation, with no sign of greed. Her air was pleasant and smiling, she never whispered in people's ears or paid attention to anyone but her host. If by chance he pressed her foot or touched her hand, she merely smiled. . . .

The wise courtesan avoided any display of anger or contempt, and she sought the company of literary men, not for their money, because they rarely had much, but because they could celebrate her beauty and advertise her charms. She contrived in this way to acquire a clientele, and sometimes she would decide to regularize her position. Such was the case with a certain courtesan who was formally married by her lover. He took her to his home and treated her with every kind of respect. She attended social functions like the other ladies of the city and went to church.

# 5 WORKERS, SLAVES, AND SERVANTS

The work of slaves or of a laboring class has supported most of the great civilizations of the past. The Egyptians, the Greeks, and the Romans all enslaved men and women in order to produce the goods and services that supported the elite. Other societies have recruited laborers from among free or partially free men. Eighteenth-century England exploited the labor of factory workers. Medieval culture rested on the backs of the serfs.

So, to some degree, it was in Florence. The woolen industry on which much of the city's prosperity depended probably employed about thirty thousand workers during most years in the fifteenth century. Many woolworkers earned a pittance, although they worked for long hours. Occasionally they revolted to demand better treatment. Profits from the labor of these exploited workers supported the good life of the elite.

Moreover, the villas and palaces of the elite required large staffs of servants. Until the middle of the fourteenth century, free men and women drawn from the poor of the city or the surrounding countryside filled these jobs. But in 1366 an epidemic of the plague, called the Black Death, swept the city and wiped out about half its population. An acute shortage of servants developed. This crisis persuaded the government and the Church to sanction the importation of slaves as long as they were infidels, not Christians. From then on, slaves formed part of the household staffs of most great families and of many Church dignitaries.

Slave labor was easily purchased. Venetian and Genoese slave traders captured refugees from the Moslem invasions of the Near East and eastern Europe. Spanish attacks on the Moors created many black refugees for the traders to capture. A number of Africans were also imported from the Sudan.

The lives of Florence's workers, slaves, and servants provide insights into the society's conception of the good life. As you read the selections that follow, think about these questions:

1.  In what ways were the woolworkers exploited? Who was responsible for this exploitation?
2.  The Florentine elite accepted the institution of slavery. What does this acceptance reveal about their conception of the good man? the good life? the good society?
3.  Were the workers, slaves, and servants satisfied with their lot? Do you think the cultural advances of the period significantly improved their lives? Explain.
4.  Suppose that a great period of cultural advancement could be made only on a basis of slave labor or exploitation of a working class. Is the gain worth the price paid? Explain.

# Workers in the Wool Industry

*The wool industry of Florence provided the city's elite with much of their wealth. The following selection describes the structure of the industry and the lives of its workers in the fourteenth century. A modern scholar compiled this information as part of an economic history of Europe.*

Eleanora Carus-Wilson, "The Renaissance Woolen Industry," in **Cambridge Economic History of Europe**, Vol. II, ed. by M. Postan and E. E. Rich (Cambridge: Cambridge University Press, 1952), Chapter 6, pp. 393–398.

. . . [B]y the early fourteenth century all other Tuscan towns had been outstripped by Florence [in the manufacture of woollen cloth]. . . . The Florentine woollen industry, as the contemporary historian Villani proudly relates, then produced each year some 80,000 pieces of cloth and employed some 30,000 persons. Over the Ponte Vecchio in the suburb of Oltrarno, where in 1200 there had been but a few houses, there now lived many thousands of wool workers, and there too many firms of the *Arte della Lana* had their headquarters.

In all these towns the structure of the industry was highly capitalistic. . . . The Italian *lanaiuolo* . . . was an entrepreneur, supplying

The **Arte della Lana** was the guild of wool merchants, or dealers. In Italian **lana** means wool. **Arte** means skill, but skill had little to do with the matter, since by 1200 the skilled artisans, disgusted with the merchants' control of the guild, had formed their own guild.

**Lanaiuolo** means wool merchant, or dealer.

capital and skilled direction, employing anything from a few only to many hundreds of craftsmen, and joining together with his fellow *lanaiuoli* in the *Arte della Lana* which controlled the production of the cloth . . . closely. . . . In Florence in 1338 there were, according to Villani, 200 such woollen manufacturing firms, employing on an average 150 operatives each. . . .

. . . [T]he growth of a class of industrial capitalists was everywhere accompanied by the growth of a hired proletariat of workers. . . . Least independent . . . were the workers engaged in the preliminary processes of beating, combing and carding. These possessed not even the tools of their trade; they worked mostly in the entrepreneur's central shop, and were under the immediate supervision of his foremen. Propertyless and rightless, they were forbidden to assemble together or to combine in their own fraternities, even for religious purposes, without the permission of the consuls of the gild, to whose jurisdiction they were wholly subjected but in whose election they had no voice. Threatened with mass unemployment and starvation in times of slump, in times of boom or of labour shortage their prospects might materially improve. With the scarcity of workers after the Black Death, for instance, they were in [a] . . . favourable . . . position to bargain for higher wages. . . . Paid mostly by the hour or by the day, they had no security of employment. . . .

The spinners also were by the fourteenth century wholly dependent, and tied often to a single entrepreneur whose wool alone they might spin. . . . [T]hey carried on their work in their own homes, scattered about in town and countryside, often far from the headquarters of the firm. . . . The *lanaiuolo* might cheat them with short weight wool and long delays in payment, despite laws passed for their protection, but they too had opportunities for trickery and bad workmanship. . . .

Weaving was done mostly in the city, by a cosmopolitan throng, Italian, German and Flemish, assisted often by their wives and by other members of their households. They too became increasingly dependent, working often under the direct supervision of the *lanaiuolo*. Often they ceased even to own the tools of their trade. For in times of trouble they would pledge their looms, often at rates ruinous to themselves but so profitable to the lender that an active business grew up in this form of investment; if some investors were content with 50%, others, like the artist Giotto took 120%. . . .

As the *lanaiuoli* steadily extended their control over almost all branches of the industry, so the *Arte della Lana* in which they were all united, and of which they alone were full members, grew in power and prestige. . . . [I]t strove to forestall trouble from the workers by keeping them in a position of subservience and refusing

Giotto (c. 1276–c. 1337), a Florentine painter, represents a transition between medieval and Renaissance styles. He painted religious scenes.

to them that right of assembly, of association and of corporate action that was in large measure the secret of their own success.

The gild's powers of enforcement were formidable. A large staff of inspectors was constantly occupied in the detection of any breach of the regulations. The gild had its own police officers, . . . its own gaols [jails], . . . and its own court. . . . The penalties it was permitted to impose were of the utmost severity. Fines, often exacted in the form of a postponement of wages, were the least to be feared; more serious was deprivation of work, involving ruin or exile. Such sanctions as these were a commonplace of gild regulation throughout the clothing towns of Europe, but in Florence, where industrial capitalism may perhaps be seen in its most intense and ruthless form, they frequently gave place to more savage methods of corporal punishment, from flogging to the loss of a hand and even the loss of life. The wool-carder Cinto Brandini, for instance, accused in 1345 of holding public meetings and exhorting the workers to unite, was arrested during the night with his two sons and, despite a protest strike by all his fellow wool-combers and carders, was hanged on the gallows. And when the prosperity of the first half of the fourteenth century was threatened by increasing problems and difficulties towards its close, the industrial life of Florence became as violent and sanguinary as its political life.

## Slaves and Servants in a Merchant's Family

*The account that follows describes the lives of slaves and servants in a Renaissance family. The details have been taken from the personal account-books and fragmentary diaries of Francesco Datini, a merchant in the small town of Prato, a few miles from Florence. General comments on slaves and servants follow.*

. . . [A] man of Francesco's standing required even in ordinary times a good many servants. . . . In the first years after his return to Prato, Francesco's household was modest enough: according to the census of 1383, it consisted of only three servants—a man called Antonio d'Andrea, a woman named Bartolomea, and a little serving-maid of twelve, Ghirigora. But two years later Francesco was already dissatisfied. "When I have set all in order," he wrote, "I shall need a female slave or two, or a little slave-boy, as you prefer." In 1387 his private account-book records the arrival of "a little slave-girl of 13 from Pisa, bought by Francesco di Michele & Co. of

▶ Is a protest strike good way to fight injustice?

A "violent and sanguinary" eruption occurred in 1378, when a rebellious mass of woolworkers burned homes, imprisoned politicians in the city hall, and demanded fair representation in the government. A few token demands were granted, but the elite retained control.

Iris Origo, **The Merchant of Prato, Francesco Di Marco Datini, 1335–1410** (New York: Alfred A. Knopf, Inc., 1957), pp. 205–213. Reprinted by permission.

Genoa," and the purchase of a slave called Bartolomea, "bought without a broker for 70 florins," while in the following year he bought yet another slave of thirty-six called Giovanna, who was also sent to Pisa by a Genoese slave-trader. And in 1393 the census also recorded, in addition to these slaves, the presence in Francesco's household of a man-servant called Domenico . . . , his wife, Domenica, and their little girl, Nanna; a young slave-girl of twenty, Lucia; and a blind, paralysed old woman, Monna Tinca di Simone, whom Francesco kept "for the love of God."

But even this household was not large enough. In the same year Francesco was instructing his partner in Genoa, Andrea di Bonanno, to find yet another slave.

Pray buy me a little slave-girl, young and rustic, between eight and ten years old, and she must be of good stock, strong enough to bear much hard work, and of good health and temper, so that I may bring her up in my own way. I would have her only to wash the dishes and carry wood and bread to the oven, and work of that sort . . . for I have another here who is a good slave, and can cook and serve well. . . .

Finally . . . the child was found in the Venetian market, and on New Year's Day, 1395, Francesco's private account-book records, in a list of tips to be given for the New Year, "2 *soldi* to Orenetta, the little slave who comes from Venice."

In addition to all these women, there were several men employed in the stables and cellars, and at least two or three messengers or carriers between Florence and Prato—as well as a Tartar slave called Antonetto, who had been bought as a boy from some Catalonian traders for 49 florins. And, finally, Francesco's private account-books in 1405 and 1407 record the names of four more female servants—Monna Beneassai, Monna Palma, Monna Chiara, and Monna Sandra—each of whom is referred to as "*nostra servente*," while in 1408 we even meet with a French maid, "Monna Perronetta of Avignon." Moreover, Margherita also seems to have had the help of several girls who came in by the day to help with the spring cleaning, the washing, and the unending baking, spinning, and weaving. "Your great pack of *femmine*" was Francesco's term for them, and Margherita herself would write of "my flock of little girls"—adding that they were incapable of doing anything without supervision. . . .

The story . . . of the part played in Tuscan households by . . . Tartar or African slaves—alien, uprooted creatures, the "displaced persons" of their time—is a very strange one. Their importation . . . was sanctioned by the Priors of Florence in 1366, in view of the acute labour shortage caused by the Black Death—on condition that these slaves were not Christians, but infidels. . . . Thus, during the

Tartars, or Tatars, are an Asian people, originally nomads. When they invaded eastern Europe in 1241, many were captured and enslaved. Catalonia is a region on the northeast coast of Spain.

▶ Is it all right to enslave or exploit people of another culture if their standard of living or cultural opportunities improve in the process?

158

last two centuries of the Middle Ages, Florentine society came to depend—like that of Greece and Rome, though to a lesser degree—on the services of slaves. Beneath the members of the guilds . . . , beneath even the oppressed, hungry crowd of the *popolo minuto*, the Tuscan cities held another class—formed of men without human or legal rights, without families of their own, without even a name, save that given them by their masters: the slaves. Sometimes a few of them succeeded in obtaining their freedom, but often only to form the dregs of the population who lived by robbery on the Tuscan roads, or swelled the crowd during bread-riots. Often, even after enfranchisement, they remained in their masters' houses, the necessary background of every domestic scene—waiting at every table, listening at every door, speaking a strange, incomprehensible jargon of their own—and mingling their alien blood with that of their Tuscan hosts. *Domestici hostes,* domestic enemies, was Petrarch's name for these inmates of every house, so alien and yet so close, and the author of a treatise on domestic economy in Sicily was of the same opinion. "We have," he wrote, "as many enemies as we have slaves." . . .

Popolo minuto, literally "little people" in Italian, was used during the Renaissance to mean the lowest class of workers.

Generally a slave's deed of sale warranted that she was free from disease ("healthy and whole in all her members, both visible and invisible") and sometimes also that she was not a thief, quarrelsome, bad-tempered, vicious, or prone to running away. . . . The buyer obtained over her . . . power "to have, hold, sell, alienate, exchange, enjoy, rent or unrent, dispose of in his Will, judge soul and body, and do with in perpetuity whatsoever may please him and his heirs, and no man may gainsay him." How completely, indeed, such a slave was considered a thing and not a person is shown in a list of property in the books of Datini's Pisan branch, in which a slave's value is thrown in with that of several domestic animals: "He says he has a female slave and a horse and two donkeys and three fifths of an ox. Let us put them down at 70 florins."

In spite, however, of their negligible status, these slaves, in actual practice, seem to have been treated very much like everyone else: they, too, were part of *la famiglia.* Indeed, it is impossible not to feel that slaves, servants, and children received very much the same treatment: great severity in theory, and considerable indulgence in practice. Servants and children alike were subject, in law, to the *podestas puniendi* of the head of the family; they could be beaten and starved and even sent to prison at his caprice. . . . In practice, however, as these letters testify, both children and servants were often impertinent and disobedient with complete impunity—and at all times singularly outspoken and, in the modern sense of the word, *familiar.*

In Italian podestas puniendi means "power to punish."

159

Let us see, for instance, what happened to Francesco's absolute authority when he was left alone in Florence, at the mercy of an ill-tempered cook.

I brought home to dinner the Mayor and Matteo d'Antonio. She had no more to do, for the steak and the fish were already cooked. But because those two ate with me today, and because some fish was left over, and she has also got to cook two bowlsful of beans, she complains she has too much to do! So you see what maids are, when left to themselves. . . .

It was far from unusual, too, for a slave to run away.

This morn [wrote Francesco's partner, Stoldo di Lorenzo] when Monna Lionardo and Monna Villana had gone to church, your slave Caterina went forth and away and we cannot find her. We have been to all the doors and cannot discover that she has gone forth through any of them. . . . They say she has taken naught from the house, save the gown of *romagnolo* wool she had on her, and a little purple gown for feast days. . . .

Even, however, when the slaves did not run away, they were not easy to live with. They quarrelled with the other free servants and with each other, and were extremely quick with their knives. They sometimes corrupted, by their evil ways and coarse manners, the respectable maid-servants, and even the daughters of the house. And they had even been known to use magic arts and poison against their masters—for indeed, in an age when poison was a common weapon, who was in a better position to administer it than a slave?

Moreover—according to the unanimous report of their mistresses—they stole all they could lay their hands on. To Francesco, with his morbid fear of being defrauded—in Mazzei's words—"even of the shoe-buckle of the wench that serves your slave," the dread of their thefts became a veritable obsession. "Lock the door behind you with three keys," he adjured his wife when she was going to Florence for the day. . . .

. . . All Francesco's free servants received, in addition to their board, lodging, and clothing, a regular yearly salary. . . . The cost of a slave, on the other hand—even if fairly high—was paid off by a very few years' work.

# Florence: The Ideals

## STATING THE ISSUE

Like fifth-century Athens, Renaissance Florence still speaks to modern man. Its public buildings and magnificent sculpture draw throngs of tourists each year to the banks of the Arno. Paintings by Florentines hang in the world's museums. The works of Florence's poets, essayists, and storytellers appear in modern anthologies, and the ideas of its political philosophers remain influential more than four centuries after they were conceived.

Like the Athenians, the Florentines asked questions that lie at the heart of human existence. Throughout the Middle Ages, most men let their faith and the word of church officials define what was good. Renaissance Florence broke firmly with this tradition. To Florentines, any question was open for discussion, and any answer worthy of study. Out of this intellectual ferment came a rich heritage.

The Florentines of the Renaissance came to share the confidence in man that characterized the ancient Greeks. Like the Athenians, they were humanists, who asserted the dignity and worth of man and emphasized his capacity for self-realization through the use of reason. They were also individualists, who stressed the sanctity of the individual personality and the responsibility of each person to develop his capabilities to the limit. These ideals helped to shape the thought of many Renaissance men.

The readings in Chapter 2 were written by men who lived and worked in Renaissance Florence, and they touch directly or indirectly on ideals. How do these writers define the good man? the good life? the good society? To what extent do they agree with each other? What implications do their ideals have for modern men? These are the major issues in this chapter.

# 6  WHAT IS MAN?:
# A HUMANIST'S ANSWER

Renaissance scholars spent much of their time on Greek and Latin manuscripts, which they preserved, copied, corrected, and imitated. Interest in the classics had developed in the Middle Ages, but medieval scholars were chiefly monks and priests concerned with using classical ideas and languages to study Christian theology. Renaissance scholars, on the other hand, brought a man-centered spirit to classical studies, and called themselves humanists, a term they learned from ancient Roman writings. By "humanism" they meant the study of classical grammar, history, literature, and philosophy. Among the concerns of humanism was the place of man in the universe.

"Humanism" in modern usage has a more general meaning. The word usually refers to the liberal arts, or to any philosophical or ethical system based on the freedom and dignity of man.

One of the most notable of these Renaissance humanists was Giovanni Pico, Count of Mirandola, a member of the literary and intellectual circle gathered around Lorenzo at the Medici Palace. Remarkably precocious even in an age when genius bloomed early, Pico could read Greek, Latin, Arabic, and Hebrew. At the age of twenty-four, he wrote his *Oration on the Dignity of Man,* a preface to a list of nine hundred theses he was prepared to debate. Because some of the theses were pronounced heretical, Pico was forced to flee for a while from Italy. He spent the last four years of his life in Florence, however, where he died at the age of thirty-one, considered by many to be the ideal man of his time in both thought and spirit.

Pico's theses were ideas drawn from Greek, Arabic, Hebrew, and Latin thinkers. He presented them to the Church authorities and offered to defend them as consistent with Catholic doctrine. The Church declared thirteen of them to be heresy. Pico fled to France, but Lorenzo interceded for him with the Church and won permission for him to return to Florence.

In his *Oration* Pico expressed the loftiest ideals of the Italian humanists. In their life-styles and in the works they wrote, many humanists were struggling toward a conception of man much like the one Pico expressed.

As you read the following passage from the *Oration,* keep these questions in mind:

1. According to Pico, what is the place of man in the cosmic scheme of things? What determines the place that a particular man makes for himself?
2. According to Pico's philosophy, how can a man lead a good life?
3. What sort of society would best promote Pico's ideals of the good man and the good life?
4. Do you agree with Pico's estimate of the nature of man? Explain.

162

# Oration on the Dignity of Man

Most esteemed Fathers, I have read in the ancient writings of the Arabians that Abdala the Saracen on being asked what, on this stage, so to say, of the world, seemed to him most evocative of wonder, replied that there was nothing to be seen more marvelous than man. And that celebrated exclamation of Hermes Trismegistus, "What a great miracle is man, Asclepius" confirms this opinion.

And still, as I reflected upon the basis assigned for these estimations, I was not fully persuaded by the diverse reasons advanced by a variety of persons for the pre-eminence of human nature; for example: that man is the intermediary between creatures, that he is the familiar of the gods above him as he is lord of the beings beneath him; that, by the acuteness of his senses, the inquiry of his reason and the light of his intelligence, he is the interpreter of nature, set midway between the timeless unchanging and the flux of time; the living union (as the Persians say), the very marriage hymn of the world, and, by David's testimony but little lower than the angels. These reasons are all, without question, of great weight; nevertheless, they do not touch the principal reasons, those, that is to say, which justify man's unique right to such unbounded admiration. Why, I asked, should we not admire the angels themselves and the beatific choirs more? At long last, however, I feel that I have come to some understanding of why man is the most fortunate of living things and, consequently, deserving of all admiration; of what may be the condition in the hierarchy of beings assigned to him, which draws upon him the envy, not of the brutes alone, but of the astral beings and of the very intelligences which dwell beyond the confines of the world. A thing surpassing belief and smiting the soul with wonder. Still, how could it be otherwise? For it is on this ground that man is, with complete justice, considered and called a great miracle and a being worthy of all admiration.

Hear then, oh Fathers, precisely what this condition of man is; and in the name of your humanity, grant me your benign audition as I pursue this theme.

God the Father, the Mightiest Architect, had already raised, according to the precepts of His hidden wisdom, this world we see, the cosmic dwelling of divinity, a temple most august. He had already adorned the supercelestial region with Intelligences, infused the heavenly globes with the life of immortal souls and set the fermenting dung-heap of the inferior world teeming with every form of animal life. But when this work was done, the Divine Artificer still longed for some creature which might comprehend

Giovanni Pico della Mirandola, **Oration on the Dignity of Man**, trans. by A. Robert Caponigri (Chicago: Gateway Editions; Henry Regnery Co., 1956), pp. 1–4, 18–19. Reprinted by permission.

The "Fathers" are Church authorities.

Hermes Trismegistus is the Latin name for an Egyptian author of works on magic, astrology, and philosophy. Asclepius was a Greek hero who became a god of healing.

This description of man is from Psalm 8 in the Old Testament. Many of the psalms are ascribed to David, a king of the ancient Hebrews.

the meaning of so vast an achievement, which might be moved with love at its beauty and smitten with awe at its grandeur. When, consequently, all else had been completed (as both Moses and [the] *Timaeus* testify), in the very last place, He bethought Himself of bringing forth man. Truth was, however, that there remained no archetype according to which He might fashion a new offspring, nor in His treasure-houses the wherewithal to endow a new son with a fitting inheritance, nor any place, among the seats of the universe, where this new creature might dispose himself to contemplate the world. All space was already filled; all things had been distributed in the highest, the middle and the lowest orders. Still, it was not in the nature of the power of the Father to fail in this last creative *élan;* nor was it in the nature of that supreme Wisdom to hesitate through lack of counsel in so crucial a matter; nor, finally, in the nature of His beneficent love to compel the creature destined to praise the divine generosity in all other things to find it wanting in himself.

At last the Supreme Maker decreed that this creature, to whom He could give nothing wholly his own, should have a share in the particular endowment of every other creature. Taking man, therefore, this creature of indeterminate image, He set him in the middle of the world and thus spoke to him:

"We have given you, Oh Adam, no visage proper to yourself, nor any endowment properly your own, in order that whatever place, whatever form, whatever gifts you may, with premeditation, select, these same you may have and possess through your own judgment and decision. The nature of all other creatures is defined and restricted within laws which We have laid down; you, by contrast, impeded by no such restrictions, may, by your own free will, to whose custody We have assigned you, trace for yourself the lineaments of your own nature. I have placed you at the very center of the world, so that from that vantage point you may with greater ease glance round about you on all that the world contains. We have made you a creature neither of heaven nor of earth, neither mortal nor immortal, in order that you may, as the free and proud shaper of your own being, fashion yourself in the form you may prefer. It will be in your power to descend to the lower, brutish forms of life; you will be able, through your own decision, to rise again to the superior orders whose life is divine."

Oh unsurpassed generosity of God the Father, Oh wondrous and unsurpassable felicity of man, to whom it is granted to have what he chooses, to be what he wills to be! The brutes, from the moment of their birth, bring with them . . . from their mother's womb all that they will ever possess. The highest spiritual beings were, from the very moment of creation, or soon thereafter, fixed in the mode of being which would be theirs through measureless eternities. But upon man, at the moment of his creation, God bestowed seeds pregnant with all possibilities, the germs of every form of life. Whichever of these a man shall cultivate, the same will mature and bear fruit in him. If vegetative, he will become a plant; if sensual, he will become brutish; if rational, he will reveal himself a heavenly being; if intellectual, he will be an angel and the son of God. And if, dissatisfied with the lot of all creatures, he should recollect himself into the center of his own unity, he will there become one spirit with God, in the solitary darkness of the Father, Who is set above all things, himself transcend all creatures.

Who then will not look with awe upon this our chameleon, or who, at least, will look with greater admiration on any other being? This creature, man, whom Asclepius the Athenian, by reason of this very mutability, this nature capable of transforming itself, quite rightly said was symbolized . . . by the figure of Proteus. . . .

According to Greek mythology, Proteus was an old man of the sea who could change himself into any shape.

These are the reasons, most reverend Fathers, which not only led, but even compelled me, to the study of philosophy. And I should not have undertaken to expound them, except to reply to those who are wont to condemn the study of philosophy, especially among men of high rank, but also among those of modest station. For the whole study of philosophy (such as the unhappy plight of our time) is occasion for contempt and contumely, rather than honor and glory. The deadly and monstrous persuasion has invaded practically all minds, that philosophy ought not to be studied at all or by very few people; as though it were a thing [of] little worth to have before our eyes and at our finger-tips, as matters we have searched out with greatest care, the causes of things, the ways of nature and the plan of the universe, God's counsels and the mysteries of heaven and of earth, unless by such knowledge one might procure some profit or favor for oneself. . . .

. . . I address all these complaints, with the greatest regret and indignation, not against the princes of our times, but against the philosophers who believe and assert that philosophy should not be pursued because no monetary value or reward is assigned it, unmindful that by this sign they disqualify themselves as philosophers. Since their whole life is concentrated on gain and ambition, they never embrace the knowledge of the truth for its own sake. This much will I say for myself—and on this point I do not blush for praising myself—that I have never philosophized save for the sake of philosophy, nor have I ever desired or hoped to secure from my studies and my laborious researches any profit or fruit save cultivation of mind and knowledge of the truth—things I esteem more and

▶ Should a good society subsidize philosophers so that they do not have to worry about making a living?

more with the passage of time. I have also been so avid for this knowledge and so enamoured of it that I have set aside all private and public concerns to devote myself completely to contemplation; and from it no calumny of jealous persons, nor any invective from the enemies of wisdom has ever been nor ever will be able to detach me. Philosophy has taught me to rely on my own convictions . . . and to concern myself less with whether I am well thought of than whether what I do or say is evil.

# 7 THE GOOD LIFE AS STRIVING: PETRARCH

Most men of the Middle Ages admired the contemplative lives of monks. Shut off from the affairs of the world, safe within the walls of a monastery, the monk could ponder the eternal problems of man. Typical medieval men earned their living on a manor or fought as members of one of the feudal orders, and had little time for contemplation. Yet the monk remained an ideal.

Urban Renaissance life gradually brought a shift in attitude. Renaissance men threw themselves into life as vigorously as any men before or since. Lorenzo and Cellini, for example, illustrate the intense activity characteristic of so many Renaissance figures.

Francesco Petrarca, called Petrarch, ranks among the earliest of these Renaissance men of action. He was born in 1304 near Florence and lived in a number of Italian and French cities. He quickly won a European reputation as a founder of the humanistic movement in Italy. He was an indefatigable collector of ancient manuscripts, a Latin poet who imitated classical models, a distinguished poet in the vernacular, an amateur diplomat, a lover of nature, an essayist, a letter writer, and a philosopher. Still, he never freed himself completely from the medieval ideal of solitary contemplation.

The Fathers of the Church were early Christians whose writings are the basis of Church doctrine. St. Augustine (354–430) is considered the founder of Christian theology for his writings on Church doctrine. St. Jerome (c. 340–420) translated most of the Bible from Hebrew into Latin.

Like so many of the humanists who followed him, Petrarch devoted much of his time to a study of Latin and Greek manuscripts. He pored over the Latin classics, both the pagan writings of antiquity and the works of such Church Fathers as St. Augustine and St. Jerome. Frustrated because he could not read Greek, he wept over a manuscript by Homer whose pages he could not translate. The quantity of his labors and the pace he set for himself astonished his contemporaries. The letter that follows was written by Petrarch in 1336 to a professor of theology who lived in Paris. As you read, keep the following questions in mind:

1. Why did Petrarch choose to climb Mont Ventoux? How was this decision related to his personality? to his humanistic studies?
2. What obstacles did he encounter on his climb? What thoughts did the climb trigger in his mind?
3. What do the ideas in this letter imply about Petrarch's conception of the good man? the good life?
4. Should everyone try to lead the active life? Suppose someone sets his goals high and fails. Is he a better man than one who sets his goals too low? Explain.

## The Ascent of Mont Ventoux

Today I ascended the highest mountain in this region, which, not without cause, they call the Windy Peak. Nothing but the desire to see its conspicuous height was the reason for this undertaking. For many years I have been intending to make this expedition. You know that since my early childhood, as fate tossed around human affairs, I have been tossed around in these parts, and this mountain, visible far and wide from everywhere, is always in your view. So I was at last seized by the impulse to accomplish what I had always wanted to do. It happened while I was reading Roman history again in Livy that I hit upon the passage where Philip, the king of Macedon—the Philip who waged war against the Roman people—"ascends Mount Haemus in Thessaly, since he believed the rumor that you can see two seas from its top: the Adriatic and the Black Sea." Whether he was right or wrong I cannot make out because the mountain is far from our region, and the disagreement among authors renders the matter uncertain. . . . I would not leave it long in doubt if that mountain were as easy to explore as the one here. At any rate, I had better let it go, in order to come back to the mountain I mentioned at first. It seemed to me that a young man who holds no public office might be excused for doing what an old king is not blamed for.

I now began to think over whom to choose as a companion. It will sound strange to you that hardly a single one of all my friends seemed to me suitable in every respect, so rare a thing is absolute congeniality in every attitude and habit even among dear friends. One was too sluggish, the other too vivacious; one too slow, the other too quick; this one too gloomy of temper, that one too gay. One was duller, the other brighter than I should have liked. This man's taciturnity, that man's flippancy; the heavy weight and obesity of the next, the thinness and weakliness of still another

Mont Ventoux is a ridge of the Alps in southeastern France, overlooking the Rhône River. It is 6,273 feet high.

Petrarch, "The Ascent of Mont Ventoux," in The Renaissance Philosophy of Man, ed. by Ernst Cassirer, et al. (Chicago: University of Chicago Press, 1948), pp. 36–41, 45–46. Reprinted by permission.

This explanation puts Petrarch into the ranks of such natural-born mountaineers as George Leigh Mallory, who climbed one of the lower peaks of Mount Everest in 1921. When asked why he wanted to climb Everest, he replied, "Because it is there."

Livy (59 B.C.–17 A.D.) was an ancient Roman historian.

167

were reasons to deter me. The cool lack of curiosity of one, like another's too eager interest, dissuaded me from choosing either. All such qualities, however difficult they are to bear, can be borne at home: loving friendship is able to endure everything; it refuses no burden. But on a journey they become intolerable. Thus my delicate mind, craving honest entertainment, looked about carefully, weighing every detail, with no offense to friendship. Tacitly it rejected whatever it could foresee would become troublesome on the projected excursion. What do you think I did? At last I applied for help at home and revealed my plan to my only brother, who is younger than I and whom you know well enough. He could hear of nothing he would have liked better and was happy to fill the place of friend as well as brother.

▶ Why are old friends or relatives sometimes the best companions?

We left home on the appointed day and arrived at Malaucène at night. This is a place at the northern foot of the mountain. We spent a day there and began our ascent this morning, each of us accompanied by a single servant. From the start we encountered a good deal of trouble, for the mountain is a steep and almost inaccessible pile of rocky material. However, what the Poet says is appropriate: "Ruthless striving overcomes everything."

The "Poet" is Virgil (or Vergil) (70–19 B.C.), the Roman whose epic **The Aeneid** describes the adventures of a Trojan hero after the fall of Troy.

The day was long, the air was mild; this and vigorous minds, strong and supple bodies, and all the other conditions assisted us on our way. The only obstacle was the nature of the spot. We found an aged shepherd in the folds of the mountain who tried with many words to dissuade us from the ascent. He said he had been up to the highest summit in just such youthful fervor fifty years ago and had brought home nothing but regret and pains, and his body as well as his clothes torn by rocks and thorny underbrush. Never before and never since had the people there heard of any man who dared a similar feat. While he was shouting these words at us, our desire increased just because of his warnings; for young people's minds do not give credence to advisers. When the old man saw that he was exerting himself in vain, he went with us a little way forward through the rocks and pointed with his finger to a steep path. He gave us much good advice and repeated it again and again at our backs when we were already at quite a distance. We left with him whatever of our clothes and other belongings might encumber us, intent only on the ascent, and began to climb with merry alacrity. However, as almost always happens, the daring attempt was soon followed by quick fatigue.

Not far from our start we stopped at a rock. From there we went on again, proceeding at a slower pace, to be sure. I in particular made my way up with considerably more modest steps. My brother endeavored to reach the summit by the very ridge of the mountain on a short cut; I, being so much more of a weakling, was bending down toward the valley. When he called me back and showed me the better way, I answered that I hoped to find an easier access on the other side and was not afraid of a longer route on which I might proceed more smoothly. With such an excuse I tried to palliate my laziness, and, when the others had already reached the higher zones, I was still wandering through the valleys, where no more comfortable access was revealed, while the way became longer and longer and the vain fatigue grew heavier and heavier. At last I felt utterly disgusted, began to regret my perplexing error, and decided to attempt the heights with a wholehearted effort. Weary and exhausted, I reached my brother, who had been waiting for me and was refreshed by a good long rest. For a while we went on together at the same pace. However, hardly had we left that rock behind us when I forgot the detour I had made just a short while before and was once more drawing down the lower regions. Again I wandered through the valleys, looking for the longer and easier path and stumbling only into longer difficulties. Thus I indeed put off the disagreeable strain of climbing. But nature is not overcome by man's devices; a corporeal thing cannot reach the heights by descending. What shall I say? My brother laughed at me; I was indignant; this happened to me three times and more within a few hours. So often was I frustrated in my hopes that at last I sat down in a valley. There I leaped in my winged thoughts from things corporeal to what is incorporeal and addressed myself in words like these:

"What you have so often experienced today while climbing this mountain happens to you, you must know, and to many others who are making their way toward the blessed life. This is not easily understood by us men, because the motions of the body lie open, while those of the mind are invisible and hidden. The life we call blessed is located on a high peak. 'A narrow way,' they say, leads up to it. Many hilltops intervene, and we must proceed 'from virtue to virtue' with exalted steps. On the highest summit is set the end of all, the goal toward which our pilgrimage is directed. Every man wants to arrive there. However, as Naso says: 'Wanting is not enough; long and you attain it.' You certainly do not merely want; you have a longing, unless you are deceiving yourself in this respect as in so many others. What is it, then, that keeps you back? Evidently nothing but the smoother way that leads through the meanest earthly pleasures and looks easier at first sight. However, having strayed far in error, you must either ascend to the summit of the blessed life under the heavy burden of hard striving, ill deferred, or lie prostrate in your slothfulness in the valleys of your sins. If

Throughout this paragraph, Petrarch quotes from the Bible and from Ovid's poetry.

▶ Is a difficult task necessarily more worthwhile than an easy one?

169

'darkness and the shadow of death' find you there—I shudder while I pronounce these ominous words—you must pass the eternal night in incessant torments."

You cannot imagine how much comfort this thought brought my mind and body for what lay still ahead of me. Would that I might achieve with my mind the journey for which I am longing day and night as I achieved with the feet of my body my journey today after overcoming all obstacles. And I wonder whether it ought not to be much easier to accomplish what can be done by means of the agile and immortal mind without any local motion "in the twinkling of the trembling eye" than what is to be performed in the succession of time by the service of the frail body that is doomed to die and under the heavy load of the limbs.

There is a summit, higher than all the others. The people in the woods up there call it "Sonny," I do not know why. However, I suspect they use the word in a sense opposite to its meaning, as is done sometimes in other cases too. For it really looks like the father of all the surrounding mountains. On its top is a small level stretch. There at last we rested from our fatigue. . . .

How often, do you think, did I turn back and look up to the summit of the mountain today while I was walking down? It seemed to me hardly higher than a cubit [about 18 inches] compared to the height of human contemplation, were the latter not plunged into the filth of earthly sordidness. This too occurred to me at every step: "If you do not regret undergoing so much sweat and hard labor to lift the body a bit nearer to heaven, ought any cross or jail or torture to frighten the mind that is trying to come nearer to God and set its feet upon the swollen summit of insolence and upon the fate of mortal men?" And this too: "How few will ever succeed in not diverging from this path because of fear of hardship or desire for smooth comfort? Too fortunate would be any man who accomplished such a feat—were there ever such anywhere. This would be him of whom I should judge the Poet was thinking when he wrote:

Happy the man who succeeded in baring the causes of things
And who trod underfoot all fear, inexorable Fate and
Greedy Acheron's uproar. . . .

How intensely ought we to exert our strength to get under foot not a higher spot of earth but the passions which are puffed up by earthly instincts."

Such emotions were rousing a storm in my breast as, without perceiving the roughness of the path, I returned late at night to the little rustic inn from which I had set out before dawn. The

This quotation is from St. Augustine's **Confessions,** in which he described his conversion to Christianity and repented for his wild youth. Petrarch took a copy of this book along with him on the climb.

The poetry is from Virgil.

170

moon was shining all night long and offered her friendly service to the wanderers. While the servants were busy preparing our meal, I withdrew quite alone into a remote part of the house to write this letter to you in all haste and on the spur of the moment. I was afraid the intention to write might evaporate, since the rapid change of scene was likely to cause a change of mood if I deferred it.

And thus, most loving father, gather from this letter how eager I am to leave nothing whatever in my heart hidden from your eyes. Not only do I lay my whole life open to you with the utmost care but every single thought of mine. Pray for these thoughts, I beseech you, that they may at last find stability. So long have they been idling about and, finding no firm stand, been uselessly driven through so many matters. May they now turn at last to the One, the Good, the True, the stably Abiding.

Farewell.

On the twenty-sixth day of April, at Malaucène.

▶ Does writing out one's thoughts sometimes clarify them?

# 8 A RELIGIOUS REFORMER: GIROLAMO SAVONAROLA

Renaissance men never confined themselves to secular interests, as the popularized picture of a lusty Renaissance would have us believe. Few of the elite abandoned traditional Catholicism. Their religious activities, however, tended to be more perfunctory than passionate. A vigorous secular life and a spirit of free inquiry competed with religion for the attention of Rennaissance humanists.

Outside Florence's circle of aristocrats, artists, and intellectuals, the Church retained a stronger hold on the minds and lives of ordinary people. Still, religion played a lesser role than it did in the Middle Ages. The otherworldliness of medieval Catholicism began to seem unsuited to bustling urban life. And the Church itself, governed from Rome by mortal men, failed to set a particularly pious example, being as vulnerable to secular influences as any other institution. The only significant religious movement of the Renaissance was directed against Church leaders instead of being inspired by them.

The leader of this movement was a Dominican friar, Girolamo Savonarola, who virtually ruled Florence for four years during the 1490's. Born in Ferrara in 1452, Savonarola received a typical humanist education and tried to blend new trends with the ancient

Catholic faith. But the worldly life in Ferrara repelled and shocked him, and he entered a monastery.

In 1491 Lorenzo de' Medici made Savonarola the prior of the Dominican monastery in Florence. There, Savonarola began to preach against the worldliness of Florentine life and its leaders, the Medici, and to predict punishment at the hands of an avenger. When an invading French army crossed the Alps in 1494, Savonarola's prophecy seemed to have come true. The Medici's rivals for power saw their opportunity and supported Savonarola; in the ensuing revolution, they expelled the Medici from the city. Savonarola became the head of the popular party in the government. For four years he was the most influential spiritual and political leader of Florence.

Piero de' Medici, Lorenzo's son, was the expelled ruler.

Like most leaders who capture the imagination of a people, Savonarola was a complex and compelling figure. Women fainted at his sermons. At Savonarola's urging, bands of young people scoured the city for symbols of vanity and high living to burn in huge bonfires. Although these burning symbols included a painting by Botticelli, this painter himself became a convert to Savonarola's ideals and renounced "pagan" ways. Eventually these activities and Savonarola's support of the French invaders aroused the anger of the pope and the Florentine elite. They combined against Savonarola, arrested him, brought him to trial for heresy, and finally hanged him and burned his body in 1498.

The Church trumped up these heresy charges in return for money paid to Pope Alexander VI by Savonarola's enemies.

Savonarola's ideals differ from those of the Renaissance humanists whose works you have read. As you examine the following selections from Savonarola's sermons, think about these questions:

1. Which aspects of Renaissance life offended Savonarola? Why?
2. What was Savonarola's conception of the good man? the good life? the good society? Did Savonarola believe in an active life? Explain.
3. According to Savonarola, how could the citizens of Florence reach the standards he set for them? Are Savonarola's ideals practical ones for modern man? Why, or why not?

# Savonarola's Sermons

Pasquale Villari, **Life and Times of Girolamo Savonarola,** trans. by Linda Villari (London: T. Fisher Unwin, Ltd., 1888), pp. 137, 140, 180–184.

### ON THE RULERS OF ITALY

. . . These wicked princes are sent to chastise the sins of their subjects; they are truly a sad snare for souls; their courts and palaces are the refuge of all the beasts and monsters of the earth, for they give shelter to ribalds and malefactors. These wretches flock to their halls because it is there that they find ways and means to satisfy their evil passions and unbridled lusts. There are the false councillors, who continually devise new burdens and new taxes to drain the blood of the people. There are the flattering philosophers and poets, who, by force of a thousand lies and fables, trace the genealogy of those evil princes back to the gods; but, and worse than all, there are the priests who follow in the same course. This is the city of Babylon, O my brethren, the city of the foolish and the impious, the city that will be destroyed of the Lord. . . .

Babylon, a city in ancient Mesopotamia, was famous as a center of luxury and worldly pleasure before it was captured by the Persians in 538 B.C.

## ON THE LEADERS OF THE CHURCH

. . . [W]e are now living in . . . evil days; the devil has called his followers together, and they have dealt terrible blows on the very gates of the temple. It is by the gates that the house is entered, and it is the prelates who should lead the faithful into the Church of Christ. Therefore the devil hath aimed his heaviest blows at them, and hath broken down these gates. Thus it is that no more good prelates are to be found in the Church. . . . Seest thou not that they do all things amiss? They have no judgment; . . . good things they deem evil, true things false, sweet things bitter, and *vice versa.* . . . See, how in these days prelates and preachers are chained to the earth by love of earthly things; the cure of souls is no longer their concern; they are content with the receipt of revenue; the preachers preach for the pleasure of princes, to be praised and magnified by them. . . . And they have done even worse than this, inasmuch as they have not only destroyed the Church of God, but built up another after their own fashion. This is the new Church, no longer built of living rock, namely, of Christians steadfast in the living faith and in the mould of charity; but built of sticks, namely, of Christians dry as tinder for the fires of hell. . . . Go thou to Rome and throughout Christendom; in the mansions of the great prelates and great lords, there is no concern save for poetry and the oratorical art. Go thither and see, thou shalt find them all with books of the humanities in their hands, and telling one another that they can guide men's souls by means of Virgil, Horace, and Cicero. Wouldst thou see how the Church is ruled by the hands of astrologers? And there is no prelate nor great lord that hath not intimate dealings with some astrologer, who fixeth the hour and the moment in which he is to ride out or undertake some piece of business. For these great lords venture not to stir a step save at their astrologer's bidding. . . .

Horace was an ancient Roman poet and satirist. Cicero was an ancient Roman orator, statesman, and philosopher around the time of Julius Caesar. He is credited with having formed the classical style of Latin writing.

At the birth of a child, an elite family commissioned an astrologer to draw up the child's horoscope.

173

But in this temple of theirs there is one thing that delighteth us much. This is that all therein is painted and gilded. Thus our Church hath many fine outer ceremonies for the solemnization of ecclesiastical rites, grand vestments and numerous draperies, with gold and silver candlesticks, and so many chalices that it is a majestic sight to behold. There thou seest the great prelates with splendid mitres of gold and precious stones on their heads, and silver crosiers in hand; there they stand at the altar decked with fine copes and stoles of brocade, chanting those beautiful vespers and masses, very slowly, and with so many grand ceremonies, so many organs and choristers, that thou art struck with amazement; and all these priests seem to thee grave and saintly men, thou canst not believe that they may be in error, but deem that all which they say and do should be obeyed even as the Gospel; and thus is our Church conducted.

Men feed upon these vanities and rejoice in these pomps, and say that the Church of Christ was never so flourishing, nor divine worship so well conducted as at present. . . . Likewise that the first prelates were inferior to these of our own times. . . . The former, it is true, had fewer gold mitres and fewer chalices, for, indeed, what few they possessed were broken up to relieve the needs of the poor; whereas our prelates, for the sake of obtaining chalices, will rob the poor of their sole means of support. But dost thou know what I would tell thee? In the primitive Church the chalices were of wood, the prelates of gold; in these days the Church hath chalices of gold and prelates of wood. These have introduced devilish games among us; they have no belief in God, and jeer at the mysteries of our faith!

What doest Thou, O Lord? Why dost Thou slumber? Arise, and come to deliver Thy Church from the hands of the devils; from the hands of tyrants, the hands of iniquitous prelates. . . . Be ye not scandalized, O my brethren, by these words; rather, when ye see that the righteous desire chastisement, know that it is because they seek to banish evil, so that the kingdom of our Blessed Lord, Jesus Christ, may flourish in the world. The only hope that now remains to us, is that the sword of God may soon smite the earth.

### AN APPEAL TO FLORENTINES

. . . Oh! would that I might persuade ye to turn away from earthly things, and follow after things eternal! Would God grant this grace to me and to ye, I should assuredly deem myself happy in this life. But this is a gift from God. None may come unto me, sayeth the Lord, unless he be brought by the Father. I cannot enlighten ye inwardly, I can only strike upon your ears; but what may that avail if your intellect be not enlightened, nor your affections kindled? . . . And how may this be done, save by the word of God? Labour, then, to comprehend His word, and do with yourselves as with corn, which to be made into flour must first be pounded and ground. Otherwise what would it avail to have full granaries, what to have the treasures of the Holy Spirit unless ye draw out their spiritual meaning? Therefore will I strive to do the work of the Apostles, making the Holy Scriptures known to ye; and to ye it behoves to be doers, and not only hearers of the word of God.

## ON THE BLESSED LIFE

. . . A human word is formed in separate and different ways by a succession of syllables, and therefore when one part of a word is pronounced, the others cease to exist; when the whole word has been uttered, it too ceases to exist. But the Divine Word is not divided into parts; it issues united in its whole essence; is diffused throughout the created world, living and enduring in all eternity, even as the heavenly light of which it is the companion. Wherefore it is *the word of life,* or rather is *the life,* and is one with the Father. It is true that we accept this word in various senses; sometimes by life we mean the state of being of living men, sometimes we regard it as meaning the occupation of living men: wherefore we say, The life of this man is knowledge, the life of the bird is song. But, truly, there is but one life, and it is God, since in Him alone have all things their being. And this is the blessed life that is the end of man, and in which infinite and eternal happiness is found. The earthly life is not only deceptive, but cannot all be enjoyed, inasmuch as it lacks unity. If thou lovest riches, thou must renounce the senses; if thou givest thyself up to the senses, thou must renounce knowledge; and if thou wouldst have knowledge, thou canst not enjoy offices. But the pleasures of the heavenly life may all be enjoyed in the vision of God, which is supreme felicity.

## A PARABLE

O Florence, the young man who went out on the high seas and complains that he is out of sight of the haven, stands here before you. To me it was told: Come, . . . leave thy home and thy land, leave everything. And I was led to the port—that is, to the religious life, which is the safe and sure haven for all who seek their salvation. I came to this port when I was twenty-three years of age. Two things I loved beyond all others, and it was they [who] led

Roberto Ridolfi, **The Life of Girolamo Savonarola** (New York: Alfred A. Knopf, Inc., 1959), pp. 103–105.

175

me to this port: freedom and peace. To keep my freedom I never took a wife, and to obtain peace I fled from the world and came to this port of religion, where I found freedom; and here I was able to do just as I wished, for I wanted and desired to do nothing but that which was told or commanded me.

I would not have wished to be a priest merely for my own greater peace; but because I wanted to do as I was told, for this I felt to be my freedom and my peace, I was led to become a priest. And so having reached that happy haven, I looked upon the waters of the sea of this world, and I saw that many fish swam around there, and, desiring to fish for them, I began to take a few small ones with my hook—that is, to draw with my preaching some souls to the port and the way of salvation. And because this pleased me well enough, the Lord set me in a ship and took me to fish in the high seas, and gently and gradually he brought me here, as you see; so that since I have come into the high seas, I see no port to which I might turn back, and where I may again find peace. ...
[T]roubles surround me on every side, and I cannot see what I should do. ...

O Lord, whither hast Thou led me? I say with Jeremiah: ... Lord, thou hast deceived me, and I was deceived. ... Thou art stronger than I, and hast prevailed. I, for wanting to catch these fish for You that they might be Yours, find myself on these high seas, and I see no port to which I might return to find my peace again. ... [W]oe is me, O my mother. ... [W]herefore came I forth out of the womb to see labour, and sorrow throughout the world? I was free and at peace. Now I am everyone's slave. I see everywhere war and discord coming upon me. ...

You see our ship where she is now, and yet the end of the voyage on which the Lord takes her is not in sight. Last night I disputed with Him, and I will tell you part of our discussion. He exhorted me to keep on my course, and I said: "Nay, Lord, take me back to the port and give me back my peace." And He answered: "There is no turning back: dost thou not see the contrary wind that drives thee on?" and I said: "Because Thou, Lord, dost not wish it, yet Thou art just, tell me if I may dispute with Thee awhile, though I am dust and ashes and Thou art Lord of all. Tell me, if I must go on over the seas of the world fishing for Thee, why here rather than elsewhere? What have I to do with Florence? I was born, as Thou knowest, in Ferrara and brought up there, and not in Florence." The Lord answered and said: "Dost thou not remember having read of the man who came down from Jerusalem to Jericho, and was assailed and wounded by thieves on the road, and there passed by men of his own people, and none of them helped him,

Jeremiah (c. 600 B.C.) was a prophet who preached in Jerusalem, advocating moral reform and predicting doom in a manner similar to Savonarola's.

▶ Does a good man have an obligation to persuade others to live a good life?

but only the Samaritan, a foreigner and a stranger, cared for him? . . . That is why thou, a stranger, hast come to preach here, outside thine own country." I answered the Lord reverently, and said: "Lord, I am not satisfied with this. I am happy to preach in the ordinary way to reprove vice and further the cause of virtue, here in Florence or whatever Thou wilt. But what have I to do with the state of Florence, to preach on it? . . ."

# 9 IDEALS OF LOVE: LYRIC POETRY OF THE RENAISSANCE

Two ideals of the relationships between men and women existed during the Middle Ages. One was the ascetic ideal of the monk or the nun who gave up marriage for service to God. The other was chivalric devotion of the knight to his lady fair, a theme that dominates minstrels' songs and much medieval popular literature. Renaissance Italians tended to emphasize the second of these ideals, the love of man for woman. They often expressed their love in an appropriate form, lyric poetry.

Renaissance society has often been pictured as thoroughly licentious. Many Renaissance personalities, even members of the clergy, took one mistress after another, some of whom bore children. Homosexuality was common among the elite. Renaissance men and women were not inclined to deny themselves the delights of the body. Much Renaissance poetry, however, stresses a love that transcends physical gratification. Many poets worshipped their women chastely from afar, comparing them to angels. Unrequited love of an ideal woman was a popular subject. To these themes, Renaissance poets added a worldly interest in the varieties of human emotion.

Instead of writing in Latin as medieval poets had done, Renaissance poets usually turned to the Italian vernacular, transforming everyday speech into a medium for the graceful expression of emotion. Reading 9 contains poems by four writers who were associated with Florence, and one anonymous poem. As you read them, think about the following questions:

1. How would you describe the careers of these poets? What do their careers tell us about the Renaissance ideal of the good man?

2. What poetic images describe the relationships of men and women in these poems? What do these images imply about the ideal of the good life?
3. Is there any way to combine the two major ideals of the relationships between men and women in these poems? Is it possible—and desirable—to have both at once?

# Six Lyric Poems

*A professor of medieval history reports that a student once described Dante thus: "He stands with one foot in the Middle Ages while with the other he salutes the rising star of the Renaissance." The thought is accurate if awkwardly expressed. Dante Alighieri was born in Florence in 1265. He was a politician and political theorist as well as the greatest poet in Italian history. His masterpiece, a long poem called the* Divine Comedy, *reflects many medieval ideals. But it was the first major poem written in the Italian vernacular, and it gave rise to a vast body of Renaissance poetry, particularly influencing the work of Petrarch. The following lyric is one of Dante's many poems to Beatrice, the woman he loved.*

Trans. by Dante Gabriel Rossetti, in **Lyric Poetry of the Italian Renaissance**, collected by L. R. Lind (New Haven: Yale University Press, 1954), p. 137.

**He will gaze upon Beatrice, by DANTE**

Because mine eyes can never have their fill
Of looking at my lady's lovely face,
I will so fix my gaze
That I may become blessed beholding her.

Even as an angel, up at his great height
Standing amid the light,
Becometh blessed by only seeing God:—
So, though I be a simple earthly wight,
Yet none the less I might,
Beholding her who is my heart's dear load,
Be blessed, and in the spirit soar abroad.
Such power abideth in that gracious one;
Albeit felt of none
Save of him who, desiring, honors her.

"Wight" is an archaic word for living creature.

*The next two poems were written by Petrarch to Laura, the wife of a French count. Petrarch first saw her in a church in 1327. He admired her from afar, for twenty-one years, until her*

178

*death. The poems are sonnets, lyric poems of fourteen lines. They illustrate two aspects of Renaissance poetry: the worship of a beautiful and unattainable lady, and the poet's interest in accurately describing his own emotions.*

## The divine Laura, by PETRARCH

She used to let her golden hair fly free
  For the wind to toy and tangle and molest;
  Her eyes were brighter than the radiant west.
  (Seldom they shine so now.) I used to see
Pity look out of those deep eyes on me.
  ("It was false pity," you would now protest.)
  I had love's tinder heaped within my breast;
  What wonder that the flame burned furiously?
She did not walk in any mortal way,
  But with angelic progress; when she spoke,
  Unearthly voices sang in unison.
She seemed divine among the dreary folk
  Of earth. You say she is not so today?
  Well, though the bow's unbent, the wound bleeds on.

Love Rimes of Petrarch, trans. by Morris Bishop (Ithaca, N.Y.: The Dragon Press, 1932). Reprinted by permission.

Pity, in the chivalric tradition, referred to the relief an ardently wooed lady gave or promised to give to her suitor, who suffered as though from a disease.

## The poet's grief, by PETRARCH

I find no peace and bear no arms for war,
  I fear, I hope; I burn yet shake with chill;
  I fly the Heavens, huddle to earth's floor,
  Embrace the world yet all I grasp is nil.
Love will not close nor shut my prison's door
  Nor claim me his nor leave me to my will;
  He slays me not yet holds me evermore;
  Would have me lifeless yet bound to my ill
Eyeless I see and tongueless I protest,
  And long to perish while I succor seek;
  Myself I hate and would another woo.
I feed on grief, I laugh with sob-racked breast,
  And death and life alike to me are bleak:
  My lady, thus I am because of you.

Trans. by T. G. Bergin, in **Lyric Poetry of the Italian Renaissance**, collected by L. R. Lind, p. 195. Reprinted by permission.

*Lorenzo de' Medici wrote many delightful poems and often had them set to melodies by court composers. Here he advises youth to enjoy the years that flee so swiftly by.*

Trans. by J. Arthur Symons, in **Poems by Arthur Symons** (New York: Dodd, Mead & Co., 1902).

**A carnival song, by LORENZO DE' MEDICI**

Fair is youth and void of sorrow;
    But it hourly flies away.
      Youths and maids, enjoy today;
Nought ye know about tomorrow.

Bacchus was the Greek god of wine and ecstasy. Ariadne, a princess, was his bride.

This is Bacchus and the bright
    Ariadne, lovers true!
They, in flying time's despite,
    Each with each find pleasure new;
These their Nymphs, and all their crew
    Keep perpetual holiday.
      Youths and maids, enjoy today;
Nought ye know about tomorrow.

The satyrs, in Greek mythology, were half man, half-horse, and highly sexed.

These blithe Satyrs, wanton-eyed,
    Of the Nymphs are paramours:
Through the caves and forests wide
    They have snared them mid the flowers;
Warmed with Bacchus, in his bowers,
    Now they dance and leap alway.
      Youths and maids, enjoy today.
Nought ye know about tomorrow.

These fair Nymphs, they are not loth
    To entice their lovers' wiles.
None but thankless folk and rough
    Can resist when Love beguiles.
Now enlaced, with wreathed smiles,
    All together dance and play.
      Youths and maids, enjoy today;
Nought ye know about tomorrow.

Silenus, in Greek mythology, was an elderly relative of the satyrs.

See this load behind them plodding
    On the ass! Silenus he,
Old and drunken, merry, nodding,
    Full of years and jollity;
Though he goes so swayingly,
    Yet he laughs and quaffs alway.
      Youths and maids, enjoy today;
Nought ye know about tomorrow.

Midas treads a wearier measure:
  All he touches turns to gold:
If there be no taste of pleasure,
  What's the use of wealth untold?
What's the joy his fingers hold,
  When he's forced to thirst for aye?
  Youths and maids, enjoy today:
Nought ye know about tomorrow.

Listen well to what we're saying;
  Of tomorrow have no care!
Young and old together playing,
  Boys and girls, be blithe as air!
Every sorry thought forswear!
  Keep perpetual holiday.
  Youths and maids, enjoy today;
Nought ye know about tomorrow.

Ladies and gay lovers young!
  Long live Bacchus, live Desire!
Dance and play; let songs be sung;
  Let sweet love your bosoms fire;
In the future come what may!
Youths and maids, enjoy today!
Nought ye know about tomorrow.
Fair is youth and void of sorrow;
  But it hourly flies away.

Midas, in Greek mythology, was granted by Dionysus the power to turn things to gold by touching them. Dionysus gave Midas that dangerous gift because Midas took care of a drunken satyr who staggered into his garden.

    *The famous painter, sculptor, and architect Michelangelo Buonarotti, like many other Renaissance artists, was also a fine poet. This poem is addressed to Vittoria Colonna, a close friend of Michelangelo's and the leading poetess of Renaissance Italy.*

### To Vittoria Colonna: the model and the statue, by MICHELANGELO

When divine Art conceives a form and face,
  She bids the craftsman for his first essay
  To shape a simple model in mere clay:
This is the earliest birth of Art's embrace.
From the live marble in the second place
  His mallet brings into the light of day
  A thing so beautiful that who can say
  When time shall conquer that immortal grace?

Trans. by J. Arthur Symons, in **Poems by Arthur Symons.**

Thus my own model I was born to be—
  The model of that nobler self, whereto
  Schooled by your pity, lady, I shall grow.
Each overplus and each deficiency
  You will make good. What penance then is due
  For my fierce heat, chastened and taught by you?

*The following anonymous poem is from fourteenth-century Italy. The speaker is clearly a young lady, and her words add another facet to the picture of Renaissance love.*

Trans. by L. R. Lind, in **Lyric Poetry of the Italian Renaissance,** collected by L. R. Lind, p. 251. Reprinted by permission.

**An arranged marriage**
Would it had pleased the Lord that I never was born!
O wretched, dolorous,
Fresh am I more than a rose,
And here I'm married to an old man, forlorn!

Ah, grief is mine! I'm lively, without a care,
I feel Love's tender arrow whizz my way.
Seeing myself in the mirror blonde and fair,
I look on a lovable girl;
And I pray that Jesus may hurl
His wrath upon those who gave me
My husband; he's old as can be,
And his beard is white and worn.

Would it had pleased the Lord that I never was born!
I might have stayed home alone,
Poor little girl I was then,
Than to live deprived of every joy that's known,
For I'll never be able to see the Springtime again!
Would it had pleased the Lord that I never was born!

▶ Should parents have the right to arrange marriages for their daughters? What are the pros and cons of such arrangements?

# 10  BOCCACCIO'S STORIES
# OF RENAISSANCE LIFE

Giovanni Boccaccio, like so many other humanists, spread his talents over a number of fields. His fame rests, however, upon one of the earliest prose works written in Italian, the *Decameron,* a collection of humorous, instructive, and sometimes ribald tales.

Boccaccio was born out of wedlock in Paris in 1313. His father, a minor Florentine banker and merchant, took his infant son back to Florence, married a Florentine woman, and raised Giovanni as a member of the family. Between the ages of seven and fifteen, the young Boccaccio studied under tutors in his parents' home, and then went to learn business under acquaintances of his father in Naples, where he stayed for thirteen years. Hating business, he continued his humanist studies there and had a passionate but platonic love affair with the daughter of the king of Naples; in his writings he immortalized her under the name Fiammetta. Boccaccio finished the *Decameron* when he was about forty years old. He became a close friend of Petrarch's and devoted the remainder of his life to classical studies. He died in 1375.

The *Decameron* is fiction. It cannot be used as absolute historical evidence about the way people lived, because the incidents in each story did not actually take place. Nevertheless, with one major exception—the lack of a moral sense—the *Decameron* represents the values of its time. Most Renaissance men and women recognized the importance of moral standards far more than Boccaccio reveals.

The *Decameron* is set in Florence in 1348, when the Black Death struck the city. In the book, seven ladies and three youths flee the plague, taking refuge in a great villa on a mountainside. There they while away their time by telling tales, one hundred in all, over a period of ten days. Each member of the group of ten tells a tale each day. Typical stories begin by connecting one tale to the next. These introductions have been included in this version. The excerpts below include three tales and part of the conclusion to the book. As you read, think about the following questions:

1. What are the personal characteristics of the men and women who emerge as heroes in the *Decameron*? What is the conception of the good life in these stories?
2. What sort of life do Boccaccio's characters lead? Is it active or contemplative? secular or otherworldly? What seems to be their conception of the good life?
3. Do you think Boccaccio had the same standards for the good man and the good life as the characters in his tales? Explain.

# Tales from the *Decameron*

## THE FIFTH DAY, THE NINTH TALE

*Federigo degli Alberighi loves, but is not beloved. He spends all his money in courtship and has nothing left but a falcon, and this*

Giovanni Boccaccio, **The Decameron,** trans. by Richard Aldington (New York: Doubleday & Company, Inc., 1930). Copyright, © 1930 by Mme. Catherine Guillaume. Reprinted by permission of Doubleday.

*he gives his lady to eat when she comes to visit him because there is nothing else to give her. She learns of this, changes her mind, takes him as her husband, and makes him a rich man.*

Filomena had ceased speaking, and the queen, seeing that nobody was left to speak except Dioneo (who had his privilege) and herself, began cheerfully as follows:

It is now my turn to speak, dearest ladies, and I shall gladly do so with a tale similar in part to the one before, not only that you may know the power of your beauty over the gentle heart, but because you may learn yourselves to be givers of rewards when fitting, without allowing Fortune always to dispense them, since Fortune most often bestows them, not discreetly but lavishly.

You must know then that Coppo di Borghese Domenichi, who was and perhaps still is one of our fellow citizens, a man of great and revered authority in our days both from his manners and his virtues (far more than from nobility of blood), a most excellent person worthy of eternal fame, and in the fullness of his years delighted often to speak of past matters with his neighbours and other men. And this he could do better and more orderly and with a better memory and more ornate speech than anyone else.

Among other excellent things, he was wont to say that in the past there was in Florence a young man named Federigo, the son of Messer Filippo Alberighi, renowned above all other young gentlemen of Tuscany for his prowess in arms and his courtesy. Now, as most often happens to gentlemen, he fell in love with a lady named Monna Giovanna, in her time held to be one of the gayest and most beautiful women ever known in Florence. To win her love, he went to jousts and tourneys, made and gave feasts, and spent his money without stint. But she, no less chaste than beautiful, cared nothing for the things he did for her nor for him who did them.

Now as Federigo was spending far beyond his means and getting nothing in, as easily happens, his wealth failed and he remained poor with nothing but a little farm, on whose produce he lived very penuriously, and one falcon which was among the best in the world. More in love than ever, but thinking he would never be able to live in the town any more as he desired, he went to Campi where his farm was. There he spent his time hawking, asked nothing of anybody, and patiently endured his poverty.

Now while Federigo was in this extremity it happened one day that Monna Giovanna's husband fell ill, and seeing death come upon him, made his will. He was a very rich man and left his estate to a son who was already growing up. And then, since he had

184

greatly loved Monna Giovanna, he made her his heir in case his son should die without legitimate children; and so died.

Monna Giovanna was now a widow, and as is customary with our women, she went with her son to spend the year in a country house she had near Federigo's farm. Now the boy happened to strike up a friendship with Federigo, and delighted in dogs and hawks. He often saw Federigo's falcon fly, and took such great delight in it that he very much wanted to have it, but did not dare ask for it, since he saw how much Federigo prized it.

While matters were in this state, the boy fell ill. His mother was very much grieved, as he was her only child and she loved him extremely. She spent the day beside him, trying to help him, and often asked him if there was anything he wanted, begging him to say so, for if it were possible to have it, she would try to get it for him. After she had many times made this offer, the boy said:

"Mother, if you can get me Federigo's falcon, I think I should soon be better."

The lady paused a little at this, and began to think what she should do. She knew that Federigo had loved her for a long time, and yet had never had one glance from her, and she said to herself:

"How can I send or go and ask for this falcon, which is, from what I hear, the best that ever flew, and moreover his support in life? How can I be so thoughtless as to take this away from a gentleman who has no other pleasure left in life?"

Although she knew she was certain to have the bird for the asking, she remained in embarrassed thought, not knowing what to say, and did not answer her son. But at length love for her child got the upper hand and she determined that to please him in whatever way it might be, she would not send, but go herself for it and bring it back to him. So she replied:

"Be comforted, my child, and try to get better somehow. I promise you that tomorrow morning I will go for it, and bring it to you."

The child was so delighted that he became a little better that same day. And on the morrow the lady took another woman to accompany her, and as if walking for exercise went to Federigo's cottage, and asked for him. Since it was not the weather for it, he had not been hawking for some days, and was in his garden employed in certain work there. When he heard that Monna Giovanna was asking for him at the door, he was greatly astonished, and ran there happily. When she saw him coming, she got up to greet him with womanly charm, and when Federigo had courteously saluted her, she said:

"How do you do, Federigo? I have come here to make amends for the damage you have suffered through me by loving me more

185

than was needed. And in token of this, I intend to dine today familiarly with you and my companion here."

"Madonna," replied Federigo humbly, "I do not remember ever to have suffered any damage through you, but received so much good that if I was ever worth anything it was owing to your worth and the love I bore it. Your generous visit to me is so precious to me that I could spend again all that I have spent; but you have come to a poor host."

So saying, he modestly took her into his house, and from there to his garden. Since there was nobody else to remain in her company, he said:

"Madonna, since there is nobody else, this good woman, the wife of this workman, will keep you company, while I go set the table."

Now, although his poverty was extreme, he had never before realised what necessity he had fallen into by his foolish extravagance in spending his wealth. But he repented of it that morning when he could find nothing with which to do honour to the lady, for love of whom he had entertained vast numbers of men in the past. In his anguish he cursed himself and his fortune and ran up and down like a man out of his senses, unable to find money or anything to pawn. The hour was late and his desire to honour the lady extreme, yet he would not apply to anyone else, even to his own workman; when suddenly his eye fell upon his falcon, perched on a bar in the sitting room. Having no one to whom he could appeal, he took the bird, and finding it plump, decided it would be food worthy such a lady. So without further thought, he wrung its neck, made his little maid servant quickly pluck and prepare it, and put it on a spit to roast. He spread the table with the whitest napery, of which he had some left, and returned to the lady in the garden with a cheerful face, saying that the meal he had been able to prepare for her was ready.

The lady and her companion arose and went to table, and there together with Federigo, who served it with the greatest devotion, they ate the good falcon, not knowing what it was. They left the table and spent some time in cheerful conversation, and the lady, thinking the time had now come to say what she had come for, spoke fairly to Federigo as follows:

"Federigo, when you remember your former life and my chastity, which no doubt you considered harshness and cruelty, I have no doubt that you will be surprised at my presumption when you hear what I have come here for chiefly. But if you had children, through whom you could know the power of parental love, I am certain that you would to some extent excuse me.

"But, as you have no child, I have one, and I cannot escape the common laws of mothers. Compelled by their power, I have come

186

to ask you—against my will, and against all good manners and duty—for a gift, which I know is something especially dear to you, and reasonably so, because I know your straitened fortune has left you no other pleasure, no other recreation, no other consolation. This gift is your falcon, which has so fascinated my child that if I do not take it to him, I am afraid his present illness will grow so much worse that I may lose him. Therefore, I beg you, not by the love you bear me (which holds you to nothing), but by your own nobleness, which has shown itself so much greater in all courteous usage than is wont in other men, that you will be pleased to give it me, so that through this gift I may be able to say that I have saved my child's life, and thus be ever under an obligation to you."

When Federigo heard the lady's request and knew that he could not serve her, because he had given her the bird to eat, he began to weep in her presence, for he could not speak a word. The lady at first thought that his grief came from having to part with his good falcon, rather than from anything else, and she was almost on the point of retraction. But she remained firm and waited for Federigo's reply after his lamentation. And he said:

"Madonna, ever since it has pleased God that I should set my love upon you, I have felt that Fortune has been contrary to me in many things, and have grieved for it. But they are all light in comparison with what she has done to me now, and I shall never be at peace with her again when I reflect that you came to my poor house, which you never deigned to visit when it was rich, and asked me for a little gift, and Fortune has so acted that I cannot give it to you. Why this cannot be, I will briefly tell you.

"When I heard that you in your graciousness desired to dine with me and I thought of your excellence and your worthiness, I thought it right and fitting to honour you with the best food I could obtain; so, remembering the falcon you ask me for and its value, I thought it a meal worthy of you, and today you had it roasted on the dish and set forth as best I could. But now I see that you wanted the bird in another form, it is such a grief to me that I cannot serve you that I think I shall never be at peace again."

And after saying this, he showed her the feathers and the feet and the beak of the bird in proof. When the lady heard and saw all this, she first blamed him for having killed such a falcon to make a meal for a woman; and then she inwardly commended his greatness of soul which no poverty could or would be able to abate. But, having lost all hope of obtaining the falcon, and thus perhaps the health of her son, she departed sadly and returned to the child. Now, either from disappointment at not having the falcon or because his sickness must inevitably have led to it, the child died not many days later, to the mother's extreme grief.

Although she spent some time in tears and bitterness, yet, since she had been left very rich and was still young, her brothers often urged her to marry again. She did not want to do so, but as they kept on pressing her, she remembered the worthiness of Federigo and his last act of generosity, in killing such a falcon to do her honour.

"I will gladly submit to marriage when you please," she said to her brothers, "but if you want me to take a husband, I will take no man but Federigo degli Alberighi."

At this her brothers laughed at her, saying:

"Why, what are you talking about, you fool? Why do you want a man who hasn't a penny in the world?"

But she replied:

"Brothers, I know it is as you say, but I would rather have a man who needs money than money which needs a man."

Seeing her determination, the brothers, who knew Federigo's good qualities, did as she wanted, and gave her with all her wealth to him, in spite of his poverty. Federigo, finding that he had such a woman, whom he loved so much, with all her wealth to boot, as his wife, was more prudent with his money in the future, and ended his days happily with her.

► Which is more important in a husband, wealth or good character?

One of O. Henry's stories, "The Gift of the Magi," has a similar plot: A husband sells his watch to buy his wife an expensive comb for Christmas, and the wife sells her beautiful long hair to buy her husband a watch-fob.

### THE SIXTH DAY, THE FOURTH TALE

*Chichibio, cook to Currado Gianfigliazzi, changes Currado's anger to laughter, and so escapes the punishment with which Currado had threatened him.*

Lauretta was silent, and they all praised Nonno; whereupon the queen ordered Neifile to follow next. And she said:

Amorous ladies, although quick wits often provide speakers with useful and witty words, yet Fortune, which sometimes aids the timid, often puts words into their mouths which they would never have thought of in a calm moment. This I intend to show you by my tale.

As everyone of you must have heard and seen, Currado Gianfigliazzi was always a noble citizen of our city, liberal and magnificent, leading a gentleman's life, continually delighting in dogs and hawks, and allowing his more serious affairs to slide. One day near Peretola his falcon brought down a crane, and finding it to be plump and young he sent it to his excellent cook, a Venetian named Chichibio, telling him to roast it for supper and see that it was well done.

Chichibio, who was a bit of a fool, prepared the crane, set it before the fire, and began to cook it carefully. When it was nearly done and giving off a most savoury odour, there came into the kitchen a young peasant woman, named Brunetta, with whom Chichibio was very much in love. Smelling the odour of the bird and seeing it, she begged Chichibio to give her a leg of it. But he replied with a snatch of song:

"You won't get it from me, Donna Brunetta, you won't get it from me."

This made Donna Brunetta angry, and she said:

"God's faith, if you don't give it me, you'll never get anything you want from me."

In short, they had high words together. In the end Chichibio, not wanting to anger his lady-love, took off one of the crane's legs, and gave it to her. A little later the one-legged crane was served before Currado and his guests. Currado was astonished at the sight, sent for Chichibio, and asked him what had happened to the other leg of the crane. The lying Venetian replied:

"Sir, cranes only have one leg and one foot."

"What the devil d'you mean," said Currado angrily, "by saying they have only one leg and foot? Did I never see a crane before?"

"It's as I say, Sir," Chichibio persisted, "and I'll show it you in living birds whenever you wish."

Currado would not bandy further words from respect to his guests, but said:

"Since you promise to show me in living birds something I never saw or heard of, I shall be glad to see it tomorrow morning. But, by the body of Christ, if it turns out otherwise I'll have you tanned in such a way that you'll remember my name as long as you live."

When day appeared next morning, Currado, who had not been able to sleep for rage all night, got up still furious, and ordered his horses to be brought. He made Chichibio mount a pad, and took him in the direction of a river where cranes could always be seen at that time of day, saying:

"We'll soon see whether you were lying or not last night."

Chichibio, seeing that Currado was still angry and that he must try to prove his lie, which he had not the least idea how to do, rode alongside Currado in a state of consternation, and would willingly have fled if he had known how. But as he couldn't do that, he kept gazing round him and thought everything he saw was a crane with two legs. But when they came to the river, he happened to be the first to see a dozen cranes on the bank, all standing on one leg as they do when they are asleep. He quickly pointed them out to Currado, saying:

"Messer, you can see that what I said last evening is true, that cranes have only one leg and one foot; you have only to look at them over there."

"Wait," said Currado, "I'll show you they have two."

And going up closer to them, he shouted: "Ho! Ho!" And at this the cranes put down their other legs and, after running a few steps, took to flight. Currado then turned to Chichibio, saying:

"Now, you glutton, what of it? D'you think they have two?"

In his dismay Chichibio, not knowing how the words came to him, replied:

"Yes, messer, but you didn't shout 'ho! ho!' to the bird last night. If you had shouted, it would have put out the other leg and foot, as those did."

Currado was so pleased with this answer that all his anger was converted into merriment and laughter, and he said:

"Chichibio, you're right; I ought to have done so."

So with this quick and amusing answer Chichibio escaped punishment, and made his peace with his master.

### THE SEVENTH DAY, THE FIRST TALE

*Gianni Lotteringhi hears a knock at his door by night, he wakes his wife and she makes him think it is a ghost. They go and exorcise it, and the knocking ceases.*

It would have pleased me better, Sir, if such had been your pleasure that some other person than I should have begun on the excellent topic of which we are to speak. But since you wish me to set an example to the others, I shall gladly do so. And I shall endeavour, dearest ladies, to say something which may be useful to you in the future; for if other women are as timorous as I am, especially of ghosts—though God knows I don't know what they are and never found anyone who did, and yet we all equally fear them—by carefully listening to my tale you will learn a good and holy prayer which will be most useful in driving them away when they come to you.

In the district of San Brancazio in Florence there lived a wool-comber named Gianni Lotteringhi, a man who was more skilled in his art than wise in other matters. Being a simple sort of man he was often made leader of the singers of Santa Maria Novella, and had to oversee their school. He filled many other such trivial offices, which gave him a high opinion of himself. This came about because he was a fairly wealthy man, and frequently made presents to the good friars. Now since he gave some of them hose, and some hoods, and some scapularies, they taught him useful prayers and the Paternoster in the vulgar tongue and the song of Saint Alesso, and the lament of San Bernardo, and the lauds of Madonna Matelda,

A scapulary is a monk's sleeveless outer garment. **Paternoster** is Latin for "Our Father," the first words of the Lord's Prayer. Laments and lauds are hymns.

190

and the like idiocies, which he esteemed greatly, and made much use of for the salvation of his soul.

His wife was a very beautiful, clever and charming woman, by name Monna Tessa, the daughter of Mannuccio de la Cuculia. Perceiving that her husband was a simpleton, and having fallen in love with a handsome young man named Federigo di Neri Pegolotti who was also in love with her, she arranged with her maid servant that Federigo should come to speak with her in a house which her husband had in Camerata. She spent the whole summer in this place; and Gianni sometimes came to stay there, and next morning returned to his business and his church singing.

Federigo, who desired her greatly, went there one evening by arrangement when Gianni was away, and with great delight dined and slept with the lady; and as she lay in his arms that night she taught him six of her husband's psalms. But, since neither she nor Federigo intended this to be the last time they were together, and since they did not want to send the servant for him each time, they made the following arrangement: every day when he visited or returned from a house he owned near there, he was to look into a vineyard near her house where he would see the skull of a donkey on one of the poles in the vineyard, and when the skull was turned in the direction of Florence he could come to her that evening in all security, and if he did not find the door open, he was to knock softly three times and she would open it for him; but when he saw the donkey's skull turned towards Fiesole, he was not to come, because Gianni would be here. And in this way they often managed to see each other.

But on one occasion when Federigo was to sup with Monna Tessa it happened that Gianni arrived late at night, after saying that he would not come. The lady was greatly distressed, and he and she supped on a little salted meat which she had had cooked separately; she ordered the servant to put into a white napkin two boiled fowls and a number of new laid eggs and a flask of good wine, and to lay them down at the foot of a peach tree which stood beside a lawn in the garden, that could be reached without going through the house—a place where she had more than once supped with Federigo. And she was so upset about all this that she quite forgot to tell the servant to wait until Federigo came and to tell him that Gianni was there, and that he was to take the things she had put in the garden. She and Gianni and the servant had not been long in bed when along came Federigo and tapped gently at the door, but she feigned sleep to prevent any suspicion of herself in Gianni's mind. After waiting a little, Federigo tapped a second time, and Gianni in surprise poked his wife, and said:

"Tessa, can you hear what I hear? Someone seems to be knocking at our door."

The lady, who had heard it better than he had, pretended to wake up, and said:

"What? Eh?"

"I say," persisted Gianni, "that someone seems to be knocking at our door."

"Knocking?" said the lady. "Why, dear Gianni, don't you know what it is? It's the ghost which has terrified me so much these last nights that as soon as I hear it I put my head under the clothes, and haven't dared to look out again until it was broad daylight."

"Come now," said Gianni, "don't be afraid. Before we went to bed I said the *Te lucis* and the *Intemerata* and other prayers, and blessed the bedposts in the name of the Father, the Son and the Holy Ghost; so there's no need to fear that it can do us any harm, whatever power it has."

The lady did not want Federigo to feel any suspicions about her and be angry, so she determined to get up and let him know that Gianni was there. She therefore said to her husband:

"Your words may have made you safe, but I shall never think myself safe and sound until we have exorcised it while you are here."

"But how can it be exorcised?" said Gianni.

"I know how to exorcise it," said the lady, "for when I went to the special church service at Fiesole the other day, one of those woman hermits—who is the most holy woman in the world, Gianni —seeing me so much terrified, taught me a holy and efficacious prayer; and she said she had made use of it more than once before she became a hermit, and had always found it worked. But God knows I never dared to go and test it by myself; but now that you are here, let us go together and exorcise it."

Gianni said he was quite ready; so they got up and went softly to the door where Federigo, already rather suspicious, was waiting. Said the lady to Gianni:

"Spit when I tell you to."

"Right!" said Gianni.

The lady then began the exorcism, and said:

"Spirit, spirit, who goest by night, by the path you came here, depart. Go to the garden, and there at the foot of the peach tree you will find a filthy dirty thing and a hundred droppings of my hen. Put a cork in the wine flask and depart, and do no harm to me and my Gianni."

She then said to her husband: "Spit, Gianni"; and Gianni spat. Federigo outside the door heard all this, and immediately recovered

192

from his jealousy and consequent ill-temper; indeed he was bursting with laughter and when Gianni spat he said softly:

"Your teeth!"

When the lady had exorcised the ghost three times in this way, she returned to bed with her husband.

Federigo, who had been expecting a supper and had none, understood the words of the exorcism perfectly well. He went into the garden, found the two fowls, the wine, and the eggs, at the foot of the large peach tree, took them home, and supped heartily. And afterwards, when he was with the lady, he often laughed over the exorcism with her.

True it is that some people say that the lady had turned the donkey's skull in the direction of Fiesole but that a workman passing through the garden gave it a knock with his stick, and turned it round in the direction of Florence, so that Federigo thought she had given the signal, and therefore came, and that lady's exorcism was after this fashion:

"Spirit, spirit, depart in God's name, for I didn't turn the donkey's skull, someone else did, God punish him, and I'm here with my Gianni."

And so Federigo had to go away without supper or bed. But a neighbour of mine, a very old lady, tells me that both versions are true, according to what she heard when a child. But the second did not happen to Gianni Lotteringhi but to a man named Gianni di Nello, who lived by the Porta San Piero, and was as big a fool as Gianni Lotteringhi.

And so, dear ladies, it is for you to choose which of the two you like the best, or both of them. They are most useful in such cases, as you have just heard. Try them, and you may yet be glad of them.


## THE AUTHOR'S CONCLUSION

Some of you may say that in writing these tales I have taken too much license, by making ladies sometimes say and often listen to matters which are not proper to be said or heard by virtuous ladies. This I deny, for there is nothing so unchaste but may be said chastely if modest words are used; and this I think I have done.

But suppose it to be true—and I shall not strive with you, for you are certain to win—I reply that I have many arguments ready. First, if there is any license in some of them, the nature of the stories demanded it; and if any understanding person looks at them with a reasonable eye he will see that they could not be related otherwise, unless I had altered them entirely. . . .

▶ Can pornographic literature lead young people astray?

In addition, anyone can see that these things were not told in church, where everything should be treated with reverent words and minds (although you will find plenty of license in the stories of the church); nor were they told in a school of philosophers, where virtue is as much required as anywhere else; . . . but they were told in gardens, in pleasure places, by young people who were old enough not to be led astray by stories, and at a time when everyone threw his cap over the mill and the most virtuous were not reproved for it.

But, such as they are, they may be amusing or harmful, like everything else, according to the persons who listen to them. . . .

No corrupt mind ever understands words healthily. And . . . so the well-disposed cannot be harmed by words which are somewhat less than virtuous. . . .

Those who have to say paternosters and play the hypocrite to their confessor can leave . . . [my tales] alone; my tales will run after nobody asking to be read. . . .

I suppose some people will say that some of the tales are too long. I reply that for those who have something else to do it is folly to read the tales, even when they are short. . . . To those who read for pastime, no tale can be too long if it succeeds in its object. Brevity befits students, who labour to spend time usefully, not to make it pass; but not you, ladies, who have unoccupied all that time you do not spend in love pleasures. . . .

I have no doubt that others will say that the things related are too full of jests and jokes, and that it ill befits a grave and weighty man to write such things. . . . Considering that the friars' sermons, which are made to censure men's sins, are full of jokes and jests and railleries, I think that such things do not go ill in my tales, which are written to drive away ladies' melancholy. However, if the tales make them laugh too much, they can easily cure that by reading the lamentations of Jeremiah, the passion of the Saviour and the penitence of Mary Magdalene. . . .

I leave it to every lady to say and think what she pleases; for me it is time to end my words, giving thanks humbly to Him who by His aid and after so much labour has brought me to the desired end.

And you, fair ladies, rest in peace in His grace; and if in reading any of these tales you find any pleasure, remember me.

194

# 11  THREE ARTISTS
# DISCUSS THEIR ART

Many people have never consciously assessed the quality of a work of art. And why should they? If a painting touches a responsive chord in the viewer, what need does he have for esthetic criteria? In reply to this question, art critics point to the new levels of appreciation that accompany knowledge. Experience with color, form, line, and texture can help you understand why an artist painted or sculptured a subject in a certain way, just as knowledge of the structure of language and verse forms can help you to understand poetry.

Renaissance artists understood this relationship between knowledge and enjoyment. In fact, many of them wrote art criticism, in which they expressed esthetic ideals. To the classical ideals of harmony and proportion, Renaissance artists added something new: a striving for the perfect representation of the real world. As wealthy Renaissance bankers and politicians began to demand portraits of themselves, artists learned to paint and carve natural-looking representations of living men. As scientists discovered laws that gave order to the world, artists began to discover laws that gave order to their work. Artists became mathematicians, calculating ways to depict distance as seen by the human eye, devising formulas to guide them in showing the human body in its correct proportions.

In Reading 11, three Florentine artists describe their ideals and standards. As you read their statements, think about the following questions:

1. What criteria for good portrait painting are implied by Vasari's praise of the *Mona Lisa*? Do you agree with Vasari's criteria? Why or why not?
2. What criteria for good sculpture are implied by Cellini's criticism of Bandinello's *Hercules and Cacus*? Do you agree with Cellini's criteria? Why or why not?
3. What seem to be Alberti's criteria for beauty in architecture? Do you think any of his criteria could be used to judge modern architecture? Explain.
4. What difference would it make in a person's life if he failed to develop criteria for judging painting, sculpture, and architecture? Have you developed criteria not mentioned by Vasari, Cellini, and Alberti? Explain.

# *Mona Lisa:* The Ideal Portrait

*Giorgio Vasari, himself a sixteenth-century painter and architect, is best known for the biographies he wrote of other Renaissance artists. In the following selection from his biography of Leonardo da Vinci, Vasari describes the* Mona Lisa *and suggests some criteria for the perfect portrait.*

Vasari's Lives of the Artists, ed. by Betty Burroughs (New York: Simon and Schuster, Inc., 1946), p. 194 Copyright, © 1946, by Betty Burroughs. Reprinted by permission of Simon & Schuster, Inc. British rights controlled by George Allen & Unwin Ltd.

For Francesco del Giocondo, Leonardo undertook to paint the portrait of Mona Lisa, his wife [La Gioconda], but, after loitering over it for four years, he left it unfinished. . . . Whoever desires to see how far art can imitate nature, may do so by observing this head wherein every subtlety and every peculiarity have been faithfully reproduced. The eyes are bright and moist, and around them are those pale, red, and slightly livid circles seen in life, while the lashes and eyebrows are represented with the closest exactitude with the separate hairs drawn as they issue from the skin, every turn being followed and all the pores exhibited in the most natural manner. The nose with its beautiful and delicately red nostrils might easily be believed to be alive. The mouth, admirable in outline, is rose tinted in harmony with the carnation of the cheeks, which seems not painted, but of flesh and blood. He who looks earnestly at the pit of the throat must fancy he sees the beating of the pulse. It is a marvel of art. Mona Lisa was very beautiful, and while he painted her, Leonardo had someone near at hand to sing or play to her, or to amuse her with jests, to keep from her that look of melancholy so common in portraits. . . .

# Cellini Attacks a Rival

*The following passage from Cellini's* Autobiography *describes an exchange between Cellini and a third-rate sculptor named Bandinello. In criticizing his rival, Cellini expressed some of his own ideals as well as those of other Florentine artists.*

Benvenuto Cellini, **Autobiography,** trans. by George Bull (Baltimore: Penguin Books, Ltd., 1956), pp. 336–337. Reprinted by permission.

The Duke stood there, listening with great enjoyment, and while I was talking Bandinello kept twisting and turning and making the most unimaginably ugly faces—and his face was ugly enough already. Suddenly the Duke moved off, making his way through some ground-floor rooms, and Bandinello followed him. The chamberlains took me by the cloak and led me after them. So we followed the Duke till his Most Illustrious Excellency reached an apartment where he sat down with Bandinello and me on either side of him.

Bandinello, *Hercules and Cacus*
Photo by Nino Mascardi, Manité

Michelangelo, *David*
Photo by Luis Villota,
Photo Researchers

In Roman mythology, Cacus was a fire-breathing monster who dared to steal some cattle from Hercules. In revenge Hercules slew him.

Traditionally, Italian Renaissance poets wrote sonnets in celebration of the unveiling of a public work of art.

A sacristy is a room in a church where sacred vestments and vessels are kept. Cellini is here referring to the sacristy of the church of San Lorenzo in Florence, usually called the Medici Chapel. Michelangelo adorned it with a magnificent group of sculpturés of the Medici family. Lorenzo and his brother Giuliano are buried here, their tombs flanked by Michelangelo's sculptures of saints.

I stood there without saying anything, and the men standing round —several of his Excellency's servants—all stared hard at Bandinello. . . . Then Bandinello began to gabble.

"My Lord," he said, "when I uncovered my Hercules and Cacus I am sure that more than a hundred wretched sonnets were written about me, containing the worst abuse one could possibly imagine this rabble capable of."

Replying to this, I said: "My lord, when our Michelangelo Buonarroti revealed his Sacristy, where there are so many fine statues to be seen, our splendid, talented Florentine artists, the friends of truth and excellence, wrote more than a hundred sonnets, every man competing to give the highest praise. As Bandinello's work deserved all the abuse that he says was thrown at it, so Buonarroti's deserved all the good that was said of it."

Bandinello grew so angry that he nearly burst: he turned to me and said: "And what faults can you point out?"

"I shall tell you if you've the patience to listen."

"Go on then."

The Duke and all the others who were there waited attentively, and I began.

First I said: "I must say that it hurts me to point out the defects in your work: but I shall not do that, I shall tell you what the artists of Florence say about it."

One moment the wretched fellow was muttering something unpleasant, the next shifting his feet and gesticulating; he made me so furious that I began in a much more insulting way than I would have done had he behaved otherwise.

"The expert school of Florence says that if Hercules' hair were shaven off there wouldn't be enough of his pate to hold in his brain; and that one can't be sure whether his face is that of a man or a cross between a lion and an ox; that it's not looking the right way; and that it's badly joined to the neck, so clumsily and unskilfully that nothing worse has ever been seen; and that his ugly shoulders are like the two pommels of an ass's pack-saddle; that his breast and the rest of his muscles aren't based on a man's but are copied from a great sack full of melons, set upright against a wall. The loins look as if they are copied from a sack of long marrows. As for the legs, it's impossible to understand how they're attached to the sorry-looking trunk; it's impossible to see on which leg he's standing, or on which he's balancing, and he certainly doesn't seem to be resting his weight on both, as is the case with some of the work done by those artists who know something. What can be seen is that he's leaning forward more than a third of a cubit; and this by itself is the worst and the most intolerable error that useless, vulgar craftsmen can make. As for the arms, it's said that they both stick out awkwardly, that they're so inelegant that it seems you've never set eyes on a live nude; that the right leg of Hercules is joined to that of Cacus in the middle in such a way that if one of the two were removed both of them—not merely one—would be without a calf. And they say that one of the feet of the Hercules is buried, and the other looks as if someone has lit a fire under it."

# An Architect's Standards of Beauty

*Leone Battista Alberti was a painter, musician, and scholar, but primarily an architect, among the greatest of fifteenth-century Italy. His emphasis on classical ideals was derived from his humanist studies, and he followed these ideals in his own work.*

It is my opinion that beauty, majesty, gracefulness, and the like charms consist in those particulars which, if you alter or take away, the whole would be made homely and disagreeable. . . . For every body consists of certain peculiar parts, of which if you take away any one, or lessen, or enlarge it, or remove it to an improper place, the beauty and grace of this body will at once be lamed and spoiled. . . .

What gives the beauty and grace to the whole . . . is that which we will call congruity, which we may consider as the original of all that is graceful and handsome. The business of congruity is to put together members differing from each other in their natures in such a manner that they form a beautiful whole. . . . This is what architecture chiefly aims at, and by this she obtains her beauty, dignity, and value.

The ancients . . . tried to imitate nature, as the greatest artist at all manner of compositions; and for this purpose the ancients labored, as far as the industry of man could reach, to discover the laws upon which nature herself acted in the production of her works. These laws the ancients transferred to architecture. . . . They found . . . that bodies were not always composed of equal parts or members; so it happens that, of the bodies produced by nature, some are smaller, some larger, and some middling. Considering that one building differed from another, because of the function it was to serve, . . . they found it necessary to make them of various kinds. Thus from an imitation of nature they invented three manners of adorning a building and gave them names drawn from their first inventors. One was better contrived for strength and duration: this they called Doric; another was more tapered and

Leon Battista Alberti, "The Art of Building," in **The Portable Renaissance Reader**, ed. James Bruce Ross and Mary Martin McLaughlin, pp. 528–531. Language simplified.

▶ Do you know a beautiful person whose individual features are only ordinary?

199

beautiful: this they named Corinthian; another was a kind of medium composed from the other two, and this they called Ionic. . . .

From the imitation of nature, they never made the ribs of their structure, that is to say, the columns, angles, and the like, in uneven numbers; as you shall not find any animal that stands or moves upon an odd number of feet. On the contrary, they made their doors and windows always in uneven numbers, as nature herself has done in some instances; for though in animals she has placed an ear, an eye, and a nostril on each side, yet the great aperture, the mouth, she has set singly in the middle.

# 12   THE ARTIST AS SCIENTIST: LEONARDO DA VINCI

In Leonardo da Vinci, the spirit of scientific inquiry that informed Renaissance art found its greatest genius. Today most artists study anatomy, but in Renaissance times religious zealots often charged students of anatomy with witchcraft, saying the body was the temple of the soul and should not be examined by inquisitive eyes. Nevertheless, Leonardo devoted himself to the study of the physical world. He dissected human cadavers as well as flowers, other plants, and animals, convinced that if he knew how something worked, he would be more able to draw it accurately.

Leonardo continually expanded his investigations and experiments. He studied geology, engineering, mathematics, botany, and architecture. He devised and sketched numerous inventions—military equipment, underwater vessels, flying machines—often prophetic, but mostly undeveloped in his lifetime. His *Notebooks*, twenty thousand pages of sketches, calculations, and notes, combine disorder with closely reasoned scientific solutions to problems of all kinds. They were written backward so that they can be read only in a mirror, a precaution Leonardo took to keep his ideas from the attention of fanatics who might accuse him of witchcraft.

Leonardo's fame rests largely on his paintings and drawings. He spent so much time collecting scientific data that he completed only a few major works of art. But his greatest paintings show the perfect naturalism that was the Renaissance ideal. Leonardo made thousands of sketches of heads, torsos, arms, legs, and features, both still and in motion, to achieve his masterful representation of the human body. He also showed himself a keen observer of human psychology: The lady called Mona Lisa has intrigued men for four centuries, and Leonardo was the first artist to paint the Last Supper as a study in human reactions to the personality of Christ. Yet, despite his great achievements, Leonardo was never satisfied. On page after page in the last of his *Notebooks* he wrote despairingly, "Tell me if anything at all was done."

This extraordinary man was born in a village outside the small town of Vinci near Florence in 1452. He was the illegitimate son of a lawyer and a woman who was probably a servant. Leonardo never received a classical education. He learned Latin in middle life but never mastered Greek. At thirty he left Florence to seek the patronage of the duke of Milan. He lived in Milan for twenty years, working as the duke's engineer, scenery designer, architect, and all-around resident artist. Later he found patrons in other cities. He died in France in 1519.

Reading 12 begins with a selection from Vasari's biography of Leonardo, then moves on to some selections from Leonardo's *Notebooks*. As you read, keep the following questions in mind:

1. List the activities to which Leonardo turned his attention. What does the list imply about Leonardo's view of the good man and the good life?
2. What Renaissance ideals does Vasari express in his evaluation of Leonardo?
3. How did Leonardo make a living? What does your conclusion tell you about how his patrons viewed the good life and the good society?
4. How did Leonardo seem to define his duty to himself? to his society? What personal values and ideals appear in the selection from his *Notebooks*?

# A Sixteenth-Century Account
# of Leonardo's Life

*Giorgio Vasari wrote biographies of sixty Renaissance artists. The account that follows is from his book.*

Truly admirable, indeed, and divinely endowed was Leonardo da Vinci, the son of Ser Piero da Vinci. He might have been a scientist if he had not been so versatile. But the instability of his character caused him to take up and abandon many things. In arithmetic, for example, he made such rapid progress during the

Vasari's Lives of the Artists, ed. by Betty Burroughs, pp. 187–197.

short time he studied it that he often confounded his teacher by his questions. He also began the study of music and resolved to learn to play the lute, and as he was by nature of exalted imagination, and full of the most graceful vivacity, he sang and accompanied himself most divinely, improvising both verses and music.

Though he divided his attention among pursuits so varied, Leonardo never abandoned his drawing, and also continued to model in relief, occupations which attracted him more than any others. His father, Ser Piero, observing this and taking into account the extraordinary character of his son's genius, took some of Leonardo's drawings to Andrea del Verrocchio, his intimate friend. He begged Andrea to tell him whether the boy showed promise. Verrocchio was amazed at these early efforts of Leonardo's and advised Ser Piero to see to it that his son become a painter. Leonardo was therefore sent to study in the shop of Andrea, whither he went most willingly. He studied not one branch of art only, but all. Admirably intelligent, and an excellent geometrician besides, Leonardo not only worked in sculpture—certain terra-cotta heads of smiling women and others of children done in early boyhood seem to be the work of a master—but, as an architect, designed ground plans and entire buildings; and, as an engineer, was the one who first suggested making a canal from Florence to Pisa by altering the river Arno. Leonardo also designed mills and water-driven machines. But, as he had resolved to make painting his profession, he spent most of his time drawing from life. He sometimes modeled clay figures on which he draped soft cloth dipped in plaster, and from these he made careful drawings on fine linen. He drew on paper also with so much care and so perfectly that no one has equaled him. Leonardo, imbued with power and grace, was endowed with so marvelous a facility, and his mind, his memory, and his hand were so efficient in the service of his intellect, that he confounded every antagonist.

Leonardo was frequently occupied in the preparation of plans to remove mountains or to pierce them with tunnels from plain to plain. By means of levers, cranes, and screws, he showed how to lift or move great weights. Designing dredging machines and inventing the means of drawing water from the greatest depths were among the speculations from which he never rested. Many drawings of these projects exist which are cherished by those who practice our arts. . . . Among Leonardo's models and drawings is one by means of which he sought to prove to the ruling citizens of Florence, many of them men of great discernment, that the church of San Giovanni could be raised and mounted upon a flight of steps without injury to the building. . . .

Though his patrimony was a mere pittance, . . . Leonardo kept many servants and horses, taking extraordinary delight in the latter. He was fond of all animals, and it is told that he used to buy caged birds only to set them free. Leonardo, in mind and spirit, gave evidence of such admirable power and perfection that whatever he did bore an impress of harmony, truthfulness, goodness, sweetness, and grace, beyond all other men.

Leonardo, with his profound comprehension of art, began many things that he never completed, because it seemed to him that perfection must elude him. He frequently formed in his imagination enterprises so difficult and so subtle that they could not be entirely realized and worthily executed by human hands. His conceptions were varied to infinity. In natural philosophy, among other things, he examined plants and observed the stars—the movements of the planets, the variations of the moon, and the course of the sun.

Leonardo afterward gave his attention to human anatomy, in company with Messer Marcantonio della Torre, an eminent philosopher. . . . Leonardo filled Marcantonio's book with drawings in red crayon outlined with the pen. These were drawn with the utmost care from bodies dissected by his own hand. He set forth the structure, arrangement, and disposition of the bones. Later he added the nerves in their due order, and then the muscles. He wrote an explanation, left-handed and backward, that can be read only with a mirror. . . . It seems almost incredible that this sublime genius could discourse, as he had done, of art, and of the muscles, nerves, veins, and every other part of the frame. There are besides, other writings of Leonardo's, also written with the left hand. They treat of painting and design in general and his theory of color. . . .

There was constant discord between Michelangelo Buonarroti and Leonardo. Michelangelo even left Florence because of it, and Duke Giuliano excused him by saying that the pope had summoned him to Rome. When Leonardo heard of this, he departed for France to the court of the King [Francis I] who already owned several of his works and wished him to paint the cartoon of Saint Anne. Leonardo kept him waiting according to his custom, a long time. Finally, being old, he lay sick for many months. When he found himself near death he made every effort to acquaint himself with the doctrine of the Catholic ritual. Then he confessed himself with great penitence and devoutly received the sacrament, sustained, because he could not stand, by his servants and friends. The King, who used to visit him often, came immediately afterward to his room. Leonardo was lamenting to him his fear that he had offended God and man, since he had not labored in art as he should have

▶ Do you like to look at lions or tigers pacing restlessly in their cages at the zoo?

A cartoon, in this sense, is a preliminary sketch over which the artist does a final tapestry, mosaic, or fresco (painting in wet plaster).

203

done, when he was seized with a violent paroxysm, the forerunner of death. The king rose and supported his head to assist him, in the hope of alleviating his pain, and Leonardo departed this life in the arms of the monarch.

# The *Notebooks*

*Each of the following short quotations comes from one of Leonardo's* Notebooks, *in which he recorded many of his ideas about art and man. The quotations represent Leonardo's thoughts about a variety of subjects.*

The Notebooks of Leonardo da Vinci, ed. by Pamela Taylor (New York: The New American Library, Inc., 1960), pp. 189, 190, 197, 198–201.

▶ Should society condemn capital punishment?

Obstacles cannot crush me.

Every obstacle yields to stern resolve.

He who is fixed to a star does not change his mind.

And you, O Man, who will discern in this work of mine the wonderful works of Nature, if you think it would be a criminal thing to destroy it, reflect how much more criminal it is to take the life of a man; and if this, his external form, appears to thee marvelously constructed, remember that it is nothing as compared with the soul that dwells in that structure; for that indeed, be it what it may, is a thing divine. Leave it then to dwell in His work at His good will and pleasure, and let not your rage or malice destroy a life—for, indeed, he who does not value it, does not himself deserve it.

All our knowledge has its origin in our perceptions.

Science is the observation of things possible, whether present or past. . . .

Avoid studies of which the result dies with the worker.

Men wrongly complain of Experience; with great abuse they accuse her of leading them astray, but they set Experience aside, turning from it with complaints as to our ignorance causing us to be carried away by vain and foolish desires to promise ourselves, in her name, things that are not in her power; saying that she is fallacious. Men are unjust in complaining of innocent Experience, constantly accusing her of error and of false evidence.

To lie is so vile, that even if it were in speaking well of godly things it would take off something from God's grace; and truth is so excellent that if it praises but small things they become noble.

Learning acquired in youth arrests the evil of old age; and if you understand that old age has wisdom for its food, you will so conduct yourself in youth that your old age will not lack for nourishment.

The acquisition of any knowledge is always of use to the intellect, because it may thus drive out useless things and retain the good.

For nothing can be loved or hated unless it is first known.

As a day well spent procures a happy sleep, so a life well employed procures a happy death.

The water you touch in a river is the last of that which has passed, and the first of that which is coming. Thus it is with time present.

Just as eating against one's will is injurious to health, so study without a liking for it spoils the memory, and it retains nothing it takes in.

It seems to me that men of coarse and clumsy habits and of small knowledge do not deserve such fine instruments nor so great a variety of natural mechanisms as men of speculation and of great knowledge; but merely a sack in which their food may be stowed and whence it may issue, since they cannot be judged to be anything else than vehicles for food; for it seems to me they have nothing about them of the human species but the voice and the figure, and for all the rest are much below beasts.

▶ Do highly talented people deserve more of the world's goods?

That is not riches, which may be lost; virtue is our true good and the true reward of its possessor. That cannot be lost; that never deserts us, but when life leaves us. As to property and external riches, hold them with trembling; they often leave their possessor in contempt, and mocked at for having lost them.

That man is of supreme folly who always wants for fear of wanting; and his life flies away while he is still hoping to enjoy the good things which he has with extreme labor acquired.

We ought not to desire the impossible.

Ask counsel of him who rules himself well.

The man who does not restrain wantonness, allies himself with beasts.

You can have no dominion greater or less than that over yourself.

He who thinks little, errs much.

The memory of benefits is a frail defense against ingratitude.

Reprove your friend in secret and praise him openly.

A simile for patience. Patience serves us against insults precisely as clothes do against the cold. For if you multiply your garments as the cold increases, that cold cannot hurt you; in the same way increase your patience under great offenses, and they cannot hurt your feelings.

Threats alone are the weapons of the threatened man.

He who walks straight rarely falls.

It is ill to praise, and worse to reprimand in matters that you do not understand.

# 13   THE STATE AND THE GOOD SOCIETY

Niccolò Machiavelli, author of the selections in this reading, was born in 1469 into a poor but distinguished Florentine family. Largely self-educated, Machiavelli started his political career in 1498, just after Savonarola was executed, by winning an appointment as secretary and diplomatic agent for one of the councils that headed the republican government. He later undertook diplomatic missions all over Europe.

In 1512 the Medici returned to power. Machiavelli, as a member of the overthrown government, was removed from office and accused of conspiring against the state. Although he insisted upon his innocence, even under torture, his political career seemed ruined. Impoverished and disheartened, he retreated to a small country home. There, during the year 1513, he wrote most of two books.

The shorter of those books, called *The Prince,* was dedicated to the new Medici ruler of Florence. Its immediate purpose was to flatter the ruler into offering Machiavelli a government job. Although *The Prince* failed to achieve that purpose, it became one of the most famous and controversial books in the history of political theory.

Part of the controversy surrounds the very meaning of *The Prince.* In form, it is a guidebook written in a cold-blooded and straightforward tone and full of advice for an Italian prince. Whether Machiavelli meant *The Prince* to be a guidebook for a new savior of Italy or a sardonic commentary on the degraded level of Italian politics remains uncertain. Whatever Machiavelli's motives, however, *The Prince* stands as the first keenly realistic analysis of how politics actually works. A modern scholar has summarized the book as follows:

The quotation is from Garrett Mattingly, "Machiavelli," in **Renaissance Profiles,** ed. by J. H. Plumb (Harper Torchbook Series; New York: Harper & Row, Publishers, 1961), pp. 31–32.

As for its contents: *The Prince* lays it down as a major premise that men in general are selfish, treacherous, cowardly, greedy, and, above all, gullible and stupid. It therefore advises a prince, and particularly a new prince who hopes to destroy the liberties of those he rules, to employ hypocrisy, cruelty, and deceit, to make himself feared even at the risk of making himself hated, to divide the people and destroy their natural leaders, and to keep faith with no one, since no one will keep faith with him. It views the world of politics as a jungle in which moral laws and standards of ethical conduct are merely snares for fools, a jungle in which there is no reality but power, and power is the reward of ruthlessness, ferocity, and cunning. . . . To a society which regarded the relations between its parts as ruled by justice and equity and sanctified by religion, all this was more shocking than we can quite imagine.

While Machiavelli was writing *The Prince*, he was also working on another volume, *The Discourses on the First Ten Books of Livy*. In this work, longer and more scholarly than *The Prince*, Machiavelli spelled out his ideas of what government ought to be if it were to foster a good society. As you read the following excerpts from *The Discourses*, keep these questions in mind:

1.  According to this account, what would a good government be like? What would it give to citizens? What sort of political institutions would it have?
2.  Who is responsible for maintaining the sort of government that can contribute to a good society? Are all of these people government officials?
3.  What does Machiavelli imply about the connection between the good man and the good society? What can the good man contribute to the society of which he is a part? Why should he make a contribution?
4.  On what sort of reasoning does Machiavelli base his conclusions? Does he argue from an ethical position? Does he base his arguments on historical examples? Do you find the basis of his reasoning satisfactory as a guide to conduct? Why?

## *The Discourses on the First Ten Books of Livy*

. . . Those who have written about states say that there are to be found in them one of three forms of government, called by them *Principality*, *Aristocracy*, and *Democracy*, and that those who set up a government in any particular state must adopt one of them, as best suits their purpose.

Others—and with better judgment many think—say that there are six types of government of which three are very bad, and three are good in themselves but easily become corrupt, so that they too must be classed as pernicious. Those that are good are the three above mentioned. Those that are bad are the other three, which depend on them, and each of them is so like the one associated with it that it easily passes from one form to the other. For *Principality* easily becomes *Tyranny*. From *Aristocracy* the transition to *Oligarchy* is an easy one. *Democracy* is without difficulty converted into *Anarchy*. So that if anyone who is organising a commonwealth sets up one of the three first forms of government, he sets up what will last but for a while, since there are no means whereby to prevent it passing into its contrary. . . .

Niccolò Machiavelli, **The Discourses**, trans. by Leslie J. Walker (New Haven: Yale University Press, 1950), Vol. I, pp. 212, 214–215, 220–222, 450–463. Reprinted by permission of Routledge & Kegan Paul, Ltd.

I maintain that all the forms of government mentioned above are far from satisfactory, the three good ones because their life is so short, the three bad ones because of their inherent malignity. Hence prudent legislators, aware of their defects, refrained from adopting as such any one of these forms, and chose instead one that shared in them all, since they thought such a government would be stronger and more stable, for if in one and the same state there was principality, aristocracy, and democracy each would keep watch over the other.

Lycurgus was a Spartan ruler of the ninth century B.C.

Lycurgus is one of those who have earned no small measure of praise for constitutions of this kind. For in the laws which he gave to Sparta, he assigned to the kings, to the aristocracy, and to the populace each its own function, and thus introduced a form of government which lasted for more than eight hundred years to his very great credit and to the tranquillity of that city.

Solon governed Athens in the sixth century B.C.

It was not so in the case of Solon, who drew up laws for Athens, for he set up merely a democratic form of government, which was so short lived that he saw before his death the birth of a tyranny . . . ; and though, forty years later, . . . Athens returned to liberty because it again adopted a democratic form of government in accordance with Solon's laws, it did not retain its liberty for more than a hundred years. For, in spite of the fact that many constitutions were made whereby to restrain the arrogance of the upper class and the licentiousness of the general public, for which Solon had made no provision, nonetheless Athens had a very short life as compared with that of Sparta because with democracy Solon had not blended either princely [or aristocratic] power. . . .

▶ Can any democracy survive without institutions that protect minority rights?

Those who have displayed prudence in constituting a republic have looked upon the safeguarding of liberty as one of the most essential things for which they had to provide, and according to the efficiency with which this has been done liberty has been enjoyed for a longer or a shorter time. And, since in every republic there is an upper and a lower class, it may be asked into whose hands it is best to place the guardianship of liberty. By the [Spartans], and in our day by Venice, it was entrusted to the nobles, but by the Romans it was entrusted to the plebs [common people].

▶ Which is the more dangerous group in our society, the wealthy who want to cut taxes or the poor who demand a better life?

It is necessary, therefore, to enquire which of these republics made the better choice. If we appeal to reason arguments may be adduced in support of either thesis; but, if we ask what the result was, the answer will favour the nobility, for the freedom of Sparta and of Venice lasted longer than did that of Rome.

Let us deal first with the appeal to reason. It may be urged in support of the Roman view that the guardianship of anything should be placed in the hands of those who are less desirous of appropriating it to their own use. And unquestionably if we ask what it is the nobility are after and what it is the common people are after, it will be seen that in the former there is a great desire to dominate and in the latter merely the desire not to be dominated. . . . So that if the populace be made the guardians of liberty, it is reasonable to suppose that they will take more care of it, and that, since it is impossible for them to usurp power, they will not permit others to do so. . . .

Turning now to the question as to which are more harmful in a republic, the "have-nots" who wish to have or the "haves" who are afraid of losing what they have, I would point out that when Marcus Menenius was appointed dictator and Marcus Fulvius master of horse, both of them plebeians, in order to investigate certain conspiracies formed in Capua against Rome, the people empowered them to enquire also about those in Rome who, moved by ambition, had sought to obtain the consulship and other posts in the city by other than the accepted methods. To the nobility it looked as if the authority thus vested in the dictator was a hit at them, so they spread it about in Rome that it was not the nobles who had ambitioned these positions and used out of the way means to get them, but commoners who, having neither blood nor virtue on which to rely, sought to obtain these posts by roundabout methods, and in particular they accused the dictator of this. So much weight was attached to this accusation that Menenius, having made a speech in which he refuted the calumnies spread by the nobles, resigned the dictatorship, and submitted his actions to the judgment of the people. He defended his own case and was acquitted.

At the trial there arose considerable discussion as to whether the "haves" or the "have-nots" were the more ambitious, for the appetites of both might easily become the cause of no small disturbance. Actually, however, such disturbances are more often caused by the "haves," since the fear of losing what they have arouses in them the same inclination we find in those who want to get more, for men are inclined to think that they cannot hold securely what they possess unless they get more at others' expense. Furthermore, those who have great possessions can bring about changes with greater effect and greater speed. And yet again their corrupt and grasping deportment arouses in the minds of the "have-nots" the desire to have, either to revenge themselves on those who have despoiled them, or that they may again share in those riches and honours in regard to which they deem themselves to have been badly used by the other party. . . .

It is . . . essential that men who live together under any constitution should frequently have their attention called to it either by some external or by some internal occurrence. When internal, such occurrences are usually due to some law which from time to time causes the members of this body to review their position; or again to some good man who arises in their midst and by his example and his virtuous deeds produces the same effect as does the constitution.

Such benefits, therefore, are conferred on a republic either by the virtue of some individual or by the virtue of an institution. In regard to the latter, the institutions which caused the Roman republic to return to its start were the introduction of plebeian tribunes, of the censorship, and of all the other laws which put a check on human ambition and arrogance; to which institutions life must needs be given by some virtuous citizen who co-operates strenuously in giving them effect despite the power of those who contravene them. . . .

In regard to this, those who governed the state of Florence from 1434 to 1494 used to say that it was necessary to reconstitute the government every five years; otherwise it was difficult to maintain it; where by "reconstituting the government" they meant instilling men with that terror and that fear with which they had instilled them when instituting it in that at this time they had chastised those who, viewed from the standpoint of this regime, had misbehaved. As, however, the remembrance of this chastisement disappears, men are emboldened to try something fresh and to talk sedition. Hence provision has of necessity to be made against this by restoring that government to what it was at the start.

Such a return to their starting-point in republics is sometimes due to the simple virtue of one man alone, independently of any laws spurring [him] to action. For of such effect is a good reputation and good example that men seek to imitate it, and the bad are ashamed to lead lives which go contrary to it. . . . If then effective action of the kind described above, together with this setting of good example, had occurred in . . . Rome at least every ten years, it necessarily follows that it would never have been corrupt. But when both the one and the other began to occur more rarely, corruption began to spread. For, after the time of Marcus Regulus, there appeared no examples of this kind, and, though in Rome there arose the two Catos, between them and any prior instance there was so great an interval, and again between the Catos themselves, that they stood alone and their good example could have no good effect; especially in the case of the younger Cato who found the greater part of the city so corrupt that he could not by his example

Cosimo, Lorenzo, and Piero de' Medici ruled from 1434 to 1494.

Marcus Regulus was a Roman hero of the third century B.C. Cato the Elder was a Roman statesman of the second century B.C. Cato the Younger lived in the first century B.C.; he was a statesman and philosopher. All three fought against corruption in Rome.

effect any improvement amongst the citizens. So much then for republics.

As to religious institutions one sees here again how necessary these renovations are from the example of our own religion, which, if it had not been restored to its starting-point by St. Francis and St. Dominic, would have become quite extinct. For these men by their poverty and by their exemplification of the life of Christ revived religion in the minds of men in whom it was already dead, and so powerful were these new religious orders that they prevented the depravity of prelates and of religious heads from bringing ruin on religion. They also lived so frugally and had such prestige with the populace as confessors and preachers that they convinced them it is an evil thing to talk evilly of evil doing, and a good thing to live under obedience to such prelates, and that, if they did wrong, it must be left to God to chastise them. And, this being so, the latter behave as badly as they can, because they are not afraid of punishments which they do not see and in which they do not believe. It is, then, this revival which has maintained and continues to maintain this religion. . . .

The conclusion we reach, then, is that there is nothing more necessary to a community, whether it be a religious establishment, a kingdom, or a republic, than to restore to it the prestige it had at the outset, and to take care that either good institutions or good men shall bring this about rather than that external force should give rise to it. For though this on occasion may be the best remedy, as it was in Rome's case, it is so dangerous that in no case is it what one should desire.

St. Francis of Assisi (1182–1226) founded the Franciscan friars in Italy. He preached humility, simplicity, and joy in God's creation; one of the most popular stories about him is that he preached a sermon to the birds. At about the same time, St. Dominic (1170–1221) founded a similar order of friars in France.

# 14 LIVING THE GOOD LIFE IN THE GOOD SOCIETY

Francesco Guicciardini, a Florentine diplomat, politician, and historian, kept an informal diary in which he jotted down at odd moments his thoughts about government and society. He left these notes, called *Ricordi*, to his descendants to read and contemplate.

Francesco Guicciardini was born in Florence in 1483 to an aristocratic family. He became a lawyer and was elected to several minor governmental posts in Florence. In 1511 he was elected ambassador to Spain. Later he held similar posts for the government of Florence and for the pope. The *Ricordi* reflect his experiences as a diplomat and an administrator who had to deal with men.

Guicciardini wrote histories of Florence and Italy, kept elaborate family records, and carried on an extensive correspondence with the great and near great of the early decades of the sixteenth century. To the modern reader, however, his *Ricordi* are by far the most interesting of his works. They have been called the most practical handbook ever written for gaining and keeping power in a society where groups compete for the reins of government. Keep in mind that Guicciardini did not always act on his ideals of freedom and republicanism. To prosper under the government in power was his principal goal.

Imagine that you are about to enter the world and assume a responsible position. Your father has passed the *Ricordi* on to you as a practical guide to behavior. As you read and study them, think about the following questions:

1. What are the characteristics of a man who follows Guicciardini's maxims? Is he a good man?
2. Which is the better guide to public life, the study of political and social theory or examples drawn from the actual experiences of other men?
3. What kind of government is most likely to bring about a good society in Guicciardini's opinion? Why this type and not another?
4. Will Guicciardini's advice be useful in other circumstances than sixteenth-century Florence? What warning about his maxims would you give to a reader who lives in a democracy in the twentieth century?

# Maxims and Reflections of a Renaissance Statesman

*Each of the short paragraphs that follow has been taken in its entirety from the fourth collection of maxims compiled by Guicciardini in 1530. They are numbered as they were in the original collection, which totaled 221.*

Francesco Guicciardini, **Maxims and Reflections of a Renaissance Statesman,** trans. by Mario Domandi (Harper Torchbook Series; New York: Harper & Row, Publishers, 1965), **passim.** Copyright, © 1965, by Mario Domandi. Reprinted by permission of Harper & Row, Inc.

5. If men were respectful or grateful enough, it would be the duty of a master to benefit his servants on every occasion, as much as he could. But experience shows—and I have seen this to be the case with my own servants—that as soon as they get their fill, or

as soon as the master is unable to treat them as generously as he has in the past, they leave him flat. Thus, to best serve his own interests, a master must be tight-fisted, more readily inclined to be stingy rather than liberal. He must retain their allegiance with hopes rather than deeds. Now, for that to be successful, he must occasionally be very generous to just one of them; and that is enough. For the nature of men is such that hope, as a rule, is stronger than fear. They are more excited and pleased by the sight of one man well rewarded than they are frightened by seeing many men treated poorly.

8. If either necessity or contempt induces you to speak ill of another, at least be careful to say things that will offend only him. For instance, if you want to insult a particular person, do not speak ill of his country, his family, or his relatives. It is great folly to offend many if you only want to insult one man.

10. Let no one trust so much in native intelligence that he believes it to be sufficient without the help of experience. No matter what his natural endowments, any man who has been in a position of responsibility will admit that experience attains many things which natural gifts alone could never attain.

14. Nothing is more precious than friends; therefore, lose no opportunity to make them. Men will always get together to talk; and friends can help, and enemies can harm you, in times and places you would never have expected.

17. Do not believe those who say they have voluntarily relinquished power and position for love of peace and quiet. Nearly always, their reason was either levity [lack of seriousness] or necessity. Experience shows that, as soon as they are offered a chance to return to the former life, they leave behind their much vaunted peace and quiet, and seize it with the same fury that fire seizes dry or oily things.

25. Be careful not to do anyone the sort of favor that cannot be done without at the same time displeasing others. For injured men do not forget offenses; in fact, they exaggerate them. Whereas the favored party will either forget or will deem the favor smaller than it was. Therefore, other things being equal, you lose a great deal more than you gain.

30. If you consider the matter carefully, you cannot deny that Fortune has great power over human affairs. We see these affairs constantly being affected by fortuitous circumstances that men could neither foresee nor avoid. Although cleverness and care may accomplish many things, they are nevertheless not enough. Man also needs good Fortune.

32. Ambition is not a reprehensible quality, nor are ambitious

men to be censured, if they seek glory through honorable and honest means. In fact, it is they who produce great and excellent works. Those who lack this passion are cold spirits, inclined more toward laziness than activity. But ambition is pernicious and detestable when it has as its sole end power, as is generally the case with princes. And when they make it their goal, they will level conscience, honor, humanity, and everything else to attain it.

46. In my administrations I never liked cruelty or excessive punishments. Nor are they necessary. Except for certain cases that must serve as example, you can sufficiently maintain fear if you punish crimes with three quarters of the penalty, provided you make it a rule to punish all crimes.

49. Tell no one anything you want kept secret, for there are many things that move men to gossip. Some do it through foolishness, some for profit, others through vanity, to seem in the know. And if you unnecessarily told your secret to another, you need not be surprised if he does the same, since it matters less to him than to you that it be known.

62. People generally—and inexperienced men always—are more easily moved by the hope of gain than by the danger of loss. And yet the contrary should be true, for the desire to keep is more natural than the desire to gain. The reason for the mistake is that, ordinarily, hope is stronger than fear. Men easily allay their fears, even when they are warranted; and hope, even when there is no hope.

74. Revenge does not always stem from hate or from an evil nature. Sometimes it is necessary so that people will learn not to offend you. It is perfectly all right to avenge yourself even though you feel no deep rancor against the person who is the object of your revenge.

86. If you are involved in important affairs or are seeking power, you must always hide your failures and exaggerate your successes. It is a form of swindling and very much against my nature. But, since your fate more often depends upon the opinion of others rather than on facts, it is a good idea to create the impression that things are going well. The opposite reputation will be harmful to you.

100. If you live under a tyrant, it is better to be his friend only to a certain extent rather than be completely intimate with him. In this way, if you are a respected citizen, you will profit from his power—sometimes even more than do those closer to him. And if he should fall, you may still hope to save yourself.

101. There is no rule or prescription for saving yourself from a bestial and cruel tyrant, except the one that applies for the plague. Run as far and as fast as you can.

109. The fruit of liberties and the end for which they were instituted is not government by everyone—for only the able and deserving should govern—but the observance of just laws and order, both of which are more secure in a republic than under the rule of one or few. And therein lies the difficulty that so troubles our city. Men are not satisfied to be free and secure: they also want to govern.

▶ Do you agree with this view of government? Who chooses the able and deserving?

132. I have been of a very easy-going nature, very opposed to bargaining. Men who have had to deal with me have had an easy time of it. Nevertheless, I have learned the most advantageous way to negotiate in all matters: namely, do not reveal immediately the ultimate point to which you would be willing to go. Rather remain distant from it, let yourself be pulled toward it step by step, reluctantly. If you do this, you will often get more than you had expected. But if you deal as I have dealt, you will never get anything but the bare minimum necessary for an agreement.

You can test the timelessness of this maxim by applying it to the next well-publicized set of diplomatic or labor-management negotiations.

134. All men are by nature inclined towards good rather than evil. Nor is there anyone who would not rather do good than evil, unless other factors induce him to the contrary. But human nature is so fragile, and temptations are so many, that men let themselves be easily deviated from the good. For that reason, wise legislators invented rewards and punishments, which amount to nothing more than using hope and fear to keep men firm in their natural inclination.

158. You can see at every turn the benefits you derive from having a good name, a good reputation. But they are few compared to those you do not see. These come of their own accord, without your knowing the cause, brought about by that good opinion people have of you. It was said most wisely: a good name is worth more than great riches.

172. Princes were ordained not for their own sake but for the common good, and their revenues and profits were meant to be used for the well-being of their dominions and their subjects. Parsimony, therefore, is more detestable in princes than in private citizens. For a prince who hoards wealth is appropriating to himself that over which, properly speaking, he was made, not master, but guardian and administrator for the benefit of many.

179. When I was young, I used to scoff at knowing how to play, dance, and sing, and at other such frivolities. I even made light of good penmanship, knowing how to ride, to dress well, and all those things that seem more decorative than substantial in a man. But later, I wished I had not done so. For although it is not wise to spend too much time cultivating the young toward the perfection of these arts, I have nevertheless seen from experience that these ornaments and accomplishments lend dignity and reputation even

215

to men of good rank. It may even be said that whoever lacks them lacks something important. Moreover, skill in this sort of entertainment opens the way to the favor of princes, and sometimes becomes the beginning or the reason for great profit and high honors. For the world and princes are no longer made as they should be, but as they are.

190.   To comfort those who are not what they would like to be, the proverb says: Look behind you and not before you. In other words, look how many more people there are worse off than you. It is a very true saying and should have the effect of making men happy with their lot. And yet it is very hard to accept, because nature placed our face in such a way that, unless we strain ourselves, we can only look ahead.

200.   One of the ways to make a supporter out of someone who would otherwise be hostile to a plan of yours, is to make him head of it and to make him think he were, so to say, its author or director. Lighthearted men are generally won over by this device because it flatters their vanity, and that is more important to them than real gains.

220.   Whenever a country falls into the hands of a tyrant, I think it is the duty of good citizens to try to cooperate with him and to use their influence to do good and avoid evil. Certainly it is in the interests of the city to have good men in positions of authority at all times. Ignorant and passionate Florentines have always thought otherwise, but they should recognize how disastrous the rule of the Medici would be if there were no one around them but foolish and evil men.

▶ Can a good man accept a political appointment from a ruler he considers unjust?

# Florence: Ideal and Reality

## STATING THE ISSUE

The ideal Florentine was well-born, although talent rather than birth earned him prestige among the elite. He read both Greek and Latin, and played a musical instrument. Although not a soldier, he was skilled in the use of arms. His living came from inherited wealth, banking, or trade, and his job left him with time for civic affairs. Although he was married and raised his children to carry on family traditions, he still enjoyed the company of ladies other than his wife. Not otherworldly, he was nevertheless a churchgoer and believed in Christianity. He was equally at home in a drawing room, an artist's studio, the counting house of a banker, the suite of a courtesan, the halls of government, the nave of a cathedral, or the barracks room of a professional soldier. In short, he was a many-sided individual.

These characteristics imply criteria for the good life and the good society. To lead the good life, the ideal Renaissance man required good health, a substantial income, a keen mind, an appealing personality, a family, and a group of distinguished friends. He needed an economy that supplied him with money without requiring too much of his time for business. He needed a government sympathetic to his way of life, even if he did not participate actively as a decision maker. And he needed a system of social classes that gave privileges to the elite even at the cost of the welfare of others.

Renaissance man faced difficult choices. Florence could not afford to give all its citizens a high standard of living and at the same time make substantial expenditures for humanistic endeavors. As you have seen, not all Renaissance men agreed about the nature of the good society and how to achieve it. What kind of society emerged in Renaissance Florence? To what extent did this society foster good men and the good life? Did it make the good life available to all? Chapter 3 focuses on these issues.

CHAPTER

3

217

# 15  THE GEOGRAPHIC SETTING

Climate, topography, and natural resources help to shape the daily life and the character of a people. True, geography alone does not determine culture. England built an industrialized society on a slender resource base while Russian peasants were ignoring many of the rich resources that surrounded them. Still, temperature, terrain, rainfall, the presence or absence of forests and minerals, and the fertility of the soil help to set limits on a society and to give it direction.

Tuscany, the region in central Italy of which Florence is the chief city, was settled by the Etruscans around the eighth century B.C. No one knows certainly where the Etruscans came from; they may have been native Italians, or settlers from Asia Minor or northern Europe. During the fourth century B.C., however, the Romans took over Tuscany. They founded the city of Florence in about the first century B.C.

The Apennines run the length of the Italian peninsula, forming its spine.

Bounded by the mountain peaks of the Apennines on the north and northeast, Tuscany is a land of swelling hills and valleys punctuated by plains and by a few large, rocky outcroppings along its Mediterranean coast. Both summer and winter are brief. During the rest of the year, a temperate climate encourages fields and gardens that bloom with flowers; in fact, the city's name, Florence, means "City of the Flower." Because Florence was built where the river Arno narrows and becomes easy to bridge, and because the city is near three mountain passes through the Apennines, it became a center of communication and trade.

Reading 15 consists of three selections: a modern historian's description of the geography around Florence; an interpretation of how geography helped Florence to achieve economic prosperity; and a discussion of how the landscape may have influenced Italian Renaissance thought. As you read, keep these questions in mind:

1. Did the geographic setting of Florence help to make the city a place where the good man, the good life, and the good society might flourish? Explain.
2. What geographic characteristics of Florence made it a likely place for industry and commerce? How did these characteristics help to shape the nature of the Florentine economy?
3. What reason does Burckhardt give for the fact that Renaissance men appreciated the landscape? From your study of art and literature in Chapter 2, what evidence can you bring to support or reject his theory?

# A View of Florence

*The following description is by a modern scholar who also wrote one of the evaluations of Lorenzo in Reading 2.*

There is no better introduction to Florence than to mount one of the many hills by which it is surrounded and to let the quickened eye take in the noble physical setting in which the town is framed. For in the close relation of city, river, plain, and mountains lies the earliest and the most abiding clue to the history [of Florence]. . . . Let us, therefore, after settling among a dozen possible lookouts on ancient Fiesole . . . , take the steep path that leads to the summit.

From this incomparable outlook we command the whole dominion ruled by the Arno from the river's source in the lofty mountains of the Casentino to its junction with the Mediterranean at its journey's end. First in abrupt descents, then by more gradual inclines the crowded highlands fall away, hiding from sight the rushing river until it reaches the foothills directly under our eye and again disappears among the dense mass of roofs, domes, and towers constituting Florence. Beyond the city the valley gradually widens and the hills decline in height, though their march in ordered double file continues westward as far as the eye can reach. Between the diminishing elevations we trace the narrow ribbon of the Arno, flashing silver as it picks up the sun and sky, and visible almost to the western sea.

Turning again to the east, we note that the great chain of the Apennines . . . sweeps on proudly, not only to the south but to the north as well, curving westward around Fiesole until its columns encounter the north-south line of the marble-bearing Carrara group raising their sharp peaks along the Mediterranean shore. And suddenly we become aware that all this land of Tuscany, of which the Arno is the vivifying artery and Florence the natural focus, is a well-marked geographic unit constituting a broken plateau declining gently from the towering bastion of the Apennines to the low-lying Mediterranean Sea. While the Arno is the main stream, it has many tributaries coming from both north and south and the province is the home of a numerous and energetic farming population. An intense cultivation, conducted by means of terraces on which the vine and olive flourish, often extends to a considerable altitude before the too precipitous plunge of the upper levels with their mass of sliding rock defeats the effort of the industrious peasants to gain a living from the soil. . . . In spite of the arid mountain peaks, this Tuscany with its fertile bottom-lands, with

Ferdinand Schevill, **History of Florence** (New York: Harcourt, Brace & World, Inc., 1936), pp. 3–4.

Fiesole is a town overlooking Florence. It boasts villas and gardens, as well as Roman ruins. It was the home of the Renaissance painter, Fra Angelico.

The Carrara region is noted for its marble, a pure white variety used by Michelangelo and by modern sculptors as well.

219

its opulent vineyards and olive groves climbing every slope, . . .
with gracious Florence spread beneath our feet, . . . this seductive
and infinitely various Tuscany, we are moved gladly to declare, is
one of earth's garden spots in which God still walks as in the days
of creation.

## Geography and Economy

*The following account of the rise of Florentine industry
and commerce links economic life to geographical conditions.*

Gordon East, **An Historical
Geography of Europe**
(London: Methuen & Co., Ltd.,
1935), pp. 317–318.

The economic activity of Italy was by no means characteristic
of its maritime cities alone, and in contrast to the trading sea-
states of Pisa, Venice and Genoa were many inland cities which
flourished alike in industry and trade. Florence in Tuscany . . .
was an outstanding example of this class of city. Florence stood on
the upper Arno in the midst of a broad upland basin which the
river entered and left by way of rocky defiles. The Sieve and
Ombrone headwaters of the Arno, which joined some distance
above the town, brought down abundant water—an indispensable
factor in the great cloth industry which was built up in the town.
Moreover, the basin itself was highly productive of cereal food-
stuffs, the vine and the olive, whilst the Tuscan hills provided
pasture for sheep from which was derived part of the wool for
the textile industry. Situated on a hill site and guarding its bridge
across the Arno, Florence was well placed in relation to the main
route-ways of central Italy. . . .

. . . Florence became to a remarkable degree a city of specialized
industries . . . : both for its textile products and its finance it was
famous throughout Europe. Every branch of the cloth industry,
and in particular the art of dyeing, [was] practised with great skill.
Wool was imported from Sardinia, Algarve in southern Portugal,
Languedoc and elsewhere in France; dyes and alum, both of which
were essential to the cloth industry, reached Florence via Pisa or
Genoa or were imported directly by Florentines themselves. . . .
Its merchants carried Florentine wares throughout western Europe
and the Mediterranean, whilst some even carried fine cloth to
China. . . .

## Geography as Beauty

*The author of this selection, Jacob Burckhardt, was a
nineteenth-century Swiss art historian. His book,* Civilization of the
Renaissance in Italy, *from which the following excerpt is taken,*

*was an attempt to present the spirit of the Renaissance as the beginning of the modern world. By 1900 Burckhardt's ideas were under attack by other experts, but his work is still valuable for its immense scholarship, wealth of historical examples, and insights into Renaissance life. And, as a modern professor has said, most scholars involved with the Renaissance "are discussing their problems (consciously or unconsciously) with Jacob Burckhardt."*

The quotation is from Denys Hay, ed., **The Renaissance Debate** (New York: Holt, Rinehart and Winston, Inc., 1965), p. 1.

Jacob Burckhardt, **Civilization of the Renaissance in Italy**, trans. by S. G. C. Middlemore, rev. and ed. by Irene Gordon (New York: The New American Library, Inc., 1960), pp. 220–223.

. . . [In] addition to scientific investigation, there was still another way to draw near to nature, and in a special sense. The Italians were the first among modern peoples by whom the outward world was seen and enjoyed as something beautiful.

The faculty is always the result of a long and complicated development, and its origin is not easily detected, since a dim feeling of this kind may exist long before it betrays itself in poetry and painting and thereby becomes a conscious process. . . . [From] the time of Homer, the powerful impression made by nature upon man is evidenced by countless verses and chance expressions. The Germanic tribes, which founded their States on the ruins of the Roman Empire, were thoroughly and specially fitted to understand the spirit of natural scenery; and though Christianity compelled them for a while to see the shapes of evil demons in the springs and mountains, in the lakes and woods that they had revered, this transitional state was certainly soon outgrown. By the year 1200, at the height of the Middle Ages, a genuine, hearty enjoyment of the external world was again in existence, and found lively expression in the minstrelsy of different nations, which gives evidence of the sympathy felt with all the simple phenomena of nature—spring with its flower, the green fields and the woods. But it is all foreground without perspective, particularly when we realize that the crusaders, who traveled so far and saw so much, are barely recognizable as such in their poems. Even epic poetry, which describes armor and costumes so fully, does not attempt more than a sketch of outward nature. . . .

To the Italian mind, at all events, nature had by this time lost its taint of sin and had shaken off all trace of demonical powers. St. Francis of Assisi, in his Canticle of the Sun, frankly praises the Lord for creating the heavenly bodies and the four elements.

But the unmistakable proofs of a profound effect of nature on the human spirit begin with Dante. Not only does he awaken in us by a few vigorous lines the sense of the morning air and the trembling light on the distant ocean, or of the storm-beaten forest, but he climbs lofty peaks with the only possible object of enjoying the view—perhaps one of the first men since the days of antiquity

The "Canticle of the Sun" is a simple, folk-like hymn composed by St. Francis of Assisi.

to do so. Boccaccio suggests rather than depicts how landscape affected him; yet in his pastoral romances we cannot fail to recognize that in his imagination, at least, nature had a powerful presence. But the significance of nature for a receptive spirit is fully and clearly displayed by Petrarch. . . .

Petrarch was not only a distinguished geographer and cartographer—the first map of Italy is said to have been drawn under his direction—and a reproducer of the sayings of the ancients; he was a man who felt the influence of natural beauty. The enjoyment of nature was, for him, the favorite accompaniment of intellectual pursuits; it was to combine the two that he lived in learned retirement . . . , that from time to time he fled from the world and from his age. We should do him wrong by inferring from his weak and undeveloped power of describing natural scenery that he did not feel it deeply. . . . [He] is . . . conscious of the beauty of rock scenery, and is perfectly able to distinguish the picturesque quality of a landscape from the utilitarian. During his stay in the woods of Reggio, the sudden sight of an impressive landscape so affected him that he resumed a poem he had laid aside long before. But the deepest impression of all was made on him by the ascent of Mont Ventoux. . . . An indefinable longing for a distant panorama grew stronger and stronger in him. . . . The ascent of a mountain for its own sake was unheard of, and there could be no thought of the companionship of friends or acquaintances. . . . It would be vain to look for a description of the view from the summit, not because the poet was insensible to it, but, on the contrary, because the impression was too overwhelming. . . . [He] opened a book which was then his constant companion, the *Confessions* of St. Augustine, and his eye fell on the passage in the tenth book, "and men go forth to admire lofty mountains and broad seas, and roaring torrents, and the ocean, and the course of the stars, and yet forget their own selves." . . .

Here, as in scientific geography, Aeneas Sylvius [Pope Pius II] is one of the most important voices of his time.

He interests us here as the first who not only enjoyed the magnificence of the Italian landscape, but described it with enthusiasm down to its minutest details. The ecclesiastical State and the south of Tuscany—his native home—he knew thoroughly, and after he became Pope he spent his leisure during the favorable season chiefly in excursions to the country. Then at last the gouty man was rich enough to have himself carried in a litter across the mountains and valleys. . . .

His eye seems as keen and practiced as that of any modern observer. He enjoys with rapture the panoramic splendor of the view from Monte Cavo, the summit of the Alban Hills, from where he could survey the coast . . . and the wide expanse of country with the ruined cities of the past and the mountain-chains of Central Italy; and then his eye would turn to the green woods below and the mountain lakes among them. He feels the beauty of the situation of Todi, crowning the vineyards and olive-clad slopes, looking down on distant woods and the valley of the Tiber, where towns and castles rise above the winding river. The lovely hills around Siena, with villas and monasteries on all of them, are his own home, and his descriptions of them are touched with a special feeling. But individual picturesque motifs charm him, too, as, for example, the little promontory of Capodimonte that stretches out into the Lake of Bolsena: "Rocky steps, shaded by vines, descend to the water's edge, where the evergreen oaks stand between the cliffs, alive with the singing of thrushes." On the path round the Lake of Nemi, beneath the chestnuts and fruit trees, he feels that here, if anywhere, a poet's soul must awake—here in Diana's hiding place. He often held consistories or received ambassadors under huge old chestnut trees, or beneath the olives on the greensward by some gurgling spring. A view like that of a narrowing gorge, with a bridge arched boldly over it, awakens at once his artistic sense. Even the smallest details delight him by something beautiful, or perfect, or characteristic in them—the blue fields of waving flax, the yellow gorge that covers the hills, even tangled thickets, or single trees, or springs, which seem to him like wonders of nature. . . .

# 16   SOCIAL STRUCTURE

All complex societies divide people into social classes. In some societies, class membership follows from one's birth. In the Middle Ages, for example, most men were born either nobles or serfs, and lived their entire lives without changing their position in the social scale. In other societies, people move from one class to another with relative ease. Social class helps to determine a person's status in society, the roles he performs, and the norms that society expects him to follow.

The class structure of Renaissance Florence profoundly influenced the city's artistic and humanistic endeavors. For example, the willingness of the elite to treat scholars as equals, to spend part of their fortunes for books, and to devote their leisure to study influenced the entire period. The culture of the Renaissance cannot be understood apart from the social structure out of which it grew.

Reading 16 describes the social structure of Florence during the Renaissance and suggests ways in which the organization of society was related to its artistic productivity. As you read, keep the following questions in mind:

1.  How many classes were there in Renaissance Florence? What were the main characteristics of each class? Was there mobility between one class and another?
2.  Which social classes contributed most to the artistic advances of the period? What forms did these contributions take?
3.  Why did the members of some classes invest so much time, energy, and money in artistic and humanistic endeavors? What returns did they get from this investment? Why did other classes fail to make such extensive contributions?
4.  Can you justify a great period of cultural advancement if it is restricted to a minority of the population and achieved at the economic expense of the majority?

# Social Classes in Renaissance Florence

By Edwin Fenton.

By the year 1300 the Italian peninsula was becoming a predominantly urban-centered society. The transition from an agricultural economy to an economic system based on trade and manufacturing had been taking place for centuries. The urban centers of trade and manufacturing had attracted many landed aristocrats, who saw new economic possibilities in the prospering cities. As the nobility left the countryside, the bonds that had tied man to the soil in the Middle Ages were dissolving, and many peasants abandoned their fields to seek jobs in the city. Thus, new social groups—an aristocratic class and an urban proletariat—developed alongside the businessmen and artisans who had earlier settled the cities.

An upper class of magnates emerged in the cities. Many magnates had been landed aristocrats, who had moved to the city and retained their country estates as investments. Some of them eventually entered banking and trade, or bought urban property to rent for a profit. Other magnates, like the Medici, were bankers or merchants who had become sufficiently rich and successful to be accepted as magnates. No matter what their origin, however, the magnates had power and helped to run Florentine politics.

The next group in the social scale—and the most important, because of its impact on the arts—consisted of rich merchants, bankers, lawyers, and judges, who formed a class commonly called the *popolo grasso* ("fat people"). Although they were not nobles, their wealth tied them more closely to the magnates than to any other group in society. During the late Middle Ages and the early Renaissance, most of the *popolo grasso* had become wealthy in trade or banking. Later, many of them bought country estates or city property, investments with a minimum of risk and a maximum of prestige. The *popolo grasso* also began to lead a leisurely existence, imitating the magnates. Many devoted themselves to learned professions and the arts.

The members of these two classes, the magnates and the *popolo grasso*, composed perhaps ten per cent of the population of fifteenth-century Florence. By and large, men who won fame as humanists came from these classes. They had enough wealth to spend most of their time at humanistic study. Although many of them followed a trade or profession, they often could merely supervise affairs, leaving day-to-day business in other hands. Thus, humanism in Florence was a product primarily of the ruling classes. It became identified with high position in the society, with power, and with good breeding.

The new culture of the upper classes hardly touched the urban middle class—the shopkeepers and the masters of the artisans' guilds. Most middle-class Florentines could read; they had to read in order to conduct business and take part in the government. But most of them never owned books, which were shockingly expensive in an age when they had to be copied by hand. Nor did they show any particular desire for the new culture. Middle-class lives were still bounded by local horizons and by the norms set by the guilds. In each generation a few particularly talented members of this class acquired higher education or artistic training and rose above the status of an artisan, but they did not change the class itself. The willingness of the magnates and the *popolo grasso* to accept men of talent simply permitted these talented men to move away from the middle class into which they were born.

The lower class consisted of workers and servants. Below them were a few thousand slaves, mostly women. Without political power they were unable to improve their lot significantly. The high culture of the Renaissance left them virtually untouched. Although they made up the great majority of the population of Renaissance Florence, they contributed nothing to, and gained relatively little from, the great advances in art and learning that have made the age famous.

Like those above them in the social scale, however, the lower classes were constantly exposed to great art and architecture.

▶ What sorts of things do modern Americans buy partly for the prestige they bring?

225

Palaces, tenements, market places, factories, and great public buildings were scattered all over the city. Buildings were packed closely together. Hence, virtually every resident came to know every important street, to enter all the major churches many of which were filled with great paintings and statuary, and to pass through the public squares frequently. On a single walk through the city, a man might see Michelangelo's *David*, Brunelleschi's cathedral, Ghiberti's famous bronze doors on the baptistry, and several handsome palaces; he might pass and recognize a member of the Medici family and a famous artist or scholar. Although he could never contribute to the culture of the city, a worker or slave could be a passive participant.

The upper classes, on the other hand, benefited more directly from the new culture. Ambitious and confident, the merchant, banker, prince, priest, and *condottiere* flaunted their wealth. They became patrons, spending their money on building and decorating churches, promoting arts and letters, and giving public festivals that provided opportunities for competitive display. Family occasions, such as marriages and christenings, also provided opportunities for splendid entertainment. The elite dressed in fine clothes and spent fortunes on the gowns of their ladies.

This delight in wealth departed sharply from medieval attitudes. Medieval society respected the ideal of the man who was poor and virtuous, like a monk. Sacrificing riches in the service of God and of one's fellow-man was the ultimate mark of the good man. Although not all medieval nobles made this sacrifice, they at least paid lip service to the ideal. The Florentine elite, however, began to take a different view. Not only did they enjoy their wealth; they began to justify it as necessary to being a good man and a good citizen. Finding that the works of Aristotle, Cicero, and other ancients supported this view, humanist scholars published books explaining why it was good to become rich, to contribute to the prosperity of the city, and to leave a fortune to one's children. Their chief justification for the morality of money has been summed up by a modern historian: "Man is destined for active deeds, and . . . everything may be looked upon as good which increases his power of action."

Guided by this philosophy, the tastes of the upper classes became steadily more refined. In the early years of the Italian cities, nobles had built fortified towers as crude as the rural ·castles they had lived in previously. In the fourteenth and fifteenth centuries, however, they learned to build palaces with spacious, airy rooms, cool courtyards, gardens, and orchards. They hired skilled artisans to make furniture and textiles. Statues, pictures, and books

The **condottieri** (plural of **condottiere**) were independent leaders of mercenary armies. They and their followers fought for whoever would pay them most. Since Renaissance Italy was rarely without wars, the **condottieri** made a handsome, if dangerous, living.

▶ Can you lead a good life if you are poor?

The quotation is from Hans Baron, "Franciscan Poverty and Civic Wealth in Humanistic Thought," **Speculum**, Vol. XIII (January, 1938), p. 24.

decorated their homes. During the hot summer months, they spent much of their time in country villas decorated in excellent taste and maintained by staffs of servants and slaves.

Urban Renaissance society promoted individualism to a greater degree than medieval society. The medieval noble could choose only knighthood or the Church for a career and had little opportunity to develop his talents or tastes. Renaissance cities provided a greater variety of opportunities. Capitalism offered chances for individual enterprise in business; the emergence of republican government and the growing participation of Florence in world affairs revealed new opportunities in politics and the diplomatic service; the use of hired soldiers opened profitable careers in military affairs. The accumulation of substantial wealth among bankers and merchants allowed them to devote time to the cultivation of personal tastes and interests. In short, the Renaissance provided a social setting in which members of the elite could develop into the well-rounded men who were the ideal.

Great artistic and humanistic achievements have seldom been the product of an entire society. In Renaissance Florence, as in ancient Athens, these achievements were limited to a small segment of the society supported by the labor of the masses. Great as Florentine culture was, it still raises a fundamental question: Are the cultural achievements of an elite worth the price the majority of the population must pay to achieve them?

# 17 THE POLITICAL SYSTEM

The nature of the political system helps to shape a society. By passing laws—or refusing to pass them—the state can help to mold the economy, the social system, the courts, and the daily relationships of men. Hence, the political institutions of a society and the attributes of political leaders often influence people's opportunities to lead a good life and to shape a good society.

A political system implies the values of those who dominate it. Democracy implies that each individual merits a role in the governing process. Totalitarian dictatorship, on the other hand, implies that the individual counts for nothing in comparison to the demands of the state. Both implications suggest definitions of the good man and the good society.

The Italian city states developed a unique set of political institutions. Feudalism never took firm root in the peninsula. During the Middle Ages, the cities of Italy, theoretically under the control of the Holy Roman Empire, grew more and more independent and finally threw off the emperor's control. Eventually five states—Venice, Milan, Florence, Naples, and the Papal States—dominated Italy. Within some of these states, extended feuds between republican factions eventually permitted despots to seize power.

Reading 17 discusses these developments. It was written by Wallace K. Ferguson, professor of history at Western Ontario University and a leading Renaissance scholar. As you read, keep the following questions in mind:

1. Why did despots get control of the Italian city-states? What does the rise of despots imply about the definition of the good life in Florence? Did a Florentine need political power to lead a good life?
2. What were the despots and their allies like? What did they do to promote the good life? the good society?
3. Where did the government of an Italian city-state get its money? What did it spend money for? Can you think of expenditures by our own governments that Renaissance government did not make? What does your conclusion imply about how Renaissance governments defined their obligation to provide the good life for their citizens?
4. Should government patronize artists? support symphony orchestras? subsidize theaters? organize a national humanities foundation to support work in the humanities? Why or why not?

# Government in Renaissance Florence

Wallace K. Ferguson, "Toward the Modern State," in **The Renaissance** (Harper Torchbook Series; New York: Harper & Row, Publishers, 1962), pp. 18–20, 23–26. Reprinted by permission of The Metropolitan Museum of Art.

. . . [In] Italy, the Renaissance witnessed the development of a system of territorial states, though these were less than national in scope and they grew, not by the centralization of feudalism, but rather by the transformation and expansion of urban communes. The states of Renaissance Italy were necessarily different from those of the North, because the past history of Italy was so different, and that difference was partly the result of two purely political facts: first, the fact that from the tenth to the thirteenth century Italy was annexed to the German Holy Roman Empire and, second, that the popes ruled a territorial state stretching right across the center of the peninsula. Both emperor and pope claimed universal authority, and the inevitable conflict between them furnished the central theme of medieval Italian history. . . . That, however, is only half the story, and perhaps not the most important half. It was a purely economic fact—the extraordinary early and vigorous development of Italian commerce, a commerce built on the exchange of goods between the eastern Mediterranean and the lands of western Europe—that was responsible for the growth of rich and populous cities in the tenth and eleventh centuries. And it was the cities which, in the last analysis, were the decisive factor in the political life of central and northern Italy. They were the primary cause for the early decline of Italian feudalism, for as the cities grew in wealth and power the nobles were drawn into them as though by a golden magnet. And they were the real victors in the struggle between the Empire and the Papacy. . . . When imperial power in Italy was permanently broken in the second half of the thirteenth century, and when the Papacy was transferred to Avignon at the beginning of the fourteenth century, the political void was filled by dozens of quarrelsome little city-states, each ruling the land around it and each pressing against its neighbors for more land to feed its people or for the control of essential trade routes.

Originally, these little city-states were self-governing communes with a republican form of government. . . . Except for the degree of their independence and the fact that they ruled the land around them, they were not very different in actual form of government from communes elsewhere in Europe. But just at the beginning of the Renaissance a vitally significant transformation was taking place in the majority of the communes, as republican government collapsed and was replaced by the rule of despots or, to use the less prejudiced Italian term, of *signori*. This change, which marks the first clear break between the medieval commune and the Renaissance state, is the outstanding fact in the political history of Italy in the fourteenth century, as many historians have recognized by calling this period the Age of the Despots. . . . On the whole, the despots were colorful characters, patrons of the arts and much given to original sins, and they furnished inspiring material for those Romantic historians who like to think of the Renaissance as a wicked age, in which art and vice attained an equal degree of aesthetic refinement.

Once despotic government was established in a city, a new despot might take over by inheritance, conspiracy, conquest, or simply by purchasing it from the current incumbent. The question of prime interest to the historian, however, is why did republican government fail and how were the despots able, in the first place, to acquire dictatorial power? . . . [T]he fundamental factor was the division of the city population into distinct economic and social classes with divergent interests, which they were unwilling to

When the powerful king of France refused to submit to the pope's authority, the papacy found itself locked in a struggle for power. To pacify the king, the Church elected a Frenchman as pope and moved the papacy to Avignon in southern France. The subsequent popes, all French, remained there until 1378.

A commune, in medieval times, was a town given certain liberties by its feudal lord or king. The privileges included an elected council.

▶ To what extent should people entrust strong leaders with decision-making power?

sacrifice for the common good. As a rule, the *signori* first gained power in those cities in which the various classes were most evenly balanced, so that it proved impossible to maintain stable government, and the citizens, having lost faith in republican government and having grown weary of perpetual civil strife, permitted some strong man to assume control of the state. . . .

Florence was a commercial city, but it was not a seaport, and its great economic expansion in the late thirteenth and early four-teenth centuries resulted from a combination of commerce with banking and large export industries, of which the woolen cloth industry was by far the most important and employed about a third of the city's ninety thousand population. This adventurous and many-sided capitalist economy afforded unusual opportunities for the creation of new fortunes, and as a result the composition of the class of wealthy merchant bankers and industrialists who generally succeeded in dominating the city's politics was constantly chang-ing. New families rose to wealth, while old families went bankrupt or invested their inherited wealth in land and rents, or simply frittered it away. In the last years of the thirteenth century the new rich combined with the middle class of guildsmen to disen-franchise the old aristocracy and set up a government controlled by the merchant guilds, with a minor share allotted to the lesser guilds of shopkeepers and artisans. The great mass of proletarian workers in the woolen industry, who were not permitted to or-ganize in guilds, were excluded entirely from active citizenship. One of the chief reasons why the merchant employers in the great wool guilds felt it necessary to control the government was to keep these restless workers in subjection. The middle class of small guildsmen also feared the violence of the woolworkers who crowded the slums of the city, and so they generally followed the lead of the merchant industrialists. . . .

The fact that executive power in the republican government was vested in a committee of priors, elected afresh every two months, made it almost inevitable that some extra-constitutional group should direct policy and give it some continuity. As a result, the vicissitudes of Florentine politics were caused more by changes in the composition of the ruling clique than in the republican consti-tution itself. When in 1434 a group of new families headed by the banker Cosimo de' Medici took control from a clique of older families led by the Albizzi, there was no revolutionary ·change in the constitution. . . . Under four generations of Medici leadership the republic retained the semblance of democracy, although the sham became increasingly apparent, while the Medici directed affairs without holding actual public office, much after the manner of a modern municipal boss. It was in foreign policy especially, where continuity was absolutely essential, that the Medici made themselves indispensable. They were not *signori* in the ordinary sense of the word, but they took their place as equals among the princes of Italy.

Foreign policy was becoming a matter of increasing importance to every Italian state in the fifteenth century, for by the beginning of that century the whole political structure of Italy had changed radically and was still changing. During the fourteenth century most of the petty despotisms of northern Italy had disappeared, swallowed up by the more powerful lordships of Padua, Verona, or Milan. . . . Nearly half a century of warfare finally ended with the Peace of Lodi in 1454, by which time all of Italy north of the papal states was divided between Venice, Milan, and Florence, with three or four small states maintaining a precarious existence between them. For the next forty years, until the arrival of the French invaders under Charles VIII, these states, together with the Papacy and the Kingdom of Naples, kept a fair degree of peace by carefully maintaining the balance of power. It is, I think, the first example of consciously calculated balance-of-power politics in the history of modern Europe.

In conclusion, I should like to say something about the interrelated problems of military force and revenue in the Italian states, . . . for herein is the secret of much of their strengths and their weaknesses. The Italian states of the Renaissance had no such difficulty with the introduction of a system of regular taxation as did the feudal kingdoms. The medieval communes had grown up with a money economy and the citizens were accustomed to taxation as a normal instrument of political life. The oligarchical republics like Venice and Florence merely rationalized and refined older customs. As for the despots, they took over going concerns and had only to use reasonable discretion to operate them at a profit. The successful despot was necessarily a good businessman, with a sharp eye on income, for in the Renaissance states money was the indispensable source of power. The citizens still paid taxes, but they no longer served in the armed forces of the state, as they had done in the heroic age of the communes. Instead, the states of the fourteenth and fifteenth centuries depended for military force entirely on hired mercenaries, homeless soldiers of fortune from every country in western Europe. The *condottieri*, who commanded these mercenaries and sold their services to the highest bidder, were essentially capitalist entrepreneurs. They conducted war as a business, for a profit. They fought only for pay, and the pay was high. From this situation two things followed: first, that whoever controlled

An oligarchy is a government controlled by a few men for their own ends. In the classic Greek political model, oligarchy was the corruption of aristocracy.

231

▶ What would happen to a nation if no one volunteered for the armed forces and everyone refused to be drafted?

the treasury of the state, whether despot or oligarchy, also controlled the state's only armed force, before which the citizens were helpless; and, second, that small and poor states could not compete with larger and richer states which could hire more soldiers. The conquest of the poorer states by the richer was an inevitable result, as was demonstrated by the expansion of Venice, Milan, and Florence. At the same time, any mercenary army these states could afford was inadequate protection against the national armies of France and Spain. The invasion and subjection of Italy in the sixteenth century resulted not only from the inability of the Italians to unite against the foreigner, but also in large part from the fact that the Italian people had long since left the business of warfare to mercenaries and had lost the art of self-defense.

# 18   THE ECONOMY

The economy of the Middle Ages was based on agriculture. Most men, both serfs and their lords, drew their living from the soil. Only a tiny percentage of people, a percentage that increased steadily during the twelth and thirteenth centuries, was tied to the market through either manufacturing or trade—except in Italy, where traces of the old urban trading economy persisted.

In contrast to the Middle Ages, the Renaissance had an economy based on manufacturing, trade, and banking. One third of the residents of Renaissance Florence made their living either directly or indirectly from the wool trade. Thousands earned their bread in other industries. The Renaissance could never have taken place without this shift in the economy from a rural-agricultural to an urban-industrial base.

By the fifteenth century, the old landed nobility had lost power in the city. Merchants and bankers like the Medici picked up the reins of government. The upper classes used much of their wealth to beautify the city and to support the writers and artists who flocked to the palaces and villas. The artistic renaissance had its base in these economic conditions.

Historians and economists have usually interpreted the Renaissance as a period of steadily rising prosperity that enabled the elite to spend their surplus funds on the arts. In Reading 18, Professor Robert Lopez, chairman of the department of medieval studies at Yale University, presents a different view, one that has caused considerable scholarly controversy. As you read, think about the following questions:

1. What argument does Lopez present about the relationship between economic depression and the development of great artistic works during the Renaissance?
2. According to Lopez, did the Florentine elite feel any obligation to assure the mass of citizens an opportunity to lead the good life? Explain.
3. How would you answer the question with which Lopez ends his article: Would it not be a good thing if we devoted a larger proportion of our increased leisure and of our immense wealth to fostering humanistic culture?

## Hard Times
## and Investment in Culture

. . . The notion that wherever there was an economic peak we must also find an intellectual peak, and vice versa, has long enjoyed . . . unquestioned authority. . . . In an examination book of a sophomore which I graded not so long ago, the postulate entailed these deductions: Double-entry bookkeeping in the Medici Bank goaded Michelangelo to conceive and accomplish the Medici Chapel; contemplation of the Medici Chapel in turn spurred the bankers to a more muscular management of credit. But these statements, even if they were more skilfully worded, are quite misleading. . . .

[In the intervening paragraphs, Professor Lopez points out that the economy of Europe reached a peak in the late Middle Ages, went through a depression in the fourteenth century, and then stabilized on an economic plateau somewhat lower than the peak of the thirteenth century. He attributes the economic decline to a number of factors, including a drop in population, few technical innovations, the interruption of trade routes, war, inflation, and high taxes that drained away capital. He cites figures about population, the resources of banks, and the wool industry to suggest that Florence was particularly hard hit by the depression. For example, the population of Florence was about 100,000 in 1300, but only about 70,000 in the middle of the fifteenth century. The capital of the Medici Banks in 1458 was 30,000 florins compared to 100,000 florins held by the Peruzzi Bank early in the fourteenth century. Moreover the woolen industry in the last quarter of the fifteenth century was only about one third the size of what it had been forty years before.]

Robert S. Lopez, "Hard Times and Investment in Culture," in **The Renaissance** (Harper Torchbook Series; New York: Harper & Row, Publishers, 1962), pp. 29, 45–52. Reprinted by permission of The Metropolitan Museum of Art.

233

▶ Do you think that some past ages, such as the Renaissance, offered more to man than the present does?

▶ Should everyone in a society actively confront reality?

We have seen that the essential phases of Renaissance economy were first a depression, then stabilization at a lower level than the highest medieval summit. The implicit opposition between those two trends, depression and stabilization, may perhaps help us to understand a certain dualism in the general outlook of the Renaissance. . . . Some Renaissance men were pessimists: they thought of the lost heights rather than of the attained platform. Others, especially those who had managed to settle down in sufficient comfort, felt that they had definitely and finally arrived.

The pessimists may not have been the larger group, but they seem to have included some of the most significant personalities, ranging from Savonarola to Machiavelli, from Leonardo da Vinci to Michelangelo. . . . Some pessimists joined the medieval preachers in demanding an earnest return to God, or they imitated the pagan writers in exalting the golden age of primitive mankind. . . . Still others built political theories upon the assumption that men are basically gullible and corrupt, and that a statesman must adapt his strategy to human imperfection. . . . Quite a few pessimists voiced the plight of the poor and the weak, or portrayed them in the background—but seldom in the forefront, because the forefront was reserved for the rich and the strong who purchased the work of art. . . . A . . . number sought an escape from reality, not in Heaven but in a world of artistic, literary, philosophical, or even mathematical dreams. All of these diverse trends may of course be detected during any historical period, but they seem more pronounced during the Renaissance. It is easier to link them with economic depression than with any other economic trend.

The optimists in the Renaissance were not as different from the pessimists as one might think at first. Usually they shared with the pessimists a widespread belief in the flow and ebb of civilization, and a tendency to look for an ideal of perfection in the past and not in the future. Their standard, however, was nothing like the coarse emotionalism of the Middle Ages or the naive primitiveness of the mythical Golden Age. It was classic antiquity—another age of stability and poise in aristocratic refinement. The optimists thought that antiquity had been one of the high tides in human history, and that their own time was another high tide, intimately close to antiquity and utterly unrelated to the recent past. Now was the time to stretch one's hand for the riches which the high tide brought within reach. . . . Private individuals and political leaders were equally impatient. Their drive for self-fulfillment was humanitarian and peaceful so long as they strove to discover and develop their own selves, their own moral and material resources. But it had to become aggressive individualism and political ruthlessness

234

when success depended upon conquest of resources claimed by other individuals or nations. All of these characteristics, too, can be found in other ages, but they seem to predominate in the Renaissance. They are not surprising in an economic stagnation which still offers a good life to the elite but little hope for the outcast.

The moods of the Renaissance are so many and so various that they seem almost to defy definition. That is exactly why the Renaissance looks so modern to us—it was almost as rich and diversified as the contemporary scene. One important modern trait, however, was lacking. Most of its exponents had little faith and little interest in progress for the whole human race. Indeed this idea seems to be germane to economic expansion. . . . The secular ideal of the progress of mankind through the diffusion of decency and learning was seldom emphasized before the late sixteenth century, when economic stagnation began at last to be broken. In between there were nearly two hundred years—the core of the Renaissance—during which any hope for progress was generally held out not to the vulgar masses but [instead] to individual members of a small elite. . . .

Contrary to widespread popular belief, the society of the Renaissance was essentially aristocratic. It offered economic, intellectual, and political opportunities to only a small number. But it lacked a universally accepted standard of nobility. The commercial revolution of the high Middle Ages and the social changes connected with it already had undermined the aristocracy of blood. The great depression of the mid-fourteenth century, and the stagnation which followed shook the security and whittled down the income of the aristocracy of wealth. Blood and money, of course, were still very useful . . . but neither insured durable distinction by itself. Too many landowners, merchants, and bankers had lost or were threatened with losing their wealth, and high birth without wealth was of little avail in the age which has been called "the heyday of illegitimate children." . . .

Perhaps this was why culture, what we still call humanistic culture, tended to become the highest symbol of nobility, the magic password which admitted a man or a nation to the elite group. . . . Statesmen who had tried to build up their power and prestige by enlarging their estates now vied with one another to gather works of art. Businessmen who had been looking for the most profitable or the most conservative investments in trade now invested in books. The shift was more pronounced in Italy because in Italy businessmen and statesmen were the same persons. And it is in this field, I believe, that we can most profitably investigate the relation between economic and intellectual trends of the Renais-

▶ Would you be satisfied to live in a society where only the elite could live a good life?

sance. We ought to explore briefly the increased value of humanistic culture as an economic investment.

Quite probably the increase was relative and not absolute. It is doubtful that the Renaissance invested in humanistic culture more than any period of the Middle Ages. The precious metals which early medieval artists lavished in their works were a staggering proportion of the available stocks of gold and silver. The cathedrals and castles of the twelfth century probably absorbed a greater amount of raw materials and manpower-hours than the churches and palaces of the Renaissance. Medieval universities were far greater investments, in strictly economic terms, than the humanistic schools. But universities, cathedrals and castles were not built primarily—or, at least, not exclusively—for the sake of pure humanistic culture. Universities aimed at preparing men for professional careers, such as those of clergyman, lawyer, and physician. Castles were insurances against accidents in this life. It is not surprising that shrewd rulers and thrifty businessmen were prepared to invest part of their capital in functional works of art and in practical culture. . . .

The evolution from the state as a business affair to the state as a work of art, . . . went together with the depression and the stagnation of the Renaissance. The decline of aristocracy and the recession of plutocracy left a gap through which culture . . . could more easily shine. That culture was placed so high—higher, perhaps, than at any other period in history—is the undying glory of the Renaissance.

The transition was smooth because the seeds had been planted in the high Middle Ages. Already in the thirteenth century, culture was a creditable pastime to the nobleman and a useful asset to the merchant. It was then the fashion for kings and courtiers to write elegant lyric poems . . . on very subtle matters of love and courtship. So did the merchants who traded in and ruled over the Italian towns. They did still more: they elaborated a formula which vaguely anticipated the Renaissance notion that humanistic culture is the true noblesse. Real love, polite love, they said, can dwell only in a gentle heart. Though a gentle heart is not yet the well-rounded personality of the Renaissance, it resembles it in at least two ways. It is unconnected with birth or riches, and it is attainable by cultivating one's soul. . . .

Let us take a great merchant, indeed the head of the world's greatest financial organization in the fifteenth century, Lorenzo the Magnificent. He was at the same time the head of the Medici Bank, the uncrowned king of Florence, a patron of art, and a poet in his own right. His record shows that, unlike his medieval forefathers, he was an amateur in business and a professional in literature. His mismanagement of the bank, or, rather, the mismanagement of the men he entrusted with running it, precipitated its downfall. But his patronage of the arts gave his illegitimate power a halo of respectability. His poems endeared him to his subjects . . . and made him famous among intellectual aristocrats throughout the world. Niccolò Machiavelli, the great historian of Florence, lauded Lorenzo for governing the state as an artist but blamed him for his poor conduct of business. Yet was this shortcoming not the inevitable counterpart of his artistic achievements? Today we no longer suffer from the ruin of the Medici Bank, while we still are enchanted by the verse of Lorenzo de' Medici. It is easier for us to be indulgent and to observe that business at that time was so bad that even a skilful management would not have brought many dividends. Perhaps Lorenzo may be forgiven for overlooking some opportunities to invest in trade at five per cent interest since he invested in art at a rate which will never be exhausted. . . .

Every age is a blending of virtues and shortcomings. Today we strive for unlimited human progress, and we invest colossal sums in functional scientific culture. Humanistic culture does not fare equally well. Not so long ago, when the American economy was hit by a great depression, art went on WPA rolls. What a sad decline! I certainly do not advocate that the bankers of New York neglect their depositors to enrich the Metropolitan Museum. I do not even propose that our businessmen write love lyrics, or that our presidents brush up on their musical criticism. Still, would it not be a good thing if we devoted a larger proportion of our increased leisure and of our immense wealth to the fostering of humanistic culture?

▶ Are artists more impractical and temperamental than other people?

The Work Projects Administration (WPA), established in 1935 during the Great Depression, put millions of Americans to work on a wide variety of federal projects. One of the agencies that made up the WPA was the Federal Art Project, which commissioned thousands of paintings, sculptures, and post-office murals.

# 19  THE IDEAS
# OF THE RENAISSANCE

Historians invented the idea of the Renaissance. Although such men as Lorenzo, Leonardo, and Cellini believed that their world differed from ancient and medieval times, they would have been surprised to learn that they lived in a historical period called the Renaissance, marked with certain well-defined characteristics. A century from now historians may decide that our age had characteristics we have not perceived clearly, and they may give the last half of the twentieth century a name we might find surprising. Such are the dangers—and the delights—of historical generalization.

Because historians differ in their techniques and their frames of reference, they often disagree. The idea of the Renaissance has provoked disagreement ever since Giorgio Vasari used the word *riniscata* to mean the rebirth of classical art. During the nineteenth century, Jacob Burckhardt and other scholars boldly identified some of the characteristics of the age, such as secularism, individualism, and classicism, and argued that the Renaissance began the modern world. Burckhardt's work touched off a vigorous debate about the nature of Renaissance life, a debate that still continues.

In Reading 19, William Fleming, professor of fine arts at Syracuse University, summarizes some of the major ideas that most historians attribute to the Renaissance. As you read, keep the following questions in mind:

1. What were the major intellectual trends of the Renaissance?
2. Were the major ideas of the Renaissance new, or did they have origins in classical times? How widespread were these ideas during the Middle Ages?
3. Suppose the major ideas identified in the reading accurately reflect the characteristics of the Renaissance elite. Would they also reflect the characteristics of other social classes?
4. What do these ideas imply about the nature of the good man? the good life? the good society?

# A Summary of Renaissance Thought

William Fleming, **Arts and Ideas,** 3rd ed., (New York: Holt, Rinehart and Winston, Inc., 1968), pp. 256–258, 260–261. Reprinted by permission.

The Gothic period is another name for the late Middle Ages.

The dominating ideas of the Florentine Renaissance cluster around three concepts—classical humanism, scientific naturalism, and Renaissance individualism. In their broadest meaning, humanism, naturalism, and individualism were far from new. Humanism . . . was a carryover from the 13th and 14th centuries; naturalism stemmed from late Gothic times; and some form of individualism is always present in any period. The term *Renaissance,* implying as it does a rebirth, is a source of some confusion. To the early 16th-century historians, it meant an awakening to the values of ancient classical arts and letters after the long medieval night. But just what, if anything, was *reborn* has never been satisfactorily explained. Since all the principal ideas were present in the Gothic period, one might do better to speak of a maturation of certain tendencies present in late medieval times. Yet there was a specific drive that gave an extraordinary impetus and color to the creative life and thought of this small Tuscan city-state in the 15th century. It is important, therefore, to discover just what it was, and what it was not, that gave Florence its special flavor.

That the Renaissance meant a secularization of life as opposed to the predominantly religious outlook of the medieval period has often been asserted. The secular spirit may indeed have been stronger during the Renaissance, but in medieval times there was a secular tradition in the architecture of castles, guild halls, and market buildings, in such pictorial works as the Bayeux Tapestry, in such epics as the *Chanson de Roland*, . . . in the aristocratic poetry of the troubadours, and in the music of the minstrels. The fact that so little of this has survived has led too often to the conclusion that secular works did not exist. And a look at the record of the 15th century will reveal that the great majority of the statuary, paintings, and music were religious works intended for placement or performance in churches. . . .

. . . Florentine humanism . . . [took] on a consciously classical coloration. Here again, however, a word of caution is necessary when speaking of a "rebirth" of the spirit of antiquity. In Italy, much more than in northern Europe, the classical tradition had been more or less continuous. Roman remains were everywhere in evidence. Many arches, aqueducts, bridges, and roads were still in use, while fragments of ancient buildings, such as columns, were used and reused over and over again as building materials. . . . Aristotle was still the official philosopher of the church, and ancient musical theory was still studied. What was new to Florence was the study of the Greek language, the setting up of Ciceronian rather than medieval Latin as a standard, and a passionate interest in Plato. In spite of a certain antiquarianism, however, the net result was less a revival of things past than a step forward. It was— as such movements usually are—a search for past precedents to justify present practices.

Much has been said also about the pagan aspect of this interest in antiquity. Here again it was less anti-Christian than appears on the surface. . . . There was . . . a certain amount of anticlericalism in Florence, as there was elsewhere at this time. Lorenzo, however, as the papal banker and as a father who chose the Church for his son Giovanni's career, was not so much a religious skeptic as he was a political realist. It is important to keep in mind that the Florentine humanists were a small band of learned men, whose Platonic disputations have made much more noise in the corridors of history than they did in their own time. Actually, they never had, nor did they seek, a large audience. . . .

The Bayeux Tapestry, an embroidery in eight colors, depicts on a strip of linen 230 feet by 20 inches William the Conqueror's invasion of England in 1066. It was done in the eleventh century, perhaps by William's wife. It is now in a museum in the town of Bayeux, France. The **Chanson de Roland,** an epic song written in the eleventh or twelfth century, describes the great battles fought by the knights of Charlemagne.

One of the favorite proposals of Renaissance humanists was that Plato be declared a saint.

"Platonic disputations" here refers to the sort of discussion favored by Plato: well-reasoned, and concerned with absolute ideals.

Naturalism, in the sense of fidelity to nature, appears in a well-developed form both in the northern Gothic sculpture and in the poetry of St. Francis, who had died as long before as 1226. . . . Florentine 15th-century naturalism took a noticeably scientific turn. Careful observation of natural phenomena and the will to reproduce objects as the eye sees them was evidence of an empirical attitude; dissection of cadavers in order to see the structure of the human body revealed a spirit of free inquiry; and the study of mathematics so as to put objects into proper perspective involved a new concept of space. Thus, while Fra Angelico's religious and Botticelli's pagan dreams are ample evidence that the visionary element was still present, clearly a new scientific spirit was now afoot.

▶ What role should a desire for fame play in a person's life?

While individualism as such is practically universal, the distinctive feature of its Florentine expression was that conditions in this small city-state were almost ideal for artists to come into immediate and fruitful contact with their patrons and audience. Competition was keen; desire for personal fame was intense; and a high regard for personality is seen in the portraiture, biographies, and autobiographies. . . .

. . . The religious nature of the vast majority of the works of art has already been pointed out, but personal patronage was in the ascendancy. Brunelleschi built the Pazzi Chapel, Masolino and Masaccio decorated the Brancacci Chapel, and Benozzo Gozzoli and Filippo Lippi did the paintings for the Medici Chapel on commission from private donors as memorials to themselves and their families. . . . Squarialupi and Isaac were on the payroll of the Medici when they played the organ in the cathedral, in a church, or in the family palace. Piousness and the desire for spiritual salvation were not the only motives for such munificence; a knowledge that the donor's present and posthumous fame depended on his building of monuments and his choice of artists to decorate them was also present.

▶ Do you think it would be better for artists to be supported by patrons or by the state?

In addition to the circumstances of patronage, certain technical considerations within the arts themselves point in the same individualistic direction. The development of perspective drawing, for instance, implied that the subject in the picture—whether a Madonna, a saint, or an angel—was definitely placed in this world rather than symbolically in the next, and hence was more on a par with the observer. The unification of space by having all the lines converge at one point on the horizon tended to flatter the spectator. . . . The central-type church that Alberti, Bramante, and later Michelangelo . . . preferred to design, in which the space is unified under a dome, is the architectural expression of the same idea. The Gothic cathedral purposely led the eye and imagination outward into the transcendental beyond, while the central-type church revolves around man himself. Standing under the cupola, the observer is aware that the axis of the building is not objectively outside or transcendentally beyond, but subjectively in himself. He is, for the moment at least, the center of the architectural space. . . .

Human figures, whether intended as prophets or portraits, tended to become more personal and individual. Each statue by Donatello . . . was a human individuality who made a powerful and unique impression. Even Fra Angelico's Madonna was a personality more than an abstraction, and his figure of the Angel Gabriel possessed genuine human dignity. . . .

The higher social status accorded Florentine artists was evidenced by the inclusion of . . . self-portraits in paintings. . . . Signatures of artists on their works became the rule, not the exception; and the culmination came when Michelangelo realized that his work was so highly individual that he no longer needed to sign it. The desire for personal fame grew to such an extent that Benvenuto Cellini no longer was content to let his works speak for him but wrote a voluminous autobiography filled with self-praise. The painter Giorgio Vasari likewise took up the pen to record the lives of the artists he knew personally and by reputation. . . .

In late medieval and early Renaissance times, artists were content with their status as craftsmen. They were trained as apprentices to grind pigments, carve wooden chests, make engravings, and prepare wall surfaces for frescoes as well as to carve marble reliefs and paint pictures. In the late 15th and early 16th centuries, however, it was not enough for an artist to create works of art. He had to know the theory of art and the place of art in the intellectual atmosphere of his period. The quality most admired in Renaissance man was *virtù* (the word comes closer in the modern sense to *virtuoso* than *virtuous*). *Virtù* revealed itself in the boundless vitality and extraordinary ability that led to the achievements of a Lorenzo the Magnificent or the breathtaking conceptions of a Michelangelo. With *virtù*, the Renaissance artist could no longer confine himself to a single specialty but sought to become the *homo universale*, the universal man. . . .

From Lorenzo's time through the early 16th century, the greatest artists were intellectuals. Alberti was a scholar-architect who wrote books on the subject, designed buildings on paper, and left the actual construction to a master mason. Botticelli associated with men of letters and worked elaborate allegories into his pictures. Leonardo da Vinci thought sculpture inferior to painting because of the physical labor involved, and in his later years devoted himself more to science than to painting. . . . Michelangelo hated the workshop, even though the realization of his grandiose designs depended on the work of many hands. He was to become the ideal of the modern individualistic artist, consciously an intellectual, dealing with popes and princes as equals, insisting that he painted with his brains not with his hands, and rejecting all offers of noble titles. When people began calling him "the divine," the cycle was complete.

# 20   THE RENAISSANCE:
# AN ASSESSMENT

Twentieth-century America, on the surface, bears little resemblance to Renaissance Florence. Yet, as you have seen in the preceding nineteen readings, Renaissance Florentines confronted many of the problems and questions that Americans do today. In a sense, one can say that Renaissance Florence seems "modern"— or should one say that twentieth-century America seems an offshoot of the Renaissance? Having studied Renaissance Florence, you should be able to make some judgments of your own about the importance of Renaissance Florence to the modern world and to your own life. You should be able tentatively to answer the question, What is the legacy of Florence to modern man?

Those who make judgments about the past must use a set of standards by which to judge. A man who believes that the economic prosperity of the common man ranks higher in a scale of values than great art and literature will judge Renaissance Florence in one way. Someone who thinks that an age can be assessed by its cultural contributions to future generations will come to a different conclusion.

Reading 20 contains an assessment of the Renaissance by Will Durant, author of a popular multivolume history of western civilization that devotes one whole volume to the Renaissance. As you read the conclusion to this volume, think about the following questions:

1.  By what criteria has Durant judged the contribution of the Renaissance? Does he make his criteria clear?
2.  According to this assessment, for whom did the Renaissance provide a good life in a good society? What groups did not lead a good life?

3. Do you agree with Durant's assessment? What criteria would you use to write your own assessment?

# The Renaissance in Perspective

It is difficult to judge . . . [the Renaissance] calmly, and we grudgingly rehearse the charges that have been brought against it. First of all, the Renaissance (limiting that term to Italy) was based materially upon the economic exploitation of the simple many by the clever few. The wealth of papal Rome came from the pious pennies of a million European homes; the splendor of Florence was the transmuted sweat of lowly proletaires who worked long hours, had no political rights, and were better off than medieval serfs only in sharing in the proud glory of civic art and the exciting stimulus of city life. Politically the Renaissance was the replacement of republican communes with mercantile oligarchies and military dictatorships. Morally it was a pagan revolt that sapped the theological supports of the moral code, and left human instincts grossly free to use as they pleased the new wealth of commerce and industry. Unchecked by censorship from a Church herself secularized and martial, the state declared itself above morality in government, diplomacy, and war.

Renaissance art (the indictment continues) was beautiful, but seldom sublime. It excelled Gothic art in detail, but fell short of it in grandeur, unity, and total effect; it rarely reached Greek perfection or Roman majesty. It was the voice of an aristocracy of wealth that divorced the artist from the artisan, uprooted him from the people, and made him dependent upon upstart princes and rich men. It lost its soul to a dead antiquity, and enslaved architecture and sculpture to ancient and alien forms. What an absurdity it was to put false Greco-Roman fronts upon Gothic churches, as Alberti did in Florence and Rimini! Perhaps the whole classical revival in art was a grievous mistake. A style once dead cannot properly be revitalized unless the civilization that it expressed can be restored; the vigor and health of the style lie in its harmony with the life and culture of its time. There was, in the great age of Greek and Roman art, a stoic restraint idealized by Greek thought and often realized in Roman character; but that restraint was quite foreign to the Renaissance spirit of freedom, passion, turbulence, and excess. What could be more contrary to the Italian temper in the fifteenth and sixteenth centuries than the flat roof and ceiling, the regular rectangular facade, the dreary rows of identical windows, that stigmatized the Renaissance palace? When Italian

Will Durant, **The Story of Civilization: Part V, The Renaissance** (New York: Simon and Schuster, Inc., 1953), pp. 724–728. Copyright, © 1953, by Will Durant. Reprinted by permission of Simon & Schuster, Inc.

architecture tired of this monotony and artificial classicism, it let itself go, like a Venetian merchant robed for Titian, in excessive ornament and splendor, and fell from the classic into the baroque. . . .

Neither could classic sculpture express the Renaissance. For restraint is essential to sculpture; the enduring medium does not fitly embody a contortion or an agony that by its nature must be brief. Sculpture is motion immobilized, passion spent or controlled, beauty or form preserved from time by metal congealed or lasting stone. Perhaps for this reason the greatest sculptures of the Renaissance are mostly tombs or *pietàs,* in which restless man has at last achieved tranquillity. Donatello, try as he might to be classic, remained striving, aspiring, Gothic; Michelangelo was a law to himself, a Titan imprisoned in his temperament, struggling through *Slaves* and *Captives* to find esthetic peace, but ever too lawless and excited for repose. The recovered classic heritage was a burden as well as a boon; it enriched the modern soul with noble exemplars, but it almost smothered that youthful spirit—just come of age— under a falling multitude of columns, capitals, architraves, and pediments. Perhaps this resurrected antiquity, this idolatry of proportion and symmetry (even in gardens), halted the growth of a native and congenial art, precisely as the revival of Latin by the humanists impeded the development of literature in the vernacular.

Renaissance painting succeeded in expressing the color and passion of the time, and brought the art to a technical refinement never surpassed. But it too had its faults. Its stress was on sensuous beauty, on lordly raiment and rosy flesh; even its religious pictures were a voluptuous sentimentality, more intent upon corporeal forms than upon spiritual significance; and many a medieval crucifix reaches deeper into the soul than the demure Virgins of Renaissance art. Flemish and Dutch artists dared to picture unattractive faces and homely dress, and to seek behind these simple features the secrets of character and the elements of life. How superficial the nudes of Venice—even the Madonnas of Raphael—seem beside the Van Dycks' *Adoration of the Lamb!* Raphael's *Julius II* is unexcelled, but is there anything in the hundred self-portraits by Italian artists that can compare with Rembrandt's honest mirrorings of himself? The popularity of portraiture in the sixteenth century suggests the rise of the *nouveaux riches,* and their hunger to see themselves in the glass of fame. The Renaissance was a brilliant age, but through all its manifestations runs a strain of show and insincerity, a flaunting of costly costumes, a hollow fabric of precarious power unsupported by inner strength, and ready to fall into ruins at the touch of a merciless rabble, or at the distant cry of an obscure and angry monk.

Well, what shall we say to this harsh indictment of an epoch that we have loved with all the enthusiasm of youth? We shall not try to refute that indictment: though it is weighted with unfair comparisons, much of it is true. Refutations never convince, and to pit one half-truth against its opposite is vain unless the two can be merged into a larger and juster view. Of course the Renaissance culture was an aristocratic superstructure raised upon the backs of the laboring poor; but, alas, what culture has not been? Doubtless much of the literature and art could hardly have arisen without some concentration of wealth; even for righteous writers unseen toilers mine the earth, grow food, weave garments, and make ink. We shall not defend the despots; . . . many of them wasted in vain luxury the revenues drawn from their people; but neither shall we apologize for Cosimo and his grandson Lorenzo, whom the Florentines obviously preferred to a chaotic plutocracy. As for the moral laxity, it was the price of intellectual liberation; and heavy as the price was, that liberation is the invaluable birthright of the modern world, the very breath of our spirits today.

The devoted scholarship that resurrected classic letters and philosophy was chiefly the work of Italy. There the first modern literature arose, out of that resurrection and that liberation; and though no Italian writer of the age could match Erasmus or Shakespeare, Erasmus himself yearned for the clear free air of Renaissance Italy, and the England of Elizabeth owed to Italy—to "Englishmen Italianate"—the seeds of its flowering. . . .

Yes, Renaissance architecture is depressingly horizontal, always excepting the lordly cupolas that rise over Florence and Rome. The Gothic style, ecstatically vertical, reflected a religion that pictured our terrestrial life as an exile for the soul, and placed its hopes and gods in the sky; classic architecture expressed a religion that lodged its deities in trees and streams and in the earth, and rarely higher than a mountain in Thessally; it did not look upward to find divinity. That classic style, so cool and calm, could not fitly represent the turbulent Renaissance, but neither could it be allowed to die; rightly a generous emulation preserved its monuments, and transmitted its ideals and principles to be a part—a sharer but not a dictator—of our building art today. Italy could not equal Greek or Gothic architecture, nor Greek sculpture, nor, perhaps, the noblest flights of Gothic sculpture at Chartres and Reims; but it could produce an artist whose Medici tombs were worthy of Phëidias, and his *Pietà* of Praxiteles.

One may assume that Durant is here referring to Savonarola.

▶ What sorts of judgments should historians try to make? Should they comment on the life-style of an era, or should they restrict themselves to the facts?

Erasmus was a sixteenth-century Dutch scholar and humanist, leader of the Renaissance in northern Europe.

Well-to-do young Englishmen were sent on a "Grand Tour" of the European continent—with emphasis on Italy, where they learned the latest fashions in dress, manners, and philosophy.

Durant is here comparing the work of Michelangelo to that of two ancient Greek sculptors, Pheidias (or Phidias) and Praxiteles.

▶ Should artists concern themselves only with beauty and joy? Or should they use their influence to point out the ugliness and despair in society?

Francis Bacon, an English philosopher, developed the modern scientific method. René Descartes was a French philosopher and mathematician, known for the phrase "I think; therefore I am." Baruch Spinoza was a Dutch philosopher. All three lived during the seventeenth century.

For Renaissance painting there shall be no word of apology; it is still the high point of that art in history. Spain approached that zenith in the halcyon days of Velasquez, Murillo, . . . and El Greco; Flanders and Holland came not quite so close in Rubens and Rembrandt. Chinese and Japanese painters scale heights of their own, and at times their pictures impress us as especially profound, if only because they see man in a large perspective; yet their cold, contemplative philosophy or decorative elegance is outweighed by the richer range of complexity and power, and the warm vitality of color, in the pictorial art of the Florentines, of Raphael and Correggio and the Venetians. Indeed, Renaissance painting was a sensual art, though it produced some of the greatest religious paintings, and—as on the Sistine ceiling—some of the most spiritual and sublime. But that sensuality was a wholesome reaction. The body had been vilified long enough; woman had borne through ungracious centuries the abuse of a harsh asceticism; it was good that life should reaffirm, and art enhance, the loveliness of healthy human forms. The Renaissance had tired of original sin, breast-beating, and mythical post-mortem terrors; it turned its back upon death and its face to life; and . . . it sang an exhilarating, incomparable ode to joy.

The Renaissance, by recalling classic culture, ended the thousand-year rule of the Oriental mind in Europe. From Italy by a hundred routes the good news of the great liberation passed over mountains and seas to France, Germany, Flanders, Holland, and England. . . . The flow of ideas, morals, and arts continued to run northward from Italy for a century. From 1500 to 1600 all western Europe acknowledged her as the mother and nurse of the new civilization of science and art and the "humanities;" even the idea of the gentleman, and the aristocratic conception of life and government, came up from the south to mold the manners and states of the north. So the sixteenth century, when the Renaissance declined in Italy, was an age of exuberant germination in France, England, Germany, Flanders, and Spain.

For a time the tensions of Reformation and Counter Reformation, the debates of theology and the wars of religion, overlaid and overwhelmed the influence of the Renaissance; men fought through a bloody century for the freedom to believe and worship as they pleased, or as pleased their kings; and the voice of reason seemed stilled by the clash of militant faiths. But it was not altogether silent; even in that unhappy desolation men like Erasmus, Bacon, and Descartes echoed it bravely, gave it fresh and stronger utterance; Spinoza found for it a majestic formulation; and in the eighteenth century the spirit of the Italian Renaissance was re-

246

born in the French Enlightenment. . . . Everywhere today in Europe and the Americas there are urbane and lusty spirits—comrades in the Country of the Mind—who feed and live on this legacy of mental freedom, esthetic sensitivity, friendly and sympathetic understanding; forgiving life its tragedies, embracing its joys of sense, mind, and soul; and hearing ever in their hearts, amid hymns of hate and above the cannon's roar, the song of the Renaissance.

## SUGGESTED READINGS

Listings preceded by an asterisk (*) are published in paperback. If the paperback imprint differs from the hardback imprint, the paperback imprint is in parentheses.

*Histories and Biographies*

* ADY, CECILIA M., **Lorenzo dei Medici and Renaissance Italy.** New York: The Macmillan Company, 1962 (Collier). A short and well-written description of the life and times of Il Magnifico.

* BURCKHARDT, JACOB, **The Civilization of the Renaissance in Italy,** translation ed. by IRENE GORDON. New York: The New American Library, Inc., 1960 (Mentor). An eloquent, classic study by the nineteenth-century Swiss scholar credited with having invented the idea of the Renaissance.

* BUTTERFIELD, HERBERT, **The Statecraft of Machiavelli.** New York: The Macmillan Company, 1962 (Collier). A concise analysis of Machiavelli's method, statecraft, and aims by a leading English historian.

* DANNENFELDT, KARL H., ed., **The Renaissance: Medieval or Modern?** Boston: D. C. Heath & Company, 1959. A collection of essays by leading modern scholars.

* FERGUSON, WALLACE K., **The Renaissance.** New York: Holt, Rinehart and Winston, Inc., 1940. An excellent, short account of the Renaissance throughout Europe.

* GILMORE, MYRON P., **The World of Humanism: 1453–1517.** New York: Harper & Row, Publishers, 1952 (Torchbook). A survey of main trends and ideas in European humanism. Not a chronological history.

* HALE, JOHN R., **Machiavelli and Renaissance Italy.** New York: The Macmillan Company, Inc., 1963 (Collier). A short and readable biography.

\* HAY, DENYS, **The Italian Renaissance in Its Historical Background.** New York: Cambridge University Press, 1961. Lucid and learned essays, including one on "Renaissance Values."

\* HAY, DENYS, ed., **The Renaissance Debate.** New York: Holt, Rinehart and Winston, Inc., 1965. A collection of Renaissance source material and analyses by later historians, all centered on the meaning of the Renaissance.

\* McCARTHY, MARY, **The Stones of Florence.** New York: Harcourt, Brace & World, Inc., 1959 (Harvest). An impressionistic guidebook and tribute by a novelist and journalist to Florence and its people, past and present.

\* MARTIN, ALFRED VON, **Sociology of the Renaissance.** New York: Harper & Row, Publishers, 1963 (Torchbook). A short, complex, and highly original examination of the evolution of the Renaissance merchant capitalist. First published in 1932.

\* MATTINGLY, GARRETT, **Renaissance Diplomacy.** Boston: Houghton Mifflin Company, 1955 (Peregrine). A readable analysis of the origins of modern diplomacy.

\* ROEDER, RALPH, **The Man of the Renaissance.** New York: The World Publishing Company, 1963 (Meridian). A long but lively portrayal of the Renaissance through the lives of four of its most eminent representatives—Savonarola, Machiavelli, Castiglione, and Aretino. First published in 1933.

\* SCHEVILL, FERDINAND, **The Medici.** New York: Harper & Row, Publishers, 1960 (Torchbook). An engrossing, brief account of the Medicis and their influence on Renaissance Italy.

\* TAYLOR, HENRY OSBORN, **The Humanism of Italy.** New York: The Macmillan Company, Inc., 1962 (Collier). An excellent short study by an outstanding European historian.

### Picture Histories

AMERICAN HERITAGE, ed., **The Horizon Book of the Renaissance.** New York: American Heritage Publishing Co., Inc., 1959. A beautiful portrait in words and pictures of Renaissance Italy.

HALE, JOHN R. and THE EDITORS OF TIME-LIFE BOOKS, **Great Ages of Man: Renaissance.** New York: Time, Inc., 1965. A handsome book which catches the excitement of the Renaissance in text and fine illustrations. Includes maps, a time line, and a bibliography.

### Literature and Statecraft

\* BOCCACCIO, GIOVANNI, **The Decameron,** tr. by RICHARD ALDINGTON. New York: Dell Publishing Co., Inc., 1962. A complete and unexpurgated translation by a novelist and poet of the tales told by seven ladies and three young men who fled Florence when the Black Plague swept the city.

* BRUCKER, GENE, ed., **Two Memoirs of Renaissance Florence: The Diaries of Buonaccorso Pitti and Gregorio Dati,** tr. by JULIA MARTINES. New York: Harper & Row, Publishers, 1967 (Torchbook). Diaries of two dynamic businessmen, one of an aristocratic family and the other of modest origins.

* CASTIGLIONE, BALDESAR, **The Book of the Courtier,** tr. by GEORGE BULL. Baltimore, Md.: Penguin Books, Inc., 1967. The most vivid account of Renaissance court life.

* LIND, L. R., ed., **Lyric Poetry of the Italian Renaissance.** New Haven: Yale University Press, 1954. A collection of 165 poems in both Italian and English.

* MACHIAVELLI, NICCOLÒ, **Mandragola,** tr. by ANNE and HENRY PAOLUCCI. Indianapolis, Ind.: The Bobbs-Merrill Co., Inc., 1957 (Library of Liberal Arts). A masterful comedy whose theme is seduction, by the author of **The Prince.**

* MACHIAVELLI, NICCOLÒ, **The Prince,** tr. by A. ROBERT CAPONIGRI. Chicago: Henry Regnery Company, 1963 (Gateway). The most famous—and infamous—of Renaissance treatises on statecraft.

* PETRARCH, FRANCESCO, **Selected Sonnets, Odes and Letters,** ed. by THOMAS G. BERGIN. Des Moines, Ia.: The Meredith Publishing Co., 1966 (Appleton-Century). A comprehensive selection of Petrarch's works, together with an introduction and a bibliography.

* ROSS, JAMES BRUCE and MARY MARTIN McLAUGHLIN, eds., **The Portable Renaissance Reader.** New York: The Viking Press, 1953. A 756-page collection of fiction, poetry, essays, and nearly every other sort of literary work from the Renaissance in Italy and northern Europe.

*Arts and Philosophy*

* ALAZARD, JEAN, **The Florentine Portrait.** New York: Schocken Books, Inc., 1968. A study of the Florentine portrait before and after Leonardo by a leading French art historian. Sixty-three illustrations.

* ARGAN, G. C., **Renaissance Painting.** New York: Dell Publishing Co., Inc., 1968. Many illustrations with short commentaries on each picture.

* CELLINI, BENVENUTO, **Autobiography,** tr. by GEORGE BULL. Baltimore, Md., Penguin Books, Inc., 1956. The most famous Renaissance autobiography, by a brilliant artist whose adventures extended to love and politics.

* CASSIRER, ERNST, ET AL., eds., **The Renaissance Philosophy of Man.** Chicago: University of Chicago Press, 1948. Essays by such leading Renaissance philosophers as Petrarch and Pico.

* CLARK, KENNETH, **Leonardo da Vinci.** Baltimore, Md.: Penguin Books, Inc., 1967 (Pelican). A splendidly written short study of Leonardo as an artist. Includes sixty-four pages of plates.

* DE SANTILLANA, GIORGIO, ed., **Age of Adventure: The Renaissance Philosophers.** New York: The New American Library, Inc., 1956 (Mentor). Selections from the writings of Renaissance philosophers in Italy and in other parts of Europe.

* **Discoveries and Opinions of Galileo,** tr. by STILLMAN DRAKE. Garden City, N.Y.: Doubleday & Company, Inc., 1957 (Anchor). Four of Galileo's major scientific works translated by a leading Galileo scholar.

* FERGUSON, WALLACE K., ET AL., **The Renaissance.** New York: Harper & Row, Publishers, 1962 (Torchbook). Six essays, each by an outstanding scholar, about politics, economic life, science, religion, literature, and art.

* MURRAY, PETER, **The Architecture of the Italian Renaissance.** New York: Schocken Books, Inc., 1963. Sound, readable, and well-illustrated.

* MURRAY, PETER and LINDA, **Art of the Renaissance.** New York: Frederick A. Praeger, Inc., 1963. A first-rate and handsome survey. Includes 251 plates, 51 of them in color.

* PATER, WALTER, **The Renaissance.** New York: The New American Library, Inc. (Mentor). A classic, nineteenth-century analysis of the art and literature which symbolize the spirit of the Renaissance. Includes chapters on Pico, Botticelli, Della Robbia, Michelangelo, and Leonardo.

* ROLLAND, ROMAIN, **Michelangelo.** New York: The Macmillan Company, Inc., 1962 (Collier). A short biography of Michelangelo by a leading French novelist. First published in 1905.

* STONE, IRVING and JEAN, eds., **I, Michelangelo, Sculptor.** The New American Library, Inc., 1962 (Signet). An autobiography of Michelangelo told mainly through his letters to his family, patrons, and friends.

* TAYLOR, PAMELA, ed., **The Notebooks of Leonardo da Vinci.** New York: The New American Library, Inc., 1960 (Mentor). A new arrangement of the **Notebooks,** in which Leonardo exhibits many facets of his powerful mind and personality. Sixteen pages of drawings.

* VASARI, GIORGIO, **The Lives of the Artists,** selected and tr. by GEORGE BULL. Baltimore, Md.: Penguin Books, Inc., 1965. Perceptive biographies and appreciations of Renaissance painters by a fellow painter. Includes a long chapter on Michelangelo.

# Unit III:

# The Humanities in New York

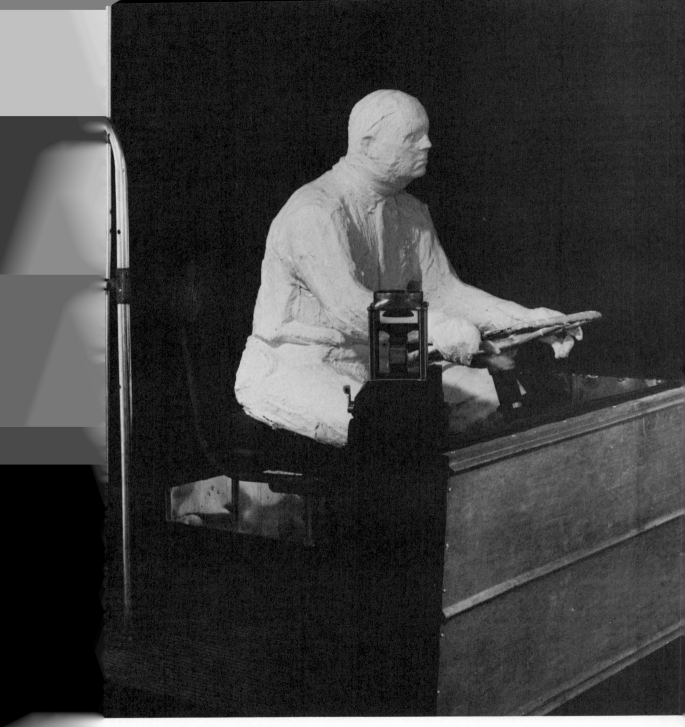

rge Segal, *The Bus Driver* (1962)
Museum of Modern Art, Philip Johnson Fund
to by Eric Pollitzer

# New York and Its Citizens

## STATING THE ISSUE

Compared to ancient Athens or Renaissance Florence, modern New York City is complexity compounded. Its population may serve as an example. New York has drawn its citizens from every corner of the world. It has more blacks than Alabama, two-thirds as many Jews as all of Israel, more people of Irish ancestry than Dublin, and more of Italian ancestry than all but four Italian cities. The tumbled array of all these strains sometimes startles visitors who themselves add significantly to the polyglot nature of the world's greatest city.

New Yorkers see their city from markedly different perspectives. Old New York families who winter in town houses and summer in Newport, Rhode Island mansions surround their lives with private schools, the Metropolitan Opera, riding lessons, social service organizations, trips abroad, and other privileges and responsibilities of great wealth. Puerto Rican immigrants fight roaches, rats, slumlords, and the vicious grind of poverty. In neighboring apartments live black nationalists who seek to establish an all-black society, and young black attorneys stretching for a higher rung on the social and economic ladder. Since so many different groups view New York from such varied perspectives, no generalization can accurately describe the New Yorker's view of his world. The "typical New Yorker" does not exist.

Chapter 1 introduces the study of humanities in New York through the viewpoint of a variety of its citizens. The first reading describes the city as one of its great writers knew it just after World War II. It is followed by accounts of New York as seen by a young Jewish boy, a black welfare client, some poor Puerto Rican families, three career women, some members of the business elite, and a young hippie. As you read these accounts, think about the variety of ways in which these people define the good man, the good life, and the good society. Do they agree about any issues? What do they disagree about? What do their opinions add to your own thoughts about these issues? Chapter 1 will focus on these three questions.

# 1 NEW YORK THROUGH
# A WRITER'S EYES

New York City is about 350 years old. It was settled originally by Dutch burghers, who are said to have bought Manhattan Island from the Indians for a few dollars worth of beads, and was conquered by the English in 1664. Standing at the mouth of the Hudson River and blessed with a deep and sheltered harbor, New York grew steadily. By 1810 it was the largest city in the United States. By 1969 its population was greater than eight million people.

During the nineteenth and early twentieth centuries, New York was the major port of entry for millions of immigrants from Europe who worked their patient way through the endless lines at Ellis Island to touch at last an eager foot on the streets of America. Millions of them never left. When restrictive laws cut off immigration from Europe in the 1920's, a new influx of black immigrants from the American South began. Since World War II, Puerto Ricans have swelled the tide. Moreover, throughout its entire history New York has pulled the talented from the entire nation—aspiring writers, artists, dancers, musicians, businessmen. Many of them failed to meet New York's harsh standards; those who succeeded have left a rich heritage.

One of the most successful was E. B. White. Like so many other writers, he found the literary life of the metropolis irresistible. As a major contributor to *The New Yorker* magazine whose famous weekly column, "The Talk of the Town," was enlivened by hundreds of his short pieces, he became one of the major essayists of the twentieth century. In 1949, White published an essay entitled "Here Is New York" in *Holiday* magazine. Republished as a short book, it has become famous.

As you read excerpts from White's essay, think about the following questions:

1.  According to White's account, is New York a good or a bad place? Is it equally good or bad for everyone? Explain your answer.
2.  How many New Yorks are there? How large is New York in its largest sense? in its smallest?
3.  What sort of man can best take advantage of what New York has to offer? What does your conclusion imply about the nature of the good man in New York City? the good life?

# "Here Is New York"

On any person who desires such queer prizes, New York will bestow the gift of loneliness and the gift of privacy. It is this largess that accounts for the presence within the city's walls of a considerable section of the population; for the residents of Manhattan are to a large extent strangers who have pulled up stakes somewhere and come to town, seeking sanctuary or fulfillment or some greater or lesser grail. The capacity to make such dubious gifts is a mysterious quality of New York. It can destroy an individual, or it can fulfill him, depending a good deal on luck. No one should come to New York to live unless he is willing to be lucky.

New York is the concentrate of art and commerce and sport and religion and entertainment and finance, bringing to a single compact arena the gladiator, the evangelist, the promotor, the actor, the trader and the merchant. It carries on its lapel the unexpungeable odor of the long past, so that no matter where you sit in New York you feel the vibrations of great times and tall deeds, of queer people and events and undertakings. I am sitting at the moment in a stifling hotel room in 90-degree heat, halfway down an air shaft, in midtown. No air moves in or out of the room, yet I am curiously affected by emanations from the immediate surroundings. I am twenty-two blocks from where Rudolph Valentino lay in state, eight blocks from where Nathan Hale was executed, five blocks from the publisher's office where Ernest Hemingway hit Max Eastman on the nose, four miles from where Walt Whitman sat sweating out editorials for the Brooklyn Eagle, thirty-four blocks from the street Willa Cather lived in when she came to New York to write books about Nebraska, one block from the spot where Marceline used to clown on the boards of the Hippodrome, thirty-six blocks from where the historian Joe Gould kicked a radio to pieces in full view of the public, thirteen blocks from where Harry Thaw shot Stanford White, five blocks from Where I used to usher at the Metropolitan Opera, and only a hundred and twelve blocks from the spot where Clarence Day the Elder was washed of his sins in the Church of the Epiphany (I could continue this list indefinitely); and for that matter I am probably occupying the very room that any number of exalted and somewise memorable characters sat in, some of them on hot, breathless afternoons, lonely and private and full of their own sense of emanations from without. . . .

There are roughly three New Yorks. There is, first, the New York of the man or woman who was born here, who takes the city for

Rudolph Valentino was a movie idol of the 1910's and '20's.

Ernest Hemingway socked Max Eastman, the essayist and poet, because Eastman had written a scathing review of Hemingway's novel about bullfighting, **Death in the Afternoon**.

Joe Gould, a fabulous character prominent in Greenwich Village, lived as a Bohemian and often recited excerpts from his unpublished Oral History, which seemed to be about everything. Harry Thaw shot Stanford White, a leading architect, in 1906 in the roof garden of the second Madison Square Garden, designed by White. Mrs. Thaw was the apex of the triangle.

The elder Clarence Day was portrayed in **Life with Father** by Clarence Shepard Day.

▶ Does everyone need a private world into which he can retreat in order to be happy?

granted and accepts its size and its turbulence as natural and inevitable. Second, there is the New York of the commuter—the city that is devoured by locusts each day and spat out each night. Third, there is the New York of the person who was born somewhere else and came to New York in quest of something. Of these three trembling cities the greatest is the last—the city of final destination, the city that is a goal. It is this third city that accounts for New York's high-strung disposition, its poetical deportment, its dedication to the arts, and its incomparable achievements. Commuters give the city its tidal restlessness; natives give it solidity and continuity; but the settlers give it passion. And whether it is a farmer arriving from Italy to set up a small grocery store in a slum, or a young girl arriving from a small town in Mississippi to escape the indignity of being observed by her neighbors, or a boy arriving from the Corn Belt with a manuscript in his suitcase and a pain in his heart, it makes no difference: each embraces New York with the intense excitement of first love, each absorbs New York with the fresh eyes of an adventurer, each generates heat and light to dwarf the Consolidated Edison Company.

The commuter is the queerest bird of all. The suburb he inhabits has no essential vitality of its own and is a mere roost where he comes at day's end to go to sleep. Except in rare cases, the man who lives in Mamaroneck or Little Neck or Teaneck, and works in New York, discovers nothing much about the city except the time of arrival and departure of trains and buses, and the path to a quick lunch. He is desk-bound, and has never, idly roaming in the gloaming, stumbled suddenly on Belvedere Tower in the Park, seen the ramparts rise sheer from the water of the pond, and the boys along the shore fishing for minnows, girls stretched out negligently on the shelves of the rocks; he has never come suddenly on anything at all in New York as a loiterer, because he has had no time between trains. He has fished in Manhattan's wallet and dug out coins, but has never listened to Manhattan's breathing, never awakened to its morning, never dropped off to sleep in its night. About 400,000 men and women come charging onto the Island each week-day morning, out of the mouths of tubes and tunnels. Not many among them have ever spent a drowsy afternoon in the great rustling oaken silence of the reading room of the Public Library, with the book elevator (like an old water wheel) spewing out books onto the trays. They tend their furnaces in Westchester and in Jersey, but have never seen the furnaces of the Bowery, the fires that burn in oil drums on zero winter nights. They may work in the financial district downtown and never see the extravagant plantings of Rockefeller Center—the daffodils and grape

Con Edison is New York City's gas and electric company.

Mamaroneck is in Westchester County, Little Neck at the outer edge of Queens, and Teaneck in New Jersey. All are comfortable suburbs.

The Belvedere Tower, an imitation medieval castle in Central Park, is now used as a weather station. It overlooks the New Lake and the Delacorte Theater, where Shakespeare is presented free in the summer.

The Bowery, a street on Manhattan's Lower East Side, has a large population of alcoholic derelicts.

hyacinths and birches and the flags trimmed to the wind on a fine morning in spring. Or they may work in a midtown office and may let a whole year swing round without sighting Governors Island from the sea wall. The commuter dies with tremendous mileage to his credit, but he is no rover. His entrances and exists are more devious than those in a prairie-dog village; and he calmly plays bridge while buried in the mud at the bottom of the East River. The Long Island Rail Road alone carried forty million commuters last year; but many of them were the same fellow retracing his steps.

The terrain of New York is such that a resident sometimes travels farther, in the end, than a commuter. Irving Berlin's journey from Cherry Street in the lower East Side to an apartment uptown was through an alley and was only three or four miles in length; but it was like going three times around the world.

A poem compresses much in a small space and adds music, thus heightening its meaning. The city is like poetry: it compresses all life, all races and breeds, into a small island and adds music and the accompaniment of internal engines. The island of Manhattan is without any doubt the greatest human concentrate on earth, the poem whose magic is comprehensible to millions of permanent residents but whose full meaning will always remain elusive. At the feet of the tallest and plushiest offices lie the crummiest slums. The genteel mysteries housed in the Riverside Church are only a few blocks from the voodoo charms of Harlem. The merchant princes, riding to Wall Street in their limousines down the East River Drive, pass within a few hundred yards of the gypsy kings; but the princes do not know they are passing kings, and the kings are not up yet anyway—they live a more leisurely life than the princes and get drunk more consistently.

New York is nothing like Paris; it is nothing like London; and it is not Spokane multiplied by sixty, or Detroit multiplied by four. It is by all odds the loftiest of cities. It even managed to reach the highest point in the sky at the lowest moment of the depression. The Empire State Building shot twelve hundred and fifty feet into the air when it was madness to put out as much as six inches of new growth. (The building has a mooring mast that no dirigible has ever tied to; it employs a man to flush toilets in slack times; it has been hit by an airplane in a fog, struck countless times by lightning, and been jumped off of by so many unhappy people that pedestrians instinctively quicken step when passing Fifth Avenue and 34th Street.)

Manhattan has been compelled to expand skyward because of the absence of any other direction in which to grow. This, more

Governors Island is located south of Manhattan in New York Harbor. Since colonial days, it has been a fort or military installation. Today it is under the jurisdiction of the U.S. Coast Guard.

Irving Berlin, whose first big hit was "Alexander's Ragtime Band" (1911), was probably the most successful popular-song composer of the first half of the twentieth century.

The Riverside Church is a prominent liberal Protestant church on the Upper West Side of Manhattan. It is about five blocks from Harlem and just across Riverside Drive from Grant's Tomb.

The Empire State Building was completed in 1931, during the Great Depression.

257

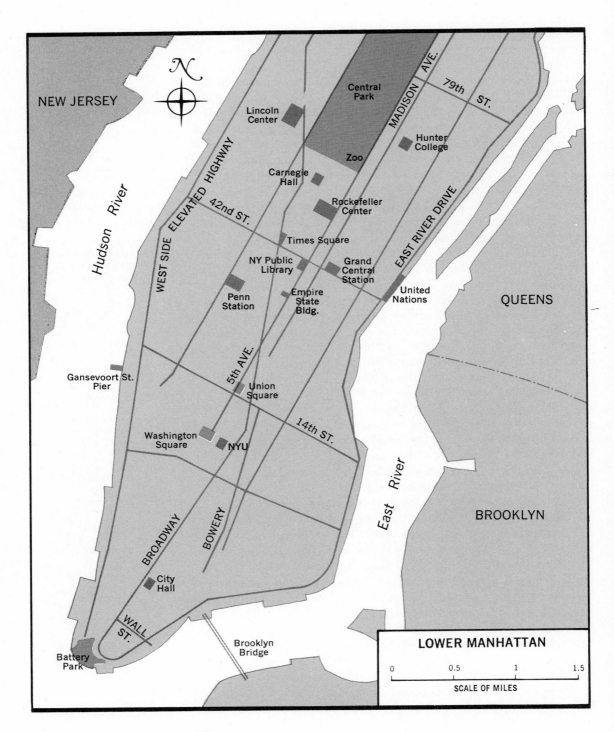

NEW JERSEY

Hudson River

Lincoln Center

Central Park

MADISON AVE.

79th ST.

Zoo

Hunter College

WEST SIDE ELEVATED HIGHWAY

42nd ST.

Carnegie Hall

Rockefeller Center

EAST RIVER DRIVE

Times Square

NY Public Library

Grand Central Station

United Nations

QUEENS

Penn Station

Empire State Bldg.

5th AVE.

Gansevoort St. Pier

Union Square

14th ST.

East River

Washington Square

NYU

BROOKLYN

BROADWAY

BOWERY

City Hall

WALL ST.

Brooklyn Bridge

Battery Park

**LOWER MANHATTAN**

0        0.5        1        1.5

SCALE OF MILES

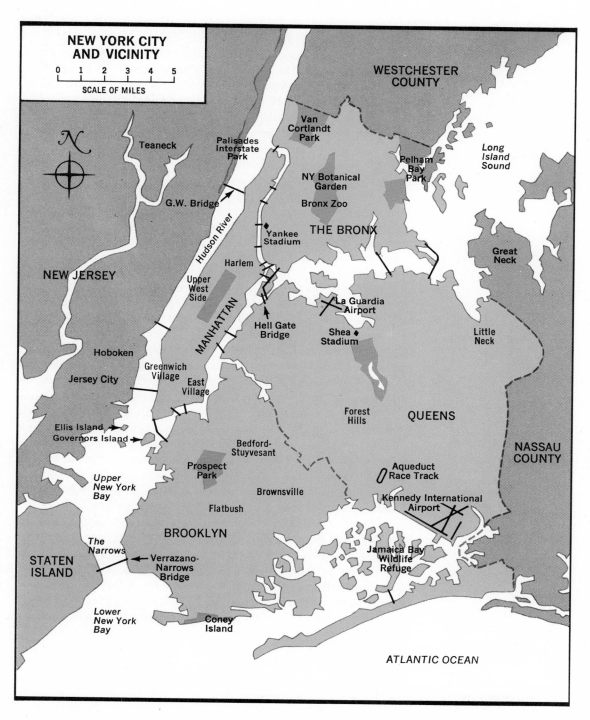

NEW YORK CITY
AND VICINITY

0 1 2 3 4 5
SCALE OF MILES

N

Teaneck

Palisades
Interstate
Park

G.W. Bridge

WESTCHESTER
COUNTY

Van
Cortlandt
Park

Pelham
Bay
Park

Long
Island
Sound

NY Botanical
Garden

Bronx Zoo

THE BRONX

Hudson River

NEW JERSEY

Yankee
Stadium

Harlem

Upper
West
Side

Great
Neck

La Guardia
Airport

MANHATTAN

Hell Gate
Bridge

Shea
Stadium

Little
Neck

Hoboken

Greenwich
Village

Jersey City

East
Village

Ellis Island
Governors Island

Upper
New York
Bay

Prospect
Park

Bedford-
Stuyvesant

Forest
Hills

QUEENS

NASSAU
COUNTY

Brownsville

Flatbush

Aqueduct
Race Track

Kennedy International
Airport

BROOKLYN

The
Narrows

STATEN
ISLAND

Verrazano-
Narrows
Bridge

Jamaica Bay
Wildlife
Refuge

Lower
New York
Bay

Coney
Island

ATLANTIC OCEAN

than any other thing, is responsible for its physical majesty. It is
to the nation what the white church spire is to the village—the
visible symbol of aspiration and faith, the white plume saying
that the way is up. The summer traveler swings in over Hell Gate
Bridge and from the window of his sleeping car as it glides above
the pigeon lofts and back yards of Queens looks southwest to where
the morning light first strikes the steel peaks of midtown, and he
sees its upward thrust unmistakable: the great walls and towers
rising, the smoke rising, the heat not yet rising, the hopes and
ferments of so many awakening millions rising—this vigorous spear
that presses heaven hard. . . .

The oft-quoted thumbnail sketch of New York is, of course: "It's
a wonderful place, but I'd hate to live there." I have an idea that
people from villages and small towns, people accustomed to the
convenience and the friendliness of neighborhood over-the-fence
living, are unaware that life in New York follows the neighborhood
pattern. The city is literally a composite of tens of thousands of
tiny neighborhood units. There are, of course, the big districts and
big units: Chelsea and Murray Hill and Gramercy (which are
residential units), Harlem (a racial unit), Greenwich Village (a
unit dedicated to the arts and other matters), and there is Radio
City (a commercial development), Peter Cooper Village (a housing
unit), the Medical Center (a sickness unit) and many other sections each of which has some distinguishing characteristic. But the
curious thing about New York is that each large geographical unit
is composed of countless small neighborhoods. Each neighborhood
is virtually self-sufficient. Usually it is no more than two or three
blocks long and a couple of blocks wide. Each area is a city within
a city within a city. Thus, no matter where you live in New York,
you will find within a block or two a grocery store, a barbershop,
a newsstand and shoeshine shack, an ice-coal-and-wood cellar
(where you write your order on a pad outside as you walk by), a
dry cleaner, a laundry, a delicatessen (beer and sandwiches delivered at any hour to your door), a flower shop, an undertaker's
parlor, a movie house, a radio-repair shop, a stationer, a haber-
dasher, a tailor, a drugstore, a garage, a tearoom, a saloon, a hard-
ware store, a liquor store, a shoe-repair shop. Every block or two,
in most residential sections of New York, is a little main street.
A man starts for work in the morning and before he has gone two
hundred yards he has completed half a dozen missions: bought a
paper, left a pair of shoes to be soled, picked up a pack of cig-
arettes, ordered a bottle of whiskey to be dispatched in the opposite direction against his home-coming, written a message to the

unseen forces of the wood cellar, and notified the dry cleaner that a pair of trousers awaits call. Homeward bound eight hours later, he buys a bunch of pussy willows, a Mazda bulb, a drink, a shine —all between the corner where he steps off the bus and his apartment. So complete is each neighborhood, and so strong the sense of neighborhood, that many a New Yorker spends a lifetime within the confines of an area smaller than a country village. Let him walk two blocks from his corner and he is in a strange land and will feel uneasy till he gets back.

Storekeepers are particularly conscious of neighborhood boundary lines. A woman friend of mine moved recently from one apartment to another, a distance of three blocks. When she turned up, the day after the move, at the same grocer's that she had patronized for years, the proprietor was in ecstasy—almost in tears—at seeing her. "I was afraid," he said, "now that you've moved away I wouldn't be seeing you any more." To him, *away* was three blocks, or about seven hundred and fifty feet. . . .

I've been remembering what it felt like as a young man to live in the same town with giants. When I first arrived in New York my personal giants were a dozen or so columnists and critics and poets whose names appeared regularly in the papers. I burned with a low steady fever just because I was on the same island with Don Marquis, Heywood Broun, Christopher Morley, Franklin P. Adams, Robert C. Benchley, Frank Sullivan, Dorothy Parker, Alexander Woollcott, Ring Lardner and Stephen Vincent Benét. I would hang around the corner of Chambers Street and Broadway, thinking: "Somewhere in that building is the typewriter that archy the cockroach jumps on at night." New York hardly gave me a living at that period, but it sustained me. I used to walk quickly past the house in West 13th Street between Sixth and Seventh where F. P. A. lived, and the block seemed to tremble under my feet—the way Park Avenue trembles when a train leaves Grand Central. This excitation (nearness of giants) is a continuing thing. The city is always full of young worshipful beginners—young actors, young aspiring poets, ballerinas, painters, reporters, singers—each depending on his own brand of tonic to stay alive, each with his own stable of giants. . . .

. . . In Turtle Bay there is an old willow tree that presides over an interior garden. It is a battered tree, long suffering and much climbed, held together by strands of wire but beloved of those who know it. In a way it symbolizes the city: life under difficulties,

Incandescent light bulbs used to be known as "Mazda bulbs."

▶ Have supermarkets, department stores, and shopping centers helped to destroy a sense of neighborhood?

Don Marquis was a satiric columnist in several New York newspapers. Many of his columns featured the adventures of archy the cockroach and mehitabel the cat.

Turtle Bay is a section of Manhattan along the East River. It is now occupied mainly by the United Nations Headquarters.

growth against odds, sap-rise in the midst of concrete, and the steady reaching for the sun. Whenever I look at it nowadays, and feel the cold shadow of the planes, I think: "This must be saved, this particular thing, this very tree." If it were to go, all would go—this city, this mischievous and marvelous monument which not to look upon would be like death.

# 2 THE BOYHOOD
# OF ALFRED KAZIN

Jews had lived in New York City for two centuries before the great influx of Jewish immigration. Most of these early settlers had emigrated from Spain or Germany; many had risen to prominence. Then, in the early 1880's, the governments of the Austro-Hungarian Empire and Russia increased their persecution of the Jews. At the same time, economic opportunities for Eastern European Jews seemed limited. In increasing numbers they sold their property, loaded a few possessions onto carts and trains, and began the trek to the New World. Soon the long beards of the orthodox were a common sight on city streets.

Jews were forbidden to own land in central Europe. Most of them earned livings as artisans or merchants. Persecuted for centuries by Europe's governments, Jews had learned to look to family, synagogue, and community organizations for succor and to rely on their community spirit to keep their ancient culture alive. This culture emphasized love for learning and respect for the scholar. In Europe, whole families had struggled to support one son studying for the rabbinate. This family solidarity and respect for the book helped to prepare Jewish immigrants to grasp the opportunities of the New World.

Most of the first generation of Jewish immigrants became tradesmen or workers in New York City's factories, particularly in the garment industry. There they helped to build the International Ladies Garment Workers Union and the Amalgamated Clothing Workers of America, two of the nation's outstanding labor unions. But the sons of these garment workers—and of the other tradesmen so prominent among the Jewish immigrants—went to the public schools, enrolled in New York's colleges, especially the tuition-free College of the City of New York (CCNY), and entered the professions. Out of their ranks have grown a disproportionate number of leading American musicians, writers, historians, actors, and artists.

One of the most notable of these men is Alfred Kazin, a distinguished American critic who has written a number of books about American literature. Although his autobiography speaks only for one man and not for all of New York's Jews, it still describes many typical aspects of life among Jewish immigrants and their children. As you read this account from his autobiography which describes life in the Brownsville section of Brooklyn, think about the following questions:

1. What gave Kazin security? What was the base from which he reached for opportunity in New York City? What was available for him to grasp?
2. Would Kazin agree with White that a New York neighborhood is only a block or so long? What took him out of this neighborhood? What did he see out there?
3. What was the good man from the point of view of the Jewish family as represented in Kazin's autobiography? the good life? the good society? Might Kazin himself answer these questions in the same way a generation later?

## A Walker in the City

Every time I go back to Brownsville it is as if I had never been away. From the moment I step off the train at Rockaway Avenue and smell the leak out of the men's room, then the pickles from the stand just below the subway steps, an instant rage comes over me, mixed with dread and some unexpected tenderness. It is over ten years since I left to live in the "city"—everything just out of Brownsville was always "the city." Actually I did not go very far; it was enough that I could leave Brownsville. Yet as I walk those familiarly choked streets at dusk and see the old women sitting in front of the tenements, past and present become each other's faces; I am back where I began. . . .

All my early life lies open to my eye within five city blocks. When I passed the school, I went sick with all my old fear of it. . . .

It was never learning I associated with . . . school: only the necessity to succeed, to get ahead of the others in the daily struggle to "make a good impression" on our teachers, who grimly, wearily, and often with ill-concealed distaste watched against our relapsing into the natural savagery they expected of Brownsville boys. . . .

Alfred Kazin, **A Walker in the City** (New York: Harcourt, Brace & World, Inc., 1951), pp. 5–6, 17–19, 43–44, 64–66, 83–84, 94–96. Reprinted by permission.

All teachers were to be respected like gods, and God Himself was the greatest of all school superintendents. Long after I had ceased to believe that our teachers could see with the back of their heads, it was still understood, by me, that they knew everything. They were the delegates of all visible and invisible power on earth—of the mothers who waited on the stoops every day after three for us to bring home tales of our daily triumphs; of the glacially remote Anglo-Saxon principal, whose very name was King; of the incalculably important Superintendent of Schools who would someday rubberstamp his name to the bottom of our diplomas in grim acknowledgment that we had, at last, given satisfaction to him, to the Board of Superintendents, and to our benefactor the City of New York—and so up and up, to the government of the United States and to the great Lord Jehovah Himself. My belief in teachers' unlimited wisdom and power rested not so much on what I saw in them—how impatient most of them looked, how wary—but on our abysmal humility, at least in those of us who were "good" boys, who proved by our ready compliance and "manners" that we wanted to get on. The road to a professional future would be shown us only as we pleased *them. Make a good impression the first day of the term, and they'll help you out. Make a bad impression, and you might as well cut your throat.* This was the first article of school folklore, whispered around the classroom the opening day of each term. You made the "good impression" by sitting firmly at your wooden desk, hands clasped; by silence for the greatest part of the live-long day; by standing up obsequiously when it was so expected of you; by sitting down noiselessly when you had answered a question; by "speaking nicely," which meant reproducing their painfully exact enunciation; by "showing manners," or an ecstatic submissiveness in all things; by outrageous flattery; by bringing little gifts at Christmas, on their birthdays, and at the end of the term—the well-known significance of these gifts being that they came not from us, but from our parents, whose eagerness in this matter showed a high level of social consideration, and thus raised our standing in turn. . . .

The little wooden synagogue was "our" place. . . . All good *Dugschitzer* were expected to show up in it at least once a year, had their sons confirmed in it as a matter of course, and would no doubt be buried from it when their time came. Members of the congregation referred to each other in a homely familiar way, using not the unreal second names so many Jews in Russia had been given for the Czar's census, but the first names in their

"Obsequiously" means servilely.

▶ Should the schools permit students to bring Christmas presents to teachers?

**Dugschitzer** refers to people from the Polish village of Dugschitz, where Kazin's mother was born. Kazin's synagogue was made up almost entirely of **Dugschitzers**. Like other immigrants to New York City, Jews from particular villages often settled near each other.

familiar order—Dovid Yossel's or Khannah Sorke's; some were known simply by some distinguishing physical trait, the Rakhmiel lame in one foot. There were little twists and turns to the liturgy that were strictly "ours," a particularly nostalgic way of singing out the opening words of prayers that only *Dugschitzer* could possibly know. If the *blind* Rakhmiel—the Rakhmiel in the back bench who was so nearsighted that he might fairly be described as blind—skipped two lines in the prayer book, the sexton would clutch his hands in despair and call out mockingly, *"Beneshalélem; Bless the Lord!* Will you just listen to the way he *reads?"* There were scornful little references to the way outsiders did things—people from Warsaw, for example, who gave every sound a pedantic roll; or Galicians, who, as everyone knew, were coarse-grained, had no taste, took cream with herring, and pronounced certain words in so uncouth a manner that it made you ache with laughter just to hear them. What did it matter that our congregation was poor, our synagogue small and drab? It was sufficient to the handful of *us* in Brownsville, and from birth to death would regather us in our ties to God, to the tradition of Israel, and to each other. On a Saturday when a boy had been confirmed, and the last loving proud *Amen!* had been heard from the women where they sat at the back separated from us by a gauze curtain, and a table in an open space between the pews had been laden with nut-cake, fruit, herring, and wine, and the brethren had gathered to toast the boy and his parents and each other in their rejoicing for Israel, we were all—no matter what we knew of each other or had suffered from each other—one plighted family. . . .

In Brownsville tenements the kitchen is always the largest room and the center of the household. As a child I felt that we lived in a kitchen to which four other rooms were annexed. . . . The kitchen held our lives together. My mother worked in it all day long, we ate in it almost all meals except the Passover *seder*, I did my homework and first writing at the kitchen table, and in winter I often had a bed made up for me on three kitchen chairs near the stove. On the wall just over the table hung a long horizontal mirror that sloped to a ship's prow at each end and was lined in cherry wood. It took up the whole wall, and drew every object in the kitchen to itself. The walls were a fiercely stippled whitewash, so often rewhitened by my father in slack seasons that the paint looked as if it had been squeezed and cracked into the walls. A large electric bulb hung down the center of the kitchen at the end of a chain that had been hooked into the ceiling; the

The sexton serves as custodian of synagogue property.

Galicians refers to Jews from the area called Galicia. That region is in what is now southern Poland and eastern Czechoslovakia.

▶ Are some of your fond childhood memories focused on a place where your family gathered?

**Passover** is a Jewish festival which commemorates the hardships of the Israelites during their Egyptian bondage, and their deliverance from that bondage. **Seders**— ceremonial dinners—are celebrated on the first and second nights of the seven- or eight-day festival.

When Kazin was growing up, many American homes had only recently changed from gas to electric lighting.

The Workmen's Circle was a Jewish fraternal and mutual aid association.

"New York" to Kazin, as to many New Yorkers today, could refer to Manhattan alone.

old gas ring and key still jutted out of the wall like antlers. In the corner next to the toilet was the sink at which we washed, and the square tub in which my mother did our clothes. Above it, tacked to the shelf on which were pleasantly ranged square, blue-bordered white sugar and spice jars, hung calendars from the Public National Bank on Pitkin Avenue and the Minsker Progressive Branch of the Workmen's Circle; receipts for the payment of insurance premiums, and household bills on a spindle; two little boxes engraved with Hebrew letters. One of these was for the poor, the other to buy back the Land of Israel. Each spring a bearded little man would suddenly appear in our kitchen, salute us with a hurried Hebrew blessing, empty the boxes (sometimes with a sidelong look of disdain if they were not full), hurriedly bless us again for remembering our less fortunate Jewish brothers and sisters, and so take his departure until the next spring, after vainly trying to persuade my mother to take still another box. We did occasionally remember to drop coins in the boxes, but this was usually only on the dreaded morning of "midterms" and final examinations, because my mother thought it would bring me luck. She was extremely superstitious, but embarrassed about it, and always laughed at herself whenever, on the morning of an examination, she counseled me to leave the house on my right foot. "I know it's silly," her smile seemed to say, "but what harm can it do? It may calm God down." . . .

The block: *my* block. It was on the Chester Street side of our house, between the grocery and the back wall of the old drugstore, that I was hammered into the shape of the streets. Everything beginning at Blake Avenue would always wear for me some delightful strangeness and mildness, simply because it was not of my block, *the* block, where the clang of your head sounded against the pavement when you fell in a fistfight, and the rows of storelights on each side were pitiless, watching you. Anything away from the block was good: even a school you never went to, two blocks away: there were vegetable gardens in the park across the street. Returning from "New York," I would take the longest routes home from the subway, get off a station ahead of our own, only for the unexpectedness of walking through Betsy Head Park and hearing the gravel crunch under my feet as I went beyond the vegetable gardens, smelling the sweaty sweet dampness from the pool in summer and the dust on the leaves as I passed under the ailanthus trees. On the block itself everything rose up only to test me. . . .

Museums and parks were related, both oases to stop in "beyond." But in some way museums and parks were painful, each an ex-

plosion of unbearable fullness in my brain. I could never go home
from the Brooklyn Museum, a walk around the reservoir in Central
Park, or sit in a rowboat Sunday afternoons in Prospect Park—where
your voice hallooed against the stone walls of the footbridge as
you waited in that sudden cold darkness below, boat against boat,
to be pushed on to the boathouse and so end the afternoon—
without feeling the same sadness that came after the movies. The
day they took us to Children's Museum—rain was dripping on the
porch of that old wooden house, the halls were lined with Audubon
prints and were hazel in the thin antique light—I was left with
the distinct impression that I had been stirring between my fingers
dried earth and fallen leaves that I had found in between the red
broken paving stones of some small American town. I seemed to
see neighborhood rocks and minerals in the dusty light of the late
afternoon slowly stirring behind glass at the back of the village
museum. But that same day they took us to Forest Park in Queens,
and I saw a clearing filled with stone picnic tables—*nothing* had
ever cried out such a welcome as those stone tables in the clearing
—saw the trees in their dim green recede in one long moving tide
back into dusk, and gasped in pain when the evening rushed upon
us before I had a chance to walk that woodland through.

There was never enough time. The morning they had led us
through the Natural History Museum, under the skeletons of
great whales floating dreamlike on wires from the ceiling, I had
to wait afterward against the meteor in the entrance yard for my
dizziness to pass. Those whales! those whales! But that same morning they took us across Central Park to the Metropolitan, and
entering through the back door in from the park, I was flung
spinning in a bewilderment of delight from the Greek discus-
throwers to the Egyptians to the long rows of medieval knights to
the breasts of Venus glistening in my eyes as she sat—some curtain
drawn before her hiding the worst of her nakedness—smiling with
Mars and surrounded by their children.

The bewilderment eased, a little, when we went up many white
steps directly to the American paintings. There was a long, narrow corridor-looking room lined with the portraits of seventeenth-
century merchants and divines—nothing for me there as they coldly
stared at me, their faces uninterruptedly rosy in time. But far in
the back, in an alcove near the freight elevator, hung so low and
the figures so dim in the faint light that I crouched to take them
in, were pictures of New York some time after the Civil War—
skaters in Central Park, a red muffler flying in the wind; a gay
crowd moving round and round Union Square Park; horse cars
charging between the brownstones of lower Fifth Avenue at dusk.

Prospect Park in Brooklyn, like Central Park in Manhattan, was designed by Frederick Law Olmsted, the landscape architect and author. In the latter capacity, Olmsted is best known for **The Cotton Kingdom**, published in 1861.

"Metropolitan" refers to the Metropolitan Museum of Art.

I could not believe my eyes. Room on room they had painted my city, my country—Winslow Homer's dark oblong of Union soldiers making camp in the rain, tenting tonight, tenting on the old camp ground as I had never thought I *would* get to see them when we sang that song in school; Thomas Eakins's solitary sculler on the Schuylkill, resting to have his picture taken in the yellow light bright with patches of some raw spring in Pennsylvania showing on the other side of him; and most wonderful to me then, John Sloan's picture of a young girl standing in the wind on the deck of a New York ferryboat—surely to Staten Island, and just about the year of my birth?—looking out to water.

# 3 STAYING ALIVE ON WELFARE

Almost a million New Yorkers, one out of every eight residents of the city, live on welfare. City, state, and Federal governments all contribute funds to their support. Because New York pays among the highest welfare benefits in the nation, many poor people move there from areas where welfare benefits are lower. Every ethnic and racial group has contributed names to the welfare rolls. The highest proportion of welfare recipients, however, are recent immigrants from Puerto Rico and blacks who have migrated from rural areas.

As restriction cut immigration from Europe in the 1920's, a new wave of immigrants began to flow from the American South. Only 150,000 blacks lived in New York City in 1920. This number more than doubled by 1930 and jumped another 150,000 by 1940, when the census takers counted 458,000 blacks. By 1950, the black population was 748,000; in 1960, 1,088,000. It continued to rise through the early 1960's, but by 1969, the rate of black migration was decreasing.

Blacks live all over New York City. Every borough except Richmond (Staten Island) has a large ghetto, the most famous of which are Manhattan's Harlem and Brooklyn's Bedford–Stuyvesant. In addition to these major concentrations, smaller predominantly black areas have grown up. Moreover, individual black families or clusters of families live throughout the city in otherwise all-white neighborhoods. Many of the suburbs which surround New York have substantial black minorities as well.

Southern blacks are as much immigrants to New York as any Europeans have been. They have been uprooted from a subculture which puts them at a disadvantage in white, middle-class society.

Although they speak English, they come mainly from the rural South, and from a heritage marked by slavery, persecution, and discrimination. Partly because they lack education and economic skills, many black men often cannot find jobs in an economy which places a premium on educated manpower. Black women, on the other hand, have found jobs more easily, but often in menial positions such as housework.

Black people coming to New York have often lacked the advantages which strong family ties gave to other immigrant groups. In addition, blacks have been relatively slow to develop strong communal, self-help organizations. Nor have many blacks founded small businesses—groceries, funeral parlors, and so forth—of the sort which provided a first step into American capitalism for many European immigrants. Blacks from the West Indies who suffered psychologically milder forms of slavery and racism, however, have been more successful in business, on the whole, than blacks from the South.

This heritage and the continuing pressure of white racism have bred social tragedy. The unemployment rate among blacks is about twice the rate among whites. Juvenile delinquency rates and drug addiction rates are also appallingly high. Despite its many individual members who have built full and happy lives for themselves, New York's black community is sick, a victim primarily of white racism stretching more than three centuries into the past.

Reading 3 describes the life of a black New Yorker who knows the degradation of public assistance from bitter experience. It was written from an interview with a welfare recipient on the Lower East Side of Manhattan in the middle 1960's. As you read, think about the following questions:

1. What does Barbara Dugan want out of life? What chance does she have of getting it?
2. How does Mrs. Dugan spend her days? How does she cope with the system within which she lives?
3. What admirable qualities do you find in Mrs. Dugan? What qualities do you find which you do not admire?
4. What should a good society do to help to bring a good life within the reach of people who live on welfare?

## Barbara Dugan's Story

"I wish I could remember when I got this sickle-cell anemia. A lot of us here have got it. They say we got in down South, but when you got it you just don't feel like doing too much. It makes your blood slow. Hard not to do too much when you are on

Sickle-cell anemia is a hereditary condition in which the oxygen-carrying capacity of the blood is reduced, leaving the victim weak and listless. Treatment usually consists of prescribing pills and special diets with high-iron content.

Richard M. Elman, **The Poorhouse State: The American Way of Life on Public Assistance** (New York: Dell Publishing Co., Inc., 1966), pp. 117–126. Copyright © 1966 by Richard M. Elman. Reprinted by permission of Pantheon Books, a Division of Random House, Inc., and Gunther Stuhlmann, Author's Representative.

the Welfare. They give you the pills and the special diets, and they send you to homemaking classes if they think it will help you, but they don't help you otherwise, so you still have a lot to do. They is picking up the kids after school because you don't want them walking home alone in a neighborhood like this . . . and they's cooking and shopping and laundry and housecleaning, and then well-baby clinic and sick-baby clinic and the clinic for yourself and that sickle-cell anemia. It's a full day.

"What I mean by a neighborhood like this is they's a lot of junkies and queers around here. Well, you just don't want to take a chance on them. So you carry your kids to school in the morning, and you carry them home after school. My kids live ten blocks away from the school. Ain't no buses down here . . .

"Ain't no lazy people on Welfare. Oh, maybe they is a few, but they ain't many. Seems like you got to pull your lazy butt from one place to the next, and you got to pull your kids with you wherever you go because they ain't no place you can leave them where they be safe . . . And sometimes you just don't feel like doing too much, but you still got to do it if you don't want them to take your kids away from you. *They find you lying in bed with nothing to do that's just what they going to do—sickle-cell anemia and all.* I got two sick kids like me and another in the Kennedy Home in the Bronx . . . I don't know about him . . . and sometimes you get pretty tired, but you just got to do certain things. After all, they say, if you don't take care of these kids, who will? They got a point. Ain't nobody else around here . . . and, after all, they's givin' you a special diet . . .

"But every time you want something extra from them, it's a whole nuisance. Like carfare. Sometimes I got to spend ninety cents for carfare for me and the kids to go off to Bellevue, because, as I told you, you can't leave them alone if you got to go there for some reason. And when I come back from Bellevue clinic, I got to rush over here to 28th Street for that carfare money or else I'm going to run short on food. Well, even so, they don't just give you your money like that. Sometimes they want proof. Sometimes they say they will owe it to you. You got to be careful about the ones who say that. I learned you got to insist right then and there you want that carfare or else you don't get it. So you just got to sit there and wait for the man until he gives it to you. You think they care? Sometimes I think I spend half my life waiting somewhere for ninety cents. . . .

"Barbara Ann goes to the psychiatrist because they said so at school but if you ask me, it's because we've been pushed down for so long even the kids know it. She cries a lot. I used to be that

The Kennedy Home cares for mentally retarded children.

Bellevue is a large municipal hospital.

▶ Should welfare officials treat their clients politely and with kindness?

270

way. You mustn't believe them when they say we get something for nothing. You may not have to work when you are on the Welfare, but you don't get anything for nothing. They make it hard as dirt. If you want something, you got to go and get it. And you can't ask the man to help because how should he know. He don't even know you're alive half the time, and the other half it's always so much this and that...

"Worse thing of all is when they decide you haven't done right. Then they get awful mean. They'll threaten you. Some of these women get sulky after one of those visits. They get sunk down real low. Every time they's a visit they get that way . . . real low . . . I don't get that way anymore. Any time they get after my tail, I take my kids and march right over here and I just start scuffling. They see me barging in like that, hollering for the man, and they just know I know my rights. You think they would treat me like those others?

"Well, you can't do that every day of the week when you got sickle-cell anemia. Sometimes you just wake up too tired. Sometimes you just don't want to go out looking for bargains. So, when night comes, you send your kids out for some of the *cuchifritos* or maybe delicatessen or a pizza pie and cokes and you just sitting around having an early supper when he comes by.

"He says, 'I just wanted to see how things are coming along.' Or he says, 'I thought I would like to find out how you are getting on.'

"And then he looks at all that food and he gets real mean. Gives you a big lecture about how you got sickle-cell anemia and should eat the proper food or what is the use of the special diet anyway. And sure enough, next time you get a check they have taken away that special diet and you got to start all over again at Bellevue with a letter from the doctor.

. . . . "Worst of all, though, are the special men who come at night. Like this one man asked me, 'If you got no man in the house what you got those pills?' Well, I told him they give them over at the Planned Parenthood two years ago and I ain't used any of them, as he can plainly see. Then he says, 'You make sure you stay that way.' . . .

"Speaking of husbands, they used to come around to some of these women. Early in the morning you could hear them running down the stairs. You think they'd ask these women when they suspected something? No. They come around asking you. Well, I ain't going to tell on any of these girls when I know I'm likely to get my head split in.

. . . . "And that's the way it goes. You're always asking and being told and going from this place to that place. You're always waiting

▶ Is it fair to cause trouble in order to get better service?

Cuchifritos are popular New York snacks of Puerto Rican origin. They are made of fried pork and can be shaped in a variety of ways.

Welfare agencies will commonly stop payments to women with dependent children if they can ascertain that there is a man in the house who is capable of providing support.

Planned Parenthood is an organization devoted to limiting family size. It provides free birth control information.

271

on lines. And all you ever think about is your Welfare. You're right. The way they got it fixed, it's just like being a junkie. You get your checks twice a month, but you got to keep going over there every few days for that extra little fix, and sometimes when you need it worst of all the man ain't nowhere to be seen.

"Worst of all, though, is when you got kids. They need gym shoes. You got to go to Welfare. They need a doctor's examination for camp, and again you got to arrange it for the Welfare. If you spend the money for food to buy your girl shoes (because she needs them for school and you figure you can save yourself a trip), the next thing you know the man wants to know why you ain't got no money. Kids just don't understand budgets, and when they want something, they really want it. I'd like to see the mother who thinks differently. But it don't work that way on Welfare. I get maybe $4.00 a week for their clothes and for me, but I am always using it to do other things. So then, when I need something, I got to go down and get the money from the Welfare, and they likely to want to know why. When you got kids, it's not a good thing to be on the Welfare.

"Well, nobody wants to get rid of their kids. Least I don't see how they could. So you are always buying now and asking questions later, and then they get angry with you and you catch hell. It's the goddamnedest life. If you buy at the store, they overcharge. If you go to the supermarket, you got to carry all that stuff back— and who's taking care of your kids meanwhile? I tell you it isn't easy when you got sickle-cell anemia . . . And some of these women got worse things than that. My neighbor's daughter is an epileptic . . . so when I asked the doctor for a housekeeper because they give her one, this man say, 'You got anybody with brain damage?'. . .

"Yes, seems like they always going to make remarks. I don't care if they white or colored. They make remarks. The colored's the worst sometimes. The young ones are a little better, but the way some of them come sniffing around, you think maybe they looking for the wrong thing. Worst of all is that you got to put up with this every day of the week. Except Sunday. They can't do much to you on Sunday. Last Sunday I took my kids in the subway up to the Bronx because this social worker said I should go to visit that other boy. I made a picnic lunch because it was supposed to be a nice day. Then it rained, and then we had to eat in the classrooms. Anyway, when we got back I only had 50¢, so I made my kids hot cereal with raisins for supper, and early next morning I sent my boy with a note to the Welfare center to get us back some of that money.

"Well, my boy say the man had this white stuff all over his

Epilepsy is a chronic disorder of the nervous system, characterized by periodic seizures.

face. He had a bad sunburn. It was the week before school was supposed to close, but he say, 'What are you doing out of school?' So he called the guidance counselor and told him he had my boy in his office, and then I had to come to school the next morning with my boy and explain or else they said they would suspend him. Well, I told that man at the school that we just didn't have any money so I had to send my boy over to the Welfare to get reimbursed because I had all this laundry to do else there wouldn't be clean clothes for anybody. You know what that man say then? He say, 'Next time that happens you just telephone.' Can you imagine? He wants me to telephone. Don't he know they don't give us any money to do that?

"It's like when I first started on the Welfare, and they said I was 'mismanaging.' This nice girl—she was a social worker—heard about me and she said she would take my case. So every time I would get a check from the Welfare, I cashed it and brought the money to her and she would put it in this little metal box in her desk. Then I could come over there every day, and she would give me a few dollars for the shopping because she said it was better to shop every day on what I was earning. She was a good sweet girl and she liked me, I think. It was better leaving the money with her than leaving it at home where I could get robbed. So every day I would come to her and get some of that money. Then one day toward the end of the month I come to her and she says, 'I'm sorry, Barbara, I just haven't got any more money for you,' and she opens up that box and shows me that it is empty. Sure enough, we sit down then and do some figuring, and I've taken out more than there was, but she says it isn't my fault. There just wasn't enough to begin with. And she says, 'Let me give you something from my pocketbook until the end of the month.' But when she opens her purse, she's only got about three or four dollars and some change.

"'I don't know what we are going to do now,' I say. I look over at this girl. She's crying.

"'Barbara,' she says, 'I'm sorry. I'm really sorry. If I give you this I just won't have anything.'

"So I had to go out then and buy at the Spanish grocer, and I've been paying him back ever since. You know, because I was short. Well, after that I figured I'll hold onto my money myself because if they ain't enough, they ain't much sense to budgeting. You know what I mean? I mean it's a little silly. Course, things can change. I get this special diet now, and I get a little more money. I don't wish to sound ungrateful. I just wish it wasn't always so hard. You know what I mean. And those remarks all the time. You know what I mean, don't you?"

Small local grocery stores will frequently grant credit to customers and concurrently charge higher prices.

# 4 THE PUERTO RICANS

In the 1960's, thousands of political refugees from Cuba and Haiti also arrived in New York City.

The Puerto Ricans are New York's most recent large group of immigrants. About five hundred Puerto Ricans lived in New York in 1910. By 1920 their numbers had grown to seven thousand. In 1930, 45,000 lived in the city. A decade later the census counted seventy thousand. In 1950, however, their numbers had increased to 187,000 and by 1960 to 613,000. Pushed out of Puerto Rico by a burgeoning population and attracted by New York's economic opportunities, these most recent immigrants have added a large Spanish-speaking community to New York.

Officially, Puerto Rico is a commonwealth. It has an elected governor and legislature, and a non-voting delegate to the U.S. Congress. As long as they live in Puerto Rico, Puerto Ricans cannot vote in Presidential elections. Although Puerto Ricans pay no Federal income taxes, they are subject to the draft.

Because Puerto Rico is a possession of the United States, the Puerto Ricans are American citizens free to come and go between New York and their Caribbean island. Like black immigrants to New York City, however, Puerto Ricans face many disadvantages which earlier groups of foreign immigrants have not faced. First, many Puerto Ricans have some mixture of Negro blood. Their color has subjected them to white racist feeling. At the same time, resisting identification with blacks, Puerto Ricans have hesitated to unite with blacks to fight common problems. Second, like black immigrants, Puerto Rican immigrants have come from a culture quite different from that of the American middle class. Common law marriages are frequent in Puerto Rico; and families are often weak. Third, Puerto Rican culture is an uncertain blend of Indian, African, Spanish, and North American elements. Thus Puerto Ricans have not developed notably strong cultural organizations—though such organizations are now beginning to appear. Furthermore, the Catholic Church has not had the strong, binding influence among Puerto Rican immigrants that it had among Irish and Italian immigrants to New York City.

Indians lived in Puerto Rico before 1492; Africans came as slaves. And the Spanish controlled Puerto Rico as a colony from 1509 to 1898, when it became a U.S. possession as a result of the Spanish-American War.

Finally, like black immigrants, Puerto Ricans have come to New York at a period when there are fewer and fewer low-skilled jobs. Despite these handicaps, a growing number of Puerto Ricans are rising from poverty and attending New York's colleges and universities.

In recent years a number of anthropologists and other scholars have studied the Puerto Ricans. Among the most important of these studies is a long account of the lives of Puerto Rican families in the culture of poverty in San Juan, the capital of Puerto Rico, and New York City. Oscar Lewis, a native New Yorker and an anthropologist, tape-recorded interviews with a number of Puerto Ricans and translated them into English. Lewis wrote exclusively about poor Puerto Ricans, not men and women from the island, particularly educated ones, who have been more successful. Hence, the people he portrays do not represent the entire Puerto Rican population. As you read excerpts from these interviews, think about the following questions:

1. What are the problems of immediate concern to this Puerto Rican family? What do they really care about? What does your conclusion reveal about their conception of the good life? the good society?
2. Do you find evidence that this family took advantage of the cultural opportunities available—often free of charge—in New York City? How do you account for your answer?
3. What kind of people did this family admire? What were their qualities? What, by their standards, was the good man?
4. Should society try to do anything to improve the lives of Puerto Ricans in New York City?

## La Vida

I wish I had power in this country. The first thing I'd do would be to end the persecution of the Puerto Ricans. I'd put an end to the landlords who want to squeeze the last drop of juice from us, charging high rents for tiny apartments and rooms. And I'd impose strict discipline in the schools and wipe out those gangs of Italians and Negroes that defame the Puerto Ricans. And I'd stop all the bad vocabulary they use against us.

A Puerto Rican up here has a hard time finding a job and a safe place to live. If you're a Puerto Rican you can apply in twenty thousand places without getting a job. You can't get a job in a hospital or in the big department stores. But go to the factories, the cheap, ratty ones, and there you find Puerto Ricans, earning miserable wages. In the best places you find only Americans, never a Puerto Rican. That's why there's so much delinquency and crime among us.

In this country everyone lives his own life and takes the other fellow's dollar if he can. Whoever gets a chance to steal something, steals it. If they see anyone who is weak and old and has trouble crossing a street, they steal his bundle and run instead of helping him. They steal wallets from little old men. And they have no respect for anybody. Any young squirt will tell an old person to go to hell.

You see little girls, eleven to thirteen years old, smooching with men, smoking, and using junk. You see those kid pregnant and

Oscar Lewis, **La Vida** (New York: Random House, Inc., 1966), pp. 211–212, 220–222, 450–452, 454–455, 511–512. Reprinted by permission. Other rights controlled by Martin Secker & Warburg Ltd.

having babies by the time they're twelve. And why? Because their mothers pay no attention to them. There should be a law about that. The time will come when you won't be able to step outside because someone might kill you in the street. Then all they'll say is that the killer was crazy and they'll send him to an insane asylum. I tell you, this country, New York, is plain rotten.

The public schools here hardly teach anything at all. Nowadays the pupils hit the teachers. With women teachers, what else can you expect? Then they waste time in exercises, games, and cultivation. Why teach them to cultivate? This isn't a tropical country. Even in Puerto Rico this business of cultivating the land doesn't get you anywhere. And what good are games and exercises? Playing is not studying. Teach them to type, I say. I'd like to send my little girls to a parochial school, where they'd be taught good things.

▶ To what degree should schools stress preparation for jobs rather than general education?

I went to school in New York two years ago. I enrolled in an English course but there was so much kidding around that you can imagine what we learned! We got there at seven and they gave us half an hour to smoke. By eight-thirty the class was over. Is that a class? And what did they teach us? First-grade stuff! I quit.

I'd like to be a *beautician* or a nurse. All my life I've dreamed about being a nurse. But even if I had a nursing degree right now they wouldn't hire me at a hospital here, because I don't know English. That's an injustice. There should be hospitals here with Spanish-speaking staffs. North Americans go to Puerto Rico without knowing a word of Spanish and get jobs right away. So why can't we get a job without knowing English? You need English here to get any kind of a job, even to sweep floors.

In this reading, the italicized words were spoken in English. All the other words were translated from the Spanish by Oscar Lewis.

I say that I shouldn't have to know English because I'm a Puerto Rican, not an American. It's not our fault we don't know English. The whole burden shouldn't fall on us. Everyone speaks his own language and has his place. There's room for all. And let me tell you, if a Puerto Rican child learns only English it's because his mother wants to show off. But all she does is create problems for her children because people say, "Look at that kid. He's Puerto Rican and he thinks he's an American." I wouldn't want my children to forget their Spanish. If they came home from school saying, "*Mami*, whatchamacallit," in English, it would be a problem for me. My children learned Spanish from me and speak Spanish, and they'd better not start speaking English to me because I'd kill them. . . .

▶ Should parents encourage their children to get ahead even if doing so may open a wide cultural gulf between parent and child?

There are many good things about Soledad. She's a hard-working woman and a great helper to any man she lives with. There are no limits to what she will do. If you are sick she takes good care of you. She has her husband's clothes ready when he needs them. Of all the women I have had, I can say without hypocrisy that none can compare with Soledad. She is also a terribly passionate woman, and when a man desires her he desires her passionately.

Soledad's defects are due mostly to her lack of schooling, and to the fact that the people among whom she grew up did her more harm than good. She goes to a lot of trouble for the sake of her relatives, although the last thing they do is bother to be nice to her. She was brought up in a low kind of place among a low kind of people. And from what I hear, that holds for the places where she has worked too. I don't mean here in New York but before, in Puerto Rico. After all, once a woman goes to work at a *bar*, what can you expect? No matter how you look at it, that kind of thing is a defect in a woman. I learned all about her from Soledad herself. She has been quite open with me. Many of the things she went through before I met her would never have happened if I had known her earlier. What she needs most is a relative, or somebody, to give her advice and help her spiritually because she makes totally unnecessary mistakes.

The worst things about Soledad, as I said before, come from her lack of social opportunities. She doesn't even know how to express herself properly. Even when we are on the best of terms, I don't take her among friends who know how to behave, people who are decent, respectably married couples, because I never know when she's going to do something shocking. She's a terribly jealous woman. . . .

I have always liked to dress well and to have some nice jewelry. In my good times, I've had as many as fifteen suits, many of them made to measure, about ten pairs of shoes, and hats made to order at eighteen dollars apiece. I would like to be not necessarily a millionaire but fairly well off, for my family's sake as well as my own. Right now I have two watches and three pretty good rings in hock. One of the watches is worth two hundred dollars. The other one is worth about a hundred and twenty-five. Soledad has a wrist watch of her own in hock, a chain I gave her, a ring, her sewing machine, and a radio-victrola. I left some money with her and she spent it all and then pawned the TV set. We owe the *pawnshop* about four hundred dollars, counting the interest.

Soledad gives me material help. But spiritually speaking, she doesn't help me as she should. I have six children. They used to come to visit me, and I sent Soledad out to get clothes and things for them. But lately she has a very strange attitude. I can't explain it. She doesn't want my children to come. "No, don't bring those

When an item is "in hock," it is being held as security for a loan from a pawnbroker.

kids here," she tells me. That's what hurts me most, see? After all, I have taken on the support of her children and she should realize I care for my own too. And she should allow them to visit me at our home. . . .

We Puerto Ricans here in New York turn to each other for friendship. We go out on Fridays because that's the beginning of the *weekend*. A whole bunch of us Puerto Ricans go out together. Because as far as having friends of other races goes, the only one I have now is an American Negro who owns *un bar*.

Lots of people here have relatives in New Jersey, Pennsylvania, well, all over. So they often spend the *weekends* out of town. Others go to dances or to the beach. That's what we mostly do for entertainment in summer, have picnics at Coney Island. A big group of us Latins go together. Coney Island is full of people— all sorts mixed together. There you find white and black Americans. But many other beaches are different; they don't want Negroes or Puerto Ricans.

We have our own clubs here too. There's one that holds a meeting every Sunday over the radio. They talk about the governors, what they're like and what they have done. . . . I would like to work for the equality of Negroes and whites although I can't say that racial prejudice has really screwed me up much. But I don't agree with this business of the Negroes fighting. Many of them do it as a blind. They steal and shield themselves behind the race problem. I wouldn't get mixed up in those fights; they are Americans and understand each other. I'd let myself be drawn into something like that only if it was the Puerto Ricans who were in it. We have nothing to do with this business, so there's no need to get involved in fights.

If it were in my power to help the Puerto Ricans any way I chose, I would choose a good education for them, for the little ones who are growing up now. I would like them to have good schools where they would be taught English, yes, but Spanish too. That's what's wrong with the system up here—they don't teach Spanish to our children. That's bad, because if a child of yours is born and brought up here and then goes back to Puerto Rico, he can't get a job. How can he, when he knows no Spanish? It's good to know English. But Spanish is for speaking to your own people. That's the problem the children of Puerto Ricans have up here. They understand Spanish but they can't speak or write it.

A good education would help them to get jobs. Because sometimes Puerto Ricans come here to get a job and they can't find one. They want to work and earn money but don't have any schooling

Coney Island, in fact a peninsula, forms part of the southern shore of Brooklyn on the Atlantic Ocean. Its ocean beach, boardwalk, amusement park, and aquarium can be reached by subway.

at all. They find themselves in a tight spot and maybe they have school children to support, so they'll accept any job that comes their way, usually the worst ones. That's one cause for the delinquency there is among us.

Another thing I would like to work for is better housing. Puerto Ricans can't get good apartments here because the landlords begin raising the rent. They don't want us because they say we're dirty and messy. All pay for what a few of us do. What happens is that when a Puerto Rican rents a place he cracks the plaster on the walls by driving in nails to hang pictures. And then he paints the different rooms different colors. Americans don't like that. So if a Puerto Rican goes to look for an apartment in a pretty part of the city, he finds they charge a hundred and fifty or two hundred dollars' rent. How can we pay that? A Puerto Rican here barely earns enough to pay for rent and food. . . .

Well, I live in New York and I don't meddle with what goes on here. I do see that Kennedy, the President who was killed, was pure gold. He was a Democrat and that's the same as being a *Popular* in Puerto Rico. But even so, he was good. Do you know what he fought for? For equality between Negroes and whites. For civil rights, which are the rights that belong to us, like not allowing a cop to come into your house and search it without your leave. The privacy of the home is a right that every one of us has. And he was also for your right not to be stopped and searched by a cop for no reason at all as you walk quietly down a street, minding your own business. And for Negroes' rights to get a job as well as white men. All those are civil rights. President Kennedy was in favor of all that. . . .

The Popular Democratic Party, founded by Luis Muñoz Marín, has worked for economic development in Puerto Rico.

Life is good here but I'd rather live in Puerto Rico. I like it better. It's so beautiful! But as long as I'm here in New York, my ambition is to make money. I'm going to enroll in night school and learn to speak English well. Then maybe someday I'll get my wish, to be in the *merchant marine*. That way I could work on a ship and get the money to go back to Puerto Rico and buy a house of my own, because you never do get to own one here. You pay and keep on paying, year in and year out, and you never do get to own it. No, what I want is a little cottage in Puerto Rico where I can keep hogs, chickens, and all sorts of animals. A home. A place where I can look at the mountains.

If I'm able to build myself a house there, I'll take my *mamá* to live with me. I'll divide the house in two and keep her there. That would be a good life, living in the country in Puerto Rico with my wife and with everything that I own here, my TV set, the record player, and all. And with the rest of my family near me. Every day I wake up with that hope. Although I have doubts, too, now and then. Sometimes I have a dream. I see myself leaving New York and going back to Puerto Rico. But when I get there I find myself friendless and alone. Nobody looks at me. No one seems to know me. I'm all dirty. And in my dream I think, "What am I doing here in Puerto Rico where nobody knows me anymore?" Then I begin to cry. I feel, oh, I feel I sort of shouldn't be in Puerto Rico at all. That's when I always wake up and say, "It was only a dream. I'm still in New York."

# 5 THE BUSINESS WORLD

New York City is the capital of American business. Wall Street has long dominated American finance; the Madison Avenue area runs advertising and publishing; with the exception of Hollywood, New York also controls the entertainment industry. The central offices of almost 2500 business firms, each with a net worth of more than a million dollars are in New York; thousands of other firms keep branch offices in the skyscrapers of the business districts.

Virtually every American corporate executive with offices elsewhere visits New York at least once a year. There he borrows money, negotiates financial mergers, buys raw materials, and sells finished products. Because New York plays such a central role in American business, the folkways of New York offices spread throughout the land.

We sometimes forget the large role which work plays in our lives. Most American men spend as much time, portal-to-portal, at their work as they do sleeping, or in all the remaining activities of their lives combined. In contemporary New York, particularly among the business elite, work plays a more important role than it did among the elite in cities such as ancient Athens or Renaissance Florence. The workways of American businessmen are one of the dimensions of the good life which are well worth study.

The editors of *Fortune,* a magazine widely read by business executives, have conducted a number of studies of business folkways. The report that follows was based on interviews with 221 management men ranging from company presidents to recent college graduates in their first years as corporation trainees. As you read excerpts from this report, think about the following questions:

1. What are the attributes of a good corporate executive?
2. What do typical executives do most of the time? What do they choose not to do? How do these decisions define the good life?
3. What do executives contribute to humanistic activities? to civic endeavors? to their families? What do you think of the values which these decisions imply?
4. Do you want to be a business executive?

# The Executive Life

. . . . A study of executives' working habits—and executives' attitudes toward them—made by *Fortune* shows that:

1. Executives are working as hard as they ever did. It is difficult to see how they could possibly work harder.
2. Despite all grumbling by executives, high income taxes have had remarkably little effect on executives' drive.
3. Executives are subject to more tensions than ever before. While the swing to "human relations" and committee management has eliminated many of the old work pressures, it has substituted plenty of new ones. . . .

By the Editors of Fortune. From the January 1954 issue of Fortune Magazine. That article has appeared in a book published by Doubleday & Co., Inc. Reprinted by permission.

In most places the average executive office week runs between forty-five and forty-eight hours. Most executives arrive at the office between 8:00 and 9:00 A.M., and leave about 5:30 or 6:00 P.M. At this point the executive is past the halfway mark; the work night has begun. On the average he will work four nights out of five. One night he will be booked for business entertaining—more, probably, if he's a president. Another night he will probably spend at the office, or in a lengthy conference somewhere else.

On two other nights he goes home, not to a sanctuary so much as to a branch office. Only a minority of executives have equipped their dens with dictating machines and calculators and such, but the majority devote at least two nights a week to business reading. . . .

Putting all the commitments together, we get a work week something like this: forty-five to forty-eight hours of daytime work; one night working late at the office, two nights working at home, one night entertaining—all in all, some fifty-seven to sixty hours. And this evidently is a minimum; come convention time, a trip, a company emergency, and the week can easily go to seventy or eighty hours. . . .

Why . . . do they work so hard? The executives' motivations, it appears, essentially are what they have always been. Here are the drives identified most often when executives justified the amount of work they did:

*Self-expression.* In talking about why he works, the executive does not speak first of pressures from the organization; very rarely does he even mention his family as a goad. He speaks of himself—and the demon within him. "People are like springs," explains one company president. "The energy you have in you has to come out one way or another. I would really get in bad shape if I didn't work." "It's like baseball," another executive puts it. "A good player never stops to think of his contract when he comes to the plate. He drives for the fences." Analogies are endless—even concert pianists are alluded to—but the theme is always self-expression.

▶ Can succeeding in school, even if it involves many hours of homework, become a means of self-expression?

*Sense of contribution.* Executives see the expression of the ego as inseparable from service to others. Characteristically, the executive can generate a great sense of excitement about his particular field of work, the frontiers of the job, the saga of the industry, and the like. While a good bit of hot air is sometimes generated in the process, the fact remains that the executive who cannot identify his drives with the commonweal is likely to be a tormented one.

In this sense management men are fortunate. On the whole they are not much preoccupied with such questions as "Is management a profession?" They are so confident that their status as a group is excellent, so confident that what they do is vital, that they don't debilitate their drive by worrying about their collective prestige. Besides, they don't have the time.

*Responsibility.* The weight of responsibility can be killing; nevertheless, it is apparent from the way executives talk of it that they wouldn't be happy unless they felt the weight. "If you're in charge of an organization," goes a typical comment, "you never forget that if you fail, it's not your failure alone but a loss to lots of others."

▶ How much should a person (a father, for example) drive himself because the welfare of others depends on him?

*Prestige.* Because of the increasingly democratic class structure of the American office, many management aspirants have the mistaken idea that status and "all that sort of stuff" is an extremely minor incentive for executives. In actual fact executives love it, and they have no pious reluctance to admit the fact. "When I walk out of the building," the head of one of America's largest corporations recently told a friend, "a lot of people turn and stare at me, and whisper that there goes Mr. Big. My friends think this probably annoys and embarrasses me. Frankly, I thoroughly enjoy it. Why shouldn't I?"

*Fear.* The growing emphasis on security has convinced some executives that fear is no longer an important incentive. "Men used to work with a strong feeling of fear," says a company president, with just a trace of nostalgia. "They put in terrible hours and were afraid to ask for a day off. Most of that has been eliminated. Now I don't say it's a bad thing, this change; it's not good to have people fearful and apprehensive. But, well . . . we have a complacency today, a sense of security we didn't used to have."

But is not preoccupation with security a form of fear? As middle-management executives point out, worries about security now take different forms, but people worry just the same. It's nice to know that today there are built-in restrictions about being sacked, but one effect of this is to allow the executive to fret all the more over the possibility of being pigeonholed. The office geniality, furthermore, only makes the task of estimating one's own standing in this respect more difficult. "You get into a certain bracket," goes a typical explanation, "and you start getting a scare that somebody else is going to get what you want. But who is he? You can't tell—it's a game of checkers. So you take on a protective coloring to look like the lower brackets. You're afraid of slipping and being surpassed."

The best defense, the executive knows, is to surpass somebody else. Since he also knows that every other executive thinks likewise, he can never feel really secure. "I like to take my vacation in three- or four-day stretches, instead of the full three weeks," one executive says. "Now why do I do that? For my health? You go away for three weeks and you find when you come back that they've rearranged your entire job. Someone has to carry on while you are gone and they are in your files and when you get back the boss will ask you questions about your job on account of what others did while you were away. I don't blame them, mind you. I'd do exactly the same thing." . . .

Do they really want leisure? When executives talk of such extra-curricular functions as entertaining, and civic work, and reading, they betray a curiously split attitude. They profess to deplore the impulse that bedevils them into thinking about work after hours. Yet, as their self-diagnoses demonstrate, they would not have it otherwise. . . .

Executives are well aware that this absorption means less time with their wives and children. Younger executives, in particular, accuse themselves; they are not, they say, the fathers they should be, and they often mention some long-planned project to do something with the little boy, like building a boat. But, they add ruefully, they probably never will. "I sort of look forward to the day when my kids are grown up," says one sales manager. "Then I won't have to have such a guilty conscience about neglecting them."

Executives' attitudes toward entertaining show the same overwhelming preoccupation with work. They do so much of it that one might wonder whether most of it is not mere play thinly disguised as work—a way of enjoying the good life without paying for it. To a degree it is; in his first years with the company the management man finds the expense account a heady contrast to life in the ranch house at 7111 Crestmere Drive.

But not for very long. "For the first five years or so it's wonderful to play the big shot when you are out on the road," explains one Chicago executive, "but after a while you realize that all you are doing is lousing up your regular standard of living. You forget there are balconies in theaters."

All this does not mean that executives as they go up come to dislike entertaining; they merely grow more choosy. Increasingly, play that is play and no more, irritates them. What they enjoy is the kind of after-hours socializing that has some relevance to their business—the kind, as they so often put it, where you can't tell whether it's work or play. . . .

Civic work, theoretically, should be a good change of pace from regular business. One of the most surprising disclosures in this survey, however, is the attitude corporation executives privately express about community activity. They don't particularly like it. When they engage in it they do so more out of a sense of obligation, or on order from their company, than for any inward satisfaction they expect from the participation. Older executives are often heavily involved in good works, but the involvement, many confess, is more entrapment than free choice. "I had looked forward to taking it easy," says one sixty-five-year-old executive, "but the trouble is that as soon as you get more free time the word gets around. Then they put the finger on you."

Rightly or wrongly, most executives consider civic work a diffusion of their energies, and only when they see a clear relation between civic work and their careers do they perform it with enthusiasm. Significantly, the businessmen who plunge into civic work with gusto usually are the bankers and merchants and others for whom it is virtually part of their job.

Culture? Executives do tend to have broader tastes in music, reading, and the like than their less successful contemporaries. But that, as executives themselves concede, isn't saying very much. Most of those questioned were conscious that they didn't read enough good books about something besides business, and some executives went out of their way to berate themselves on that score.

But where, the executive asks, can he find time? Much as he might like to read more history or take in more plays, he looks on this as too marginal, too little relevant to his career to warrant making the time. His judgment is debatable on this point, but that is another story; the fact is that he doesn't see much relationship, and thus, as with the long-deferred project to build a boat with the boys, he will keep on planning that reading he hopes to get around to. One of these days.

Hobbies? Even here, the executive applies the yardstick of business relevance. While some executives are genuinely absorbed in a hobby for the sheer creative bang of it, for a larger number the pursuit carries strong therapeutic overtones. For them the hobby is not a joy in itself but simply a means of restoring themselves between rounds. To this end some executives go through an almost compulsive ritual—like watering the flowers at a regular weekend time whether or not it has just rained. To borrow an old phrase, they are never less at leisure than when they are at leisure.

▶ Should a hobby be similar to or quite different from what one does on a job?

# 6 THREE CAREER WOMEN

The modern world has at last made a place for women outside the home. A few exceptional women—the Cleopatras or Saint Joans—have always managed to break through the hard crust of male-dominated society. But in the past, the overwhelming majority of women have been relegated to kitchen and nursery, if not to the fields. Even today, most women lead rewarding lives as wives and mothers, but many work before and after their child-rearing years, and others choose careers instead of marriage and a family.

New York draws these ambitious, bright, imaginative young women. They fill Manhattan's businesses and theaters. Many arrive after they have completed college, clutching copies of articles they wrote for college newspapers or portfolios of drawings done for art courses to serve as passports to the world of business or the arts.

Reading 6 contains short autobiographical accounts by three women who became successes in New York City. These accounts are taken from a book whose authors interviewed eighteen successful women, asking them to reminisce about what their life was like when they were sixteen. As they did so, they often commented on their earlier childhood and their later careers. As you read excerpts from these tape-recorded interviews, think about the following questions:

1. What were the personal characteristics of each of these three women?
2. What rewards did they find in their careers? What did they have to give up in order to earn these rewards?
3. To what degree does a good life for a woman involve marriage and a family? To what degree does it require a career independent of the home?

# A Designer, a Psychiatrist, and a Businesswoman

From **When I Was Sixteen** by Mary Brannum and the Editors. Copyright © 1967 by The Platt and Munk Company, Inc.

## BETSEY JOHNSON

*Born in Wethersfield, Connecticut, in 1942, Betsey Johnson became, in the mid-1960's, a top designer for Paraphernalia, a trend-setting mod boutique. In the selection that follows, Miss Johnson describes her first years working in New York.*

With me, nothing I was doing in college began to pull together until . . . my roommate persuaded me to enter the *Mademoiselle* magazine Guest Editor contest [in my senior year]. It was the first [contest] I really cared about winning, because it would bring me to New York. I didn't think about making it straight to the top after college. Just being a runaround girl in a fashion magazine, anything as long as I was on the scene—that was enough for a beginning. If I could win this contest, I could get to New York and be an assistant to one of the editors for a month. Maybe there'd be an opening, maybe something would break. At least I'd be taken care of for a month. They set you up in a hotel, they introduce you to all kinds of people. I'd be started out. . . .

. . . .[O]ne day I got a telegram that I'd won. I had to miss my graduation exercises. They flew me to New York, and they made me assistant fabric editor!

I was *furious.* I guess it's very hard for *Mademoiselle* to find someone to be fabric editor, and because I'd taken fabric design in college and did these big splashy prints and made clothes out of them, they thought, "Aha! We have someone for the fabric department." So they threw me in there, and I was so mad because it had nothing to do with art. I wanted to get close to the art department. Boy, did I work—in at nine o'clock, doing the editor's fabric files. I got to know every fabric house, every fabric, different weaves, different blends. There was so much work that I was kept on for another month.

286

And while I was making a little salary at *Mademoiselle,* I took my portfolio around to places during my lunch hour. The very first man I saw . . . looked at my book, and he said, "What do you want to do?" And I said, "Me? What do you mean? I don't know what I want to do." There I was with that portfolio—every different kind of work in it, the fabric designs, the fashion illustrations, and everything looked like it had been done by a different artist. I'd done everything to please all my instructors, to get my little A. He said I'd really have to work hard to get my own style, because that's the only thing for a person to have in a professional field; it has to be very personal, unique.

He said I could be very successful in this city, and quickly, too. I'd always believed that if you're going to be good, it doesn't take ten, twenty years to get there. If you've got it you can do it in five years at the most. New York is too hard on you physically and mentally to knock yourself out for ten years. So he said I could do it in like two years, but in those two years I'd have to work so hard. He really got very emotional: "Tears, sweat, blood!" I didn't know what he meant by that kind of work. But now, well, it's all very lovely now. I sit here and have tea and talk, but my first year after the two months at *Mademoiselle* I got a job as runaround girl in an art department. That didn't pay me enough money, so I had a sweater business. I made sweaters and got mail orders. I made three hundred of those things by hand. But I wanted more work, so I started up a fashion illustration business, and there was a lot of response. I worked nine to five, I had to make a sweater every night—that took four hours—and a minimum of four on the weekends, I had to do the fashion illustration assignments, keep up my own portfolio, and I was making my own clothes.

When I think of how hard I worked—I could count the parties I went to and the people I knew on one hand. But I was so happy. In New York everything is exaggerated. If you do something here, you get such a great feeling if it's the least bit successful. Whereas if I were in, say, Wethersfield, Connecticut, and I did something, who'd know about it? There's just not the same satisfaction. I do have something to offer people and I want to offer it to as many people as I can. For that I must be in New York. . . .

The thing about New York is that there are so many opportunities here, something has to work for you if you try hard enough. If you have something to offer people, they don't care how old you are. . . .

## RUTH FULLER

*Dr. Ruth Fuller, born in 1937, is a black child psychiatrist living with her husband on Manhattan's Upper West Side. In the excerpts that follow, Dr. Fuller describes mainly what her friendships as an adolescent meant to her.*

When I turned sixteen, . . . I was a senior at Newtown High School in Queens, New York. . . . All I knew about my future at sixteen was that I was headed into the sciences, probably one of the applied sciences, but I wasn't sure which one. I started college the second half of my sixteenth year. That was at Howard University in Washington, D.C. I took a pre-med major, beginning with chemistry and zoology. After college I went on to medical school. I took one careful step at a time.

There were many influences affecting my decision to become a doctor—teachers, family, people who had attained their goals in life in various professions. The people who were most important to me were interested in me in a very freeing way. They said, "These are the kinds of things that you might be able to do. Take a look at them and try them on for size and see what fits best." My parents wanted a life and a kind of work for me that I would enjoy and find rewarding, intellectually stimulating. How I attained it, though, depended on my finding my particular lifestyle. They were willing to let me discover the one that suited me. It was an open-ended approach from everyone. But I think that's truly helpful when you're moving in many, many directions and you're not quite sure which is going to be best. I liked the freedom to be able to experiment a little. I enjoyed that freedom, and I also felt that learning was important, no matter what use I put it to. . . .

[My friends and I] really cared for each other, and caring and being cared for are crucial at sixteen. The great bursts of creativity and feeling, the sudden sense of being acutely aware that you are you, of an intense need to communicate with someone, and with someone that you feel understands, can sometimes be extremely frustrating and frightening. You begin to wonder, "Am I the only person in the world that feels this? . . ." And the answer seems to be, "Yes, I am," and then you are finally very worried or very lonely. Then you wish for somebody to see what you see, to recognize it and share it with you. But there's a two-way street that develops. You feel the trauma and magic of being able to care about someone and knowing that someone cares about you. Then the world looks much lovelier. Terribly unhappy things do happen, but there's a kind of faith that there are other people who feel the same way. Then you begin to realize that people aren't so unique and that somewhere others like you exist. . . .

I was an only child, but I never felt like one. We had a large, close family of uncles and aunts and cousins. Of course, I couldn't make regular visits to those living on the West Coast but there were enough in the New York area, and even enough in Queens, to give me the feeling that I wasn't exactly alone in the world. Both my parents came from large families and they all migrated north and west out of the Carolinas.

My mother was—and still is—a seamstress, fitter, and designer. She loved me and paid attention to what I said, but she wasn't, in many ways, a very conventional mother. She was interested in my safety and my education, all the things parents are usually interested in, but her approach was often pretty original. One night the group was determined to go to a party in a terrible blizzard. The party was in the far reaches of Queens and our ride had disappeared, of course—he showed a little sense about the weather! At first, Mother just refused to let me go, and painted wild pictures of being stranded all night in the snow. But when we got a substitute ride and were obviously going no matter what, Mother's solution was to go with us. She said it would be better to be lost and cold together. So we took off, and we made it to the party.

But it was the trip back that was really marvelous. The snow stopped, and a full moon came out. It's hard to find white unbroken snow in New York, but there it was, beautiful and quiet. It was worth dragging my mother out into a blizzard just to see that. It was a nice evening and I was glad my mother was there. I realized that evening how much, even though I was sixteen, I still needed her, although I would have promptly denied it. . . .

Through the years I have been especially fortunate—there were so many teachers who were good to me, interested in me. They always made me feel that they wanted from me the best I had to give, and I in turn felt that they gave me the best they had. I know that not every student has teachers like that. In fact, I think most of them don't; I've seen more teachers who don't belong in the profession than I can count. But getting that encouragement from an extraordinary group of people has left me with the feeling that I can ask the questions and get the answers which help me to do my job well. There is no more valuable gift they could have given me.

## EILEEN FORD

*Born in 1925, Eileen Ford grew up in Great Neck, Long Island, a well-to-do suburb of New York City. Mrs. Ford, together with her husband, now runs the Ford Agency, New York's most glamorous model agency. Besides running her business, Mrs. Ford has raised four children. In the following excerpts, Mrs. Ford tells how she came to be a New York career woman, and gives a brief description of the modeling business.*

If I could have gone to Stanford, I wouldn't have minded the idea of college at all, but my mother thinks there are Indians west of Princeton, and I never had a prayer. She took me to Barnard, and that's where I went. Then my life began to alter. Gradually I became aware of other things besides bandleaders and sweater collections.

But at sixteen, during my last year of high school, I was very content and very confident. I had everything it took to make me, Eileen Otte, happy. My parents thought I was fine. I had reasonable marks, nice clothes and a car, a home where I could give a party every week, plenty of boyfriends. I wasn't skinny and I wasn't fat, I had no skin problems. I was just me. There was none of this problem of wondering "Who am I?" which we hear about endlessly now. None of my friends had identity problems either. I didn't know any lost teenagers. We all had perfectly marvelous lives. . . .

In a way I just drifted when I got out of school. I had lots of jobs because I had eloped and my husband and I were very young and very poor. I had one terrible job rationing priorities for American Export, and then I became a stylist and all-around secretary for a photographer. I ran errands and typed things—badly—and messed up the bookkeeping beyond all repair, but the point is I got the job as a stylist without any experience whatsoever. I just said I could do it, and I could—all for the grand sum of $35 a week. I used to have to mail the film to Eastman Kodak in Rochester, New York, and I'd go down into the underground concourse at Radio City every day. There was a talking myna bird there, and he and Charles, the doorman, were my best friends. But I was a career girl, right?

Well, I worked for Arnold Constable as a copywriter, and later in the advertising and photography department. When I started this agency I was only twenty-one, and my husband and I were expecting a baby and we were broke. I knew a lot of models and I sort of rounded them up and that's how it started. I'm sorry it couldn't be more dramatic.

My husband runs this whole place; he does all the financial part. I'm just an agent, but he's very clever. He has a marvelous sense of order and finance. Were it left to me, we'd have been out of business the first day we started. I don't care about money. It doesn't interest me except that I like to make it for people. Money is very hard to understand, so I don't bother with it.

Beneath Rockefeller Center, of which Radio City is a part, is a labyrinthine network of underground concourses lined with shops.

Arnold Constable is a New York clothing store.

▶ Is money really unimportant, or does it seem unimportant only when a person has lots of it?

I *care* about my models' careers, that's what I really care about. I've got a total absorption in it. I care about this business so much it's difficult to describe, and it's a very nice business. It enables you to do things for people. Probably if I weren't a model agent, I'd be a social worker. It's a very rewarding feeling to know you've helped girls through college. Oh, sure, lots of girls go through college on what they make with us in the summer. And then I get invitations to their children's weddings, or I see them getting married to nice boys and see them start another life. It's wonderful.

Of course the work is interesting for the models, too. It's never the same—every job is a different dress or a different coat—imagine wearing the nicest dresses! And modeling is certainly lucrative. For example, four of my girls earn upwards of $75,000 a year. They work for about ten to twelve years, which is fine. Many women would like to retire anyway by then to raise a family and have a home. Also, the demand of the business is for youth.

Models are girls, and their lives are basically the same as other girls'. There is the difference in their looks, of course, and in the clothes that they wear modeling. A model may be a gem of sophistication to the photographer, but when she takes off the sable coat and the emeralds, she's another young girl going home very tired from having worked like a stevedore. What are they tired from? Well, they're tired from having stood on their feet all day with every muscle stretched from end to end. They're bent like pretzels.

# 7 THE HIPPIES

Like Haight–Ashbury in San Francisco, the East Village in New York has become a mecca for hippies. A few live there year round. Each summer their numbers swell with self-imposed exiles from the entire nation who have turned their scornful backs on middle-class parents, middle-class homes, middle-class schools, and middle-class values. The true hippies—those who pass out free clothing in the Diggers' store or organize the Be-Ins—strive to create a new society with drastically different values from those of their parents. The ones who spend an adventurous couple of weeks in the East Village during the warm summer months— plastic hippies, the pure breed calls them—often cut their hair and return to school and hearthside after Labor Day.

The transition from childhood to adult has always been painful. Society requires parents to socialize their children—that is, to teach them how to live in acceptable ways. Socialization involves rewards and punishments to encourage some sorts of behavior and to discourage others. To put the case mildly, children often resist doing what their parents think proper. Parents, in turn, shake their worried heads in dismay at the rebellious ways and questionable wisdom of boys and girls whose diapers mother and father once changed.

No one knows whether the present generation is more restless than others have been in the past. Benjamin Franklin ran away from home in Boston to seek fame and fortune in Philadelphia— and he turned out all right. In the nineteenth century, boys shipped out on clipper ships around the Horn or took off for the West to become cowboys or die facing down a gunman. In the 1930's, college students by the thousands joined left-wing groups to work against the economic system which supplied their tuition money. Today's hippies, however, represent a revolt with far deeper meaning for the society.

The excerpts which follow have been taken from an interview by Lewis Yablonsky, a sociologist, with a twenty-two year old New York hippie named Sonny. Sonny grew up in a wealthy eastern suburb. His father was a $50,000 a year executive, and in Sonny's words "a proper super-straight cat." As you read the interview, think about the following questions:

1. What was Sonny rebelling against? Why did he rebel?
2. What is Sonny's image of a good society? of a good man? of a good life?
3. What parts, if any, of Sonny's philosophy appeal to you? Is it possible for an entire society to be organized in the way that he suggests?

# The Values of a Hippie

From **The Hippie Trip,** by Lewis Yablonsky, published by Pegasus, A Division of Western Publishing Co., Inc. Copyright © 1968 by Western Publishing Co., Inc.

*Sonny:* I was a super-straight young man from respectable parents in a middle-class Roman Catholic home. We, of course, belonged to the country club. My eyes were on the commercial stars of America. I had a nice little sports car—the whole scene. Well, for a good period of time, I thought I'd be a marine biologist and I always had an interest in writing. It was kind of a toss-up between the two. I was going to be something very earth-shattering, very noble, very respected.

*Yablonsky:* What kind of hangups did you have? What things bugged you? . . .

*Sonny:* . . . . I had the main hassle of our time. My refusal to accept the life that my parents picked for me. Most parents within the society are doing something they don't really want to do. You know, there's always some dream that they always wanted, yet they can't do it. And they're caught up in a very materialized sort of game structure. And they excuse this or they rationalize that by saying, "Well, we're going through this so our children can have a better life." That's the excuse that every parent uses, you know, when he isn't leading the type of life that he'd like. And so, when a child grows up and decides that he doesn't want what they've had in their mind for him for all these years, they kind of forget that perhaps he has the right to decide his own form of life. And so you get into a real conflict with them and yourself at that point.

The whole society's based on a very egocentric form of game structure. All the games within the society are ego games. Of prime importance within this society is the self-image and the image presented to others. It just becomes a . . . paramount thing in everybody's life. It's influenced by movies. People try and be a movie star like John Wayne or somebody like that. They stroll down the street looking tough. They grab onto certain concepts of masculinity and femininity which have nothing to do with what's masculine at all . . . it's just a facade. This allows the self, or ego, to dominate feelings and true expressions. So you become not really yourself, but just kind of a shallow mirror image of some originally false idea. The games would break down if the people became aware that they are games. . . .

Here's how I came around to this way of thought. When I was young, I was kind of a mind worshiper. You know, I was a very young, snotty intellectual and I went through that whole academic rap game. An intellectual just reads for the sake of later talking to others and impressing them. But eventually, if you read enough, it begins to sink in. So when I got to college, I went into philosophy. It completely disappointed me. Western philosophy has broken down. The questions that it . . . it originally tried to answer . . . metaphysics, ontology, etc. . . . had broken down to the point where now it was just an intellectual semantic word game.

I found the educational system ridiculous. I'll tell you how ridiculous the educational system is. Everybody there is there only for a degree. For example, whenever I need money badly all I have to do is go to a college town and let it be known that I write term papers and I can make around $150 a week. That, I think, is comment enough on the attitude of most students. The curriculum and the courses themselves—they're just absurd. I think it's a waste of time for anybody who wants to learn anything to go to college, really. . . .

▶ Should parents sacrifice their own happiness for their children's future?

Metaphysics is a division of philosophy which includes ontology (which relates to the nature and relations of being) and epistemology (the study of the theory of the nature of knowledge). Semantics refers, broadly, to language and its meaning. Sonny's view of post-World War II Western philosophy is shared by many university scholars.

▶ How high is the nonsense quotient in education: that is, how much nonsense must a student endure to get what is worthwhile from school?

▶ Why don't more people run and skip in the streets?

*Yablonsky:* In your opinion how did the hippie movement start?

*Sonny:* The hippie movement, if you want to call it that, is a natural outgrowth of the '50's beatnik movement plus the important extra ingredient—acid.

Beat people like Kerouac, Miller, Gregory Corso, Allen Ginsberg are still with us. These are people who have become dissatisfied with American society and the American way of life. At that point, they were beginning to see the ridiculousness of it. That's pretty much all they were seeing. They were looking at the negative side of society and they weren't reacting really by trying to change anything positive. They were associated, of course, with the left. The beatnik movement of the '50's was basically just a commentary movement. A group of people expressing themselves principally through the arts. They said, "This is ridiculous; we want no part of it." . . .

. . . . Society exists, I think, almost . . . as an entity in itself. For its own self-preservation and perpetuation it has to install certain attitudes within the people who are in it. These attitudes may be fine for maintaining *that* form of society and keeping *that* form of society alive and functioning. But it [can ruin] the personalities and the minds of the people within it.

The hippies or the flower people or whatever you want to call 'em are nothing but people who've dropped [their] hangups People who can behave as children when they want to, unashamedly. And I don't think there is any human being alive who wouldn't want to just run and skip in the streets like a kid. Swing from light posts, climb trees. People who aren't afraid of loving each other. People who aren't suspicious.

Friendship no longer becomes a thing of dominance, you know, where one friend dominates the other or where you're always suspicious that maybe someone's out to get you or knife you in the back. It's . . . it's just open. It's dropping all the false trappings of society.

If you need money or anything, you ask somebody for it. If you want to, people turn you on free. I went to three different places last night. Every place I went, I got stoned. I had some grass this morning so I found some people in the park and came up here and got nicely stoned. . . .

The concept now is to try and get away from trading and bartering. I kind of feel that everybody has one thing which they like to do. Sometimes more than one thing. One function that makes them happy. And to a lot of people that are here in the Village the only reason that they got the courage to come here is because that thing is in the arts. If you're serious about art, you can't really exist in this society because there's just no way to live. This society isn't geared for serious poets, artists, painters.

The people here have their thing. But there are also other people. For example, people down on Wall Street—maybe they would really dig being farmers. Nothing would make them more happy than to till the land, till the soil. To other people, they have a thing like they keep building things. All the frustrated little fix-it shops out in suburbia. Those people would really be happy if they could make something beautiful. And although it isn't very practical in this society now, or in the very near future, it's plausible to envision a society where everybody could just go out and "do their thing." The only way that that could work, each one doing his own thing, is if you do away with the whole concept of pay.

These ideas are working now. It's working down here and it's working in the communities and tribes out in the country. When you do your thing. If you dig farming, you give the food away, except for what you need to eat. If you're making things—chairs, tables, or anything like that—you give them away to those who need it. And if you need help on something, you just ask somebody, "Hey, I'm doing this today," and so they come and help you. It's sort of a total sharing.

I don't think it's a socialistic idea at all. I think it's more a humanist idea. And it will work 'cause it works down here. If you're hungry now, I'd tell you where to go where people have food. You just walk in the door and they'd give you a plate of food. If you wanted to get stoned now, I could tell you where to go. . . .

The power of the movement is through artistic expression and through just being. That's what the Be-In concept is. The whole idea of a Be-In is just to have a whole bunch of hippies, or people who feel like this, in a group—happy and doing their thing. When straight people go by and see somebody else happy when they themselves aren't, maybe they'll begin to question why they aren't. I've expressed these feelings in a poem. Would you like to hear the poem?

[Yablonsky said he would like to hear the poem, so Sonny read it:]

Some hippies have established small communal settlements in the countryside.

### The Children of the Flowers
a parable of parts

The Children of the flowers
burst from their winter caves
gathering in fields of spring
to lift their collective mind
                in song.

They run—
                    smiling color
                         through the trees:
dancing down dirt warmed
roads.
Toes curling the warmth of
                                        earth
swirling dust devils
          and
shimmering waves of heat
past fields of magic mushrooms.
Their world
          the land of elves and hobbits
the sparkle colored
                              being
of aware.
Their smell
          the odor of fresh earth,
                              spring rains
                    and roan goats skipping
through dew-covered fields.
They come
          an army of joy
viewing new worlds
          through the open doors of perception.

## II

Entering the town
fences vanish
at the touch of flowered seed.
Laughing down yesterday's somber
                                        streets
to the splash of
smiling bodies
churning, swirling,
          in the shimmering crystal water
dissolved in village
                    green.
Their thoughts flee unseen
          down dimlit alleys
building barricades of love
to bar the passage of blind hostility;
the time of flowers is at hand

296

the tribes of coral-colored gypsies
have descended
        from the hills
to blot the games with billboards
            of awareness.

III

Playing
      the mad music of alive
           on violins of cosmic energy
they
  run through streets
        turning pushcarts into apples
and mending holes in old men's shirts.
The merchants
      standing in their doors
scream their indignation
with
the bellow panting of bald cigars.
Faces red
    with neck veins bulging
they stamp their feet in
        hollow fury
at the impertinence of love
between nine and five.
"What is the meaning
    (of all this)"
one mumbles around the chomped-down end of a
fine Havana
ten dollar bill.
The children of the flowers
      laugh
and dance through the plastic
rain forest
along one wall.
They go
  from shop to shop
spreading good Karma.
The merchants
close their shops
with strings of summer flowers
feet dancing unaided
to the sounds
of the mad calliope-player.

In Hinduism and Buddhism, karma is the force a person's actions generate which is the motive power for reincarnation.

297

IV

Who are
        the Children of the Flowers?
They gather in small tribes
among the cliffs—
                children of the chemical goddess.
I
        the ego
                is dead
killed during its last hysterical
                                ravings
        to become we.
Words are nothing
                lost
amidst sunlit fields of
                empty water towers.
It is whispered among the trees
and through the
                swirling ocean mist
that the time of flowers
                is at hand.
Rocks upon the hillside
are
scattered of their own volition;
fish hawks glide among
                the cliffs
searching for the memory
                of a dying youth.
The tide is sweeping inland
the ancient sea walls crumble
before the cleansing sea.
We
are the Children of the flowers—
the Children of the flowers
                        are
                        now.

[Yablonsky told Sonny how much he liked the poem. After a
short break, the discussion continued:]

*Yablonsky:* To go back to the community reaction thing—why
do you think middle-class people are so hostile toward hippies?

*Sonny:* Mr. Jones is hostile in large part because he sees joy and
happiness where joy and happiness shouldn't be. He isn't so much
worried about it for himself, but he's worried about it for his sons

and daughters. Because Mr. Jones is basically not a happy person. Mr. Jones comes home at night, he's tired—he has a beer, he watches TV, and goes to bed. He gets up the next morning and goes through the same thing. Mr. Jones is caught up in a very depressing sort of life and he knows that his children would say that he is not basically a happy man. Mr. Jones drinks too much. . . . He grumbles and complains a lot.

And then he sees these people out there having fun, Mr. Jones doesn't believe, because he's very skeptical, that they're really happy. But he's afraid that his sons and daughters will see "the flower children" and believe that they really are happy. Perhaps his children do not want to grow up and be grumbling and mumbling like Mr. Jones. They may want to go out dancing in the streets and do what they want to do. . . .

*Yablonsky:* Where do you see the movement heading?

*Sonny:* I see a lot of people coming to the rather obvious conclusion that cities are an unnatural place to live. Cities breed hostility. Cities as a human environment are architecturally negative. I think a lot of hip people are coming to the conclusion that the cities, for them at least, are a very unnatural way to live. And people who have the kind of ideas I've been telling you about have decided to get out into small tribes, find an open area of open land or woods somewhere, do their thing, and live in the country.

# New York: The Ideals

## STATING THE ISSUE

New York is the capital of literary America. Many of the great publishing houses which bless a book of poems or a novel by an unknown writer cluster on or near Madison Avenue. Close to one hundred legitimate theaters, thirty-four of them on Broadway, dominate the American stage; New York reviewers can sound the death knell over almost any play. Manhattan's office buildings house many of our great periodicals as well as the off-beat literary magazines which have published the first works of a score of famous writers.

Many modern writers earn their living behind a typewriter, although many others also teach, lecture, or edit to support their families. Unlike the men of the Renaissance, many of whom wrote as an avocation, the modern novelist, poet, or essayist lives partly on royalties from his published works. Our society has become so specialized and the demands of work so insistent that few members of the business elite turn a hand to creative literature. Royalties have freed artists from the need for private patrons who supported them during the Renaissance; they may also have widened the gap which separates the financial and intellectual elites of the society.

Great literature does not express the ideals of Everyman. If it did, more people would read it. Americans buy more detective stories than serious novels, more tabloids than great newspapers like *The New York Times,* more magazines that regale the lives of movie stars than those that analyze the aspirations of man. Still, great literature raises basic questions which trouble sensitive people.

Chapter 2 contains a series of short essays on New York, a group of poems, the lyrics to a number of songs, a portion of the autobiography of a famous playwright, two short stories, and an essay by a black nationalist. How do these perceptive people define the good man? the good life? the good society?

# 8 FINDING BEAUTY IN NEW YORK

We see what we look for. Each of us has his vision limited by a frame of reference which filters what he perceives through his senses. What may strike an artist as beautiful—smoke from a factory chimney—may be only a civic problem to a city planner worried about air pollution. A musician may hear the germ of a symphony in the cacophony of city traffic; a policeman may register the same sounds as meaningless noise to be abated. The sounds and sights and smells of a city affect everyone differently.

How our environment affects us helps to determine the quality of the life we lead. Head down, intent on getting there, impatient with every traffic light, we can ramrod down a street oblivious to everything except impediments. In a receptive mood, however, we can find beauty, laughter, and meaning crowding us on every side. To find them, then, we must learn to look.

E. B. White honed sharp his ability to take delight in the commonplace around New York. In "The Talk of the Town," the collection of essays and commentaries that opens each issue of *The New Yorker,* White published a number of little articles triggered by the sights and sounds of the city. As you read the collection below, think about the following questions:

1. Why did each of the incidents described by White make an impression on him? Would they strike most people in the same way? Explain.
2. Who is more likely to take joy in incidents like those which White described, an advocate of the active and strenuous life or someone who is more contemplative?
3. What incidents like those described by White have you experienced? Have they enriched your life? If so, how?

Abridgment of "Notes on the City" from **The Second Tree from the Corner** (1954) by E. B. White: "High Noon," copyright 1937, 1950; "Transient," copyright 1935; "Business Show," copyright 1936; "Rediscovery," copyright 1948; "Impasse in the Business World," copyright 1936; "In an Elevator," copyright 1938; "Twins," copyright 1948. All, copyright by E. B. White. Originally appeared in **The New Yorker,** and reprinted by permission of Harper & Row, Publishers. British rights held by Hamish Hamilton Ltd.

## Notes on the City

### HIGH NOON

We lunched alone today, as is our wont. It has its peptic advantages and induces a disconsolate attitude which has some slight literary value. Looking about the room, though, at the tables of twos, threes, and fours, we realized how important a function lunch is in New York, how drastic and purposeful. There was a dark pall of gain hanging over every table—everyone there for some

301

reason of business or intrigue: salesmen, applicants, supplicants, agents provocateurs, contact executives, actresses gaming with managers, writers taking the temperature of editors, lovers sparring for their strange vantage, everywhere a sprig of personal increase garnishing the cold salmon. Next to us a burlap-bag man was convincing a poultry-feed gentleman that his particular sack kept the vitamins alive longer than usual. As we watched the interplay, we envisioned millions of hens standing in caked henyards, uttering the dreamy summer sound that hens make, unaware of the new sack, the new retention of vitamins in the laying mash, the myriad other new things which arise from lunch in town.

With nothing much else to do, we complained of the fish, which stank. "You do not like the fish?" said the captain, after the waiter had whispered about the trouble at his table. "It stinks," we said, in our simplest vein. But the captain would not smell it, despite the nose being the most valuable of all organs in the appraisal of food. He would bring us, without charge, another dish—but he wouldn't be caught sniffing his own fish. Dogs are more forthright in these situations. They not only will sniff bad fish, they will stick up for it.

## TRANSIENT

In the patchy little gardens of Turtle Bay, where half a dozen dry sycamore leaves constitute the pungent fall, a thrush appeared the other morning. We watched him from a window, exploring the tangle, dipping at the fountain, brown and unannounced. There is a special satisfaction to a city person in such a visitation; we took twice the pleasure in this thrush that we would have felt had we discovered him in the country. The city is the place for people who like life in tablet form, concentrated: a forest resolved into a single tree, a lake distilled into a fountain, and all the birds of the air embodied in one transient thrush in a small garden.

## BUSINESS SHOW

It was a soft afternoon with smoke rising in straws of light from the chimneys, and pink clouds the color of chrysanthemums folded gently against a pale sky. Even Eighth Avenue seemed to dwell in heavenly pallor when we left it to plunge into the Business Show and walk in the chattering aisles of calculators, addressographs, electric tabulation machines, where girls in purest white satin, enthroned on chromium chairs, their blonde hair gleaming like clouds, their nails shining pink the color of chrysanthemums, pushed the little shining keys—tick, tap, PULL, tick, tap, PULL—adding, subtracting, filing, assembling, addressing, dictaphoning, typing, silhouetted firmly against the pure walls of steel that was grained to look like wood, and the murmurous mysteries of business enlarged a hundred times, staggering the mind. Adoringly we paused before each machine, as a traveller before a shrine; and it all seemed more mechanistic than any play we had ever seen, even than the plays produced by the little groups who take the theatre seriously. But what we noticed was that the seeming dominance of the machines was an illusion of the senses, that the electric current was in fact impotent, for everywhere we saw men standing gravely talking to the girls in purest white satin, and always something passed between them, something a little extra in their look, the eyes of the girls returning the clear, desirous gaze of the builders of the incredible machines, giving back desire for desire, and that the current of this exchange (the exciting unfulfillment) was the thing in all the room, and not the chattering mysteries of the addition, tabulation, punctuation, subtraction, which were as nothing, which were as an accompaniment (tick, tap, PULL) to the loud, insistent, throbbing song of beauty unattainable, hair (like clouds) infinitely desirable (in a hall on Eighth Avenue), with smoke rising in straws of light from the chimneys.

## REDISCOVERY

Coming in from the country, we put up at a hotel in midtown for a few days recently, to give the moths free rein in our apartment. Our hotel bedroom was on an air shaft, and whenever anyone took a shower bath the sissing sound could be heard clearly. People took showers frequently, because of the heat and because a shower is one of the ways you can kill time in a hotel. Somebody would come in at five in the afternoon and take a shower, then in the evening people would be taking showers around eight or nine, then after the theatre they would come back and take one, and then the late people—the playboys and the playgirls—would return at three in the morning and cool off in a shower. One morning we woke at seven, or half woke, and lay in bed listening to the sissing. Everybody in the building seemed to be taking a shower. After a while we caught on. It was raining. Good for the crops at the bottom of the air shaft, probably.

Sometimes our affection for New York becomes dulled by familiarity. No building seems high, no subway miraculous, no avenue enchanted—all, all commonplace. Then, in a moment of rediscovery, it is as though we were meeting the city again for the first time.

▶ How can we teach ourselves to look at familiar places or people as if we were seeing them for the first time?

303

This happened a couple of days ago when we dropped into our abandoned apartment to retrieve a book. It was a shut place—a stagnant tomb of camphor, drawn shades, and green memories. No air had entered or left, no tap had been turned, no picture gazed upon. The furniture, under dust covers, seemed poised to receive the dead. A fashion magazine lay open where it had been tossed, the fashionable ladies poised in summer dresses, waiting for fall. There was no mouse in the trap, no sherry in the decanter. Silent in the middle of turmoil, a cube of heat and expectancy, the place felt exciting and we were visited by a fresh sense of the surrounding city: the salt pressure of its tides, the perfect tragedy of each of its eight million inmates—so many destinations, so many arrivals and departures, and the fares being given and received, the promises given and received, the lights being switched on and off in the innumerable chambers, the flow of electricity and blood, the arrangements, the meetings, the purposeful engagements, and the people sealed tightly in phone booths dialling Weather, the calamities, the dead ends, the air drill poised ready to open the pavement, the dentist's drill poised ready to open the tooth, the conductor's baton poised ready, the critic's pencil poised ready, the ferry chain winding on the windlass, the thieves and vegetarians in the parks—we saw them all in dazzling clarity as though the curtain had just lifted on New York. And when we quit the apartment and walked up the street, as though out upon a stage, we saw clearly the lady in black fishing in a trash can, and the sportive bachelor leaving his pointed shoes with the shoe-shine man at the corner, and we were spellbound at the majesty of ginkgoes and the courtesy of hackmen. We hadn't had anything to drink, either. Just stopped in to get a book.

A ginkgo is a type of tree which produces a yellow fruit.

## IMPASSE IN THE BUSINESS WORLD

While waiting in the antechamber of a business firm, where we had gone to seek our fortune, we overheard through a thin partition a brigadier general of industry trying to establish telephone communication with another brigadier general, and they reached, these two men, what seemed to us a most healthy impasse. The phone rang in Mr. Auchincloss's office, and we heard Mr. Auchincloss's secretary take the call. It was Mr. Birstein's secretary, saying that Mr. Birstein would like to speak to Mr. Auchincloss. "All right, put him on," said Mr. Auchincloss's well-drilled secretary, "and I'll give him Mr. Auchincloss." "No," the other girl apparently replied, "you put Mr. Auchincloss on, and *I'll* give *him* Mr. Birstein." "Not at all," countered the girl behind the partition. "I wouldn't dream of keeping Mr. Auchincloss waiting."

This battle of the Titans, conducted by their leftenants to determine which Titan's time was the more valuable, raged for five or ten minutes, during which interval the Titans themselves were presumably just sitting around picking their teeth. Finally one of the girls gave in, or was overpowered, but it might easily have ended in a draw. As we sat there ripening in the antechamber, this momentary paralysis of industry seemed rich in promise of a better day to come—a day when true equality enters the business life, and nobody can speak to anybody because all are equally busy.

## IN AN ELEVATOR

In an elevator, ascending with strangers to familiar heights, the breath congeals, the body stiffens, the spirit marks time. These brief vertical journeys that we make in a common lift, from street level to office level, past the missing thirteenth floor—they afford moments of suspended animation, unique and probably beneficial. Passengers in an elevator, whether wedged tight or scattered with room to spare, achieve in their perpendicular passage a trancelike state: each person adhering to the unwritten code, a man descending at five in the afternoon with his nose buried in a strange woman's back hair, reducing his breath to an absolute minimum necessary to sustain life, willing to suffocate rather than allow a suggestion of his physical presence to impinge; a man coming home at one A.M., ascending with only one other occupant of the car, carefully avoiding any slight recognition of joint occupancy. What is there about elevator travel that induces this painstaking catalepsy? A sudden solemnity, perhaps, which seizes people when they feel gravity being tampered with—they hope successfully. Sometimes it seems to us as though everyone in the car were in silent prayer.

Many large buildings have no thirteenth floor—they skip from the twelfth floor to the fourteenth for good luck.

## TWINS

On a warm, miserable morning last week we went up to the Bronx Zoo to see the moose calf and to break in a new pair of black shoes. We encountered better luck than we had bargained for. The cow moose and her young one were standing near the wall of the deer park below the monkey house, and in order to get a better view, we strolled down to the lower end of the park, by the brook. The path there is not much travelled. As we approached the corner where the brook trickles under the wire fence, we noticed a red deer getting to her feet. Beside her, on legs that were just learning their business, was a spotted fawn, as small and perfect as a trinket

The Bronx Zoo, with more than 250 acres of land and 2500 animals, is the second largest zoo in the world.

seen through a reducing glass. They stood there, mother and child, under a gray beech whose trunk was engraved with dozens of hearts and initials. Stretched on the ground was another fawn, and we realized that the doe had just finishing twinning. The second fawn was still wet, still unrisen. Here was a scene of rare sylvan splendor, in one of our five favorite boroughs, and we couldn't have asked for more. Even our new shoes seemed to be working out all right and weren't hurting much.

The doe was only a couple of feet from the wire, and we sat down on a rock at the edge of the footpath to see what sort of start young fawns get in the deep fastnesses of Mittel Bronx. The mother, mildly resentful of our presence and dazed from her labor, raised one forefoot and stamped primly. Then she lowered her head, picked up the afterbirth, and began dutifully to eat it, allowing it to swing crazily from her mouth as though it were a bunch of withered beet greens. From the monkey house came the loud, insane hooting of some captious primate, filling the whole woodland with a wild hooroar. As we watched, the sun broke weakly through, brightened the rich red of the fawns, and kindled their white spots. Occasionally a sightseer would appear and wander aimlessly by, but of all who passed none was aware that anything extraordinary had occurred. "Looka the kangaroos!" a child cried. And he and his mother stared sullenly at the deer and then walked on.

In a few moments the second twin gathered all his legs and all his ingenuity and arose, to stand for the first time sniffing the mysteries of a park for captive deer. The doe, in recognition of his achievement, quit her other work and began to dry him, running her tongue against the grain and paying particular attention to the key points. Meanwhile the first fawn tiptoed toward the shallow brook, in little stops and goes, and started across. He paused midstream to make a slight contribution, as a child does in bathing. Then, while his mother watched, he continued across, gained the other side, selected a hiding place, and lay down under a skunk-cabbage leaf next to the fence, in perfect concealment, his legs folded neatly under him. Without actually going out of sight, he had managed to disappear completely in the shifting light and shade. From somewhere a long way off a twelve-o'clock whistle sounded. We hung around awhile, but he never budged. Before we left, we crossed the brook ourself, just outside the fence, knelt, reached through the wire, and tested the truth of what we had once heard: that you can scratch a new fawn between the ears without starting him. You can indeed.

The **afterbirth** in a mammal consists of the placenta and fetal membranes expelled after delivery.

# 9 THE POET AND THE CITY

Poets extend sensitive antennae to the world around them. A great variety of impulses touch these antennae and set them in motion. A beam of sunlight, the flash of a child's smile, or man's inhumanity to man may all become the subjects of poems. More sensitive than most of us, better read, and more devoted to the arts, poets sometimes feel divorced from the rough-and-tumble of life in an aggressively competitive society. But typical or not, they frequently express sentiments which the rest of us can recognize and share.

Thousands of people study, read, and write poetry in New York. Poetry is taught as a subject in English courses in New York's nearly two thousand elementary and secondary schools and its forty colleges and universities. Poetry magazines appear on newsstands in many parts of the city; in addition, general periodicals and newspapers carry occasional poems. University professors, poets who make a living partly from their verse, and thousands of gifted amateurs take up their pens to compose poetry each year.

The poems in Reading 9 are all about New York and have been written by New Yorkers. Many of them have been studied in New York's schools and colleges and enjoyed by thousands of general readers in the city. As you read them, keep the following questions in mind:

1. What are these poems about? Why do you suppose that the poets chose to write about these particular subjects? Do the poets seem to be contemplative people?
2. What images of the good man, the good life, and the good society do these poems reveal?
3. Why read poetry? Why write it?

## New York Poems

*Born on Long Island in 1819, Walt Whitman lived in or near New York City for most of his life. In "Mannahatta," Whitman celebrates the bustling commercial city of the mid-nineteenth century.*

### Mannahatta

I was asking for something specific and perfect for my city.
Whereupon lo! upsprang the aboriginal name.

"Aboriginal" means first or native. Mannahatta is an Algonquin Indian word which means "island of the hills."

From **Leaves of Grass** (Garden City, N.Y.: Doubleday & Company, 1924). Reprinted by permission.

Now I see what there is in a name, a word, liquid, sane, unruly, musical, self-sufficient,
I see that the word of my city is that word from of old,
Because I see that word nested in nests of water-bays, superb,
Rich, hemm'd thick all around with sailships and steamships, an island sixteen miles long, solid-founded,
Numberless crowded streets, high growths of iron, slender, strong, light, splendidly uprising toward clear skies,
Tides swift and ample, well-loved by me, toward sundown,
The flowing sea-currents, the little islands, larger adjoining islands, the heights, the villas,
The countless masts, the white shore-streamers, the lighters, the ferry-boats, the black sea-steamers well model'd,
The down-town streets, the jobbers' houses of business, the houses of business of the ship-merchants and money-brokers, the river-streets,
Immigrants arriving, fifteen thousand in a week.
The carts hauling goods, the manly race of drivers of horses, the brown-faced sailors,
The summer air, the bright sun shining, and the sailing clouds aloft,
The winter snows, the sleigh-bells, the broken ice in the river, passing along up or down with the flood-tide or ebb-tide,
The mechanics of the city, the masters, well-form'd, beautiful-faced, looking you straight in the eyes,
Trottoirs throng'd, vehicles, Broadway, the women, the shops and shows,
A million people—manners free and superb—open voices—hospitality —the most courageous and friendly young men,
City of hurried and sparkling waters! city of spires and masts!
City nested in bays! my city!

*James Agee, author of the next poem, was born in Tennessee in 1909. He was an extraordinarily sensitive novelist, poet, and screen-writer who lived most of his short life in New York City.*

## Rapid Transit

Squealing under city stone
   The millions on the millions run,
Every one a life alone,
   Every one a soul undone:

There all the poisons of the heart
   Branch and abound like whirling brooks,

Lighters are flat-bottomed barges usually used to load and unload ships when large piers are not available.

Trottoirs are sidewalks.

In Louis Untermeyer, ed., **Modern American Poetry** (New York: Harcourt, Brace & World, Inc., 1950), p. 641. Reprinted by permission of the James Agee Trust Fund (David McDowell, Literary Trustee, c/o Crown Publishers, Inc.).

And there through every useless art
   Liked spoiled meats on a butcher's hooks

Pour forth upon their frightful kind
   The faces of each ruined child:
The wrecked demeanors of the mind
   That now is tamed, and once was wild.

*John Updike is one of the best of the younger writers for* The
New Yorker *magazine. Updike's poetry, stories, and novels are
noted for their delicate craftsmanship and feeling for language. In
the next poem, Updike writes of Manhattan's Upper West Side.*

## Summer: West Side

When on the coral-red steps of old brownstones
Puerto Rican boys, their white shirts luminous,
gather, and their laughter
conveys menace as far as Central Park West,

When the cheesecake shops on Broadway
keep open long into the dark,
and the Chinaman down in his hole of seven steps
leaves the door of his laundry ajar,
releasing a blue smell of starch,

When the indefatigable lines of parked cars
seem embedded in the tar,
and the swish of the cars on the Drive
seems urgently loud—

Then even the lapping of wavelets
on the boards of a barge on the Hudson
is audible,
and Downtown's foggy glow
fills your windows right up to the top.

And you walk in the mornings with your cool suit
sheathing the fresh tingle of your shower,
and the gratings idly steam,
and the damp path of the street-sweeper evaporates

And—an oddly joyful sight—
the dentists' and chiropractors' white signs low
in the windows of the great ochre buildings on
   Eighty-sixth Street
seem slightly darkened
by one more night's deposit of vigil.

From John Updike,
**Telephone Poles and
Other Poems** (New York:
Alfred A. Knopf, Inc., 1963).
Copyright © 1960 by John
Updike. Originally appeared
in **The New Yorker**.
Reprinted by permission.
Other rights controlled by
André Deutsch Limited
Publishers.

**Brownstones** are four- or
five-story row buildings
fronted with reddish-brown
sandstone.

"The Drive" here refers to
Riverside Drive, which runs
along Riverside Park and the
Hudson River on Manhattan's
West Side.

Lawrence Ferlinghetti, **A Coney Island of the Mind.** Copyright © 1955, 1958 by Lawrence Ferlinghetti. Reprinted by permission of New Directions Publishing Corporation.

*Born in Yonkers, New York, in 1919, Lawrence Ferlinghetti became a leading avant-garde poet in the 1950's.*

## "Fortune Has its Cookies . . ."

Fortune
     has its cookies to give out
which is a good thing
       since it's been a long time since
    that summer in Brooklyn
when they closed off the street
   one hot day
    and the

           FIREMEN
      turned on their hoses
and all the kids ran out in it
    in the middle of the street
and there were
     maybe a couple dozen of us
        out there
with the water squirting up
       to the
        sky
         and all over
          us

▶ Why do so many adults lose the capacity for joy which, as children, they once had?

there were maybe only six of us
       kids altogether
running around in our
     barefeet and birthday
   suits
    and I remember Molly but then
the firemen stopped squirting their hoses
   all of a sudden and went
     back in
     their firehouse
     and
     started playing pinochle again
       just as if nothing
      had ever
       happened
while I remember Molly
       looked at me and
    ran in
because I guess really we were the only ones there

310

*Born in Baltimore, Suzanne Ostro Zavrian lives in New York City where she writes poetry and co-edits* Extensions, *a magazine of poetry and fiction. Like most New Yorkers in the mid-1960's, she experienced the annoyances of a power blackout, a garbage strike, and many minor stoppages of "essential" services.*

## Postcard

What can I tell you?

The subways stopped
and we couldn't use the tunnels;
the buses broke down, fell apart
  a few went
out of
   control
    into

  the power failed
and we ran out of candles.
(do not go out during New Moon)

I am writing this to you
on top of sixteen feet of garbage,
taking a sunbath as I watch
the Saint Patrick's Day parade.

Copyright ©, 1969, by Suzanne Ostro Zavrian. Reprinted by permission of the poet.

*Langston Hughes, born in Missouri in 1902, lived most of his life in New York City where he wrote poetry, plays, novels, song lyrics, children's books, and a popular newspaper column for the* Amsterdam News, *New York's leading black newspaper. Perhaps more than any other writer, Hughes spoke for Harlem in prose, and in poems like the two that follow.*

## Migration

A little Southern colored child
Comes to a Northern school
And is afraid to play
With the white children

At first they are nice to him,
But finally they taunt him
And call him "nigger."

The colored children
Hate him, too,
After awhile.

From Langston Hughes, **Fields of Wonder** (New York: Alfred A. Knopf, Inc. 1947). Reprinted by permission.

▶ Why are little children sometimes so terribly cruel to each other?

He is a little dark boy
With a round black face
And a white embroidered collar.

Concerning this
Little frightened child
One might make a story
Charting tomorrow.

From Langston Hughes,
**The Panther and the Lash**
(New York: Alfred A. Knopf,
Inc., 1967). Copyright 1951
by Langston Hughes.
Reprinted by permission
of Alfred A. Knopf, Inc.
and Harold Ober Associates
Incorporated.

## A Dream Deferred

What happens to a dream deferred?

Does it dry up
Like a raisin in the sun?
Or fester like a sore—
And then run?
Does it stink like rotten meat?
Or crust and sugar over—
Like a syrupy sweet?

Maybe it just sags
Like a heavy load.

*Or does it explode?*

*LeRoi Jones was born in Newark, New Jersey, within sight of
Manhattan's skyline, in 1934. He has written powerful plays as well
as poetry. In the mid-1960's, he also became one of Newark's leading black militants. In the poem that follows, Jones writes about
the Gansevoort Street pier, which juts out into the Hudson River
from the northwest corner of Greenwich Village.*

From **New Negro Poets: USA**
edited by Langston Hughes.
Copyright © 1964 by
Langston Hughes. Reprinted
by permission of Indiana
University Press.

## Each Morning

(Section 4 From "Hymn for Lanie Poo")

Each morning
I go down
to Gansevoort St.
and stand on the docks.
I stare out
at the horizon
until it gets up
and comes to embrace
me. I

312

make believe
it is my father.
This is known
as genealogy.

*Philip Booth, born in New Hampshire in 1925, studied at Colum-
bia University in New York City before becoming an English
professor at Syracuse University in upstate New York.*

## Was a Man

Was a man, was a two-
faced man, pretended
he wasn't who he was,
who, in a men's room,
faced his hung-over
face in a mirror hung
over the towel rack.
The mirror was cracked.
Shaving close in that
looking glass, he nicked
his throat, bled blue
blood, grabbed a new
towel to patch the wrong
scratch, knocked off
the mirror and, facing
himself, almost intact,
in final terror hung
the wrong face back.

From **The Islanders** (New York: The Viking Press, Inc., 1958). Copyright © 1958 by Philip Booth. Reprinted by permission of The Viking Press, Inc.

# 10 SONGS AND GRAFFITI

Not all of today's young rebels have become hippies like Sonny, the young man whose interview appears in Reading 7. Many rebel only to the extent of growing long hair or trying pot. Others take part in peace marches, participate in sit-ins, or tutor young ghetto children in an attempt to remake society in conformity with their ideals. By far the majority of young people, however, have not rebelled at all. But even many of these young people question some aspects of the society in which they live.

Some of the issues which trouble young people emerge in the music they play and listen to. Many of the songs that drive parents crazy as they blare at top volume from the bedroom record player have little more than a catchy tune, a good beat, and slick lyrics to recommend them. But the words of many others reveal deep-seated feelings and basic discontents. So does popular literature —the paperbacked books young people read, the movies they go to, even the sayings they scrawl on the walls of restrooms. Indeed, the humanities may be studied in strange places!

Reading 10 consists of two parts. The first contains the words of a number of pop songs and folk songs which have been hits among young people in New York City during the late 1960's. The second is made up of graffiti, sayings scrawled on the walls of johns in New York bars, coffee houses, and restaurants. As you read, think about the following questions:

1. What are these lyrics and graffiti saying? Why do you think they were popular during the late 1960's?
2. How accurately do popular music and folk literature indicate what young people think? How do these songs and sayings define the good man, the good life, and the good society?
3. What current popular song do you think has meaningful lyrics? Bring a recording of your favorite to class as a focus for discussion tomorrow.

# Songs of the City

*Born in New York in 1919, Pete Seeger became the leader in the American folk song revival of the 1940's and '50's. Seeger's repertoire is immense, ranging from chain gang songs he learned from Leadbelly and Dust Bowl songs he learned from Woody Guthrie in the 1940's, to Vietnam protest songs he himself composed in the 1960's. The following song, one of Seeger's favorites, was composed by Malvina Reynolds, a San Francisco song writer, in 1962.*

## Little Boxes

*Words and Music by Malvina Reynolds*

Little boxes on the hillside,
Little boxes made of ticky tacky
Little boxes on the hillside,
Little boxes all the same.
There's a green one and a pink one
And a blue one and a yellow one

And they're all made out of ticky tacky
And they all look just the same.

And the people in the houses
All went to the university,
Where they were put in boxes
And they came out all the same.
And there's doctors and there's lawyers,
And business executives,
And they're all made out of ticky tacky
And they all look just the same.

And they all play on the golf course
And drink their martinis dry,
And they all have pretty children
And the children go to school.
And the children go to summer camp
And then to the university,
Where they are put in boxes
And they come out all the same.

And the boys go into business
And marry and raise a family
In boxes made of ticky tacky
And they all look just the same.
There's a green one and a pink one
And a blue one and a yellow one
And they're all made out of ticky tacky
And they all look just the same.

*Born in 1937, Tom Paxton was raised in Oklahoma. He came to New York in 1961, and began his career as a modern folk singer and composer at The Gaslight in Greenwich Village.*

## *What Did You Learn in School?*

### *by Tom Paxton*

What did you learn in school today, dear little boy of mine?
What did you learn in school today, dear little boy of mine?
I learned that Washington never told a lie
I learned that soldiers seldom die
I learned that everybody's free.
That's what the teacher said to me.
And that's what I learned in school today. That's what I learned in school.

What did you learn in school today, dear little boy of mine?
What did you learn in school today, dear little boy of mine?
I learned that policemen are my friends
I learned that justice never ends,
I learned that murderers die for their crimes
Even if we make a mistake sometimes
And that's what I learned in school today. That's what I learned in
    school.

What did you learn in school today, dear little boy of mine?
What did you learn in school today, dear little boy of mine?
I learned our government must be strong,
It's always right and never wrong,
Our leaders are the finest men,
And we elect them again and again,
And that's what I learned in school today. That's what I learned in
    school.

What did you learn in school today, dear little boy of mine?
What did you learn in school today, dear little boy of mine?
I learned that war is not so bad,
I learned of the great ones we have had
We fought in Germany and in France,
And someday I might get my chance,
And that's what I learned in school today. That's what I learned in
    school.

*Len Chandler, born in Akron, Ohio, holds a master's degree in musicology from Columbia University, and is an accomplished oboist. He has also become a leading folk performer and composer whose songs often stem from his feelings and experiences as a black American.*

# Keep on Keepin' on

### by Len H. Chandler, Jr.

While sitting on a crowded southbound train—
It happened just the other day;
I could have sworn that I was rolling back
As the train beside me slowly pulled away.
Well, my whole life long it seems I've been on that track,
With everybody rolling on and me just slipping back;
And they don't wave good-by and they don't look back;
*So I guess I've gotta keep on keepin' on.*

Some people always say what I should do:
Now that's something they seem to know so well;
Ah but it's what I've got to do that's on my mind,
And they never seem to listen when I tell.
But it really doesn't bother me that no one seems to care,
That the stairs are full of splinters, and my tender feet are bare,
And I just can't keep from thinkin' there's trouble everywhere,
*So I guess I've gotta keep on keepin' on.*

Well, I know you wish my tongue would turn to stone,
Or that I'd have kept it still the other day;
I said I'd like to see you walk the sea
And you sank just like your feet were made of clay.
But there's a mountain in the bottom of that sea we flounder in;
If we'd find that mountain-top we wouldn't need to swim;
If we'd found that mountain sooner just think where we could have
  been,
*So I guess I've gotta keep on keepin' on.*

One ship sails east, and the other sails west while the very same
  breezes blow;
It's the set of the sail and not the gale that bids them where to go.
And like the ships of the sea is the way of our fate:
The seas are getting stormy and the hour's getting late.
If that ship starts seeping water, you know how to bail;
You can't change the weather but you sure can change the sail,
And a harbor looks much better when you've made it through a
  gale—
*So I guess I've gotta keep on keepin' on.*

▶ Should an individual set his own course if the prevailing winds blow in the opposite direction?

*Paul Simon and Arthur Garfunkel, both born in Queens in 1942,
are a leading folk-rock team. (Garfunkel is the arranger.) They
are known for their originality and sophistication. Simon and Garfunkel also wrote and performed the music for the movie,* The
Graduate.

# I Am A Rock

### Words and Music by Paul Simon

A winter's day. In a deep and dark December.
I am alone, gazing from my window
To the streets below. On a freshly fallen silent shroud of snow.

*Chorus:* I Am A Rock, I am an island.

From "I Am A Rock" by Paul Simon. © 1965 Charing Cross Music, Inc. Used with permission of the publisher.

▶ Can a person lead a good life shut up within himself to avoid the pain which friendship sometimes brings?

I've built walls. A fortress steep and mighty,
That none may penetrate.
I have no need of friendship;
Friendship causes pain.
It's laughter and it's loving I disdain.

*Chorus:* I Am A Rock, I am an island.

Don't talk of love; I've heard the words before;
It is sleeping in my memory and I won't disturb the slumber
Of feelings that have died.
If I never loved I never would have cried.

*Chorus:* I Am A Rock, I am an island.

I have my books and my poetry to protect me;
I am shielded in my armor.
Hiding in my room, safe within my womb;
I touch no one and no one touches me.

*Chorus:* I Am A Rock, I am an island.

And a rock can feel no pain. And an island never cries.

*Buffy Sainte-Marie, of American Indian descent, was adopted by Cree Indians and raised in Maine and Massachusetts. She is known particularly for poignant protest and folk songs, but has also ventured into country and western.*

Jainism is an Indian religion that dates to the sixth century B.C.

## Universal Soldier

### by Buffy Sainte-Marie

He's five foot two, and he's six feet four,
He fights with missiles and with spears.
He's all of thirty-one, and he's only seventeen,
He's been a soldier for a thousand years.
He's a Catholic, a Hindu, an atheist, a Jain,
A Buddhist, and a Baptist, and a Jew.
And he knows he shouldn't kill,
And he knows he always will
Kill you for me, my friend, and me for you.
And he's fighting for Canada,
He's fighting for France,
He's fighting for the U.S.A.
And he's fighting for the Russians,
And he's fighting for Japan,
And he thinks we'll put an end to war this way.

And he's fighting for democracy,
He's fighting for the Reds.
He says it's for the peace of all.
He's the one who must decide
Who's to live and who's to die,
And he never sees the writing on the wall.
But without him how would Hitler have condemned them to
    Dachau;
Without him Caesar would have stood alone.
He's the one who gives his body as the weapon of the war,
And without him all this killin' can't go on.
He's the universal soldier, and he really is to blame,
His orders come from far away no more.
They come from here and there, and you and me,
And, brothers, can't you see
This is not the way we put the end to war.

Dachau, a town in southern Germany, was the site of one of the Nazis' largest concentration and death camps.

# Graffiti

*"Graffiti" is a fancy word for inscriptions on walls. The following graffiti are taken from a collection made by a New Yorker, mostly in Greenwich Village and the East Village.*

We are the people our parents warned us about.
*Engagé Coffee House, 339 East 10th Street*

Robert Reisner, ed., **Graffiti** (New York: Grove Press, 1968). Reprinted by permission of Grove Press, Inc. Copyright © 1967 by Robert Reisner.

Do not write on walls!
UNDERNEATH:
You want we should type maybe?
*Forum Coffee House, Avenue A*

Think ethnic.
*Blimpie's, Sixth Avenue and 11th Street*

I love grils.
UNDERNEATH THIS SOMEONE WROTE:
It's spelled girls.
TO WHICH SOMEONE REPLIED:
What about us grils?

Socrates eats Hemlock.
*Lion's Head, 59 Christopher Street*

America, rich and arrogant, founded on racism and theft.
You'll get yours this summer, 1966.
*Engagé Coffee House, 339 East 10th Street*

In an insane world the only sane men are crucified, shot, jailed, or classified as insane themselves.
*Le Metro Caffe Espresso, 149 Second Avenue*

Reality is the shifting face of need.
*Le Metro Caffe Espresso, 149 Second Avenue*

There are no answers, only mysteries.
*Le Metro Caffe Espresso, 149 Second Avenue*

Death is Nature's way of telling you to slow down.

You are fast becoming what you are going to be.

I want to be what I was when I wanted to be what I am now.
*Ladies' Room, Ninth Circle Restaurant, 139 West 10th Street*

If I had a wish I would wish that people would stop eating each other's brains out.
*Ladies' Room, Limelight Restaurant, 91 Seventh Avenue South*

Take sex, religion, and politics out of the john.
*Engagé Coffee House, 339 East 10th Street*

Don't think everyone who comes in here is clever! Actually the owners write all this to pretend this is an "IN" bar—Good try!
*Lion's Head, 59 Christopher Street*

My graffiti will fail,
Because my lipstick's so pale.
*Ladies' Room, Lion's Head, 59 Christopher Street*

## 11 TRIUMPH AND THE GOOD LIFE

Broadway symbolizes success on the American stage. Celebrated in song and story as the Great White Way, it remains the ultimate goal of thousands of aspiring playwrights, actors, directors, and technicians. Even many movie stars, as well as men and women who have won reputations in other cities or in off-Broadway shows, eventually test their talents in one of Broadway's famous theaters. Moss Hart was one of these men.

Brooklyn-born of a poor family who lived in a shabby apartment, Hart went to the public schools and read himself to sleep

320

throughout his boyhood. The theater swept its magic over him while he was still a child. Beginning as an office boy for a theatrical agent, he graduated to a position as social director of a summer camp, director of a little theater, and finally the author of a play which closed on the road.

Then he met George S. Kaufman, whose genius as a playwright and director had long graced New York theaters. Together, Hart and Kaufman toiled for an entire season on the script of *Once in a Lifetime,* a comedy about the early days of the movies. Finally, the play opened at the Music Box in 1930, in the depths of the Depression, to be greeted with rave reviews and long lines at the box office. For a man not yet out of his twenties, no wine could be sweeter.

In the excerpts from his autobiography which follow, Hart describes this great moment in his life. As you read, think about the following questions:

1. Who and what meant most to Hart when he realized that his play was a hit? What does your answer imply about his conception of the good life?
2. How alone was he? how close to others?
3. Does any other profession have a moment of triumph like that in the theater? what about sports, politics, the law, medicine, being a housewife? Do you need great moments to sustain the good life?

# Opening Night

From that moment onward, both play and audience took on something of the quality of fantasy—it was being played and received like a playwright's dream of a perfect opening night. The performance was brilliant and the audience matched it in their response. One of the theatre's most steadfast beliefs is that there is never again a sound of trumpets like the sound of a New York opening-night audience giving a play its unreserved approval. It is a valid belief. Bitter words have been written about the first-night audience, but the fact remains that there is no audience ever again like it—no audience as keen, as alive, as exciting and as overwhelmingly satisfactory as a first-night audience taking a play to its heart. It can unfurl the tricolor of its acclamation and make flags seem to wave from every box; just as in reverse its dissent can seem to dangle the Jolly Roger from the center chandelier and blanket the auditorium in leaden disapproval. . . .

Moss Hart, **Act One** (New York: Random House, Inc., 1959), pp. 426, 432–435, 435–443. Copyright © 1959 by Catherine Hart and Joseph M. Hyman, Trustees. Reprinted by permission of Random House, Inc. and Martin Secker & Warburg, Ltd. (London).

Is success in any other profession as dazzling, as deeply satisfying, as it is in the theatre? I cannot pretend to know, but I doubt it. There are other professions where the rewards are as great or greater than those the theatre offers, there are professions where the fruits of success are as immediate, and still others where the pursuit of a more admirable goal undoubtedly brings a nobler sense of fulfillment. But I wonder if success in any of them tastes as sweet. Again, I am inclined to doubt it. There is an intensity, an extravagance, an abundant and unequivocal gratification to the vanity and the ego that can be satisfied more richly and more fully by success in the theatre than in any other calling. Like everything else about the theatre, its success is emphatic and immoderate. Perhaps what makes it so marvelously satisfying is that it is a success that is anything but lonely—everyone seems to share in it, friends and strangers alike—and a first success in the theatre is the most intoxicating and beguiling time imaginable. No success afterward surpasses it. It roars and thumps and thunders through the blood the way that second drink seemed to be coursing through my veins right now, so that it seemed hardly bearable to have to wait until tomorrow to start savoring it.

I asked someone what time it was and blinked my surprise when I was told it was four thirty in the morning. It seemed but a few short minutes since we had waited impatiently for two thirty to come to be able to read the first notice in the *Times*. The morning editions appeared very much later in those days, and it was the custom to go directly to each newspaper in turn and wait for the first copies to roll off the presses. Everyone in the theatre knew what time each paper would appear and where to go for them. The *Times* appeared first at about two thirty, the *Tribune* about three, and the *Daily News* last at four o'clock in the morning. The *World* was far downtown on Park Row and would have to wait until tomorrow, but with three ecstatic notices under my arm, the *World,* in more ways than just the name of a newspaper, could wait. . . .

I protested a little during the good-byes, but I was secretly relieved that the others were going now, too, for a childish reason of my own. It satisfied my sense of drama to complete the full circle of *Once in a Lifetime* alone with Joe Hyman—the circle that had begun with a dinner alone with him before the opening in Atlantic City and would end with this dinner alone with him now after the opening in New York. It is a childish game I have always played and have never been able to resist—a game of arranging life, whenever possible, in a series of scenes that make perfect first-act or third-act curtains. When it works, and it often does, it lends an

▶ Why is it sometimes important to have approval of what one does expressed publicly by someone you respect?

322

extra zest and a keener sense of enjoyment to whatever the occasion may be where my thirst for drama has contrived to make life imitate a good third act. It worked beautifully now.

I cannot recall one word that was exchanged between us, but it must have taken a fairly long time to satisfy my sense of the dramatic entities, for when we came out of the restaurant it was six o'clock in the morning and broad daylight. For the second dawn in a row I peered down the streets of a sleeping city, searching for a taxi. This dawn, however, was going to usher in an historic moment. My last subway ride was behind me. Never again would I descend those dingy steps or hear those turnstiles click off another somber day behind me. . . .

No one has ever seen the skyline of the city from Brooklyn Bridge as I saw it that morning, with three hit notices under my arm. The face of the city is always invested with grandeur, but grandeur can be chilling. The overpowering symmetry of that skyline can crush the spirit and make the city seem forbidding and impenetrable, but today it seemed to emerge from cold anonymity and grant its acknowledgment and acceptance. There was no sunlight—it was a gray day and the buildings were half shrouded in mist, but it was a city that would know my name today, a city that had not turned me aside, and a city that I loved. Unexpectedly and without warning a great wave of feeling for this proud and beautiful city swept over me. We were off the bridge now and driving through the sprawling, ugly area of tenements that stretch interminably over the approaches to each of its boroughs. They are the first in the city to awake, and the long unending rows of drab, identical houses were already stirring with life. Laundry was being strung out to dry along roof tops and fire escapes, men with lunch boxes were coming out of the houses, and children returning from the corner grocery with bottles of milk and loaves of bread were hurrying up the steps and into the doorways.

I stared through the taxi window at a pinch-faced ten-year-old hurrying down the steps on some morning errand before school, and I thought of myself hurrying down the street on so many gray mornings out of a doorway and a house much the same as this one. My mind jumped backward in time and then whirled forward, like a many-faceted prism—flashing our old neighborhood in front of me, the house, the steps, the candy store—and then shifted to the skyline I had just passed by, the opening last night, and the notices I still hugged tightly under my arm. It was possible in this wonderful city for that nameless little boy—for any of its millions—to have a decent chance to scale the walls and achieve what they wished. Wealth, rank, or an imposing name counted for nothing. The only credential

▶ Why are marvelous extravagances—a taxi ride, a new hat, a night on the town—so much fun for some people?

323

the city asked was the boldness to dream. For those who did, it unlocked its gates and its treasures, not caring who they were or where they came from. I watched the boy disappear into a tailor shop and a surge of shamefaced patriotism overwhelmed me. I might have been watching a victory parade on a flag-draped Fifth Avenue instead of the mean streets of a city slum. A feeling of patriotism, however, is not always limited to the feverish emotions called forth by war. It can sometimes be felt as profoundly and perhaps more truly at a moment such as this. . . .

I stood in the doorway of the kitchen while I waited for the water to boil and gazed at the sleeping figure of my brother on the daybed in the dining room, and beyond it at the closed door of the one bedroom where my parents slept. The frayed carpet on the floor was the carpet I had crawled over before I could walk. Each flower in the badly faded and worn design was sharply etched in my mind. Each piece of furniture in the cramped dim room seemed mildewed with a thousand double-edged memories. The ghosts of a thousand leaden meals hovered over the dining-room table. The dust of countless black-hearted days clung to every crevice of the squalid ugly furniture I had known since childhood. To walk out of it forever—not piecemeal, but completely—would give meaning to the wonder of what had happened to me, make success tangible, decisive.

The goal behind the struggle for success is not always one goal, but many—some real, some hidden; some impossible to achieve, even with success piled upon success. The goal differs with each of us in the mysterious and wonderful way each human being is different from any other, in the way each of us is the sum total of the unexpressed longings and desires that strew the seas of childhood and are glimpsed long afterward from a safe distance—a submerged iceberg, only the tip of which is seen. . . .

I awakened my brother by dumping the papers on the bed for him to read and then called through the bedroom door to my mother and father to get up right away. I gave them barely enough time to read the notices and then plunged. "We're moving into New York today—as soon as you have a cup of coffee—and we're not taking anything with us. We're walking out of here with just the clothes on our backs and nothing else. The coffee's on the stove, so hurry up and get dressed."

My mother stared at me and then spoke quietly, as if a raised voice at this moment might send me further out of my senses. "Where are we going?" she asked logically enough.

"To a hotel," I said, "until we find an apartment and furnish it." There was a stunned silence and before anyone else could speak,

I spoke again, not impatiently but as if what I was saying was inarguable. "There's nothing to pack; we just walk out of the door. No," I added in answer to my mother's mute startled look around the room, "not a thing. We leave it all here just as it stands, and close the door. We don't take anything—not even a toothbrush, a bathrobe, pajamas, or nightgown. We buy it all new in New York. We're walking out of here and starting fresh." . . .

"I'm not walking out of here without the pictures," my mother said with great firmness.

It was my turn to be astonished. "What pictures?" I asked.

"*All* the pictures," she replied. "The baby pictures of you and Bernie and the pictures of my father and my sister, and Bernie's diploma and your letters, and all the other pictures and things I've got in the closet in that big box."

I threw my arms around her and kissed her. I had won. It was being accepted as a fact—incomprehensible but settled.

"One suitcase," I ordered. "Put it all into one suitcase, but one suitcase—that's all."

I looked at my brother, who had remained silent through all of this. He handed the papers back to me with a flourish and winked. "Don't you have to give some of the money to George Kaufman?" he said.

"Half," I replied. "But my share will be over a thousand dollars a week."

"That'll buy a lot of toothbrushes," he said. "I'm going to get ready." And he climbed out of bed.

My mother and father stared at us as if to make sure we were not indulging in some elaborate joke for their benefit.

"It's true," I said soberly. "It's not a salary. I get a percentage of every dollar that comes into the box office. Don't you understand how it works?"

Obviously, they did not, and I realized somewhat belatedly that it had never occurred to either of them to translate good fortune in the theatre into anything more than what my mother's friends defined as "making a good living." No wonder my proposal had sounded lunatic, but now as the belief came to them that what I had just said might be the literal truth, they were suddenly seized with some of my own excitement. My mother's reaction was a curious one. She burst into a peal of laughter. She had a merry and ringing laugh, and it was contagious. My father and I joined in her laughter, though we would have been hard put to tell exactly what we were laughing at. I was reminded of that moment and of her laughter long, long afterward, when I heard someone say, "Nothing makes people laugh like money—the rich get wrinkles from laughing." It was said sardonically, of course, but it is not without an element of truth. Money does generate its own kind of excitement, and its sudden acquisition creates an ambiance of gaiety and merriment that it would be nonsense to deny or not to enjoy. It induces, moreover, a momentum of its own. Everything moves with an unaccustomed and almost miraculous speed. . . .

To everyone's surprise, including my own, a strange silence fell upon us in the taxi, in spite of the fact that my brother read aloud the glowing notice in the *World,* which he had picked up on his way to get the cab. . . .

My mother, . . . silent, took out her handkerchief and wiped her eyes. They were not, I suspected, tears of joy for my success. They were not tears for the beginning of something, but for the end of something none of us could name. Not until we came within sight of Brooklyn Bridge did anyone speak. Then, as suddenly as it had fallen, the silence lifted. Crossing the bridge, as it had for me earlier that morning, seemed to put an old way of life behind us and make inevitable the new one we were rushing headlong into. We started to talk, all of us at once, almost at the same moment, as if crossing the bridge had cut the ties irrevocably and was a symbol of entry into a world as dazzling as the skyline in front of us.

Suddenly no one seemed to have an unexpressed thought. Everyone talked incessantly, oblivious of what anyone else might be saying. We were at 34th Street before I thought to glance out the window. I had told the driver to take us to the Edison Hotel on 47th Street, for no other reason except that it was practically around the corner from the Music Box and seemed more of a family hotel than any other I could think of; but as the cab moved into Times Square, I asked the driver to stop first at the Music Box.

Even through the rain-splashed windows of the cab, I could see a long double line of people extending the full length of the lobby from the box office. The line spilled out under the marquee where another line was patiently forming under umbrellas. I got out of the cab and walked into the lobby and stood gaping at all the people. It was not yet half-past nine in the morning. How long I stood there, forgetful of everything else but the wonder of that line, I do not know, but the box-office man, looking up for a moment to glance across the lobby, caught sight of me and smiled. . . .

"A year at least," he said, "It's the hottest ticket in town. What can I do for you?"

"I wanted to draw $500.00," I said quickly. "I'm moving into town."

"Sure, sure—anything you want," he said. He reached for an

I.O.U. slip and rapidly filled it in. "How do you want it?" he asked.

"A few fifties," I replied, "the rest in twenties and tens."

I signed the slip as he counted out the money, conscious that the people immediately in back of me were whispering to each other. "It is *not* George Kaufman," I heard a woman's voice say. "It must be the other one."

As nearly as I could, I tried to achieve a look of modesty with the back of my head while I waited for him to finish. He pushed the rather formidable stack of bills toward me and his smile floodlit the box office. "Come around any time," he said, "we'll be here for a long, long time."

I doubled the bills in my fist and walked out and into the taxi. Without a word I went through the pretense of counting the money, thoroughly aware of the awed silence around me. . . .

My fatal weakness for standing aside from whatever was happening around me and translating it into vignettes of drama overcame me once more. I could hear myself telling the whole story to Sam Harris. Unresisting, I let it assemble and take shape in my mind. The wait for the notices, the first taxi ride home, the decision to walk out and leave everything behind us, the trip back to open the windows and let the rain pour in—I could hear myself telling it all to him, right down to counting the money in the cab, our paroxysm of laughter, and the cab driver turning around to add the final touch. I could see myself some time later this afternoon standing in his office in the Music Box and telling it to him with the proper embellishment, making it all come out a rounded, dramatic entity. I could see his eyes squint with amusement as I told it and hear his soft laughter afterward. I could even, I thought, hear his comment.

"Not bad, kid," he would say. "Not a bad curtain for a first act."

# 12–13 THE SHORT STORY
# AND SOCIAL JUSTICE

A democracy of talent pervades intellectual New York. Although prejudices touch America everywhere, they probably play a smaller role in television, the theater, nightclubs, education, and the world of literature than in any other set of professions or occupations. The uniquely talented generally respect their peers regardless of skin color or religious belief.

Talented New Yorkers have built a distinguished record in America's long fight for social justice. In the 1920's, a whole list of New York writers and entertainers joined hands to work for the release of Nicola Sacco and Bartolomeo Vanzetti, two Italian-American anarchists convicted in a notoriously unfair trial of murdering a payroll guard during a robbery. Talented New Yorkers supported Franklin D. Roosevelt's New Deal. Since World War II, many of them have thrown themselves into the civil rights movement, giving time, money, and prestige to the ideals it represents.

New York writers often work for the causes in which they believe through protest literature. For example, a dozen excellent plays, novels, poems, and historical accounts have been written by New Yorkers about the Sacco–Vanzetti case. In the 1930's, a stream of proletarian novels pleading for social justice flowed from the presses. The contemporary civil rights movement has triggered a fresh outburst of literary works.

Some protest literature hits directly at an issue. Other literature, such as the two short stories by Dorothy Parker which follow, suggest the same goals in a more subtle fashion. As you read them, think about the following questions:

1. Are these good short stories? Why or why not? What elements of literary craftsmanship can you find?
2. What cause, if any, does Miss Parker support in these stories? Should writers of short stories support causes?
3. What definitions of the good man, the good life, and the good society are implied by these stories?

From **The Portable Dorothy Parker.** Copyright 1927, renewed 1955 by Dorothy Parker. Originally appeared in **The New Yorker.** Reprinted by permission of The Viking Press, Inc.

# Arrangement in Black and White

The woman with the pink velvet poppies twined round the assisted gold of her hair traversed the crowded room at an interesting gait combining a skip with a sidle, and clutched the lean arm of her host.

"Now I got you!" she said. "Now you can't get away!"

"Why, hello," said her host. "Well. How are you?"

"Oh, I'm finely," she said. "Just simply finely. Listen. I want you to do me the most terrible favor. Will you? Will you please? Pretty please?"

"What is it?" said her host.

"Listen," she said. "I want to meet Walter Williams. Honestly, I'm just simply crazy about that man. Oh, when he sings! When he sings those spirituals! Well, I said to Burton, 'It's a good thing for you Walter Williams is colored,' I said, 'or you'd have lots of reason to be jealous.' I'd really love to meet him. I'd like to tell him I've heard him sing. Will you be an angel and introduce me to him?"

"Why, certainly," said her host. "I thought you'd met him. The party's for him. Where is he, anyway?"

"He's over there by the bookcase," she said. "Let's wait till those people get through talking to him. Well, I think you're simply marvelous, giving this perfectly marvelous party for him, and having him meet all these white people, and all. Isn't he terribly grateful?"

"I hope not," said her host.

"I think it's really terribly nice," she said. "I do. I don't see why on earth it isn't perfectly all right to meet colored people. I haven't any feeling at all about it—not one single bit. Burton—oh, he's just the other way. Well, you know, he comes from Virginia, and you know how they are."

"Did he come tonight?" said her host.

"No, he couldn't," she said. "I'm a regular grass widow tonight. I told him when I left, 'There's no telling what I'll do,' I said. He was just so tired out, he couldn't move. Isn't it a shame?"

"Ah," said her host.

"Wait till I tell him I met Walter Williams!" she said. "He'll just about die. Oh, we have more arguments about colored people. I talk to him like I don't know what, I get so excited. 'Oh, don't be so silly,' I say. But I must say for Burton, he's heaps broader-minded than lots of these Southerners. He's really awfully fond of colored people. Well, he says himself, he wouldn't have white servants. And you know, he had this old colored nurse, this regular old nigger mammy, and he just simply loves her. Why, every time he goes home, he goes out in the kitchen to see her. He does, really, to this day. All he says is, he says he hasn't got a word to say against colored people as long as they keep their place. He's always doing things for them—giving them clothes and I don't know what all. The only thing he says, he says he wouldn't sit down at the table with one for a million dollars. 'Oh,' I say to him, 'you make me sick, talking like that.' I'm just terrible to him. Aren't I terrible?"

"Oh, no, no, no," said her host "No, no."

"I am," she said. "I know I am. Poor Burton! Now, me, I don't feel that way at all. I haven't the slightest feeling about colored people. Why, I'm just crazy about some of them. They're just like children—just as easygoing, and always singing and laughing and everything. Aren't they the happiest things you ever saw in your life? Honestly, it makes me laugh just to hear them. Oh, I like them.

▶ Should people get security and pleasure by keeping others in an inferior position?

329

I really do. Well, now, listen, I have this colored laundress, I've had her for years, and I'm devoted to her. She's a real character. And I want to tell you, I think of her as my friend. That's the way I think of her. As I say to Burton, 'Well, for Heaven's sakes, we're all human beings!' Aren't we?"

"Yes," said her host. "Yes, indeed."

"Now this Walter Williams," she said. "I think a man like that's a real artist. I do. I think he deserves an awful lot of credit. Goodness, I'm so crazy about music or anything, I don't care *what* color he is. I honestly think if a person's an artist, nobody ought to have any feeling at all about meeting them. That's absolutely what I say to Burton. Don't you think I'm right?"

"Yes," said her host. "Oh, yes."

"That's the way I feel," she said. "I just can't understand people being narrow-minded. Why, I absolutely think it's a privilege to meet a man like Walter Williams. Yes, I do. I haven't any feeling at all. Well, my goodness, the good Lord made him, just the same as He did any of us. Didn't He?"

"Surely," said her host. "Yes, indeed."

"That's what I say," she said. "Oh, I get so furious when people are narrow-minded about colored people. It's just all I can do not to say something. Of course, I do admit when you get a bad colored man, they're simply terrible. But as I say to Burton, there are some bad white people, too, in this world. Aren't there?"

"I guess there are," said her host.

"Why, I'd really be glad to have a man like Walter Williams come to my house and sing for us, sometime," she said. "Of course, I couldn't ask him on account of Burton, but I wouldn't have any feeling about it at all. Oh, can't he sing! Isn't it marvelous, the way they all have music in them? It just seems to be right in them. Come on, let's us go on over and talk to him. Listen, what shall I do when I'm introduced? Ought I to shake hands? Or what?"

"Why, do whatever you want," said her host.

"I guess maybe I'd better," she said. "I wouldn't for the world have him think I had any feeling. I think I'd better shake hands, just the way I would with anybody else. That's just exactly what I'll do."

They reached the tall young Negro, standing by the bookcase. The host performed introductions; the Negro bowed.

"How do you do?" he said.

The woman with the pink velvet poppies extended her hand at the length of her arm and held it so for all the world to see, until the Negro took it, shook it, and gave it back to her.

"Oh, how do you do, Mr. Williams," she said. "Well, how do you do. I've just been saying, I've enjoyed your singing so awfully much. I've been to your concerts, and we have you on the phonograph and everything. Oh, I just enjoy it!"

She spoke with great distinctness, moving her lips meticulously, as if in parlance with the deaf.

"I'm so glad," he said.

"I'm just simply crazy about that 'Water Boy' thing you sing," she said. "Honestly, I can't get it out of my head. I have my husband nearly crazy, the way I go around humming it all the time. Oh, he looks just as black as the ace of—Well. Tell me, where on earth do you ever get all those songs of yours? How do you ever get hold of them?"

"Why," he said, "there are so many different——"

"I should think you'd love singing them," she said. "It must be more fun. All those darling old spirituals—oh, I just love them! Well, what are you doing, now? Are you still keeping up your singing? Why don't you have another concert, some time?"

"I'm having one the sixteenth of this month," he said.

"Well, I'll be there," she said. "I'll be there, if I possibly can. You can count on me. Goodness, here comes a whole raft of people to talk to you. You're just a regular guest of honor! Oh, who's that girl in white? I've seen her some place."

"That's Katherine Burke," said her host.

"Good Heavens," she said. "Is that Katherine Burke? Why, she looks entirely different off the stage. I thought she was much better-looking. I had no idea she was so terribly dark. Why, she looks almost like—Oh, I think she's a wonderful actress! Don't you think she's a wonderful actress, Mr. Williams? Oh, I think she's marvelous. Don't you?"

"Yes, I do," he said.

"Oh, I do, too," she said. "Just wonderful. Well, goodness, we must give someone else a chance to talk to the guest of honor. Now, don't forget, Mr. Williams, I'm going to be at that concert if I possibly can. I'll be there applauding like everything. And if I can't come, I'm going to tell everybody I know to go, anyway. Don't you forget!"

"I won't," he said. "Thank you so much."

The host took her arm and piloted her into the next room.

"Oh, my dear," she said. "I nearly died! Honestly, I give you my word, I nearly passed away. Did you hear that terrible break I made? I was just going to say Katherine Burke looked almost like a nigger. I just caught myself in time. Oh, do you think he noticed?"

"I don't believe so," said her host.

"Well, thank goodness," she said, "because I wouldn't have embarrassed him for anything. Why, he's awfully nice. Just as nice as he can be. Nice manners, and everything. You know, so many

▶ Why do people sometimes make slips of the tongue such as this one?

colored people, you give them an inch, and they walk all over you. But he doesn't try any of that. Well, he's got more sense, I suppose. He's really nice. Don't you think so?"

"Yes," said her host.

"I liked him," she said. "I haven't any feeling at all because he's a colored man. I felt just as natural as I would with anybody. Talked to him just as naturally, and everything. But honestly, I could hardly keep a straight face. I kept thinking of Burton. Oh, wait till I tell Burton I called him 'Mister'!"

# Clothe the Naked

Big Lannie went out by the day to the houses of secure and leisured ladies, to wash their silks and their linens. She did her work perfectly; some of the ladies even told her so. She was a great, slow mass of a woman, colored a sound brown-black save for her palms and the flat of her fingers that were like gutta-percha from steam and hot suds. She was slow because of her size, and because the big veins in her legs hurt her, and her back ached much of the time. She neither cursed her ills nor sought remedies for them. They had happened to her; there they were.

Many things had happened to her. She had had children, and the children had died. So had her husband, who was a kind man, cheerful with the little luck he found. None of their children had died at birth. They had lived to be four or seven or ten, so that they had had their ways and their traits and their means of causing love; and Big Lannie's heart was always wide for love. One child had been killed in a street accident, and two others had died of illnesses that might have been no more than tedious, had there been fresh food and clear spaces and clean air behind them. Only Arlene, the youngest, lived to grow up.

Arlene was a tall girl, not so dark as her mother but with the same firm flatness of color. She was so thin that her bones seemed to march in advance of her body. Her little pipes of legs and her broad feet with jutting heels were like things a child draws with crayons. She carried her head low, her shoulders scooped around her chest, and her stomach slanted forward. From the time that she was tiny, there were men after her.

Arlene was a bad girl always; that was one of the things that had happened to Big Lannie. There it was, and Big Lannie could only keep bringing her presents, surprises, so that the girl would love her mother and would want to stay at home. She brought little bottles of sharp perfume, and pale stockings of tinny silk, and

From **The Portable Dorothy Parker.** Copyright 1938, copyright © renewed 1966 by Dorothy Parker. Reprinted by permission of The Viking Press, Inc.

Gutta-percha is a tough plastic substance resembling rubber. It comes from several types of Malaysian trees.

▶ Why should a person give presents to loved ones?

332

rings set with bits of green and red glass; she tried to choose what Arlene would like. But each time Arlene came home she had bigger rings and softer stockings and stronger perfume than her mother could buy for her. Sometimes she would stay with her mother over a night, and sometimes more than a week; and then Big Lannie would come back from work one evening, and the girl would be gone, and no word of her. Big Lannie would go on bringing surprises, and setting them out along Arlene's bed to wait a return.

Big Lannie did not know it, when Arlene was going to have a baby. Arlene had not been home in nearly half a year; Big Lannie told the time in days. There was no news at all of the girl until the people at the hospital sent for Big Lannie to come to her daughter and grandson. She was there to hear Arlene say the baby must be named Raymond, and to see the girl die. For whom Raymond was called, or if for anyone, Big Lannie never knew.

He was a long, light-colored baby, with big, milky eyes that looked right back at his grandmother. It was several days before the people at the hospital told her he was blind.

Big Lannie went to each of the ladies who employed her and explained that she could not work for some while; she must take care of her grandson. The ladies were sharply discommoded, after her steady years, but they dressed their outrage in shrugs and cool tones. Each arrived, separately, at the conclusion that she had been too good to Big Lannie, and had been imposed upon, therefore. "Honestly, those niggers!" each said to her friends. "They're all alike."

Big Lannie sold most of the things she lived with, and took one room with a stove in it. There, as soon as the people at the hospital would let her, she brought Raymond and tended him. He was all her children to her.

She had always been a saving woman, with few needs and no cravings, and she had been long alone. Even after Arlene's burial, there was enough left for Raymond and Big Lannie to go on for a time. Big Lannie was slow to be afraid of what must come; fear did not visit her at all, at first, and then it slid in only when she waked, when the night hung motionless before another day.

Raymond was a good baby, a quiet, patient baby, lying in his wooden box and stretching out his delicate hands to the sounds that were light and color to him. It seemed but a little while, so short to Big Lannie, before he was walking about the room, his hands held out, his feet quick and sure. Those of Big Lannie's friends who saw him for the first time had to be told that he could not see.

Then, and it seemed again such a little while, he could dress himself, and open the door for his granny, and unlace the shoes

"Discommoded" means inconvenienced.

333

from her tired feet, and talk to her in his soft voice. She had occasional employment—now and then a neighbor would hear of a day's scrubbing she could do, or sometimes she might work in the stead of a friend who was sick—infrequent, and not to be planned on. She went to the ladies for whom she had worked, to ask if they might not want her back again; but there was little hope in her, after she had visited the first one. Well, now, really, said the ladies; well, really, now.

The neighbors across the hall watched over Raymond while Big Lannie looked for work. He was no trouble to them, nor to himself. He sat and crooned at his chosen task. He had been given a wooden spool around the top of which were driven little brads, and over these with a straightened hairpin he looped bright worsted, working faster than sight until a long tube of woven wool fell through the hole in the spool. The neighbors threaded big, blunt needles for him, and he coiled the woolen tubes and sewed them into mats. Big Lannie called them beautiful, and it made Raymond proud to have her tell him how readily she sold them. It was hard for her, when he was asleep at night, to unravel the mats and wash the worsted and stretch it so straight that even Raymond's shrewd fingers could not tell, when he worked with it next day, that it was not new.

Fear stormed in Big Lannie and took her days and nights. She might not go to any organization dispensing relief, for dread that Raymond would be taken from her and put in—she would not say the word to herself, and she and her neighbors lowered their voices when they said it to one another—an institution. The neighbors wove lingering tales of what happened inside certain neat, square buildings on the cindery skirts of the town, and, if they must go near them, hurried as if passing graveyards, and came home heroes. When they got you in one of those places, whispered the neighbors, they laid your spine open with whips, and then when you dropped, they kicked your head in. Had anyone come into Big Lannie's room to take Raymond away to an asylum for the blind, the neighbors would have fought for him with stones and rails and boiling water.

Raymond did not know about anything but good. When he grew big enough to go alone down the stairs and into the street, he was certain of delight each day. He held his head high, as he came out into the little yard in front of the flimsy wooden house, and slowly turned his face from side to side, as if the air were soft liquid in which he bathed it. Trucks and wagons did not visit the street, which ended in a dump for rusted bedsprings and broken boilers and staved-in kettles; children played over its cobbles, and men and women sat talking in open windows and called across

▶ What should charitable organizations require as a condition for giving assistance to the needy?

to one another in gay, rich voices. There was always laughter for Raymond to hear, and he would laugh back, and hold out his hands to it.

At first, the children stopped their play when he came out, and gathered quietly about him, and watched him, fascinated. They had been told of his affliction, and they had a sort of sickened pity for him. Some of them spoke to him, in soft, careful tones. Raymond would laugh with pleasure, and stretch his hands, the curious smooth, flat hands of the blind, to their voices. They would draw sharply back, afraid that his strange hands might touch them. Then, somehow ashamed because they had shrunk from him and he could not see that they had done so, they said gentle good-bys to him, and backed away into the street again, watching him steadily.

When they were gone, Raymond would start on his walk to the end of the street. He guided himself by lightly touching the broken fences along the dirt sidewalk, and as he walked he crooned little songs with no words to them. Some of the men and women at the windows would call hello to him, and he would call back and wave and smile. When the children, forgetting him, laughed again at their games, he stopped and turned to the sound as if it were the sun.

In the evening, he would tell Big Lannie about his walk, slapping his knee and chuckling at the memory of the laughter he had heard. When the weather was too hard for him to go out in the street, he would sit at his worsted work, and talk all day of going out the next day.

The neighbors did what they could for Raymond and Big Lannie. They gave Raymond clothes their own children had not yet worn out, and they brought food, when they had enough to spare and other times. Big Lannie would get through a week, and would pray to get through the next one; and so the months went. Then the days on which she could find work fell farther and farther apart, and she could not pray about the time to come because she did not dare to think of it.

It was Mrs. Ewing who saved Raymond's and Big Lannie's lives, and let them continue together. Big Lannie said that then and ever after; daily she blessed Mrs. Ewing, and nightly she would have prayed for her, had she not known, in some dimmed way, that any intercession for Mrs. Delabarre Ewing must be impudence.

Mrs. Ewing was a personage in the town. When she went to Richmond for a visit, or when she returned from viewing the azalea gardens in Charleston, the newspaper always printed the fact. She was a woman rigorously conscious of her noble obligation; she was prominent on the Community Chest committee, and it was she who planned and engineered the annual Bridge Drive to raise funds for planting salvia around the cannon in front of the D.A.R. headquarters. These and many others were her public activities, and she was no less exacting of herself in her private life. She kept a model, though childless, house for her husband and herself, relegating the supervision of details to no domestic lieutenant, no matter how seemingly trustworthy.

Back before Raymond was born, Big Lannie had worked as laundress for Mrs. Ewing. Since those days, the Ewing wash tubs had witnessed many changes, none for the better. Mrs. Ewing took Big Lannie back into her employment. She apologized for this step to her friends by the always winning method of self-deprecation. She knew she was a fool, she said, after all that time, and after the way that Big Lannie had treated her. But still, she said—and she laughed a little at her own ways—anyone she felt kind of sorry for could always get round her, she said. She knew it was awfully foolish, but that, she said, was the way she was. Mr. Ewing, she said behind her husband's hearing, always called her just a regular little old easy mark.

Big Lannie had no words in which to thank Mrs. Ewing, nor to tell her what two days' assured employment every week could mean. At least, it was fairly assured. Big Lannie, as Mrs. Ewing pointed out to her, had got no younger, and she had always been slow. Mrs. Ewing kept her in a state of stimulating insecurity by referring, with perfect truth, to the numbers of stronger, quicker women who were also in need of work.

Two days' work in the week meant money for rent and stovewood and almost enough food for Raymond and Big Lannie. She must depend, for anything further, on whatever odd jobs she could find, and she must not stop seeking them. Pressed on by fear and gratitude, she worked so well for Mrs. Ewing that there was sometimes expressed satisfaction at the condition of the lady's household linen and her own and her husband's clothing. Big Lannie had a glimpse of Mr. Ewing occasionally, leaving the house as she came, or entering it as she was leaving. He was a bit of a man, not much bigger than Raymond.

Raymond grew so fast that he seemed to be taller each morning. Every day he had his walk in the street to look forward to and experience, and tell Big Lannie about at night. He had ceased to be a sight of the street; the children were so used to him that they did not even look at him, and the men and women at the windows no longer noticed him enough to hail him. He did not know. He would wave to any gay cry he heard, and go on his way, singing his little songs and turning toward the sound of laughter.

Then his lovely list of days ended as sharply as if ripped from some bright calendar. A winter came, so sudden and savage as to find no comparison in the town's memories, and Raymond had no clothes to wear out in the street. Big Lannie mended his outgrown garments as long as she could, but the stuff had so rotted with wear that it split in new places when she tried to sew together the ragged edges of rents.

The neighbors could give no longer; all they had they must keep for their own. A demented colored man in a near-by town had killed the woman who employed him, and terror had spread like brush fire. There was a sort of panic of reprisal; colored employees were dismissed from their positions, and there was no new work for them. But Mrs. Ewing, admittedly soft-hearted certainly to a fault and possibly to a peril, kept her black laundress on. More than ever Big Lannie had reason to call her blessed.

All winter, Raymond stayed indoors. He sat at his spool and worsted, with Big Lannie's old sweater about his shoulders and, when his tattered knickerbockers would no longer hold together, a calico skirt of hers lapped around his waist. He lived, at his age, in the past; in the days when he had walked, proud and glad, in the street, with laughter in his ears. Always, when he talked of it, he must laugh back at that laughter.

Since he could remember, he had not been allowed to go out when Big Lannie thought the weather unfit. This he had accepted without question, and so he accepted his incarceration through the mean weeks of the winter. But then one day it was spring, so surely that he could tell it even in the smoky, stinking rooms of the house, and he cried out with joy because now he might walk in the street again. Big Lannie had to explain to him that his rags were too thin to shield him, and that there were no odd jobs for her, and so no clothes and shoes for him.

Raymond did not talk about the street any more, and his fingers were slow at his spool.

Big Lannie did something she had never done before; she begged of her employer. She asked Mrs. Ewing to give her some of Mr. Ewing's old clothes for Raymond. She looked at the floor and mumbled so that Mrs. Ewing requested her to talk *up*. When Mrs. Ewing understood, she was, she said, surprised. She had, she said, a great, great many demands on her charity, and she would have supposed that Big Lannie, of all people, might have known that she did everything she could, and, in fact, a good deal more. She spoke of inches and ells. She said that if she found she could spare anything, Big Lannie was kindly to remember it was to be just for this once.

Knickerbockers, or knickers, are loose-fitting short pants gathered at the knees. They were standard dress for American boys from the 1880's through the 1930's.

An ell can be any of several units of length, used chiefly for measuring cloth.

When Big Lannie was leaving at the end of her day's work, Mrs. Ewing brought her a package with her own hands. There, she said, was a suit and a pair of shoes; beautiful, grand things that people would think she was just a crazy to go giving away like that. She simply didn't know, she said, what Mr. Ewing would say to her for being such a crazy. She explained that that was the way she was when anyone got around her, all the while Big Lannie was trying to thank her.

Big Lannie had never before seen Raymond behave as he did when she brought him home the package. He jumped and danced and clapped his hands, he tried to speak and squealed instead, he tore off the paper himself, and ran his fingers over the close-woven cloth and held it to his face and kissed it. He put on the shoes and clattered about in them, digging with his toes and heels to keep them on; he made Big Lannie pin the trousers around his waist and roll them up over his shins. He babbled of the morrow when he would walk in the street, and could not say his words for laughing.

Big Lannie must work for Mrs. Ewing the next day, and she had thought to bid Raymond wait until she could stay at home and dress him herself in his new garments. But she heard him laugh again; she could not tell him he must wait. He might go out at noon next day, she said, when the sun was so warm that he would not take cold at his first outing; one of the neighbors across the hall would help him with the clothes. Raymond chuckled and sang his little songs until he went to sleep.

After Big Lannie left in the morning, the neighbor came in to Raymond, bringing a pan of cold pork and corn bread for his lunch. She had a call for a half-day's work, and she could not stay to see him start out for his walk. She helped him put on the trousers and pinned and rolled them for him, and she laced the shoes as snug as they would go on his feet. Then she told him not to go out till the noon whistles blew, and kissed him, and left.

Raymond was too happy to be impatient. He sat and thought of the street and smiled and sang. Not until he heard the whistles did he go to the drawer where Big Lannie had laid the coat, and take it out and put it on. He felt it soft on his bare back, he twisted his shoulders to let it fall warm and loose from them. As he folded the sleeves back over his thin arms, his heart beat so that the cloth above it fluttered.

The stairs were difficult for him to manage, in the big shoes, but the very slowness of the descent was delicious to him. His anticipation was like honey in his mouth.

Then he came out into the yard, and turned his face in the gentle air. It was all good again; it was all given back again. As quickly as he could, he gained the walk and set forth, guiding himself by the fence. He could not wait; he called out, so that he would hear gay calls in return, he laughed so that laughter would answer him.

He heard it. He was so glad that he took his hand from the fence and turned and stretched out his arms and held up his smiling face to welcome it. He stood there, and his smile died on his face, and his welcoming arms stiffened and shook.

It was not the laughter he had known; it was not the laughter he had lived on. It was like great flails beating him flat, great prongs tearing his flesh from his bones. It was coming at him, to kill him. It drew slyly back, and then it smashed against him. It swirled around and over him, and he could not breathe. He screamed and tried to run out through it, and fell, and it licked over him, howling higher. His clothes unrolled, and his shoes flapped on his feet. Each time he could rise, he fell again. It was as if the street were perpendicular before him, and the laughter leaping at his back. He could not find the fence, he did not know which way he was turned. He lay screaming, in blood and dust and darkness.

When Big Lannie came home, she found him on the floor in a corner of the room, moaning and whimpering. He still wore his new clothes, cut and torn and dusty, and there was dried blood on his mouth and his palms. Her heart had leapt in alarm when he had not opened the door at her footstep and she cried out so frantically to ask what had happened that she frightened him into wild weeping. She could not understand what he said; it was something about the street, and laughing at him, and make them go away, and don't let him go in the street no more, never in the street no more. She did not try to make him explain. She took him in her arms and rocked him, and told him, over and over, never mind, don't care, everything's all right. Neither he nor she believed her words.

But her voice was soft and her arms warm. Raymond's sobs softened, and trembled away. She held him, rocking silently and rhythmically, a long time. Then gently she set him on his feet, and took from his shoulders Mr. Ewing's old full-dress coat.

# 14 A SEARCH FOR IDENTITY

A single essay can sometimes capture the spirit of an age. Pericles's Funeral Oration reflected the essence of Athenian democracy. Lincoln's Gettysburg Address spoke in similar fashion for nineteenth-century American patriots. Winston Churchill's famous phrases rallied Britain to help halt Hitler's triumphant march through Europe. Words like these have justly won a place in history.

An essay by Stokely Carmichael, although certainly not as famous as the words of Pericles, Lincoln, or Churchill, has nevertheless come to symbolize the aspirations of many young, black Americans. After World War II, the United States seemed to be moving toward a society in which blacks and whites shared equal rights. Legislatures, the courts, and executive orders by government officials struck down segregation. Sit-ins and protest marches signified widespread public support for these developments. Integration became the goal of civil rights leaders of all colors and faiths. But despite conspicuous triumphs, many doors remained firmly closed to black men and women. Slowly at first, and then at an increasing pace, young blacks began to call for a new black nationalism and a society in which black men and women could work out their own destiny. "Black Power" became the slogan for these young militants.

No one man speaks for all black militants. The call for black power has been heard throughout the nation and in a variety of forms. Much of this agitation has centered in New York City where nationalists such as Elijah Muhammed and Malcolm X won large followings. Among the leading militants is Stokely Carmichael, born in the West Indies in 1942, and raised in New York City. In 1966, *The New York Review of Books* published an essay by Carmichael, who was then national chairman of the Student Nonviolent Coordinating Committee (SNCC). Carmichael's essay spoke clearly for one segment of the black nationalist movement. As you read excerpts from his essay, think about these questions:

1. According to Carmichael, what do blacks need in order to develop a sense of self-worth and of community? What would be the characteristics of a good man who is a black American?
2. Why does Carmichael reject white American society? Are his charges accurate?
3. Why does Carmichael refuse to work toward an integrated society? How does he define a good society for black Americans?
4. What sorts of black people would be most likely to agree with Carmichael? Which sorts of black people would probably disagree? Why?

Stokely Carmichael, "What We Want," **The New York Review of Books**, Vol. 7, No. 4 (September 22, 1966), pp. 5–8. Reprinted by permission of SNCC.

# Black Power: A Radical View

One of the tragedies of the struggle against racism is that up to now there has been no national organization which could speak to the growing militancy of young black people in the urban ghetto. There has been only a civil rights movement whose tone of voice was adapted to an audience of liberal whites. It served as a sort of buffer zone between them and angry young blacks. None of its so-called leaders could go into a rioting community and be listened to. In a sense, I blame ourselves—together with the mass media—for what has happened in Watts, Harlem, Chicago, Cleveland, Omaha. Each time the people in those cities saw Martin Luther King get slapped they became angry; when they saw four little black girls bombed to death, they were angrier; and when nothing happened, they were steaming. We had nothing to offer that they could see, except to go out and be beaten again. We helped to build their frustration.

For too many years, black Americans marched and had their heads broken and got shot. They were saying to the country, "Look, you guys are supposed to be nice guys and we are only going to do what we are supposed to do—why do you beat us up, why don't you give us what we ask, why don't you straighten yourselves out?" After years of this, we are at almost the same point—because we demonstrated from a position of weakness. We cannot be expected any longer to march and have our heads broken in order to say to whites: come on, you're nice guys. For you are not nice guys. We have found you out.

An organization which claims to speak for the needs of a community—as does the Student Nonviolent Coordinating Committee—must speak in the tone of that community, not as somebody else's buffer zone. This is the significance of black power as a slogan. For once, black people are going to use the words they want to use—not just the words whites want to hear. And they will do this no matter how often the press tries to stop the use of the slogan by equating it with racism or separatism.

An organization which claims to be working for the needs of a community—as SNCC does—must work to provide the community with a position of strength from which to make its voice heard. This is the significance of black power beyond the slogan.

Black power can be clearly defined for those who do not attach the fears of white America to their questions about it. We should begin with the basic fact that black Americans have two problems: they are poor and they are black. All other problems arise from this two-sided reality: lack of education, the so-called apathy of black men. Any program to end racism must address itself to that double reality. . . .

Ultimately, the economic foundations of this country must be shaken if black people are to control their lives. The colonies of the U.S.—and this includes the black ghettos within its borders,

Carmichael is here referring to some of the major black ghetto riots of the mid-1960's. Four young black girls were killed in the bombing of a Birmingham, Alabama church in September 1963, four months after civil rights demonstrations led by the Rev. Dr. Martin Luther King, Jr.

north and south—must be liberated. For a century, this nation has been like an octopus of exploitation, its tentacles stretching from Mississippi and Harlem, to South America, the Middle East, southern Africa, and Vietnam; the form of exploitation varies from area to area but the essential result has been the same—a powerful few have been maintained and enriched at the expense of the poor and voiceless colored masses. This pattern must be broken. As its grip loosens here and there around the world the hopes of black Americans become more realistic. For racism to die, a totally different American must be born.

This is what the white society does not wish to face; this is why that society prefers to talk about integration. But integration speaks not at all to the problem of poverty, only to the problem of blackness. Integration today means the man who "makes it," leaving his black brothers behind in the ghetto as fast as his new sports car will take him. It has no relevance to the Harlem wino or to the cotton-picker making $3 a day. As a lady I know in Alabama once said, "The food that Ralph Bunche eats doesn't fill my stomach."

Integration, moreover, speaks to the problem of blackness in a despicable way. As a goal, it has been based on complete acceptance of the fact that in order to have a decent house or education, blacks must move into a white neighborhood or send their children to a white school. This reinforces, among both black and white, the idea that "white" is automatically better and "black" is by definition inferior. This is why integration is a subterfuge for the maintenance of white supremacy. It allows the nation to focus on a handful of southern children who get into white schools, at great price, and to ignore the 94 per cent who are left behind in unimproved all-black schools. Such situations will not change until black people have power—to control their own school boards, in this case. Then Negroes become equal in a way that means something, and integration ceases to be a one-way street. Then integration doesn't mean draining skills and energies from the ghetto into white neighborhoods; then it can mean white people moving from Beverly Hills into Watts, white people joining the Lowndes County Freedom Organization. Then integration becomes relevant. . . .

White America will not face the problem of color, the reality of it.

From birth, black people are told a set of lies about themselves. We are told that we are lazy—yet I drive through the Delta area in Mississippi and watch black people picking cotton in the hot sun for fourteen hours. We are told, "If you work hard, you'll

Ralph J. Bunche, Under-Secretary for Special Political Affairs of the United Nations, won the Nobel Peace Prize in 1950, for his work in setling the Arab–Israeli War of 1948. To many, Bunche became a symbol of the black man who succeeded in white society.

▶ Can any group of people who lack political power lead a full life?

The Lowndes County Freedom Organization of Alabama, started by SNCC under Carmichael's leadership, was an attempt to build a radical political party.

342

succeed"—but if that were true, black people would own this country. We are oppressed because we are black—not because we are ignorant, not because we are lazy, not because we're stupid (and got good rhythm); but because we're black.

I remember that when I was a boy, I used to go to see Tarzan movies on Saturday. White Tarzan used to beat up the black natives. I would sit there yelling, "Kill the beasts, kill the savages, kill 'em!" I was saying: Kill me. It was as if a Jewish boy watched Nazis taking Jews off to concentration camps and cheered them on. Today, I want the chief to beat hell out of Tarzan and send him back to Europe. But it takes time to become free of the lies and their shaming effect on black minds. It takes time to reject the most important lie: that black people inherently can't do the same things white people can do, unless white people help them.

The need for psychological equality is the reason why SNCC today believes that blacks must organize in the black community. Only black people can convey the revolutionary idea that black people are able to do things themselves. Only they can help create in the community an aroused and continuing black consciousness that will provide the basis for political strength. In the past, white allies have furthered white supremacy without the whites involved realizing it—or wanting it, I think. Black people must do things for themselves: they must get poverty money they will control and spend themselves, they must conduct tutorial programs themselves so that black children can identify with black people. This is one reason Africa has such importance: The reality of black men ruling their own nations gives blacks elsewhere a sense of possibility, of power which they do not now have. . . .

I have said that most liberal whites react to "black power" with the question, What about me? rather than saying: Tell me what you want me to do and I'll see if I can do it. There are answers to the right question. One of the most disturbing things about almost all white supporters of the movement has been that they are afraid to go into their own communities—which is where the racism exists—and work to get rid of it. They want to run from Berkeley to tell us what to do in Mississippi; let them look instead at Berkeley. They admonish blacks to be nonviolent; let them preach nonviolence in the white community. They come to teach me Negro history; let them go to the suburbs and open up freedom schools for whites. Let them work to stop America's racist foreign policy; let them press this government to cease supporting the economy of South Africa. . . .

Black people do not want to "take over" this country. They don't want to "get whitey;" they just want to get him off their backs, as the saying goes. It was for example the exploitation by Jewish landlords and merchants which first created black resentment toward Jews—not Judaism. The white man is irrelevant to blacks, except as an oppressive force. Blacks want to be in his place, yes, but not in order to terrorize and lynch and starve him. They want to be in his place because that is where a decent life can be had.

But our vision is not merely of a society in which all black men have enough to buy the good things of life. When we urge that black money go into black pockets, we mean the communal pocket. We want to see money go back into the community and used to benefit it. We want to see the cooperative concept applied in business and banking. We want to see black ghetto residents demand that an exploiting landlord or storekeeper sell them, at minimal cost, a building or a shop that they will own and improve cooperatively; they can back their demand with a rent strike, or a boycott, and a community so united behind them that no one else will move into the building or buy at the store. The society we seek to build among black people, then, is not a capitalist one. It is a society in which the spirit of community and humanistic love prevail. The word love is suspect; black expectations of what it might produce have been betrayed too often. But those were expectations of a response from the white community which failed us. The love we seek to encourage is within the black community, the only American community where men call each other "brother" when they meet. We can build a community of love only where we have the ability and power to do so: among blacks.

As for white America, perhaps it can stop crying out against "black supremacy," "black nationalism," "racism in reverse," and begin facing reality. The reality is that this nation, from top to bottom, is racist: that racism is not primarily a problem of "human relations" but of an exploitation maintained—either actively or through silence—by the society as a whole. Camus and Sartre have asked, can a man condemn himself? Can whites, particularly liberal whites, condemn themselves? Can they stop blaming us, and blame their own system? Are they capable of the shame which might become a revolutionary emotion?

We have found that they usually cannot condemn themselves, and so we have done it. But the rebuilding of this society, if at all possible, is basically the responsibility of whites—not blacks. We won't fight to save the present society, in Vietnam or anywhere else. We are just going to work, in the way we see fit, and on goals we define, not for civil rights but for all our human rights.

▶ Does a person need a good self-image and psychological security to love well?

Albert Camus and Jean-Paul Sartre, French existentialist philosophers and authors, were read by many young people in the 1950's and '60's.

344

# New York: Ideal and Reality

## STATING THE ISSUE

New York is not a single culture; it is a hundred, each with common elements but each distinct in its own way. Blacks, Puerto Ricans, Jews, Italians, Irish, Germans, the old white Anglo-Saxon Protestant stock—all these groups and many others—define the good man from peculiar vantage points based on lands far removed and customs stretching across oceans. No individual could capture all these strands in a single personality.

The good life encounters similar problems of definition. The hippies in the East Village have turned their backs on all of middle-class America; the heart of the establishment works in corporate offices only a few blocks away. The lives admired by these polar opposites span the spectrum. To thousands of Puerto Ricans and blacks, neither the psychedelic world of the turned-on generation nor the power in the hands of Madison Avenue executives defines an ideal life. Many of them want only a steady job, a home free of vermin, a good education for their children, and a chance to hold their heads high in a society which has long slammed the door of opportunity in their faces.

And what of the good society? New York's ideal culture should permit each group in the city to achieve its aspirations at the same time. But what one group wants, another opposes; what one needs, another refuses to grant. Giving nearly always involves giving up. Until man finds a way to repeal this basic fact of living, the ideal of the good society can never be achieved for everyone in a diverse culture.

New Yorkers are deeply concerned with the basic humanistic questions. To what degree does the city try to open a better life to everyone? How much are privileged groups willing to give up in order to meet the demands of men and women in the ghettos? What is New York and the megalopolis of which it is a part doing to merge ideal and reality? These are the questions which we will explore in Chapter 3.

CHAPTER

3

# 15 THE GEOGRAPHIC SETTING

Geography determined New York's location. When Henry Hudson dropped anchor in 1609, he correctly guessed that the mighty river which now bears his name and the deep harbor at its mouth held the key to the eastern seaboard and to a vast stretch of the interior. The Dutch burghers who settled Manhattan Island in the seventeenth century and the English lord who seized it from them in 1664 knew they held the kingpin to the North American colonies. By 1810, trade had made New York the largest city in the United States; the opening of the Erie Canal in 1825 further spurred growth. Manufacturing, which grew up because New York's access to markets and raw materials gave the city a competitive advantage, followed in turn. Immigrants poured in from every port in Europe and Asia to cluster near the garment factories and the docks on Manhattan. Soon the city's population spilled over into the Bronx, Queens, Brooklyn, Staten Island, New Jersey, and later the outlying counties north of the Bronx and on Long Island. Eventually, bridges spanned the rivers and tunnels burrowed under them to speed men and materials back and forth in trains, trucks, busses, and automobiles.

As New York grew, its political boundaries changed. Boroughs were annexed one after the other until the present five—Manhattan, the Bronx, Queens, Brooklyn, and Richmond (Staten Island)— were all in the fold. But New York City influences far more territory than it annexed. Some people who work in the city live in Connecticut or New Jersey and commute each day to the metropolis. Air taxis link New York's three major airports to satellite towns. Shuttle airlines with a flight every hour during the day connect it to Boston and Washington. New high-speed express trains have begun to compete for this business.

New York City is an example of a new phenomenon on the face of the earth, an enormous super-city stretching far beyond the formal political boundaries of city or state. In 1961, the geographer, Jean Gottmann, revived an old Greek name for a super city— megalopolis—and applied it to the urban complex of which New York is the center. His term and the ideas it stood for caught on. Reading 15 analyzes some of Gottmann's ideas and their implications. As you read, keep the following questions in mind:

1.  What does the term megalopolis mean? What does the American megalopolis include?
2.  What is the quality of material life in megalopolis? in the central cities of the area?

3. On what governmental level can the society best cope with the problems created by megalopolis? Do we need a new political entity?

# Megalopolis

The nature of cities is . . . changing. The metropolis, already huge by any earlier scale, is now giving way to the supergiant city, the megalopolis. The city of even several decades ago was a dense tangled knot of humanity. The cities emerging today are vast, sprawling complexes of suburbs and beyond these, rings of "exurbs," like the rings around the planet Saturn.

The city as a social institution reached a high state of development in ancient Greece. In fact, the Greeks dreamed beyond their powers to build, and they even coined a word for something which would not appear on the earth for two thousand years. The geographer Jean Gottmann tells the story:

"Some two thousand years before the first European settlers landed on the shores of the James River, Massachusetts Bay, and Manhattan Island, a group of ancient people, planning a new city-state in the Peloponnesus in Greece, called it *Megalopolis,* for they dreamed of a great future for it and hoped it would become the largest of the Greek cities. Their hopes did not materialize. Megalopolis still appears on modern maps of the Peloponnesus but it is just a small town nestling in a small river basin. Through the centuries the word *Megalopolis* has been used in many senses by various people, and it has even found its way into Webster's dictionary, which defines it as 'a very large city.' Its use, however, has not become so common that it could not be applied in a new sense, as a geographical place name for the *unique cluster of metropolitan areas of the northeastern seaboard of the United States.* There, if anywhere in our times, the dream of those ancient Greeks has come true."

The word *megalopolis* is a combination of two Greek words: *mega* meaning "great" and *polis,* meaning "city-state." In adapting it to contemporary use, Gottmann implies, and rightly so, that the cluster of cities along the northeastern coast of the United States is a "great city-state," with a character and personality all its own. These cities, from southern New Hampshire, down through Boston, New York, Philadelphia, Wilmington, Baltimore, Washington, D.C., and Arlington, [Virginia] form an almost continuous single urban area. Gottmann describes it further:

Robert Cook and Mitchell Gordon, **Urban America: Dilemma and Opportunity** (New York: The Macmillan Company, 1965), pp. 9–12. Reprinted by permission. The quotations in this reading are from Jean Gottmann, **Megalopolis: The Urbanized Northeastern Seaboard of the United States** (New York: Twentieth Century Fund, 1961). Reprinted by permission.

The Peloponnesus is the peninsula on which Sparta was located.

"No other section of the United States has such a large concentration of population, with such a high average density, spread over such a large area. And no other section has a comparable role within the nation or a comparable importance in the world. Here has been developed a kind of supremacy, in politics, in economics, and possibly even in cultural activities, seldom before attained by an area of this size.

"This region has indeed a 'personality' of its own. . . . [It] is difficult to single this area out from surrounding areas, for its limits cut across established historical divisions, such as New England and the Middle Atlantic states, and across political entities, since it includes some states entirely and others only partially. A special name is needed, therefore, to identify this special geographical area. . . . [The] industrialized Midwest, between the Great Lakes and the Ohio River, and the California seaboard form two other smaller but nonetheless impressive concentrations of riches, economic equipment, and educated people. Across the Atlantic are the countries of western Europe, where on both sides of the North Sea and English Channel an intensity of urban dynamism comparable to that in Megalopolis may soon be attained."

The crowding in Megalopolis creates many problems, social, economic, and political. But there are also many advantages. The problems are serious, but the advantages are great. Gottmann notes:

"Crowding of population within a small area creates shortages of various resources, and most of the crowded people are bound to suffer in some ways because of the shortages. To alleviate them, to make crowding more bearable and the population happier, ways and means of constantly better distribution must be found. Otherwise no lasting growth can develop, and the whole enterprise will soon be doomed. . . . Modern political life and its concepts of liberty, self-government, and democracy are the products of urban growth, the inheritance of cities in process of growth and development—places such as Jerusalem, Athens, Rome, Bruges, Florence, Paris, London, to mention only those that have been most studied by historians. And the same places, or similar urban centers, have contributed most of our scientific and technological developments, either because people there were struggling to solve pressing problems or because urban societies make possible a leisurely enough elite, some of whose members can devote themselves to disinterested research and a search for a better understanding of the universe.

"This urban crowding and the slums and mobs characteristic of it may be considered growing pains in the endless process of civilization.

Bruges, Belgium, was one of Europe's most important cities in the thirteenth and fourteenth centuries.

"In the same way, the picture of Megalopolis is not as dark as the outspoken pessimists and frequent protests would seem to paint it. Crowded within its limits is an extremely distinguished population. It is, *on the average,* the richest, best educated, best housed, and best serviced group of similar size (that is, in the 25-to-40-million people range) in the world. The area is still a focus of attraction for successful or adventurous people from all over America and beyond. It is true that many of its sections have seen pretty rural landscapes replaced by ugly industrial agglomerations or drab and monstrous residential developments; it is true that in many parts of Megalopolis the air is not clean any more, the noise is disturbing day and night, the water is not as pure as one would wish, and transportation at times becomes a nightmare. Many of these problems reflect the revolutionary change that has taken place as cities have burst out of their narrow bounds to scatter over the 'open' countryside. In some ways this suburban sprawl may have alleviated a crowding that had threatened to become unbearable, for residential densities of population per square mile have decreased. But new problems have arisen because of the new densities of activities and of traffic in the central cities and because the formerly rural areas or small towns have been unprepared to cope with the new demands made upon their resources. New programs are needed to conserve the natural beauty of the landscape and to assure the health, prosperity, and freedom of the people. In spite of these problems, however, available statistics demonstrate that in Megalopolis the population is on the average healthier, the consumption of goods higher, and the opportunity for advancement greater than in any other region of comparable extent."

▶ What sort of extremes does this average conceal?

The ancient Greeks were among the first to develop cities as a positive adjunct to man's life on earth. One of them has said: "The city is the teacher of the man." Another took a different but not wholly contradictory view: ". . .[N]ot houses finely roofed or the stones of walls well-built, nay, nor canals and dockyards, make the city, but men able to use their opportunity."

The city—and the story of how it has grown—has much to teach. Left to their natural course, the pressures our cities are exposed to could destroy modern civilization. Understanding and effective action can build for a future without limits. The problem is to build the best of what the past offers into the city of tomorrow, to eliminate what is bad, and to push forward to higher ground.

▶ To what degree is each individual responsible for taking action to improve his own city?

The twentieth-century city is rife with perplexities and complexities. It is a grab-bag of delights and excitements, but it suffers from a wide variety of ailments—congested living, overtaxed transportation facilities, confused political organization, and problems of economics. Most cities have outgrown their political machinery, which once was adequate. They are attempting, often with little success, to deal with their ever-growing complexities. Urban and suburban life today is a veritable maelstrom of change and challenge, of crisis and adventure.

The difficulties are without precedent. Our population is increasing faster than our planning for the future. By the year 2000, the U.S. population could be about double what it is today, nearly 400 million people. The way things are going now, 85 per cent of this multitude will be living in cities—and a far larger proportion than at present in megalopolises.

How will the story end? Will the people living in our supercities be able to fashion these new centers of industry and culture—of traffic jams and of smog—into rich and satisfying communities? Or are these sprawling giants of steel and concrete going to enslave those caught in their tentacles? Will the asphalt jungle prove in the end to be a trap, or a launching pad into a glorious future?

# 16 SOCIAL STRUCTURE

With few exceptions, every ancient Athenian was Greek and every Renaissance Florentine Italian. Like other cities, ancient Athens and Renaissance Florence attracted traders, intellectuals, and casual sightseers from around the known world, but Greek or Italian was the only language to echo around the dinner table. Moreover, most citizens were born in the city except for men from the nearby hinterland pulled irresistibly by high hopes of fame and fortune. Not so New York.

The social structure of Athens and Florence revolved around classes which primarily followed birth or occupational lines: aristocracy, merchants and manufacturers, shopkeepers, workers, slaves. These classes, at least at the top and bottom and especially in Florence, opened only when a child was born. The uniquely talented alone could climb the social ladder to hobnob with Florentine aristocrats, but not, of course, to marry their daughters. Each member of these classes played a role appropriate to the rung of the social ladder on which he found himself. Well-defined norms of behavior helped to keep each group in its accustomed place and to define the way in which members of one class should treat members of another. New York is different.

For more than a century, Americans expected New York to melt its immigrants into a homogeneous American equivalent of Athenians or Florentines. Michel-Guillaume Jean de Crèvecoeur, a naturalized New Yorker, suggested this idea in his *Letters from an American Farmer,* published in 1782. Israel Zangwill, another naturalized New Yorker, popularized it in 1908 in a poor but widely-heralded play, *The Melting Pot,* which ran for months on Broadway. School textbooks are full of it. And despite contrary evidence abounding on every side, the general public still bows at its altar.

Reading 16 comes from one of the best of an outpouring of books and articles written since the mid-1950's which take issue with the notion of a melting pot. These writings argue that New York, as well as the United States in general, can best be understood as a society whose social structure revolves essentially around ethnic, racial, and religious groups, each with its own internal class structure. As you read, keep the following questions in mind:

1. According to this account, what are the major social groups in New York City? What seems to be happening to the structure of these groups in recent years? What may the social structure be like in a decade?
2. What does this sort of social structure imply for definitions of the good man, the good life, and the good society?
3. Given this social structure, what should be done to improve the quality of the humanistic experiences of New York's citizens?

## Beyond the Melting Pot

We must begin with this image of the city. New York is more than ten times as large as San Francisco, and twice as large as Chicago, but this does not suggest how much more complicated it is. For in the affairs of men, twice as large means four or eight times as complicated. Twice as large means that the man on top is perhaps four or eight times away from what happens on the bottom. But attempts at calculation understate the complexity. When you have 24,000 policemen in a city, it not only means that you need a few additional levels of authorities to deal with them—those over hundreds, and five hundreds, and thousands, and five thousands— but it also means (for example) that there are enough Jewish or Negro policemen to form an organization. And they too can fill a hall.

The interweaving of complexity that necessarily follows from its size with the complexity added by the origins of its population, drawn from a staggering number of countries and from every race,

Reprinted from **Beyond the Melting Pot** by Nathan Glazer and Daniel Patrick Moynihan by permission of The M.I.T. Press, Cambridge, Massachusetts. Copyright 1963 by the Massachusetts Institute of Technology.

Many of the voters who supported Wagner in 1961, voted in 1965 for John V. Lindsay, who ran on the Republican, Liberal, and Independent Citizens tickets. Although New York City's registered Democrats far outnumber its registered Republicans, independent and liberal Republicans— like Lindsay and like Mayor Fiorello H. La Guardia in the 1930's and '40's—can sometimes win if they run on fusion tickets.

makes New York one of the most difficult cities in the world to understand, and helps us understand why so few books try in any serious way to understand it. . . .

Consider the politics of New York. Major changes are now taking place in the city. The power of the regular Democratic party—the "machine"—to name its candidates has been broken. In 1961 Mayor Robert F. Wagner, having been denied the nomination, ran in opposition to the regular party, and won. To explain what happened, we have to say that he won with the support of lower-class Negro and Puerto Rican voters, and middle-class Jewish voters who together were enough to overcome the opposition of Italian, Irish, and white Protestant middle-class and upper-working-class voters. One could describe his victory and the political transition now underway in the city without using ethnic labels, but one could barely explain it. For in New York City ethnicity and class and religion are inevitably tied to each other. The votes of the poor and the well-to-do cannot be understood without looking into the question of who the poor and the well-to-do are, without examining their ethnic background.

Similarly, to describe the economy of New York fully, one would have to point out that it is dominated at its peak (the banks, insurance companies, utilities, big corporation offices) by white Protestants, with Irish Catholics and Jews playing somewhat smaller roles. In wholesale and retail commerce, Jews predominate. White-collar workers are largely Irish and Italian if they work for big organizations, and Jewish if they work for smaller ones. The city's working class is, on its upper levels, Irish, Italian, and Jewish; on its lower levels, Negro and Puerto Rican. Other ethnic groups are found scattered everywhere, but concentrated generally in a few economic specialties. . . .

The census of 1960 showed that 19 per cent of the population of the city were still foreign-born whites, 28 per cent were children of foreign-born whites, another 14 per cent were Negro, 8 per cent were of Puerto Rican birth or parentage. Unquestionably, a great majority of the rest (31 per cent) were the grandchildren and great-grandchildren of immigrants, and still thought of themselves, on some occasions and for some purposes, as German, Irish, Italian, Jewish, or whatnot, as well as of course Americans.

Of the foreign-stock population (immigrants and their children), 859,000 were born in Italy or were the children of Italian immigrants; 564,000 were from the U.S.S.R. (these are mostly Jews); 389,000 from Poland (these too are mostly Jews); 324,000 from Germany; 312,000 from Ireland; 220,000 from Austria; 175,000 from Great Britain; almost 100,000 from Hungary; more than 50,000 from Greece, Czechoslovakia, Rumania, and Canada; more than 25,000 from Yugoslavia, around 10,000 from the Netherlands, Denmark, Finland, and Switzerland; more than 5,000 from Portugal and Mexico. There were more than a million Negroes, and more than 50,000 of other races, mostly Chinese and Japanese. From almost every country in the world there are enough people in the city to make up communities of thousands and tens of thousands with organizations, churches, a language, some distinctive culture. . . .

▶ What can ties to an ethnic community contribute to a good life?

Let us introduce some order into this huge buzzing confusion. The best way to do so is historically. English stock has apparently never been in a clear majority in New York City. In 1775 one-half of the white population of the state was of English origin, but this proportion was probably lower in New York City, with its Dutch and other non-English groups, and with its large Negro population. After the Revolution and the resumption of immigration, English and Scottish immigrants as well as migrants from New England and upstate New York probably maintained the British-descent group as the largest in the city through the first half of the nineteenth century.

In the 1840's Irish and Germans, who had of course been present in the city in some numbers before this time, began to enter in much larger numbers, and soon became dominant. By 1855 the Irish-born made up 28 per cent of the city, the German-born 16 per cent of the city; with their children they certainly formed a majority of the city, and they maintained this dominance until the end of the century. In 1890 Irish-born and German-born and their children made up 52 per cent of the population of New York and Brooklyn (then separate cities).

In the 1880's Jews and Italians began to come in large numbers (there were of course sizable communities of both groups in the city before this time), and this heavy immigration continued until 1924, and on a reduced scale after that.

In 1924, Congress passed the National Origins Act, which reduced immigration sharply.

The Negroes began to enter the city in great numbers after World War I, the Puerto Ricans after World War II.

Thus six great groups have entered the city two by two, in subsequent epochs; and to these we must add as a seventh group the "old stock," or the "white Anglo-Saxon Protestants." The two terms are of course not identical, but the overlap among those they comprise is great. The "old stock" includes those New Yorkers who descend from families that were here before the Revolution. They were largely of English, Scottish, and Welsh origin, but also included Dutch, French and other settlers from Northwestern Europe. It has been relatively easy for later immigrants of the same ethnic and religious background—from Canada and from Europe—to assimilate to this "old stock" group if they were in occupations of high status and of at least moderate affluence.

What is the relative size of these seven groups in the city today? For all except the Negroes and the Puerto Ricans, who are listed separately in the census, it is difficult to give more than a very general guess. The accepted religious breakdown of the city population, based on sample surveys and estimates by various religious groups, indicates that less than a quarter of the population is Protestant, and more than half of that is Negro. The white Protestants of course include many of German, Scandinavian, Czech, and Hungarian origins. It is thus not likely that more than about one-twentieth of the population of the city is "old stock," or "WASP." Public opinion polls which ask for "national origin" suggest that about a tenth of the population is Irish, another tenth German. The same sources suggest that about a sixth is Italian. Jewish organizations estimate that one-quarter of the population is Jewish. The census reports that Negroes form 14 per cent of the population, Puerto Ricans 8 per cent. We have accounted for about 90 per cent of the population. . . . These figures, aside from being inexact, . . . assume that everyone in the city can be neatly assigned to an ethnic category. Of course this is in large measure myth; many of the people in the city, as in the nation, have parents and grandparents of two or three or four groups. . . .

There is also, in New York, a nonethnic city. There are the fields that draw talent from all over the country and all over the world. There are the areas, such as Greenwich Village where those so collected congregate. On Broadway, in the radio and television industry, in the art world, in all the spheres of culture, mass or high, one finds the same mixture that one finds in every country. Those involved in these intense and absorbing pursuits would find the city described in these pages strange. Another area of mixture is politics. It is true that political life itself emphasizes the ethnic character of the city, with its balanced tickets and its special appeals. But this is in large part an objective part of the business, just as the Jewish plays on Broadway are part of the business. For those in the field itself, there is more contact across the ethnic lines, and the ethnic lines themselves mean less, than in other areas of the city's life. . . .

Religion and race seem to define the major groups into which American society is evolving as the specifically national aspect of ethnicity declines. In our large American cities, four major groups emerge: Catholics, Jews, white Protestants, and Negroes, each making up the city in different proportions. This evolution is by no means complete. And yet we can discern that the next stage of the evolution of the immigrant groups will involve a Catholic group in which the distinctions between Irish, Italian, Polish, and German Catholic are steadily reduced by intermarriage; a Jewish group, in which the line between East European, German, and Near Eastern Jews is already weak; the Negro group; and a white Protestant group, which adds to its Anglo-Saxon and Dutch old-stock elements German and Scandinavian Protestants, as well as, more typically, the white Protestant immigrants to the city from the interior.

The white Protestants are a distinct ethnic group in New York, one that has probably passed its low point and will now begin to grow in numbers and probably also in influence. It has its special occupations with the customary freemasonry. This involves the banks, corporation front offices, educational and philanthropic institutions, and the law offices who serve them. It has its own social world (epitomized by, but by no means confined to, the Social Register), its own churches, schools, voluntary organizations and all the varied institutions of a New York minority. These are accompanied by the characteristic styles in food, clothing, and drink, special family patterns, special psychological problems and ailments. For a long while political conservatism, as well as social aloofness, tended to keep the white Protestants out of the main stream of New York politics, much in the way that political radicalism tended to isolate the Jews in the early parts of the century. Theodore Roosevelt, when cautioned that none of his friends would touch New York politics, had a point in replying that it must follow that none of his friends were members of the governing classes.

There has been a resurgence of liberalism within the white Protestant group, in part based on its growth through vigorous young migrants from outside the city, who are conspicuous in the communications industry, law firms, and corporation offices of New York. These are the young people that supported Adlai Stevenson and helped lead and staff the Democratic reform movement. The influence of the white Protestant group on this city, it appears, must now grow as its numbers grow.

In this large array of the four major religio-racial groups, where do the Puerto Ricans stand? Ultimately perhaps they are to be absorbed in the Catholic group. But that is a long time away. The Puerto Ricans are separated from the Catholics as well as the Negroes by color and culture. One cannot even guess how this large element will ultimately relate itself to the other elements of the city; perhaps it will serve, in line with its own nature and genius, to soften the sharp lines that divide them. . . .

▶ Which seems riskier, to marry outside of one's ethnic group or outside of one's religious affiliation?

355

Religion and race define the next state in the evolution of the American peoples. But the American nationality is still forming; its processes are mysterious, and the final form, if there is ever to be a final form, is as yet unknown.

# 17 THE ECONOMY

Manufacturing and trade dominate New York's economy. The census classifies a tiny number of the city's residents as farmers, but overwhelmingly, manufacturing and the exchange of goods support the population. In turn, the residents of the city demand services, the third major area of employment. On this economy rests the welfare of the individual including his opportunities for humanistic expression and growth.

Money cannot assure a rich humanistic culture, but lack of money can stifle individual development and atrophy a society. New York is the world's richest city, although its per capita income falls far below that of many American suburban areas. The ways in which the city spends its tax money and private citizens allocate their incomes yield rich insights into the value systems of New York's eight million people. Reading 17 consists entirely of charts and tables containing statistical information about New York's economy. Study questions appear with each figure in the reading.

### FIGURE I  Land Use, 1959–60

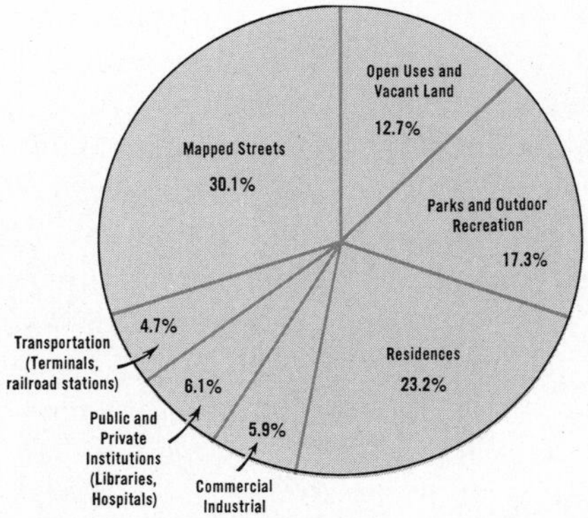

*Unless otherwise noted, all statistics in this reading are from Department of Commerce and Industrial Development, City of New York, 1965 Statistical Guide for New York City.*

1. What is most New York land used for?
2. What does this use of land indicate about the economy? about values?

356

## FIGURE II    Population Density, 1960

| | Land Area in Square Miles | Population | Population per Square Mile |
|---|---|---|---|
| The Bronx | 43.1 | 1,424,815 | 33,032 |
| Brooklyn | 78.5 | 2,627,319 | 33,446 |
| Manhattan | 22.6 | 1,698,281 | 75,072 |
| Queens | 114.7 | 1,809,578 | 15,777 |
| Richmond | 60.9 | 221,991 | 3,648 |
| Total, New York City | 319.8 | 7,781,984 | 24,333 |

1. What is the average population density of your own city?
2. To what degree does a population density as great as Manhattan's limit the ability to lead a good life?

## FIGURE III    General Economic Characteristics of the Population, 1960

| | Employed | Unemployed |
|---|---|---|
| Experienced civilian labor force | 3,479,474 | 171,926 |
|   Professional, technical, and kindred workers | 378,400 | 9,982 |
|   Managers, officials, and proprietors | 294,525 | 6,129 |
|   Clerical and kindred workers | 726,674 | 24,532 |
|   Sales workers | 239,702 | 8,670 |
|   Craftsmen, foremen, and kindred workers | 358,102 | 16,038 |
|   Operatives and kindred workers | 686,434 | 57,673 |
|   Private household workers | 67,850 | 3,015 |
|   Service workers, excluding private hsld. | 352,433 | 17,299 |
|   Laborers, excluding farm and mine | 138,954 | 28,276 |
|   Farmers and farm managers | 734 | 70 |
|   Farm foremen and farm laborers | 1,172 | 242 |
|   Not reported (employed only) | 234,494 | |
| Population not in labor force | | |
|   Total fourteen years and over | 2,524,461 | |
|   Inmate of institution | 55,093 | |
|   Enrolled in school | 397,818 | |
|   Other, sixty-five years old and over | 590,941 | |
|   Other, under sixty-five years old | 1,480,609 | |

What do most New Yorkers do for a living? What do these figures indicate about the nature of the economy?

## FIGURE IV   Employment and Earnings, 1967

| Category | Number of Employees | Average Weekly Earnings |
|---|---|---|
| All manufacturing | 849,700 | $106.60 |
|    Durable goods | 199,500 | 113.40 |
|    Non-durable goods | 650,200 | 104,71 |
| Contract construction | 105,100 | 191,75 |
| Transportation and Public Utilities | 323,700 | |
|    Electric, gas, and sanitary svce. | 26,600 | 159,64 |
|    Telephone and telegraph | 62,600 | 124.57 |
|    (other categories omitted) | | |
| Trade* | 747,800 | 113.09 |
|    Wholesale | 312,400 | 137.03 |
|    Retail | 435,400 | 89.87 |
| Finance, Insurance, and Real Estate | 408,500 | |
|    Banking | 102,500 | 114.70 |
|    (other categories omitted) | | |
| Services and Miscellaneous | 726,400 | |
|    Hotels (year-round) | 31,900 | 83.16 |
|    (other categories omitted) | | |

* *Eating and drinking places are excluded.*
*Source: Unpublished survey of the New York State Department of Labor, Division of Employment, 1968.*

1. The total employed labor force is about 3.5 million. The figures above cover about 3.2 million. How much money does the typical New Yorker make each week?
2. How good a life can a family of four live on a typical income if only one family member works?

**FIGURE V** Adequate Budget Costs for a Family of Four (est.), 1967

| | Year | Week |
|---|---|---|
| Food | $2,313 | $ 44.48 |
|    Food at home | 2,001 | 38.48 |
|    Lunches at work | 312 | 6.00 |
| Housing | 1,561 | 30.03 |
|    Rent and heat | 1,086 | 20.88 |
|    Utilities | 137 | 2.62 |
|    Housefurnishings | 211 | 4.06 |
|    Household supplies | 45 | .86 |
|    Launderette service | 83 | 1.60 |
| Clothing and upkeep | 596 | 11.45 |
| Personal care | 170 | 3.26 |
| Medical care | 371 | 7.14 |
| Transportation (non-car owner) | 319 | 6.14 |
|    To work | 208 | 4.00 |
|    Other | 111 | 2.14 |
| Other goods and services | 970 | 18.66 |
|    Reading material, recreation, | | |
|       tobacco, education, stationary supplies | 551 | 10.60 |
|    Telephone | 77 | 1.49 |
|    Life Insurance | 109 | 2.09 |
|    Union dues | 49 | .95 |
|    Gifts, contributions, misc. | 184 | 3.53 |
|     **Total, all goods and services** | **6,301** | **121.17** |
| Other costs and personal taxes | 1,109 | 21.33 |
|    FICA and disability insurance | 306 | 5.88 |
|    New York City income tax | 26 | .50 |
|    New York State income tax | 106 | 2.04 |
|    Federal income tax | 671 | 12.91 |
| **Total cost of the budget** | **$7,410** | **$142.50** |

Source: *Unpublished survey of the New York State Department of Labor, Division of Employment, 1968.*

1.  What is the quality of a life lived on this budget?
2.  As Figure IV indicates, most New Yorkers make less money than the estimated minimum needed for a family of four. What would you do in such a situation? If you had to cut, what would go first? What, if anything, should the society do about this income distribution?

**FIGURE VI    Retail Trade by Selected Types of Business, 1963**

|  | Number of Establishments | Total Sales |
|---|---|---|
| Automotive dealers | 1,097 | $  790,423,000 |
| Home furnishing stores | 3,428 | 415,678,000 |
| Radio, television stores | 341 | 60,619,000 |
| Record shops | 181 | 18,173,000 |
| Musical instrument stores | 121 | 16,559,000 |
| Eating places | 10,923 | 1,209,177,000 |
| Drinking places (alcoholic beverages) | 4,661 | 293,106,000 |
| Liquor stores | 2,053 | 334,860,000 |
| Antique stores | 339 | 26,755,000 |
| Secondhand stores | 717 | 39,334,000 |
| Book stores | 309 | 32,520,000 |
| Sporting goods stores | 197 | 30,989,000 |
| Jewelry stores | 1,148 | 96,844,000 |
| Florists | 866 | 42,252,000 |
| News dealers, newsstands | 978 | 40,695,000 |
| Camera, photographic supply stores | 202 | 38,281,000 |
| Hobby, toy, and game shops | 235 | 20,407,000 |
| Religious goods stores | 101 | 2,954,000 |
| Pet shops | 177 | 5,175,000 |

1. Do these statistics accurately represent income expenditures in New York City? What about the statistics for book and record stores, for example?
2. What do these statistics reveal about the New Yorker's conception of the good life?

## FIGURE VII    Amusement and Recreation Services, 1963

|  | Number of Establishments | Total Sales |
|---|---|---|
| Motion picture theaters | 342 | $ 98,216,000 |
| Dance halls, studios | 304 | 10,120,000 |
| Bands, orchestras, entertainers | 1,327 | 56,503,000 |
|   Dance bands, orchestras, except symphony | 369 | 23,844,000 |
|   Entertainers (radio, TV), except classical | 917 | 16,842,000 |
|   Classical music groups | 41 | 15,817,000 |
| Theatrical presentations, services | 1,026 | 196,879,000 |
| Bowling, billiards, pool | 389 | 37,560,000 |
|   Billiard, pool parlors | 180 | 3,531,000 |
|   Bowling establishments | 209 | 34,029,000 |
| Commercial sports | 205 | 123,584,000 |
|   Baseball, football clubs, promoters | 19 | * |
|   Racetrack operation, including racing stables | 186 | * |
| Public golf courses | 3 | 210,000 |
| Golf clubs, country clubs | 11 | 2,691,000 |
| Other commercial recreation | 175 | 11,890,000 |
|   Skating rinks | 12 | 716,000 |
|   Swimming pools | 34 | 2,773,000 |
|   Boat, canoe rentals | 28 | 1,182,000 |
|   Other | 101 | 7,219,000 |
| Other commercial amusements | 605 | 34,414,000 |
|   Amusement parks | 44 | 2,959,000 |
|   Concession operator of amusement devices | 8 | * |
|   Carnivals, circuses | 128 | * |
|   Coin-operated amusement devices | 146 | 9,642,000 |
|   Other | 279 | 17,879,000 |
| **Total** | **4,045** | **$473,851,000** |

* *Withheld to avoid disclosure.*

1. How do New Yorkers and New York visitors spend their money for recreation and relaxation?
2. What definition of the good life emerges from these statistics?

# 18 POLITICS

Athens and Florence governed themselves as city states. Not so New York. The complexities of New York government would have bewildered either Socrates or Machiavelli. There is a mayor, a City Council, a Board of Estimate, five borough president's offices, a Board of Education, more than a thousand other government agencies and authorities, a state government in Albany, a national government in Washington, and local governments in three states, dozens of counties, and hundreds of towns and cities within the metropolitan area of New York, New Jersey, and Connecticut. Getting things done in New York is no easy matter. Problems like transportation and air pollution cut across political boundaries. Working out the budget for New York City alone involves estimating what the financial contributions from state and Federal government will be. City officials find themselves spending much of their time traveling to the state capital of Albany or to Washington, D.C. to lobby for funds. Because of New York's size and complexity, many observers have questioned whether the city can in fact be governed satisfactorily at all.

The city government alone conducts a tremendous enterprise. During most of the Renaissance, Florence had about 70,000 citizens. New York City employs more than 60,000 schoolteachers, 25,000 policemen, and 13,000 firemen. During the fifth century B.C., Athens had a total population including slaves of about 245,000. Almost 300,000 people draw their pay from the City of New York, by far the biggest employer in the metropolitan area. New York's annual budget of about $6 billion could have built all of Florence several times over.

Just as the political system of Athens and Florence helped to shape life in those cities, politics helps to shape New York. Reading 18 presents a variety of information about politics in the city. As you study the tables and read the accounts which follow, think about these questions:

1. For what does the City of New York spend its money? What do these expenditures imply for the good life and the good society?
2. How much more money does the city think it needs to cope with its problems? How is it trying to get these funds?
3. How can a citizen get access to big government? Will more money solve all the city's problems? If more money will not solve the problems, what will?

# Governing New York

**FIGURE I   New York City Expense Budget, 1967–68***

| | |
|---|---|
| Legislative | $      1,980,600 |
| Council and City Clerk | |
| General government: City | 153,289,682 |
| Executive, elections, administrative, finance, real estate, purchasing, law, recording and reporting, planning and zoning, personnel, labor, investigation and research, public works, broadcasting, promotion | |
| Libraries | 31,860,322 |
| Education | 1,419,859,135 |
| Cultural, scientific, recreation, and memorials | 8,765,069 |
| Municipal parks | 51,940,783 |
| Public safety | 631,740,636 |
| Police, fire, civil defense, inspection, traffic | |
| Health and sanitation | 686,748,259 |
| Social Services, Dept. of (welfare) | 1,119,400,986 |
| Correction | 41,418,527 |
| Judicial: City | 39,077,242 |
| Public service and other enterprises | 47,503,021 |
| General government: County | 9,689,091 |
| Law, recording and reporting | |
| Judicial: County | 29,945,609 |
| Human Resources Program (anti-poverty) | 119,174,189 |
| Debt service | 507,389,528 |
| Miscellaneous | 342,480,494 |
| **Total Expense Budget** | **$5,242,263,173** |

* Source: Unpublished memorandum, Economic Development Administration, City of New York, 1969.

363

FIGURE II  New York City Capital Budget, 1967–68*

| Department or Agency | City Funds |
|---|---:|
| Air Pollution Control, Dept. of | $       300,000 |
| Community Mental Health Board | 3,066,667 |
| Correction, Dept. | 33,578,850 |
| Education, Board of | 193,868,190 |
| Fire Department | 5,071,000 |
| Health Department | 5,487,040 |
| Higher Education, Board of | 9,371,929 |
| Highways, Dept. of | 26,508,500 |
| Hospitals, Dept. of | 51,530,926 |
| Housing and Redevelopment Board | 9,800,000 |
| Libraries | 4,177,640 |
| Marine and Aviation, Dept. of | 22,402,950 |
| Markets, Dept. of | 71,000 |
| Mayor, Office of the | 22,000,000 |
| Museums and Institutions | 7,068,479 |
| Parks, Dept. of | 24,133,705 |
| Police Dept. | 12,890,859 |
| Borough Presidents' Offices | 1,529,000 |
| Public Works, general | 27,264,100 |
| Public Works, pollution control | 56,171,598 |
| Purchase, Dept. of | 4,500,000 |
| Real Estate, Dept. of | 4,350,000 |
| Relocation, Dept. of | 4,000,000 |
| Sanitation, Dept. of | 14,990,000 |
| Social Services, Dept. of | 1,037,000 |
| Traffic, Dept. of | 16,896,100 |
| Transit Authority | 84,543,000 |
| Water Supply, Board of | 11,367,219 |
| Water Supply, Gas and Electricity, Dept. of | 14,600,000 |
| WNYC—Municipal Broadcasting System | 355,000 |
| Total, City Funds | $  672,931,472 |
| Other Funds | 362,593,124 |
| **Total, Capital Budget** | **$1,035,524,596** |

* Source: *Unpublished memorandum of the Economic Development Administration, 1968.*

Federal Role in Urban Affairs: Hearings before the Subcommittee on Executive Reorganization of the Committee on Government Operations, U.S. Senate, 89th Congress, 2nd Session, August, 1966, Part 3 (Washington, D.C.: Government Printing Office, 1966), pp. 582, 586, 598.

*The following passage is an excerpt from a hearing before the Subcommittee on Executive Reorganization of the Committee on Government Operations of the United States Senate in August, 1966.*

*Senator [Robert F.] Kennedy:* Now the money aspects have been touched upon, but I would like to ask you this. On page 9 you say:

"There is no solution in New York. The money must come from Federal revenues."

What do you anticipate are your needs as far as Federal funds are concerned in the City of New York?

*Mayor [John V.] Lindsay:* I was just studying a brief analysis that we have made on that point, because I anticipated that it might be raised. We figure that over and above what the city does now with its own resources and with Federal and state contributions, over the next ten years in the area of $50 billion would be required to make this city thoroughly livable, with a quality to life and an exciting place in which to live. That is new money.

*Senator Kennedy:* You need on the average of $5 billion a year. . . . How would it break down? How would you spend it?

*Mayor Lindsay:* Well, in the area of housing, for example—for clearance and redevelopment—we are talking in terms of $3.5 billion; rehabilitation and maintenance, $1.7 billion. Capital facilities of various kinds, transportation $4 billion; environmental protection, nearly $2 billion; schools, in the area of $2 billion.

Various other programs lumped together, about $3 billion. Basic government services—we are talking about operational costs here as opposed to capital costs—education, 15; health, about 6; police, 6; fire, 3.

*Senator Kennedy:* Three what?

*Mayor Lindsay:* $3 billion total over a ten-year period. Parks, almost endless, but let's put it down at $1 billion. Opportunity development, about $3 billion. All that will have to go into services—again these are operating costs, not capital expenditures—somewhere between $20 and $25 billion. I didn't mention in that figure the problem of welfare, which we hope will be a decreasing problem, as the city renews itself in various areas, but this is a problem that is likely to cost $700 million over a ten-year period.

*Senator Kennedy:* $700 million what?

*Mayor Lindsay:* Per year, which means $7 billion. . . .

*Senator Kennedy:* Let me just say in closing, it seems to me that in dealing with [these] problems. . . , whether it be welfare or problems of poverty, there is no question that jobs is going to have to be the answer, and I don't think that the [Federal] government, speaking realistically about it, you talk about the government putting in $5 billion every year for the next ten years, which is ten times as much as it is putting in now, as a practical matter if you put that much in the City of New York, the amount of money that you are going to have to spend in the rest of the cities across the rest of the country is just astronomical, so as a practical matter, I don't think the answer is going to [come just from] Federal funds.

▶ What must Americans be willing to give up if they wish to spend billions of dollars on their cities?

365

The New York Times (June 14, 1964), p. 84. © 1964 by The New York Times Company. Reprinted by permission.

*The following story from* The New York Times *describes an attempt made by Mayor Robert F. Wagner to give citizens access to him.*

Every work day a courier from City Hall goes to a post office at nearby Church Street to pick up an average of seventy-five letters of complaint to Mayor Wagner about city affairs.

Without fanfare, the courier returns to City Hall and delivers his parcel to Harold Mayer, legal aide to the Mayor. Mr. Mayer reads every letter, makes certain an acknowledgment is sent to all writers, and then assigns the complaint to the proper city department for action.

Since Box 100, New York City 8, was set up by the city in January, 1961, more than 65,000 New Yorkers have written to Mayor Wagner with a wide range of complaints, tips on wrongdoing or suggestions for better city programs.

"We encourage these letters whether the writers identify themselves or not," Mr. Mayer said yesterday. "In fact, many anonymous letters have helped us to act in cases of graft or corruption by city personnel."

What kind of letters are received?

Mr. Mayer reported that most letters told of city officials accepting or offering gratuities, city employees moonlighting (working a noncity second job), and failure of certain departments to take action on complaints, such as street repairs, police protection, or building violations.

"We have made five thousand arrests as a result of tips in these letters," Mr. Mayer said. "Most of the arrests have led to convictions."

He said some arrests had resulted from letters from fathers who complained about sons who were drug addicts and named the sellers, or from wives who told of husbands betting away paychecks and listed names and addresses of the bookmakers.

But there are other letters, too, he said. "We once got a request from a citizen who said he had autographed pictures of every Mayor but James J. Walker. Could we help? he wondered. We found a picture and sent it to him.

Mr. Mayer said the most difficult request was from a writer who sent a self-addressed stamped envelope with a request for all the literature there was about the city. "That man had no idea how much literature we have," he commented.

*Some citizens took a dim view of Mayor Wagner's attempt to stay in touch with his constituents. The following passage comes*

Walker, who served from 1925 to 1932, was seen more often in nightclubs than in City Hall. He was bright, friendly, and popular as a symbol of the Roaring 'Twenties. Following investigations into corruption in city politics, Walker resigned his post under pressure from Governor Franklin D. Roosevelt.

*from a fascinating book about Manhattan's Upper West Side written by a resident of this area of the city.*

Father Browne, who often speaks in cartoons, says that New York City government is like the Empire State Building without elevators. Somewhere up on top is the administrative apparatus, the public is in the basement, and in between is a vast air space occupied by the civil service. The consequence of this three-tiered arrangement is that the unaffiliated citizen lives in nearly total bewilderment about his government and, on their side, the administrative officials work in general ignorance of what their own bureaucracies are doing to the citizen. Presumably it was a suspicion of this latter fact that impelled Mayor Wagner to rent himself a private mailbox (Box 100) to which he asked citizens to write and tell him the truth about his subordinates.

Although there was no reason to suppose that Box 100 was anything but another public-relations effort, some people took it seriously for a time. Peter Slevin . . . of the . . . Stryckers Bay Neighborhood Council, used to send off communications to Box 100 regularly. "I wrote to Wagner, I wrote to the commissioner, I wrote to everybody," he says. "I have my own typewriting machine at home, and I send letters in complaining about the block, and also the whole neighborhood—how it is run ragged and all the different illegal things that are going on. I complain about the police department and the narcotics division.

"The only answer they will ever give you if you write to that Box 100 is a little made-up-in-advance letter of the mayor's. The last time I wrote him, I complained about the Housing and Redevelopment Board and I put a note on the bottom of my card saying I didn't want the made-up letter, I wanted an answer from the mayor himself. Now, what do you think I got? I got the made-up letter. It told me that the mayor had turned my letter over to the Housing and Redevelopment Board, the same outfit I was complaining about."

Joseph Lyford, **The Airtight Cage** (New York: Harper & Row, Publishers, 1966), pp. 301–302. Copyright © 1966 by Joseph P. Lyford. Reprinted by permission of Harper & Row, Publishers.

Father Henry J. Browne, president of the Stryckers Bay Neighborhood Council, has tried to organize his community to fight for better housing and city services.

▶ Should a citizen expect the mayor of his city to pay attention personally to his complaints?

# 19 NEW YORK AND THE GOOD SOCIETY: A SUMMARY

Although New York City continues to attract immigrants, visitors, businessmen, job seekers, and students, its appeal as a place to lead a full life has dimmed. Yet New York still has the nation's best theaters, its most distinguished dance groups, one of its best orchestras, some of its most prestigious museums and galleries, its best public library, many of its finest restaurants, and dozens of other similar attractions. An old cliché—"A good place to visit, but I'd hate to live there"—sums up one set of judgments.

New York offers unique richness in each important area of humanistic endeavor. No one could possibly exhaust New York's cultural treasures in a lifetime. But millions of New York's citizens live unaware of the great humanistic resources at their fingertips. And millions of others have begun to doubt that a night at the theater is worth a week on crowded subways in a city no longer able to provide clean air, safe streets, good schools, and regular trash collection.

New York seethes with discontent. In ancient cities, slaves or a servile working class formed the base of society. If they complained, the elite crushed them. In New York, however, all citizens have the right to vote and to participate in public decision making. Moreover, no group in New York willingly accepts an inferior position in the social structure, as Stokely Carmichael's writings indicate. They struggle universally to lead the good life and to shape a society in which that life is possible.

The article which follows summarizes the problems of life in New York in the late 1960's. As you read, think about the following questions:

1. What major problems disturb the city? What has caused these problems?
2. What is New York trying to do to make a good life and a good society possible? What more can be done?
3. Can typical people hope to lead gratifying lives in the major metropolitan areas of a modern megalopolis?

# New York in Crisis

"John Lindsay's Ten Plagues," **Time** (November 1, 1968), pp. 20–21, 23–24, 29. Reprinted by permission from **TIME, The Weekly Newsmagazine,** copyright © 1968 by Time, Inc.

In Central Park the leaves turned brown and gold in the tangy weather that makes lyricists write of "autumn in New York." On Fifth Avenue an unending parade of shoppers canvassed the world's most elegant bazaar. The Broadway marquees touted yet another hectic season. From the Battery to the Bronx, the thud of dynamite and the roar of drills accompanied probably the greatest construction boom in the history of cities. No other metropolis in the world offered its inhabitants greater hope of material success or a wider variety of cultural rewards. Yet for all its dynamism and glamour, New York City, day by day, little by little, was sliding toward chaos. "The question now," said its handsome young Mayor, John Lindsay, "is whether we can continue to survive as a city."

Many New Yorkers shared that somber view. The city's plight, of course, was not one of physical survival—though some cynics argued that New York's complex ills could only be cured if the metropolis were razed and rebuilt. Its breakdown this fall was one of spirit and nerve, a malaise that affected the tacit assumptions of trust and interdependence without which no organism so vast and disparate can possibly function. In what most responsible citizens concede to be one of the ugliest situations in memory, strikes and the threat of strikes pitted not only union against employer—the city—but, worse, black against white, Jew against Gentile, middle class against poor.

In front of City Hall, two thousand picketing policemen yelled "Blue power!" and carried signs exhorting "Dump Lindsay". . . . Hundreds more paraded in front of twenty of the city's seventy-nine precinct stations. Until their union ended the practice at week's end, as many as three thousand men, one-fifth of the force scheduled for duty, reported "sick" each day with a fictitious strain of Asian flu. Cops on duty watched benignly as motorists left their cars in bus stops and no-parking zones. Minor complaints were simply ignored, and traffic became badly snarled. Possibly worst of all was the damage done to the conception of law and order, as "New York's Finest" sneered at laws they were sworn to enforce.

Firemen refused housekeeping duties, such as checking fire hydrants and inspecting buildings, and the head of the firemen's union warned that the slowdown "could escalate into a full-scale strike" that would leave alarms unanswered and homes in danger.

The least dangerous breakdown in public services was the most serious. For the third time since September, the majority of the city's 58,000 teachers defied state law to go out on strike, and more than a million students were denied the vital right of education. Teachers marched outside their schools, and children watched as picketers traded insults and obscenities with nonstrikers and parents. . . .

. . . .The sad truth is that for most of its millions, New York is an increasingly unfavorable habitat. Within the past two to three years, rents on noncontrolled apartments have risen as much as 100 per cent—with hikes of 40 per cent and 50 per cent common. Still, 800,000 units, a quarter of the city's dwellings, are listed as substandard. Replacing them would be a task equal to rebuilding two-thirds of blitz-shattered London, and several of the impoverished ghettos are as big as medium-sized cities. Traffic is scarcely

▶ Should public employees who provide essential services have the right to strike? If not, how can they make strong demands for for what they think they deserve?

The schools finally reopened in late November, 1968.

To dampen wartime inflationary pressures, price controls—price ceilings— were placed on most New York City apartments in 1943. Controls still apply to most low- and medium-priced larger apartment houses built before 1947. By statute, controls are supposed to remain as long as an apartment shortage remains. And the shortage shows no signs of abating. This explanation of rent controls is highly simplified; the intricacies of rent controls, however, are a frequent topic of conversation among New Yorkers, who are almost always in search of better apartments.

▶ What can an individual do to keep his city—or the halls of his high school—clean?

better; every day 3.5 million people crowd into nine square miles of Manhattan south of Central Park, the equivalent of transporting every man, woman and child in Connecticut into Bridgeport and out again each day. From the visible evidence, the sanitation strike [of February, 1968] might still be on, and blowing papers and scattered heaps of filth testify to perhaps the most unkempt city on the North American continent.

Even the construction boom has brought its toll in dirt, noise, and the destruction of treasured landmarks and favorite spots. The good small restaurants that were the city's pride are being torn down, to be replaced by fifteen-minute service counters in skyscraper basements. In the Wall Street area, where building activity and crowding are most intense, lines form in front of hot-dog carts at lunchtime, and a sign in a Broad Street bookstore reads: "Please—no browsing from 12 to 2." Says Architect Percival Goodman: "Size can mean healthy growth or cancer. In New York, it's become cancer."

New York has always had its detractors, and out-of-towners often find odd comfort and perverse joy in discussing its faults and inconveniences. But many people who once loved the city are now regretfully finding their passion growing cold. . . .Even Big Business is either too big, fragmented, or uninterested to offer the kind of leadership it exerts in cities like Pittsburgh and Atlanta. Extraordinarily kind on occasion, New Yorkers in the mass can be the rudest, surliest, nastiest citizens of America and, with the possible exception of Paris, the world. . . .

For the city's minorities, it is not a question of dullness or excitement, but survival in the urban jungle. Properly dissatisfied with the inferior education that most of their children were receiving, the city's Negroes long ago began pressing for local control of schools in black neighborhoods. With encouragement from Lindsay, the Central School Board last year grudgingly met them part way, offering black communities limited autonomy in three experimental districts. If the districts succeeded, the prospect was that the entire school system—a "pathological bureaucracy" in the words of New York University Professor David Rogers—would in time be decentralized so that parents all over the city would have a greater say in their children's future.

It was a bold, exciting educational venture, and a sensible scheme to bring government to the people, particularly to the blacks who felt victimized by an impacted intransigent white bureaucracy. In practice, however, it met a multitude of small problems, and one gigantic roadblock: the United Federation of Teachers, the nation's largest union local (55,000 members). After

370

years of struggling for power, the union felt endangered. Not only would decentralization break up the school system, many teachers reasoned, it would also break up the union, which would have to negotiate with thirty-three local school boards. To many teachers and indeed to many members of other unions, the Negroes' demand for community control—and the city's limited compliance—was nothing less than union busting. . . .

If the problems of New York can be compared only to the ten plagues of Egypt, as Lindsay once claimed in jest, the autumn of 1968 is clearly the time of all ten. There are more than a few who blame Lindsay himself for spreading the plague. Said Dominick Peluso, executive assistant to Frank O'Connor, Democratic City Council president and an archfoe of the Republican Mayor: "Lindsay has taken New York from a city in crisis to a city in chaos." The summary is typical, though hardly just: Lindsay's record is one of remarkable success and serious shortcomings against overpowering odds.

During the three years of the Lindsay administration, welfare rolls have risen by 40 per cent, to a point where almost 1 million people (one out of eight New Yorkers) are on relief. Some city officials would accept Richard Nixon's argument that welfare payments across the country should be standardized, on the theory that New York City, with the highest payments in the country, is a magnet for the poor of other states and communities. The city's budget since 1965 has risen 40 per cent to almost $6 billion, more than any state—including the state of New York—spends in a year. Real estate taxes have gone up 26¢ per $100 (but the assessed valuation has risen more than $2 billion), and for the first time the city has levied an income tax. Strike has followed strike, and New Yorkers can only speculate on what essential service will be cut off next. Many of the promising young men who joined Lindsay at City Hall left after the first year.

▶ When one person in eight is on relief, should a society require work from those among them who are able-bodied before it gives support?

He has labored heroically to communicate with the blacks in the ghettos. The city has had no major racial upheaval since 1964. Yet many white New Yorkers feel neglected as a result. In huge areas of the Bronx, Brooklyn, and Queens, thousands feel that Lindsay is interested only in the black and Spanish-speaking slums. Says Democratic Councilman Robert Low, a possible candidate for Mayor in 1969: "He has concentrated his attention on slum areas and raising standards for minority groups, without making the middle class feel he offers compensating programs for them." Partially as a result, the white exodus to the suburbs goes on, and the dissatisfaction grows. In a secret poll early in October, 42 per cent rated Lindsay's mayoral record as "poor."

371

Certainly, much is beyond Lindsay's or any Mayor's control. He is not only opposed on many issues by the Democratic City Council; the state legislature as well has a degree of control over city policies that is perhaps without parallel elsewhere in the United States. The spectacular hike in welfare rolls is a direct result of heavy black migration from the South and a longtime influx of Puerto Ricans. Much of the budget, including welfare, is mandated by law. Inflation causes union to vie against union in looking to the city treasury. "When one takes snuff," says Negotiator Theodore Kheel, "the others all sneeze.". . .

In cutting through other tangles that choke his city, Lindsay has done better than just about anyone else could have. Not always appreciated in New York—or in Nelson Rockefeller's Albany—he is generally regarded in Washington offices that handle urban programs as the best big-city mayor in the country.

One of his biggest accomplishments has been to restore some measure of grace to a city not noted for its civility, and to slow, if only by a fraction, the numerous forces that make New York an increasingly unlivable city. Under Lindsay, the parks have been made into attractive recreational centers, with cafes and musicales and bicycling on roadways that are closed to cars on weekends and holidays. Air pollution has been cut slightly, and the level of design in civic architecture has been raised. Plans are being pushed through for a great network of new subways, and the grandiose, frequently destructive schemes of the expressway builders have, for the most part, been restrained from running great swaths of concrete through residential areas.

The city government has been reorganized to follow the simpler federal outline, and advanced techniques of systems analysis are being applied to bureaucratic procedures that had not changed by more than a jot in a century. Still in dire need of money, the city's budget has been brought in line with income. . . . One of Lindsay's less heralded accomplishments is the tapping of the federal till with new programs and aggressive lobbying. Since he took office, federal outlays to the city have jumped more than threefold, to $892 million a year. Yet city residents still pay out far more than the city receives, $16 billion a year, or roughly 10 per cent of all income taxes paid the Federal Government. (They similarly pay more to the state than they receive, getting back 43c on the dollar.)

The police department has been humanized. . . .Most important of all is Lindsay's unique rapport with the Negroes and Puerto Ricans, a fragile yet invaluable link that the Mayor readily admits could vanish in a single night of riot and looting.

This view of course, is hotly disputed by many New York residents.

The question that is always asked about New York can be asked about any other metropolis in the United States today: Is it governable? Under its present antique structure, the answer is quickly becoming obvious: it is not.

In part, the problem is one of technology. City lines are meaningless when a commuter, on his everyday ride to work, passes through a dozen corporate boundaries from home to office. Neither are there limits to the problems technology has created: traffic jams and noise, air and water pollution do not stop at the city line. . . .

The villain generally is size. Most local governments are either too small to deal with big problems, or too big to take care of the small. In New York and other major cities, the difficulty is one of reaching down. "The city is designed to shrink people," says Leonard Fein, associate director of the M.I.T.–Harvard Joint Center for Urban Affairs, "so one doesn't feel plugged in, connected, part of a family. So at least then, let's resurrect the neighborhood, the community within the city. That's what decentralization is all about. It's not about schools. It's about neighborhood and plugging people in.". . .

Plugging people in is the goal of modern planners and urban thinkers, just as building grand boulevards and sweeping plazas was the dream a century ago. Most urban thinkers envisage a graduated form of government. A large regional body would do such things as policing the environment, building expressways, and providing police. Small organizations would provide services such as recreation and education.

. . . . A somewhat similar theme was sounded by Leonardo da Vinci. To relieve the congestion and bring order to the bedlam of sixteenth century Milan, he told its Duke, the community would have to be broken down into ten cities of 30,000 people each. . . .

Since the founding of such cities as Eridu and Kish in the valleys of Mesopotamia 5,500 years ago, the city has been the nerve and growth center of civilization. Despite their seemingly insoluble problems, cities are more than ever the creative heart of American society. Indeed, the city and its compounded quandaries—from the problem of race to the issue of law and order—dominate almost all social and political debate in the country today. Ultimately, no city can solve the problems alone, for they belong to the whole society.

Cities are immensely vulnerable: their technology is fragile and their massed populations are interdependent. Yet they also possess a stubborn, stunning, and almost blind will to endure. New York did not dissolve in chaos last week. It will probably not fall apart this week or next, or the week after that. With luck, it will never break down entirely. Nonetheless, a nation that prides itself on pragmatism and problem-solving can afford only at its peril to ignore the immense—and immensely complex—challenge of making its cities habitable, enjoyable, and governable. [Lewis] Mumford told a Senate committee last year, "Unless human needs and human interactions and human responses are the first consideration, the city, in any valid sense, cannot be said to exist. As Sophocles long ago said: 'The city is people.'"

Mumford has written on a wide variety of cultural matters, from utopias to the arts. He is best known for perceptive works on cities, such as **The City in History** (New York: Harcourt, Brace & World, Inc., 1961), and for his sharp criticisms of city design.

# 20 THE GOOD SOCIETY:

# HOW TO ATTAIN IT

In ancient Athens, private citizens contributed ships to the navy and built monuments to beautify the streets of the city. Through these streets walked 125,000 slaves, the basis of an economy which gave the elite time and money for civic service. In Renaissance Florence, a small number of aristocrats also used their fortunes to beautify a city. These fortunes grew from the labor of a large working class only a very few of whom were slaves. Neither society devoted much effort to improving the daily lives of the poor either through private charity or through governmental programs.

Private citizens have made thousands of contributions to the cultural and aesthetic life of New York City. Museums, concert halls, and college buildings bear the names of men who donated money to build them. Each year citizens launch hundreds of drives to solicit contributions for orchestras, the opera, dance groups, and similar cultural organizations as well as for charitable work among the poor and unfortunate. But the efforts of New Yorkers to bring the good life nearer to everyone extend far beyond private giving. Many of them take place through government.

The democratic ethic implies that everyone should have access to the good life. No man should be slave to another; no one should starve; no one should be forced to live in a squalid slum; everyone should have access to free public education of outstanding quality. Without decent living conditions, the rich cultural opportunities of New York City are a sham. Raising New York to minimum standards of health and decency will cost billions of dollars, as Mayor Lindsay pointed out to the Congress. Where will the money come from?

A number of scholars have set out to answer this question. One of the most notable among them is John Kenneth Galbraith, an economist, whose theory of social balance has drawn the attention of the entire intellectual community. As you read his ideas, think about the following questions:

1. What is the theory of social balance? Why does Galbraith use these words to describe his ideas?
2. Can we attain the good society entirely through private means such as charitable contributions, voluntary slum clearance, and so forth?
3. Galbraith appeals for greater public spending at the expense of private spending. About 20 per cent of the Gross National Product is now spent by government. Should government spend more? If it should, what will be the cost in terms of what private citizens have to give up? (Do not forget that the GNP has risen in nearly every year since 1933.)

## The Theory of Social Balance

The final problem of the productive society is what it produces. This manifests itself in [a]. . .tendency to provide an opulent supply of some things and a niggardly yield of others. This disparity. . .is a cause of social discomfort and social unhealth. The line which divides our area of wealth from our area of poverty is roughly that which divides privately produced and marketed goods and services from publicly rendered services. Our wealth in the first is not only in startling contrast with the meagerness of the latter, but our wealth in privately produced goods is, to a marked degree, the cause of crisis in the supply of public services. For we have failed to see the importance, indeed the urgent need, of maintaining a balance between the two.

This disparity between our flow of private and public goods and services is no matter of subjective judgment. . . .In the years following World War II, the papers of any major city—those of New York were an excellent example—told daily of the shortages and shortcomings in the elementary municipal and metropolitan services. The schools were old and overcrowded. The police force was under strength and underpaid. The parks and playgrounds were insufficient. Streets and empty lots were filthy, and the sanitation staff was underequipped and in need of men. Access to the city by those who work there was uncertain and painful and becoming more so. Internal transportation was overcrowded, unhealthful, and

John Kenneth Galbraith, **The Affluent Society** (Boston: Houghton Mifflin Company, 1958), pp. 251–253, 255–261. Copyright © 1958 by John Kenneth Galbraith. Reprinted by permission of Houghton Mifflin Company and John Kenneth Galbraith.

▶ Can a person lead a good life if he cares for his own welfare but permits the public sector to decay?

375

"Dalliance" means acting
amorously or frivolously.

dirty. So was the air. Parking on the streets had to be prohibited, and there was no space elsewhere. These deficiencies were not in new and novel services but in old and established ones. Cities have long swept their streets, helped their people move around, educated them, kept order, and provided horse rails for vehicles which sought to pause. That their residents should have a nontoxic supply of air suggests no revolutionary dalliance with socialism.

The discussion of this public poverty competed, on the whole successfully, with the stories of ever-increasing opulence in privately produced goods. The Gross National Product was rising. So were retail sales. So was personal income. Labor productivity had also advanced. The automobiles that could not be parked were being produced at an expanded rate. The children, though without schools, subject in the playgrounds to the affectionate interest of adults with odd tastes, and disposed to increasingly imaginative forms of delinquency, were admirably equipped with television sets. We had difficulty finding storage space for the great surpluses of food despite a national disposition to obesity. Food was grown and packaged under private auspices. The care and refreshment of the mind, in contrast with the stomach, was principally in the public domain. Our colleges and universities were severely overcrowded and underprovided, and the same was true of the mental hospitals.

The contrast was and remains evident not alone to those who read. The family which takes its mauve and cerise, air-conditioned, power-steered, and power-braked automobile out for a tour passes through cities that are badly paved, made hideous by litter, blighted buildings, billboards, and posts for wires that should long since have been put underground. They pass on into a countryside that has been rendered largely invisible by commercial art. (The goods which the latter advertise have an absolute priority in our value system. Such aesthetic considerations as a view of the countryside accordingly come second. On such matters we are consistent.) They picnic on exquisitely packaged food from the portable icebox by a polluted stream and go on to spend the night at a park which is a menace to public health and morals. Just before dozing off on an air mattress, beneath a nylon tent, amid the stench of decaying refuse, they may reflect vaguely on the curious unevenness of their blessings. Is this, indeed, the American genius?. . .

. . . . An increase in the consumption of automobiles requires a facilitating supply of streets, highways, traffic control, and parking space. The protective services of the police and the highway patrols must also be available, as must those of the hospitals. Although the need for balance here is extraordinarily clear, our use of privately produced vehicles has, on occasion, got far out of line with

376

the supply of the related public services. The result has been hideous road congestion, an annual massacre of impressive proportions, and chronic colitis in the cities. . . .

But the auto and the airplane, versus the space to use them, are merely an exceptionally visible example of a requirement that is pervasive. The more goods people procure, the more packages they discard, and the more trash that must be carried away. If the appropriate sanitation services are not provided, the counterpart of increasing opulence will be deepening filth. The greater the wealth the thicker will be the dirt. This indubitably describes a tendency of our time. As more goods are produced and owned, the greater are the opportunities for fraud, and the more property that must be protected. If the provision of public law enforcement services do not keep pace, the counterpart of increased well-being will, we may be certain, be increased crime. . . .

In a well-run and well-regulated community, with a sound school system, good recreational opportunities, and a good police force—in short a community where public services have kept pace with private production—the diversionary forces operating on the modern juvenile may do no great damage. Television and the violent mores of Hollywood and Madison Avenue must contend with the intellectual discipline of the school. The social, athletic, dramatic, and like attractions of the school also claim the attention of the child. These, together with the other recreational opportunities of the community, minimize the tendency to delinquency. Experiments with violence and immorality are checked by an effective law enforcement system before they become epidemic.

In a community where public services have failed to keep abreast of private consumption things are very different. Here, in an atmosphere of private opulence and public squalor, the private goods have full sway. Schools do not compete with television and the movies. The dubious heroes of the latter, not Miss Jones, become the idols of the young. The hot rod and the wild ride take the place of more sedentary sports for which there are inadequate facilities or provision. Comic books, alcohol, narcotics, and switchblade knives are, as noted, part of the increased flow of goods, and there is nothing to dispute their enjoyment. There is an ample supply of private wealth to be appropriated and not much to be feared from the police. An austere community is free from temptation. It can be austere in its public services. Not so a rich one.

Moreover, in a society which sets large store by production, and which has highly effective machinery for synthesizing private wants, there are strong pressures to have as many wage earners in the family as possible. As always all social behavior is part of a

**Colitis** is an inflammation of the colon, which is part of the large intestine.

To "synthesize" means to combine parts to form a whole, or to reason deductively.

piece. If both parents are engaged in private production, the burden on the public services is further increased. Children, in effect, become the charge of the community for an appreciable part of the time. If the services of the community do not keep pace, this will be another source of disorder.

Residential housing also illustrates the problem of the social balance, although in a somewhat complex form. Few would wish to contend that, in the lower or even the middle income brackets, Americans are munificently supplied with housing. A great many families would like better located or merely more houseroom, and no advertising is necessary to persuade them of their wish. And the provision of housing is in the private domain. At first glance at least, the line we draw between private and public seems not to be preventing a satisfactory allocation of resources to housing.

On closer examination, however, the problem turns out to be not greatly different from that of education. It is improbable that the housing industry is greatly more incompetent or inefficient in the United States than in those countries—Scandinavia, Holland, or (for the most part) England—where slums have been largely eliminated and where *minimum* standards of cleanliness and comfort are well above our own. As the experience of these countries shows, and as we have also been learning, the housing industry functions well only in combination with a large, complex, and costly array of public services. These include land purchase and clearance for redevelopment; good neighborhood and city planning, and effective and well-enforced zoning; a variety of financing and other aids to the housebuilder and owner; publicly supported research and architectural services for an industry which, by its nature, is equipped to do little on its own; and a considerable amount of direct or assisted public construction for families in the lowest income brackets. The quality of the housing depends not on the industry, which is given, but on what is invested in these supplements and supports. . . .

. . . .By failing to exploit the opportunity to expand public production we are missing opportunities for enjoyment which otherwise we might have had. Presumably a community can be as well rewarded by buying better schools or better parks as by buying bigger automobiles. By concentrating on the latter rather than the former it is failing to maximize its satisfactions. As with schools in the community, so with public services over the country at large. It is scarcely sensible that we should satisfy our wants in private goods with reckless abundance, while in the case of public goods, on the evidence of the eye, we practice extreme self-denial. So, far from systematically exploiting the opportunities to derive use and pleasure from these services, we do not supply what would keep us out of trouble.

The conventional wisdom holds that the community, large or small, makes a decision as to how much it will devote to its public services. This decision is arrived at by democratic process. Subject to the imperfections and uncertainties of democracy, people decide how much of their private income and goods they will surrender in order to have public services of which they are in greater need. Thus there is a balance, however rough, in the enjoyments to be had from private goods and services and those rendered by public authority.

It will be obvious, however, that this view depends on the notion of independently determined consumer wants. In such a world one could with some reason defend the doctrine that the consumer, as a voter, makes an independent choice between public and private goods. But given the dependence effect—given that consumer wants are created by the process by which they are satisfied—the consumer makes no such choice. He is subject to the forces of advertising and emulation by which production creates its own demand. Advertising operates exclusively, and emulation mainly, on behalf of privately produced goods and services.* Since management and emulative effects operate on behalf of private production, public services will have an inherent tendency to lag behind. Automobile demand which is expensively synthesized will inevitably have a much larger claim on income than parks or public health or even roads where no such influence operates. The engines of mass communication, in their highest state of development, assail the eyes and ears of the community on behalf of more beer but not of more schools. Even in the conventional wisdom it will scarcely be contended that this leads to an equal choice between the two. . . .

So much for the influences which operate on the decision between public and private production. The calm decision between public and private consumption pictured by the conventional wisdom is, in fact, a remarkable example of the error which arises from viewing social behavior out of context. The inherent tendency will always be for public services to fall behind private production. We have here the first of the causes of social imbalance.

▶ Should aroused citizens organize advertising campaigns in behalf of the public sector?

*Emulation does operate between communities. A new school or a new highway in one community does exert pressure on others to remain abreast. However, as compared with the pervasive effects of emulation in extending the demand for privately produced consumer's goods there will be agreement, I think, that this intercommunity effect is probably small.

# SUGGESTED READINGS

Listings preceded by an asterisk (*) are published in paperback. If the paperback imprint differs from the hardback imprint, the paperback imprint is in parentheses.

## The City: The Long View

FEININGER, ANDREAS and KATE SIMON, **New York.** New York: The Viking Press, 1964. Fine photographs and an informative text about New York City past and present.

PRITCHETT, V. S. and EVELYN HOFER, **New York Proclaimed.** New York: Harcourt, Brace & World, Inc., 1965. A perceptive and affectionate essay about the city and its people by a leading English critic. Illustrated with over one hundred photographs.

STILL, BAYRD, ed., **Mirror for Gotham.** New York: New York University Press, 1956. Writings about the city by New Yorkers and visitors from the 1620's to the 1940's. Liberally illustrated.

## City People

* BALDWIN, JAMES, **Notes of a Native Son.** Boston: Beacon Press, 1955 (Bantam). Brilliant commentaries on Harlem, America, race, and self-knowledge by one of the finest living essayists.

* BROWN, CLAUDE, **Manchild in the Promised Land.** New York: The Macmillan Company, Inc., 1955 (Signet). A moving and often brutal autobiography about growing up in Harlem.

* DECARVA, ROY and LANGSTON HUGHES, **The Sweet Flypaper of Life.** New York: Hill & Wang, Inc., 1967. Photographs by DeCarva with captions by Hughes describing the joys and sadnesses of everyday life in Harlem.

* EVANS, WALKER, **Many Are Called.** Boston: Houghton Mifflin Company, 1966. Candid photographs of people in the New York subways in the late 1930's and early '40's by a great photographer, with an introduction by James Agee.

* LARNER, JEREMY and RALPH TEFFERTELLER, eds., **Addict in the Street.** New York: Grove Press, Inc., 1966 (Zebra). Extended, tape-recorded interviews with New York drug addicts from a variety of social backgrounds.

* LOVE, EDMUND, **Subways Are for Sleeping.** New York: Harcourt, Brace & World, Inc., 1957 (Signet). Compassionate, tightly-written true stories about New Yorkers without visible means of support.

* MALCOLM X, **Autobiography.** New York: Grove Press, Inc., 1965 (Evergreen Black Cat). The searing life story of the famous black nationalist leader who was assassinated in 1965.

* MAYERSON, CHARLOTTE LEON, ed., **Two Blocks Apart.** New York: Holt, Rinehart and Winston, Inc., 1965 (Avon). Tape-recorded life stories of two adolescent boys—one of Puerto Rican heritage, the other an Irish-American—who live two blocks apart on Manhattan's Upper West Side.

* THOMAS, PIRI, **Down These Mean Streets.** New York: Alfred A. Knopf, Inc., 1967 (Signet). A fast-moving autobiography of a Puerto Rican boy growing up in the *barrio* of East Harlem.

* WOLFE, TOM, **The Kandy-Kolored Tangerine-Flake Streamline Baby.** New York: Farrar, Straus and Giroux, 1965 (Pocket Book). A subjective reporter's views of a disc jockey, a rock magnate, a Jet Setter, some East Side nannies, and other New Yorkers.

*Society and Politics*

* BUCKLEY, WILLIAM F., JR., **The Unmaking of a Mayor.** New York: The Viking Press, 1966 (Bantam). An account of the 1965 mayoral campaign by the witty and testy Conservative Party candidate who was defeated by John V. Lindsay.

* CLARK, KENNETH B., **Dark Ghetto.** New York: Harper & Row, Publishers, 1965 (Torchbook). A frank, angry, and penetrating analysis of Harlem by a leading psychologist.

* COSTIKYAN, EDWARD, **Behind Closed Doors.** New York: Harcourt, Brace & World, Inc., 1966 (Harvest). An informative and highly practical commentary on New York politics by a reform Democrat who headed Tammany Hall from 1962 to 1964.

* COX COMMISSION, **Crisis at Columbia.** New York: Random House, Inc., 1968 (Vintage). A report on the tumultuous spring of 1968 at Columbia University, with a cast including university administrators, Students for a Democratic Society, and the New York Police Department.

* GLAZER, NATHAN and DANIEL PATRICK MOYNIHAN, **Beyond the Melting Pot: The Negroes, Puerto Ricans, Jews, Italians, and Irish of New York City.** Cambridge, Mass.: The M.I.T. Press, 1963. A sympathetic survey of the experiences and problems of New York's five major ethnic groups.

\* JACOBS, JANE, **The Death and Life of Great American Cities.** New York: Random House, Inc., 1961 (Vintage). An effective analysis of what makes a city work or fail as an environment for people, with vivid examples from New York.

\* LYFORD, JOSEPH, **The Airtight Cage.** New York: Harper & Row, Publishers, 1966 (Harper Colophon). A journalist's careful but readable study of the people and problems of Manhattan's Upper West Side, a section of the city inhabited by people from almost every imaginable ethnic group and social class.

\* MANN, ARTHUR, **La Guardia Comes to Power: 1933.** Philadelphia: J. B. Lippincott Company, 1965 (Preceptor). A short and engrossing account of one of New York's most exciting political races: the 1933 mayoral election, won by Fiorello H. La Guardia.

\* VERNON, RAYMOND, **Metropolis 1985.** Cambridge, Mass.: Harvard University Press, 1960 (Anchor). Perhaps the best short description of how New York's economy works. Prepared by a commission planning for New York's needs in the 1980's.

*Literature and the Arts*

\* BARTHELME, DONALD, **Unspeakable Practices, Unnatural Acts.** New York: Farrar, Straus and Giroux, 1968 (Bantam). Wild and brilliant short stories by one of the most inventive of modern writers.

\* BELLOW, SAUL, **Seize the Day.** New York: The Viking Press, 1956 (Fawcett Premier). A masterful, short novel about a day in the life of a middle-aged businessman and his father on the Upper West Side.

\* ELLISON, RALPH, **Invisible Man.** New York: Random House, Inc., 1952 (Signet). The fictional odyssey of a black man in America. An outstanding and engrossing novel.

\* GOLDSTEIN, RICHARD, ed., **Poetry of Rock.** New York: Bantam Books, 1969. A collection of rock lyrics from the 1950's and '60's, with commentaries on stylistic developments.

KAUFMAN, GEORGE S. and MOSS HART, **Six Plays.** New York: Random House, Inc. (Modern Library), 1942. Six complete Broadway hits from the 1930's and '40's by one of the wittiest theatrical writing teams.

\* LEARY, PARIS and ROBERT KELLY, eds., **A Controversy of Poets: An Anthology of Contemporary American Poetry.** Garden City, N.Y.: Doubleday & Company, Inc., 1965 (Anchor). Recent American poetry skillfully selected by two practicing poets.

\* MILLER, ARTHUR, **Death of a Salesman.** New York: The Viking Press, 1949 (Compass). A play about a saleman who wanted love and success but knew how to find neither.

\* MILLER, ARTHUR, **A View from the Bridge.** New York: The Viking Press, 1957 (Compass). A play about love, tragedy, and the clash of generations in an Italian-American community in Brooklyn.

\* NEW YORKER MAGAZINE EDITORS, eds., **Stories from the New Yorker: 1950–1960.** New York: Simon and Schuster, 1965. A 780-page collection of short stories of the 1950's, many of them by New Yorkers or about New York.

\* PALEY, GRACE, **The Little Disturbances of Man.** New York: The Viking Press, 1968 (Bantam). Eleven finely written short stories, mostly about love and New York.

\* PERELMAN, S. J., **The Most of S. J. Perelman.** New York: Simon and Schuster, 1958. Stories, essays, dramatizations, and diversions by one of the funniest and most literate men alive.

\* ROSE, BARBARA, **American Art since 1900.** New York: Frederick A. Praeger, Inc., 1967. A readable and intelligent survey of modern American art, with a chapter on architecture. Includes 281 illustrations, 37 of them in color.

\* ROSS, LILLIAN and HELEN, **Player: A Profile of an Art.** New York: Simon and Schuster, 1962. Fifty-five interviews with actors and actresses in which they describe their profession and their careers. Moving and informative.

\* ROTH, PHILIP, **Goodbye, Columbus.** Boston: Houghton Mifflin Company, 1959 (Bantam). Compelling, superbly written short stories about Jews in New York's suburbs.

\* SALINGER, J. D., **Nine Stories.** Boston: Little, Brown and Company, 1953 (Bantam). Short stories about New Yorkers by the author of **The Catcher in the Rye.**

# Index

Page numbers in **heavy type** following an author's name indicate a selection written by that author. Page numbers followed by n. refer to marginal notes.

imperialism, Athenian, 12–13, 92, 93–97; U.S., Stokely Carmichael on, 341–342, 343

individualism, Renaissance, art and, 240–242; Cellini and, 143; cities and, 227; economy and, 234–235

industry, Florence, 220, 230, 232, 233; garment, in New York City, 262; guilds and, 156, 157, 230; housing, 378; Middle Ages, 130; New York City, 346, 358 (chart); woolen, in Florence, 133, 134, 136, 139, 154–157

integration, 340, 342

Italy, 140 (map)

Jews, 262, 263, 264–265; blacks and, 344; New York City, 264–265, 266, 355. See also ethnic groups in New York City

Johnson, Betsey, 286–287

Jones, LeRoi, 312–313

justice, Athenian, 109–110, 118; Guicciardini on, 214; Plato on, 89

Kazin, Alfred, 263–268

Kennedy, Robert F., 364–365

King, Martin Luther, Jr., 341

Kitto, H. D. F., 108–112, 121–124

labor unions, New York City, garment industry, 262; Jews and, 262; policemen's union, 369; sanitation workers' union, 370; strikes, 369, 370–371, 372; United Federation of Teachers, 369, 370–371. See also guilds

leisure, Athens, 8, 19; businessmen and, 283, 285

Leonardo da Vinci, 200–201, 234, 241–242; life, 201; Mona Lisa, 196; Notebooks, 204–

205; religious beliefs, 203–204; sculpture, 241; Vasari on, 196, 201–204

Lewis, Oscar, 274, 275–280

Lindsay, John V., 352n., 365, 369, 370, 371, 372

literature. See drama; poetry; short story

Lopez, Robert S., 232, 233–237

Lorenzo de' Medici, 136–142, 166, 198n., 236–237, 241, 245; education, 137–139; Medici business and, 139, 142, 236–237; patronage of arts, 140, 162, 237; poetry, 140, 179, 180–181, 237; religious beliefs, 141, 239; Savonarola and, 172

love, Greek ideals, 20–22; medieval ideals, 177; Renaissance ideals, 177

Lucas-Dubreton, J., 131–135, 150–154

Lyford, Joseph, 367

Machiavelli, Niccolò, 234; Discourses, 207–211; life, 206; on government, 207–211; on Lorenzo, 237; on state prison, 134; The Prince, 206-207

Manhattan, 258; (map); skyline, 257, 260, 323. See also New York City

manufacturing. See industry

mathematical proportion in art and architecture, Greek, 17, 43; Renaissance, 195, 199–200, 240, 244

mathematics, study of, Athens, 17; Renaissance artists, 195

Medici, 224, 226, 240; Cellini and, 143; government of Florence by, 136, 172, 206, 210, 230–233. See also Cosimo; Giuliano; Lorenzo; Piero

Medici business, depression and, 233; Lorenzo in, 139, 142, 236–237

Medici Chapel, 198n., 240

Medici Palace, 137, 138, 162

medicine, Greek, 118–119

Mediterranean Sea, 218, 219, 220

megalopolis, 347–350

Melos, 93–97

Menander, 46

merchants, Athens, 8; Florence, 133, 134, 135; in Renaissance government, 136, 230; in Renaissance social structure, 225. See also trade

Michelangelo, 226, 234, 241; Cellini on, 198; individualism, 242; Leonardo and, 203; poetry, 181–182; sculpture 244

Middle Ages, agriculture, 130, 224, 232; art, 239, 240–241, 245; economy, 232, 233; feudalism, 130, 227–228; humanism, 236, 239; individualism, 227; love, 177; poverty as ideal, 226; religion, 161, 166, 171, 239; slavery, 159; social structure, 223, 225; taxation, 231; trade, 229, 232; women, 149

middle class, Florence, 225, 230; hippies and, 291, 292–293, 298–299; politics of New York City and, 352, 371. See also merchants; social structure

migration to New York City, 254, 256, 268

military affairs, Athens, 89, 93–97, 109, 112; French invasion of Italy (1494), 172, 231; Greece, 114, 117; Italian city-states, 231–232, 243; Melos, 93–97; Sparta, 89, 93; wealth and, in Greece, 114. See also armed forces

monks. See friars and monks

Moynihan, Daniel Patrick, 351–356

City, 352; in politics of New York City, 352; in social structure of New York City, 354–356

racism, blacks and, 269, 340–341, 342, 344; Puerto Ricans and, 274, 275, 278; U. S. foreign policy and, 343

rationalism, Greek, 39; in art, 42–43; in music, 17

real estate, cooperative ownership, 344; exploitation of tenants by landlords, 275, 344; Florence, 224, 225, 230; Greece, 105, 114; New York City, 279, 357 (chart), 369, 371; rent control, 369n.

religion, art and, 200; burial rites, Greek, 48; death and, 24–28, 48, 104; drama and, 47, 48; Egyptian, 104; gods, Greek, 40, 42, 119; Leonardo and, 203; Lorenzo and, 141; Machiavelli on, 211; medieval, 161, 162, 221; nature and, 221; New York City, 352, 354–356; polis and, 123; Renaissance, 161, 171, 234, 243

Renaissance, characteristics of, 238–242; defined, 238

republics, Guicciardini on, 215; Italian, 136, 206, 227, 229–230, 243; Machiavelli on, 208–211; Rome, ancient, 208–210, 211

revenue, New York City, 364 (chart), 365, 372. *See also* taxation

Reynolds, Malvina, 314–315

Rome, ancient, 110, 348; art, 243; empire, 221; Florence and, 132, 218, 239; humanism in, 162; Machiavelli on government of, 208–210, 211; slavery, 154

St. Augustine, 166n. 170n., 222

St. Francis of Assisi, 221, 240. *See also* friars and monks

Sainte-Marie, Buffy, 318–319

sanitation, city, Athens, 6–7, 106–107; Florence, 131; New York City, 363 (chart), 364 (chart), 370, 375

Sappho, 46

Savonarola, Girolamo, 171–172, 172–177, 206, 234

Schevill, Ferdinand, 139–141, 219–220

science, cities and, 348; Leonardo and, 203, 204; Renaissance art and, 195, 200, 240

sculpture, Cellini on, 196–199; Gothic, 245; Greek, 40, 42, 43, 100, 102, 245; Renaissance, 196–199, 202, 243, 244, 245

sea, influence of, on Greeks, 101, 103

secularism, Renaissance, 171, 239, 243

Seeger, Pete, 314

segregation, 340. *See also* racism

servants, Florentine, 157, 160, 225, 226; Guicciardini on, 212–213

short story, Boccaccio, 183–194; Parker, Dorothy, 328–339

Simon, Paul, 317–318

Simonides, 44–45, 118

slave trade, Renaissance, 155, 158

slavery, 154; medieval, 159; Renaissance, 157–160; U.S., 269

slaves, Athens, 8, 19, 104; Florence, 154, 157–160, 225, 226; rights denied, 15, 16, 107–108, 116; treatment of, 37, 159; value of, 159

slums, 230, 348, 378. *See also* ghettos

social structure, Athens, 112, 114–116, 123, 350; despots and, 229–231; Greece, 105,

112–114; Florence, 223–227; hippies and, 294; Lorenzo and, 138, 141; Middle Ages, 223; New York City, 351–356; Renaissance economy and, 235; slavery and, 159

Socrates, 14, 119; as titular Head of State, 109; criticizes amateurism in government, 110; military service of, 40, 114; on death, 27–28; on government, 87–89, 111; on women, 20–22; rationalism in, 42

Solon, 28, 32–34, 208

Sonny, 293–299

Sophocles, 40, 110; *Antigone,* 47–86; on cities, 374; on the sea, 103

Sparta, 8; armed forces, 91; Machiavelli on, 208; Melos and, 93, 97; polis compared to Athenian, 122; war with Athens, 89, 91, 93

status, artists, 241–242; businessmen, 282. *See also* fame

Student Nonviolent Coordinating Committee (SNCC), 340, 341, 343

suburbs, blacks in, 268, 343; commuters, 256–257, 373; megalopolis and, 346, 347, 349; movement to, 371

taxation, Greece, 19, 93, 105, 106, 107, 122; Florence, 136, 231; Italian city-states, 231; New York City, 371, 372. *See also* revenue

technology, cities and, 348, 373; New York City and, 373; E. B. White on, 302–303, 305

theaters. *See* drama

Thebes (Greece), 8, 47

Themistocles, 10, 16, 111

Theognis, 45

Theophrastus, 35–38

Thucydides, 13, 90–93, 94–97,

112, 119, 122; military service of, 114; on Pericles, 11–12
trade, Athens, 8, 104; Florence, 132, 133, 230; Middle Ages, 130, 229, 232; New York City, 346, 352, 358 (chart), 360 (chart); Renaissance, 218, 220, 232; slave, 155, 158. *See also* industry; merchants
transportation, megalopolis, 349; New York City, 346, 364 (chart), 365, 369–370, 372. *See also* automobiles
Trojan War, 24–25, 28
Tuscany, 135; agriculture, 219–220; climate, 218; geography, 218–223; slavery, 159

unemployment, 269; black, 269; New York City, 357 (chart); Puerto Rican, 278–279
unions. *See* guilds; labor unions
United Federation of Teachers, 369, 370–371
Updike, John, 309

Vasari, Giorgio, 197, 238, 241; on Leonardo, 201–204; on *Mona Lisa,* 196
vernacular, rise of, in Italian literature, 140, 177, 178, 244

Vietnam, 342, 344
Virgil, 168n., 170, 173

wages, New York City, 357 (chart), 358 (chart)
Wagner, Robert F., 352, 366, 367
warfare. *See* military affairs
wealth, civic responsibility and, 105, 106, 122, 226, 284, 374; Galbraith on, 375; Greece, 114, 119; Guicciardini on, 215; Moss Hart on, 325–326; hippies and, 294, 295; kinship system in Greece and, 114; Leonardo on, 205; papal, 243; Pericles on, 91; private vs. public, 106, 375–379; Puerto Ricans and, 277, 279; Renaissance, 136, 227, 230, 235, 245; Solon on, 132–134. *See also* patronage of arts; poverty
welfare system, 268–273, 365, 371; budget for, 363 (chart), 364 (chart); immigration and migration and, 372
White, E. B., 254, **255–257, 260–262, 301–306**
white supremacy, 342, 343
Whitman, Walt, 307–308
Wilson, Eleanora Carus-, 155–157

women, 149; careers, 285–291; Cellini on, 145–146; courtesans, 153–154; Greek, 14, 16, 20; medieval, 149; Medici, 137; Renaissance, beauty and manners of, 151–152; rights denied to Greek, 107–108, 116; slaves, 157–160, 225; Socrates on, 19–22
Work Projects Administration (WPA), 237n.
workers, Athenian, 8; Florentine, 136, 154–157, 224–226, 230, 243; New York City, 352, 357 (chart), 358 (chart); rights of Florentine, 156; uprising of Florentine, 157n.; woolen industry, Florentine, 155–157, 230

Xenophon, 19–22

Yablonsky, Lewis, 293–299
youth, delinquency, 269, 275, 376, 377; Florence, 138; Greece, 40–41, 119–120; hippies, 291–299; Leonardo on, 204. *See also* education

Zavrian, Suzanne Ostro, 311
Zimmern, Alfred E., 104, **105–107**

390